AF833705

Inscribed Athenian Laws and Decrees in the Age of Demosthenes

Brill Studies in Greek and Roman Epigraphy

Editorial Board

John Bodel (*Brown University*)
Adele Scafuro (*Brown University*)

VOLUME 9

The titles published in this series are listed at *brill.com/bsgre*

Inscribed Athenian Laws and Decrees in the Age of Demosthenes

Historical Essays

By

Stephen D. Lambert

BRILL

LEIDEN | BOSTON

Cover illustration: The cover photograph shows the upper part of *IG* II^{3} 1, 312, a decree of the Athenian Assembly of 340/39 BC honouring three foreigners. It is the only extant inscribed decree proposed by the orator Demosthenes. (Fragment of proxeny decree, purchased by the Fondation Calvet in 1841, photograph courtesy of Musée Calvet, Avignon, Alban Rudelin, inv. E 28).

Library of Congress Cataloging-in-Publication Data

Names: Lambert, S. D., 1960– author.
Title: Inscribed Athenian laws and decrees in the age of Demosthenes: historical essays / by Stephen D. Lambert.
Description: Leiden ; Boston : Brill, 2018. | Series: Brill studies in Greek and Roman epigraphy ; volume 9 | Includes bibliographical references and Index.
Identifiers: LCCN 2017040852 (print) | LCCN 2017041801 (ebook) | ISBN 9789004352490 (E-book) | ISBN 9789004352483 (hardback : alk. paper)
Subjects: LCSH: Law, Greek—Sources. | Athens (Greece)—History—To 1500—Sources. | Greece—History—146 B.C—Sources. | Inscriptions, Greek—Greece—Athens.
Classification: LCC KL4115.A75 (ebook) | LCC KL4115.A75 L364 2018 (print) | DDC 340.5/38—dc23
LC record available at https://lccn.loc.gov/2017040852

Typeface for the Latin, Greek, and Cyrillic scripts: “Brill”. See and download: brill.com/brill-typeface.

ISSN 1876-2557
ISBN 978-90-04-35248-3 (hardback)
ISBN 978-90-04-35249-0 (e-book)

Copyright 2018 by Koninklijke Brill NV, Leiden, The Netherlands.
Koninklijke Brill NV incorporates the imprints Brill, Brill Hes & De Graaf, Brill Nijhoff, Brill Rodopi, Brill Sense and Hotei Publishing.
All rights reserved. No part of this publication may be reproduced, translated, stored in a retrieval system, or transmitted in any form or by any means, electronic, mechanical, photocopying, recording or otherwise, without prior written permission from the publisher.
Authorization to photocopy items for internal or personal use is granted by Koninklijke Brill nv provided that the appropriate fees are paid directly to The Copyright Clearance Center, 222 Rosewood Drive, Suite 910, Danvers, MA 01923, USA. Fees are subject to change.

This book is printed on acid-free paper and produced in a sustainable manner.

Inscribed Athenian Laws and Decrees in the Age of Demosthenes

Historical Essays

By

Stephen D. Lambert

TUTA SUB AEGIDE PALLAS · 1683 ·

BRILL

LEIDEN | BOSTON

Cover illustration: The cover photograph shows the upper part of *IG* II³ 1, 312, a decree of the Athenian Assembly of 340/39 BC honouring three foreigners. It is the only extant inscribed decree proposed by the orator Demosthenes. (Fragment of proxeny decree, purchased by the Fondation Calvet in 1841, photograph courtesy of Musée Calvet, Avignon, Alban Rudelin, inv. E 28).

Library of Congress Cataloging-in-Publication Data

Names: Lambert, S. D., 1960– author.
Title: Inscribed Athenian laws and decrees in the age of Demosthenes: historical essays / by Stephen D. Lambert.
Description: Leiden ; Boston : Brill, 2018. | Series: Brill studies in Greek and Roman epigraphy ; volume 9 | Includes bibliographical references and Index.
Identifiers: LCCN 2017040852 (print) | LCCN 2017041801 (ebook) | ISBN 9789004352490 (E-book) | ISBN 9789004352483 (hardback : alk. paper)
Subjects: LCSH: Law, Greek—Sources. | Athens (Greece)—History—To 1500—Sources. | Greece—History—146 B.C—Sources. | Inscriptions, Greek—Greece—Athens.
Classification: LCC KL4115.A75 (ebook) | LCC KL4115.A75 L364 2018 (print) | DDC 340.5/38—dc23
LC record available at https://lccn.loc.gov/2017040852

Typeface for the Latin, Greek, and Cyrillic scripts: "Brill". See and download: brill.com/brill-typeface.

ISSN 1876-2557
ISBN 978-90-04-35248-3 (hardback)
ISBN 978-90-04-35249-0 (e-book)

Copyright 2018 by Koninklijke Brill NV, Leiden, The Netherlands.
Koninklijke Brill NV incorporates the imprints Brill, Brill Hes & De Graaf, Brill Nijhoff, Brill Rodopi, Brill Sense and Hotei Publishing.
All rights reserved. No part of this publication may be reproduced, translated, stored in a retrieval system, or transmitted in any form or by any means, electronic, mechanical, photocopying, recording or otherwise, without prior written permission from the publisher.
Authorization to photocopy items for internal or personal use is granted by Koninklijke Brill nv provided that the appropriate fees are paid directly to The Copyright Clearance Center, 222 Rosewood Drive, Suite 910, Danvers, MA 01923, USA. Fees are subject to change.

This book is printed on acid-free paper and produced in a sustainable manner.

Contents

Preface

Inscribed Athenian Laws and Decrees 352/1–322/1 BC: Epigraphical Essays (Leiden, Brill, 2012) collected 18 papers which laid the groundwork for my edition of the inscriptions, *IG* II³ 1 fascicule 2, which also appeared in 2012. Simultaneously I published English translations in Attic Inscriptions Online (www.atticinscriptions.com). This volume brings together twelve papers concerned mainly with the historical interpretation of the inscriptions. At the time of writing seven of these had been published before (between 2010 and 2017), or were in press, in conference proceedings, *Festschriften* or *AIO Papers*. Five are new. Although the chapters can be read as self-standing papers, there is also a shape to the overall volume, and readers interested in obtaining an overview are invited to peruse the Introduction, which summarises my findings, seeks to delineate that shape and to fill, albeit briefly, some gaps in the overall structure not covered by the main chapters. For the republished papers it also references some important bibliography that has appeared since their first publication. The republished papers have also been lightly annotated, mainly by inserting (in square brackets) *IG* II³ references and cross-references to other papers in the book.

This phase of my work on these inscriptions has extended over a number of years and I have incurred many debts of gratitude, institutional and personal, which I gladly acknowledge here. In 2012/3 I enjoyed the privilege of Membership of the Institute for Advanced Study, Princeton, supported by the Patrons' Endowment Fund and the Loeb Foundation. Chapters 1, 2, 7, 8, 9 and 10 are based on work I did there. In addition to Angelos Chaniotis, Stephen Tracy, Christopher Jones and the audiences of early versions of some of the papers delivered that year, I am very grateful to Nino Luraghi and Marc Domingo Gygax at Princeton University for fruitful discussions and in particular to Stephen Tracy for moral support. The book was finished in 2016/7 during a year of research leave, supported by my University, Cardiff, for which I am very grateful. Work on it in the autumn of 2016 was carried out in the congenial environment of the British School at Athens, where I enjoyed, among other things, the privilege of 24 hour access to the excellent library, and use of the superb, recently refurbished, tennis court. The BSA has been a crucially important base on and off over the 17 years I have worked on this material and I take the opportunity to renew my warm thanks to successive Directors, most recently John Bennet, to the wonderful staff of the School and to the librarian, Penny Wilson. In the summer of 2016 and again between February and April

2017, I enjoyed very fruitful visits to the University of Heidelberg and the privilege of access to the superb library of the Seminar für Alte Geschichte. I am very grateful to Kai Trampedach and Christian Witschel for facilitating these visits and to the Humboldt Foundation for supporting my stay in Heidelberg in early 2017. While in Britain my work on this book over the years has benefited from the fine library resources of the Institute of Classical Studies, London.

For their academic interest in this book (including in some cases reading material in draft) and for moral support I am also variously grateful in Princeton to Glen Bowersock, Christian Habicht and Heinrich von Staden, in Athens to James Kierstead and in Britain to Peter Liddel, Robin Osborne, and especially to P.J. Rhodes. As series editor for Brill, Adele Scafuro has offered welcome (and patient) encouragement. Thomas Willis has encouraged me by his friendship and interest. Irene Vagionakis has rendered invaluable assistance behind the scenes in the final stages. I am writing this Preface on a visit to Utrecht, where Josine Blok has been a staunch friend over the years, and supportive through thick and thin.

Chapter 1 is also to be published by *Historika. Studi di Storia Greca e Romana* (Turin) as Suppl. 1, *Inscribing space: the topography of Attic inscriptions. Proceedings of the conference, Heidelberg 29–30 May 2015* (forthcoming), and I am very grateful to the editors of that volume, Irene Berti and Daniela Marchiandi, for inviting me to their conference and for approving the publication of the paper in this volume.

By the time this book appears Chapter 2 will have been published in *Hyperboreus. Festheft for Christian Habicht* (St. Petersburg, 2017) and I am grateful to the editors for approving its publication also in this volume.

Chapter 3 was first published in S. D. Lambert ed., *Sociable man. Essays on ancient Greek social behaviour in honour of Nick Fisher* (Swansea, Classical Press of Wales, 2011), 193–214. I am grateful to Anton Powell for giving his blessing to its republication here.

Chapter 4 was first published in V. Azoulay, P. Ismard, eds. *Clisthène et Lycurgue d'Athènes. Autour du politique dans la cité classique* (Paris, Publications de la Sorbonne, 2011), 175–90, and I am grateful to Publications de la Sorbonne for permission to reproduce it in this volume and to the editors for their approval.

Chapter 5 was first published in L. Foxhall, H.J. Gehrke and N. Luraghi eds., *Intentional history: spinning time in ancient Greece* (Stuttgart, Steiner, 2010), 225–38, and I am grateful to the Steiner Verlag for permission to reproduce it in this volume.

Chapter 6 was first published in J. Marincola, L. Llewellyn-Jones, and C. Maciver eds., *Greek notions of the past in the archaic and classical eras:*

history without historians. Edinburgh Leventis Studies 6 (Edinburgh, Edinburgh University Press, 2012), 253–75, and I am grateful to the editors for sanctioning republication in this volume.

Chapter 10 was first published in A. P. Matthaiou and N. Papazarkadas eds., *Axon. Studies in honor of Ronald S. Stroud* (Athens, Greek Epigraphical Society, 2015), 233–46, and I am grateful to the editors and to the Greek Epigraphical Society for approving republication.

Chapter 11 was first published as *AIO Papers* no. 6 (2015), https://www.atticinscriptions.com/papers/aio-papers-6/.

Utrecht, 7 April 2017

Introduction

This book is a collection of historical essays on the inscribed Athenian laws and decrees of 352/1–322/1 BC, which I recently edited for *Inscriptiones Graecae*.[1] They are not "historical" in the sense that they utilise the inscribed laws and decrees as a source of factual information to support, correct and supplement an account of the period written primarily from the literary evidence. Such a collection of essays could certainly be written (Demosthenes and other orators would be the major source), but this is not it. They are also not essays that deal with the historical or quasi-historical matter that lies close to the epigraphist's elbow: chronology, prosopography, onomastics.[2] Rather, they seek to explore historical matters on which the inscriptions cast light independently, from their own perspective; and they seek to pay attention to significant historical shapes and patterns, synchronic and diachronic, to the wood of the corpus as a whole rather than the trees of the individual inscriptions that comprise it.

I should begin by acknowledging some methodological issues and explain my approach to them. Demosthenes proposed his first known Assembly decree in 352/1, and 322/1, the year of his death, is also the last year of the classical democracy. The years in between are the most richly documented in Athenian history, but Athens began inscribing decrees on stone in significant numbers in the middle of the fifth century BC and continued doing so through the Roman period. Against this background these thirty-one years are a relatively short time span, and if one is attending to shapes and patterns, that ought to include diachronic ones which extend over much longer time periods. That said, there is a practical problem in that the fascicules of *IG* II³ 1 containing the inscribed laws and decrees of periods immediately neighbouring mine, 403/2–353/2 and 321/0–301/0, have yet to be published. My response has been of various kinds. There are some matters which, for evidential reasons, need to be addressed specifically in relation to these, or roughly these, years. For example, there is sufficient information for systematic analysis of proposers of inscribed laws and decrees only after 354/3, when proposers in inscriptions begin to be referred to with father's name and demotic and therefore become readily identifiable (chapter 8). Moreover, without getting drawn into detailed analysis of the inscribed decrees of immediately neighbouring periods, I have not hesitated to cast an eye both forwards and backwards in time where this seemed appropriate. Locations of inscribed laws and decrees in our period were driven partly by

1 *IG* II³ 1, fascicule 2.

2 Such matters were handled in several of the essays in *IALD*.

© KONINKLIJKE BRILL NV, LEIDEN, 2018 | DOI 10.1163/9789004352490_002

convention and tradition, partly they were innovative; but understanding the tradition and the innovation necessitates extending the perspective backwards in time, and to an extent forwards, from our core period (chapter 1). A key development in the culture of these years was an intensified focus on the past. My approach here was to begin with a study specifically of the period of my corpus (chapter 5) and to build on it a wider analysis looking across the whole of the fourth century (chapter 6). In the paper on relations between Council and Assembly, on the other hand (chapter 9), while in-depth analysis of neighbouring periods must await the publication of the new corpus fascicules, it seemed to me potentially illuminating to compare the situation in these 31 years with a comparable number of years a little over a century later, 229/8–198/7, for which the relevant new corpus has been published.[3] Finally, an intensified focus on a relatively short, but well-documented, period has in some cases proved helpful in identifying developments which had previously been lost in the broad sweep. It will be apparent to the reader of chapters 7–9, on democratic themes, that there is more to be said about diachronic developments across the fourth century democracy, especially as regards attitudes to the rule of law and relations between Council and Assembly, than previous work on this topic might have suggested. By all means there remains more to be done to extend some analyses, for example of decree proposers and relations between Council and Assembly, across a longer time span; and a systematic study of attitudes to the past displayed in the inscriptions of the hellenistic period would among other things help clarify how far the maintenance of democratic forms was supported by an idea of Athens' heritage from its past, making them a kind of "classical" façade behind which the realities of power had shifted.

Second, it might be objected that, since there are laws and decrees attested in literary sources, a relentless focus on the inscribed record is difficult to justify. Disaggregation of literary and epigraphical sources, however, enables a clearer appreciation of the distinctive perspectives inherent in the different types of evidence. This is important, for example, in chapter 2, on selectivity of inscribing, where the literary evidence serves to help define the limits of what was inscribed and the extent to which the inscribed record is representative. It is also important in the chapters on decree proposers (8) and on the balance between the Council and Assembly (9), where the epigraphical evidence has a greater claim to presenting a randomised sample, and disaggregation both facilitates identification of distortions inherent in the literary record, and enables what is I hope a more nuanced analysis of both evidence types. I readily acknowledge that in some cases the picture obtained is a partial one. A

3 *IG* II^3 1, fascicule 5.

full analysis of the decrees in the literary record is a desirable next step which promises to yield fresh insights. Peter Liddel has made a valuable start on the honorific decrees (2016), and promises a fuller study.

Finally, coverage of the territory does not claim to be systematic or complete. In general the essays are on matters on which I have something new to say, and spend little time going over ground that is well-trodden or tangential to the epigraphical record. This does not purport to be a handbook, but a book which seeks in various ways to progress our understanding of a period of history from an epigraphical perspective.

The first two essays (Part I) address some fundamentals. The conventional approach to inscribed laws and decrees as sources of factual information about the past has tended to obscure some important avenues to understanding them in the round. In particular to give a satisfactory account of what the city was doing with these inscriptions we need to comprehend them as monuments as well as texts. Two aspects of monumentality can be distinguished: location; and physicality, including features such as form, shape, size, sculpture, moulded decoration, paint and physical aspects of the writing (e.g. letter size, use of headings, stoichedon style). The first essay, while making some observations on physical aspects,[4] focuses primarily on location, exploring the acropolis as the predominant place of erection for inscribed decrees since the mid-fifth century, through the period of our corpus and beyond. In a manner that has much in common with, but also remains distinguishable from, dedications in sanctuaries, decree stelai are part of the city's commerce with the gods, one face oriented metaphorically to the divine sphere. But the space of the acropolis is not only religiously charged, it is also public, the city's space, not that of any individual or group, and its inscriptions, though very numerous by our period, were intended to be noticed by, and (importantly) have an impact on, men as well as gods. It was also monumental space. The city began regularly inscribing its inscriptions on the acropolis at the same time as the Periclean

4 For some further observations see Lambert 2006, 116–19 (= *IALD*, 95–101). I would highlight here one feature which helps understand the impact of a decree inscription on the visitor to the acropolis presented, as would have been the case by this period, with a mass of inscribed stones and other monuments competing for attention. It was patently one function of relief sculpture and/or painted decoration, headings in larger lettering (including names labelling divine and human figures in the relief, names of honorands in larger letters at the head of the decree and the word, θεοί), and, above or more usually at this period below the text, inscribed crowns, often containing the name of the awarder of the crown (as e.g. Council or Assembly) and its recipient, to help convey key information about it at a glance, by a mixture of visual (relief, crowns) and verbal signals, about the type of decree (e.g. honorific? proxeny?), the identity of individuals and cities that were the subject of the decree, and the religious context.

building programme; the inscriptions complemented on a small scale the larger scale monuments, sharing in their quality of exultation of the city and its patron goddess, making the acropolis a suitable location for inscriptions relating to the Athenian Empire, and incidentally celebrating the city as a city of the word, originally spoken and ephemeral in Council and Assembly, made now to endure in petrified writing. And it was high space, not only conspicuous, but raised from the often contentious "down to earth" debate in Council chamber and Pnyx that was the prelude to the "up"-grading that the inscription represented from mere proposal of a citizen to solemn decision of the city. By our period the acropolis had been established for a century as the "default" location and it required a strong driver to pull to other locations, a pull that could be exerted by the same religious driver that determined the acropolis as prime location, drawing sometimes to a sanctuary elsewhere; a pull that could also be exerted where the city's message was to be conveyed to a particular viewership in a particular place, occasionally a message guaranteeing or authorising or informing about something, but more often a hortatory or dissuasory one. Inscribed decrees had agency; they were designed to have an impact on the world. Finally, just as the religious driver could sometimes pull away from the acropolis as it usually pulled towards it, so the "imperial" driver, which had helped pull inscriptions to the acropolis at the height of the Athenian Empire, also had a centrifugal momentum: inscribed decrees could also express the presence of the city and the reach of its decisions outside the boundaries of Attica. There was a tendency for "message" drivers to pull to locations away from the acropolis with decrees that were the first of their kind or sui generis. Laws as a distinct category of measure from decrees were a specific feature of the fourth-century democracy and were, it seems, to be lodged in papyrus copies in the archive in the Metroon, created in the last decade of the fifth century perhaps specifically to receive them. For laws inscription was an optional extra to an extent that never applied with certain types of decree; inscribed laws are accordingly not only rare, there was no default location and where they are inscribed the "message" driver is commonly apparent in determining location.

The second essay explores another fundamental topic, selectivity. What decrees were inscribed and what were not?[5] The question is fundamental because it is intimately connected with the question, what inscribing decrees was *for*, and because if we are to answer questions on the basis of the epigraphical record, for example about the wealth and prominence of proposers and relations between the Council and the Assembly, we need to understand

5 With rare exceptions, e.g. *IG* II^3 1, 337, for the merchants of Kition, at this period decrees were inscribed at public initiative and expense.

how representative that record is of all decrees passed. Honorific decrees overwhelmingly predominate in the inscribed corpus of this period, accounting for 87%, with just a handful of religious regulations, treaties and other foreign policy related decrees and other types. Comparison with the decrees proposed by Demosthenes attested in the literary record demonstrates clearly that there were categories of decree that were not usually inscribed on stone, including those dealing with ephemeral (but not necessarily unimportant) matters, such as military dispositions; and close reading of the inscribed record shows that, even with the most common inscribed category, the honorific decree, some types were not usually inscribed, e.g. those honouring Athenian officials before the 340s, those awarding foliage (rather than gold) crowns to Athenians after that date, and those awarding crowns, but no enduring privileges (for which the inscribed decree would serve as guarantee), to foreigners. Even with commonly inscribed types, such as proxenies, the decision to inscribe a particular decree or not was at the discretion of the Assembly. Crucial drivers towards inscription were the enduring character of the measure, religiously significant subject-matter (e.g. if the decree honoured a priest or provided for sacrifices), and the potential of the inscription to deliver a message, typically, but not always, hortatory or dissuasory. The award of honours was, it is clear enough, an important part of the work of the Council and Assembly,[6] but honorific decrees did not comprise 87% of the decrees passed by those bodies; and we must bear in mind this unbalance when seeking to address questions about the behaviour of the Assembly on the basis of the inscribed record as a whole.

If inscribed laws and decrees had agency, it makes sense to enquire into the character of that agency, or simply put, to ask what the city was seeking to achieve by having them inscribed. This question is explored in the two chapters that comprise Part II; and here a paper on the inscribed treaties and decrees honouring whole cities of this period, first published in 2010, and reprinted in the companion volume to this one,[7] is also relevant. Chapter 3 of this volume (first published in 2011) explores this question primarily in relation to the most numerous category of inscribed decree at this, and indeed at all periods from the mid-5th century on, honorific decrees. It notes that the 340s witnessed three important, linked, developments in honorific decrees: the explicit recognition of *philotimia* ("honour-loving behaviour") directed

6 Clear above all from prominence of honorific decrees in the literary record as well as the epigraphical (e.g. a quarter of decrees proposed by Demosthenes attested in the literary record were honorific) and their dominance in the statistics for *graphai paranomon*. See further the discussion of this point in chapter 8.

7 Lambert 2010 = *IALD*, 377–86.

at the city as praiseworthy; the introduction of "hortatory intention" clauses, stating explicitly that the purpose of the decree, sometimes specifically the purpose of inscribing it, was to encourage the honorand to continue to behave in an honour-loving way towards the city, and more significantly, others to behave in a similar way; and the beginning of the regular practice of inscribing decrees honouring Athenian officials such as councillors, priests, secretaries, curators of the water supply, managers of festivals. These were not wholly new phenomena: the hortatory intention had always been implicit in the bestowal of honours, and, though it is difficult to pin down the extent of the practice, councillors and other Athenian officials had been honoured by the Council and Assembly before the 340s; but these developments of the 340s display, I suggested, a city straining to gain maximum leverage from honours, to encourage high performance from its officials, and maximum benefaction from foreigners, at a time when the city's position in the Greek world was increasingly threatened by the growth of Macedonian power, and honorific decrees were becoming relatively increasingly important instruments of policy as other options for action, including the exercise of military muscle, became unrealistic, especially after the defeat at Chaironeia in 338, the subsequent termination of the Second Athenian League and Athens' accession to the League of Corinth, under Macedonian leadership. As I emphasise in chapter 8, the honouring of relatively ordinary Athenian officials was also an important democratisation of *philotimia*, helping to explain how it could come to be acceptable as a praiseworthy virtue in a democracy.[8]

Lambert 2010 developed some of these points, observing that Athens ceased inscribing (and may have largely ceased making) bilateral treaties and decrees honouring whole cities (a genre of decree that, like the treaty, was an instrument of interstate diplomacy) between the battle of Chaironeia and the Lamian War.[9] Instead the only two inscribed treaties that survive from Athens at this period are copies of multilateral treaties to which Athens was a subordinate

8 On euergetism and honorific practice in archaic and classical Greece see now the study of Domingo Gygax 2016, which deals extensively with Athens, references other recent bibliography and is likely to become an important point of reference for future work on this topic.

9 Liddel 2016, 321 with n. 52, notes that the decree of the post-Chaironeia period enfranchising exiles from Troizen, attested by Hyp. *Ath.* 31, might be an exception to the rule that Athens ceased passing decrees honouring whole cities in this period, though as M. Osborne 1981–83 iii–iv, 71–72 (T37) points out, the numbers of Troizenians actually awarded privileges by this decree may well have been more limited than Hypereides suggests, and the decree honouring Akarnanian exiles of 338/7, *IG* II^3 1, 316, may supply a parallel. In that decree only the two leaders were granted citizenship (or rather had existing hereditary rights confirmed) and their followers were effectively granted *isoteleia*. See also Whitehead 2000, 341–42.

party, with other Greek cities, to Philip II (*IG* II^3 1, 318) and Alexander the Great (*IG* II^3 1, 443). The battle of Chaironeia marked, indeed, a long-term watershed, after which Athens' room for manoeuvre in interstate relations became more or less constrained, formally or informally, by the Macedonian kings and their successors, and the relative value of state-to-person relations, as represented by the honorific decree, was enhanced.

Chapter 4, also first published in 2011, draws together some of these threads and seeks to unpack a little more specifically the key changes in the political priorities and preoccupations of the Athenians as reflected in the inscribed laws and decrees of this period. The most numerous among decrees honouring foreigners are those which, directly or indirectly, concern relations with Macedon. Unsurprisingly they display a shift of direction after the battle of Chaironeia: before it aimed at encouraging and supporting enemies of Philip, while those aimed at maintaining good relations with the Macedonian regime and its friends put in an appearance only in the years after the battle. Athens does not hesitate, however, to inscribe decrees after Chaironeia which show her giving a warm welcome to enemies of Philip who had supported Athens but were now in exile from their home cities; and later in the 30s and early 20s there are other decrees which arguably express muted or suppressed resistance, or an aspiration to resist.[10] The two next most numerous categories,

10 This is implicitly also one aspect of the "anti-tyranny" law of 336, on which see further below. There is a synoptic essay to be written on developing relations with and attitudes to the Macedonians in the period between Chaironeia and the Lamian War, taking in the evidence of the orators alongside that of the inscriptions. It is clear enough from the orators that the policy of detente with Macedon, whose leading proponent was Demades, was fiercely controversial in the early years after 338; witness for example the virulent opposition, voiced by Hypereides, to Demades' proposal to honour the pro-Macedonian Euthykrates of Olynthos, to Philippides' proposal to honour the *proedroi* who had put to the vote proposals to honour one or more leading Macedonians (chapter 7 n. 22, and below n. 13), and to Diondas' *graphe paranomon* against his own and Demomeles' proposal to crown Demosthenes in 338 (which came to court in 335/4 or 334/3, Carey et al. 2008, 3), not to mention that voiced by Polyeuktos of Sphettos (chapter 8 n. 87) and Lykourgos (chapter 11.2), to the proposal of Kephisodotos to honour Demades himself with a statue. It is also clear from the orators that Demades won some of these arguments (Din. 1.101 shows that he was indeed honoured), and lost others (he was rendered *atimos* in 323 for a third conviction for making an illegal proposal, namely his proposal in 324 to honour Alexander as a god, Diod. 18.18, cf. Athen. 6.251b, Hansen 1974, 41 no. 38), but mostly the orators do not inform us about the results of cases in the courts (the results of those involving Euthykrates and Philippides are unknown, and the other two successful *graphai paranomon* against Demades are also unknown). Here the inscribed decrees have the edge, since by definition they record proposals that attracted majority support

those relating to the grain supply and the theatre, display the generalised hortatory intention, and the People's priorities, with particular clarity. The grain supply had always been high on the city's policy agenda, but it is only in the circumstances of general shortages across the eastern Mediterranean in the 330s, and anxieties generated by the defeat at Chaironeia, the "end of Empire" and the ceding of hegemony to the Macedonians, that Athens develops a systematic policy of honouring grain traders with inscribed decrees, in an attempt to encourage not only the individual traders honoured, but the whole grain-trading community, to give priority to supplying Athens. Thereby Athens was making "celebrities" of men who in every case are otherwise unknown to the historical record.[11] A similar dynamic applies to the group of decrees honouring men connected with the theatre, actors, playwrights and others. This was an era in which such men were indeed celebrities, able to demand high fees, for whose services Athens was in competition with, among others, Alexander himself.[12] Like grain traders in the post-Chaironeia years, the city adopted a policy of offering honours as an incentive to these men to ply their trade at Athens. The inscribed laws and decrees of this period also document an intense engagement with the regeneration of the religious and festival life of the city, most notably in measures to enhance the annual celebration of the Panathenaia; and, a golden thread running through a number of the developments in the political and cultural life of the city at this period, an intense engagement with the past, including the 5th century, which now acquires focus as a "classical" period, politically, as the high-point of Empire, and culturally, as a high-point of theatrical achievement.

It is this last point that I develop in Part III. In chapter 5, first published in 2010, I explore how the laws and decrees of this period manifest an impulse, stimulated by anxiety about defeat and decline, to connect paideutically with the past in general and the glory days of the fifth century in particular. The locus classicus is *IG* II^3 1, 444, a decree of this period recording a decision to

---

in the Assembly. They make clear enough in general the extent of Demades' influence, and that he and other supporters of constructive relations with the Macedonians could command a majority for key measures honouring leading Macedonians and their courtiers (including Archedikos of Lamptrai for his proposal in the late 320s to honour the "friends of the king and Antipater", *IG* II^3 1, 484), but that those ranged on the other side of the argument could also secure victories, albeit not such as to disrupt the main lines of the policy of detente (as e.g. Hegesippos' honours for Akarnanian supporters of the Athenians at Chaironeia, *IG* II^3 1, 316).

11 For a full analysis of the role of honorific decrees in the context of Athenian trade policy between 415 and 307 BC see now Engen 2010.

12 On this topic see now also Csapo and Wilson 2014; Hanink 2014.

repair and raise a statue of Athena Nike, "Athena Victory", first dedicated from the spoils of victories in the 420s; but the tendency can also be observed in other inscriptions. Chapter 6, first published in 2012, extends the scope of the enquiry to the fourth century as a whole, showing how, before ca. 350, the regime of the Thirty is the most distant past event alluded to in inscribed laws and decrees and there are no references to the 5th-century earlier than that, but from the 340s onwards the 5th century before 403 is increasingly (albeit still only occasionally) alluded to, subtly at first, but more explicitly after 338. The paper adds further examples to those discussed in chapter 5 and, finally, looks forward in this perspective to Stratokles' decree of 307/6, posthumously honouring Lykourgos of Boutadai, *IG* II^2 457 + 3207.

The period covered by this corpus can be designated as the "last phase of the classical democracy" and Part IV examines some of the many facets of that "democracy" on which the inscriptions cast light. In these years, particularly after the battle of Chaironeia, "democracy" became self-consciously part of the city's heritage from its 5th-century past, promoted and cultivated in the face of the Macedonian challenge, in the same way, in a sense, as the city's theatrical heritage, and its imperial one. Some Athenians may have voted for the famous law of 336 (*IG* II^3 1, 320) which sought to embed democracy against threats, real or imagined, from potential "tyrants", supported by a resurgent Areopagos, as a shot across the bows of Demosthenes (and others) who had contributed to that resurgence, but there is no doubt that there was a perceived ideological connection at this period between the anti-democrat and the pro-Macedonian;[13] and, as far as the reality rather than the rhetoric is concerned, it is scarcely a coincidence that the other significant fact known about the proposer of the law, Eukrates of Piraeus, is that he was among the leading Athenian opponents

13 One might take as an example Hypereides' prosecution of Philippides at a *graphe paranomon*, at around the time the anti-tyranny laws was passed (datable to between the aftermath of Chaironeia and the death of Philip II), for proposing that the *proedroi* should be honoured for putting to the vote a proposal to honour a leading Macedonian or Macedonians. Philippides, asserts Hypereides, could not claim to be a democrat (δημοτικός), because he was a slave to "tyrants" (scil. = the Macedonians) and thought it right to give instructions to the People (ἀλλὰ ἴστ' αὐτὸν τοῖς μὲν τυράννοις δουλεύειν προελόμενον, τῶι δὲ δήμωι προστάττειν ἀξιοῦντα, Hyp. *Phil.* 10 Whitehead). In the same speech the word *demokratia* occurred in the same (fragmentary) context as mention of Philip II (F11, no doubt the antipathy between the two was emphasised), and Hypereides also perhaps (I suggest in a forthcoming paper) plays with the connotations of the name of one of Philippides' supporters, Demokrates of Aphidna: "and yet, O Demokrates, you alone have no right to say anything disparaging about the Demos", καίτοι ὦ Δημ[όκρα]τες μόνωι σοὶ οὐκ [ἔνι λέγ]ειν περὶ τοῦ δήμου [φλα]ῦρον οὐδέν (2).

of Macedon who was executed on the orders of Antipater at the moment when the democracy was, in fact, dissolved,[14] and (it seems) the inscription carrying the law which had been supposed to embed it was pulled down (it was used in the fill for an early hellenistic building in the Agora). It seems clear enough that, for some Athenians, the passage of this law was motivated by anxiety about what Macedonian hegemony meant for their "democracy". The relief at the top of the law that sought to embed democracy depicted a personification of Democracy crowning a personification of the People, and it is also no surprise that one of the many manifestations of the city's intensified focus on its religious observance in these years is an enhanced public attention directed to the cult of the "goddess" Demokratia.[15]

A paper could also be written on developments at this period in the culture and practice of accountability, a cornerstone of the democratic idea since the very beginnings of political theorising,[16] a paper that would encompass Aeschines' allegation that Ktesiphon's proposed award of a crown to Demosthenes was illegal among other things because he had not submitted his accounts,[17] as well as the frequent references, in inscribed honours for Athenians, to crowns being awarded either subject to, or following, *euthynai*.[18] Aeschines 3.9–12 insinuates

---

14 Lucian, *Dem. Enc.* 31.

15 Dedication by Council, "having been crowned by the People" of a statue of Democracy in 333/2, *IG* II³ 4, 3; sacrifices to Democracy by the generals in Boedromion 332/1, *IG* II² 1496, ll. 131–32, and 331/0, ll. 140–41. Parker 1996, 228–29, aptly remarks on the implications of this for a sense among ordinary Athenians of the divine blessings bestowed by Democracy.

16 In the debate on the constitutions dramatically set in Persia in 522 BC by Hdt. 3.80, Otanes singles out accountability as a key feature of "rule of the mass" (i.e. "democracy"): ὑπεύθυνον δὲ ἀρχὴν ἔχει. An association between freedom, democracy and accountability is also implied in the decree of 307/6 honouring Lykourgos: καὶ διδοὺς εὐθύνας πολλάκις τῶν πεπολιτευμένων ἐν ἐλευθέρᾳ καὶ δημοκρατουμένῃ τῃ πόλει...([Plut.] *Lives of the Ten Orators* 852d).

17 Aeschin. 3.9–31.

18 Phanodemos of Thymaitadai to be crowned by the Council with a five hundred drachma crown for winning the competition for best speaker in the Council, not made subject to *euthynai*, but a *probouleuma* also to go forward to the People that he should be crowned with a 1,000 dr. crown, ἐπειδὰν τὰς εὐθύνας δῶι, *IG* II³ 1, 306, 13 (343/2); Eudoxos of Sypalettos, Council administrator, to be crowned with 500 dr. crowns paid for by the Council and the councillors privately, ἐπειδὰν τὰς εὐθύνας δῶι, *IG* II³ 1, 306, 30 and 46 (343/2); priests in Piraeus cults and *hieropoioi* to be crowned, ἐπειδὰν τὰς εὐθύνας δῶσι, *IG* II³ 1, 416, 22, 35 (338/7?); Chairestratos of Acharnai, secretary of the Council (?) to be crowned, ἐπειδὰν τὰς εὐθύνας δῶι, *IG* II³ 1, 323, 13 (337/6); Phyleus of Oinoe, secretary of the Council and People (?), to be crowned, ἐπειδὰν τὰς εὐθύνας δῶι, *IG* II³ 1, 327, 42 and 58–59 (336/5), and following the successful completion of his *euthynai*, *IG* II³ 1, 327 III

that the practice of making such awards subject to *euthynai* was to prejudice the *euthynai* in the office-holder's favour, though in the past, he implies, before the current law was passed, the situation was even worse, in that crowns had been actually awarded before office-holders had passed their *euthynai*. This was one, somewhat jaundiced, angle on the matter; another, more pragmatic, was that the Council needed to be able to award and recommend honours for office-holders before it demitted office at the end of its annual term. There is no doubt, however, that this very deliberate and explicit acknowledgement of the principle of accountability, inscribed so frequently on dedications and stelai honouring officials, also emphatically displayed this aspect of democratic ideology in a way that had not happened before decrees honouring Athenian officials began to be regularly inscribed in the 340s.

The focus of the three papers that comprise Part IV, however, is elsewhere. Democracy and the rule of law were ideological bed-fellows in this latest phase of the classical democracy, as they are in the modern West; but the "rule of law" had a special significance in a city in which, since 403 BC, decrees of the Council and Assembly had been required to be within the law. Chapter 7 shows how the inscribed laws and decrees of this period display a commitment to the rule of law, motivated both by a principled sense of the need for legality in a democracy, and by a more self-interested concern on the part of proposers in the Council and Assembly to protect decrees from being attacked as illegal by *graphe paranomon*. It argues that there are indications of an intensified preoccupation with the rule of law after 338, detectable both in the texts of decrees and in an increase in the frequency with which new laws were inscribed. This, I suggest, was a reaction to defeat comparable to others that are detectable in the epigraphical record, driven by a desire to embed and promote Athens' distinctive democratic identity.

The two longer chapters in this Part analyse two fundamental aspects of the workings of the democratic process: the proposers of laws and decrees; and relations between the Council and the Assembly. M. H. Hansen (1984, 1991) observed that there was a remarkable multiplicity of decree proposers in the

(335/4); Pytheas of Alopeke, curator of the water supply, to be praised, ἐπειδὰν τὰς εὐθύνας δῶι, *IG* II^3 1, 338, 19–20 (333/2); Androkles of Kerameis, priest of Asklepios, to be crowned, ἐπειδὰν τὰς εὐθύνας δῶι, *IG* II^3 1, 359, 21–22 (328/7); three councillors responsible for organising a dedication to Amphiaraos to be crowned, ἐπὰν τὰς εὐθύνας δῶσιν, *IG* II^3 1, 360, 51–52 (328/7); annual *hieropoioi* to be crowned, ἐπειδὰν τὰς εὐθύνας δῶσιν, *IG* II^3 1, 369, 46 (325/4); prytany treasurer (?) to be crowned, ἐπειδὰν τὰς εὐθύνας δῶι, *IG* II^3 1, 417, 21 (340–325); Kallikratides of Steiria, recorder (*anagrapheus*) to be crowned, ἐπειδὰν τὰς εὐθύνας δῶι, *IG* II^3 1, 469, 28 (ca. 330); cf. the fragmentary cases, 424, 3; 458, 3.

fourth-century democracy, a good number of them not very wealthy or prominent individuals. He offered two main explanations for this. First, about 50% of decrees were probouleumatic, i.e. passed by the Assembly as they came forward from the Council. Since no-one was permitted to serve more than two annual terms as councillor in a lifetime, the Council was manned largely by ordinary Athenians rather than by prominent politicians, ordinary Athenians who quite commonly, therefore, appear as decree proposers. Second, for avoidance of the *graphe paranomon*, it was convenient for prominent politicians to have their proposals put in the name of a relatively obscure individual, whether in the Council or the Assembly, a practice documented in the orators. In chapter 8 I challenge this analysis. As argued in chapter 9, the large majority of inscribed decrees of the late-350s to 322/1 were, in fact, non-probouleumatic or were debated in the Assembly; wealthy and prominent individuals are, in fact, commonly attested as proposers of decrees, including honorific ones; and it is questionable to infer common patterns of behaviour from rhetorical allegations in the orators of improper political practices. Insofar as the factors driving someone to propose a decree can be detected in the epigraphical record (and admittedly those factors are often obscure) a wider range of mostly more innocent explanations would seem to fit the case: for example, a younger citizen learning the political ropes under the tutelage of a more experienced one; a man not on the Council, but keen to pursue an issue in the Assembly, persuading a fellow demesman who was on the Council to propose a suitable *probouleuma*. The chapter identifies explanations for the two most notable patterns as regards top-flight politicians: the large number of decrees proposed by Demosthenes in the literary record in contrast to the small number in the epigraphical; and the large number of inscribed decrees proposed by Demades and Lykourgos. As regards the overall picture, on the basis of an analysis of liturgists, decree proposers, secretaries of the Council and *proedroi*, it finds that, on average, the proposers of inscribed laws and decrees were less prominent and wealthy than the average liturgist, but more prominent and wealthy than the average secretary of the Council or ordinary councillor. When we break these figures down, however, we find that they conceal a marked contrast between decrees honouring Athenians, more commonly proposed by less wealthy and prominent men who were councillors, and other kinds of decree, more commonly proposed in the Assembly by more wealthy and prominent individuals. Athenian honorands were mostly councillors, Council officers or officials whose duties had been performed under the purview of the Council, and the proposers of honours for them, like the honorands, were generally also Council members and not very prominent or wealthy. The proposers of honorific decrees for foreigners and other foreign policy decrees on the other hand mostly required a locus in high status international networks. The multiplicity of decree proposers observed by Hansen, and confirmed by my analysis, remains, however, a notable feature. I suggest that it is explicable as an aspect of a political culture which was "democratic" in promoting the active political participation of all citizens and favouring the plurilocality of power and influence, regardless of the prominence and wealth of those exercising it. In general the findings of this chapter are consonant with the observations of Ober 2008 that democratic Athens was a uniquely well-networked city, in which political knowledge and expertise came to be spread remarkably widely among its citizens.

Greek cities commonly had a Council that was responsible for preparing the business of the citizen Assembly (*probouleusis*), but the composition, organisation and relationship to eachother of Council and Assembly were crucial determinants of the extent to which a city was "democratic".[19] It is generally recognised that the constitution of the Council and Assembly in fourth-century Athens was democratically normative, and chapter 9 adds nothing new as regards the infrastracture of the institutions at that period. It does, however, present new findings on their relative roles in the formulation of decisions. The current orthodoxy, established by P. J. Rhodes (1972), is that Council and Assembly were broadly in balance in this regard across the fourth-century democracy as a whole. Chapter 9 shows that this now requires radical modification in relation to the period 352/1–322/1, when the Assembly was much more dominant than that orthodoxy would suggest. For example, the large majority of inscribed Assembly decrees were non-probouleumatic (i.e. the Council's proposal was recast in the Assembly), and all but two of the probouleumatic decrees are or may have been followed on the stone by riders, implying that they were actively debated and modified in the Assembly. Analysis of the content of the non-probouleumatic decrees indicates a clear tendency for the Assembly to reserve to itself more significant and controversial decisions.

The extent to which the Assembly was predominant over the Council would have been regarded by most contemporary Athenians as a healthy sign of a vigorous democracy; but since the Council was broadly representative of the citizen body as whole, this is more surprising to our minds, used to ideas of representative democracy. It was a notably radical feature of the democracy at this period that it was regarded as necessary for policy decisions to be taken by the collective of the citizens as a whole, in the Assembly, where every individual citizen had

19 Again in Otanes' analysis in the debate on the constitutions in Persia in 522 BC dramatised by Hdt. 3.80, it was characteristic of "rule of the mass" (= "democracy") that βουλεύματα … πάντα ἐς τὸ κοινὸν ἀναφέρει ("all proposals are referred to the collective").

the opportunity to participate. This is consonant with the observations about the multiplicity of decree proposers in chapter 8: in democracy as practised in fourth-century Athens it was felt to be essential that the many should predominate, whether in the number of individuals who made successful proposals or the relative roles of the Council and Assembly in formulating decisions.

Finally chapter 9 offers a comparison with the situation across a comparable span of years at the end of the third century BC, finding that, while some of the "democratic" features of the infrastructure of the fourth-century remained in place – the Council was still "democratically" large, with 50 members per tribe, and routinely referred its *probouleumata* for ratification by the Assembly – other aspects of that infrastructure had crumbled. The limitation on serving twice in the Council that was so crucial in ensuring that it was representative of the citizen body in the fourth century had been lifted, while it is unclear whether another crucial aspect of the fourth-century democratic system, pay for attendance at the Council and Assembly, still applied. As for frequency of Assembly meetings, another touchstone of a democratic system, the basis for the conventional view that they continued in the third century roughly at the same frequency as in the fourth (i.e. normally four times a prytany in the fourth century, three times in the shorter prytanies of the third century) is not strong, though there are indications that there continued to be at least one Assembly in each prytany. More importantly there are clear indications in the character and wording of the decrees in this later period that the real balance of power had shifted away from the many and towards the few. The balance in decision-taking has shifted markedly away from the Assembly and towards the Council. Probouleumatic decrees now predominate in the epigraphic record; other signs of an active Assembly, such as riders, are absent from the inscriptions. Moreover, honours are awarded to Athenian citizens explicitly for their financial contributions in a way that never occurred in the inscribed decrees of the fourth-century democracy. Assembly decisions are not always put into effect; and in some cases are taken explicitly because a wealthy political leader "thinks it right". This reflects a long term shift, in which the abolition of liturgies by Demetrios of Phaleron was a crucial step, from a collective system of public financing in the classical democracy, which legally imposed heavy financial obligations on the wealthy, to a system dependent, by the late third century, on voluntary euergetism. Consonant with this was a shift away from the Council and Assembly as key loci for major decision taking and towards extra-constitutional sources of power, whether super-wealthy Athenian citizens such as Eurykleides and Mikion or the hellenistic kings and their courtiers.

Part IV as a whole supplies some evidence that the Athenian democracy strengthened as the fourth-century democracy progressed: the rule of law was progressively embedded and emphasised; the Assembly, it seems, was progressively more dominant in decision-making.[20] More work would need to be done on the situation in the first half of the fourth century to show that the widespread involvement in political initiative-taking observable in the data for proposers of laws and decrees in the last generation of the classical democracy is also the result of progressive development since 403.

Part V, Postscripts, comprises two chapters which discuss inscriptions not included in *IG* II^3 1 fasc. 2, but which are nonetheless relevant to the period. In effect they supplement the essays published in *IALD*. Two Council decrees of the 330s from the sanctuary of Kekrops on the acropolis are inscribed together with decrees not of the Assembly, but of other groups, including the tribe Kekropis: *IG* II^2 1156 = *RO* 89, a dedication by the ephebes of Kekropis of 334/3 BC, including a list of the ephebes, followed by honorific decrees of the tribe, of the Council, of the deme Eleusis, where the ephebes had performed guard duty, and the deme Athmonon, to which their commander belonged; and, the subject of chapter 10, *IG* II^2 1155, a dedication of 339/8 by the soldiers of Kekropis and their tribal commander (taxiarch), and very fragmentary honorific decrees of the Council and the tribe. The paper, first published in 2015, reviews the texts and relationship to eachother of the fragments of this inscription (or inscriptions) and briefly discusses the possibility that the military service commemorated by the monument was in the context of the two skirmishes of winter 339/8 mentioned by Demosthenes 18.216–17 ("the battle by the river and the winter battle") in which the allies were victorious in the lead-up to the battle of Chaironeia. Between that battle and the Lamian War Lykourgos of Boutadai was the most influential Athenian politician in the domestic sphere, and the decree honouring him, passed posthumously on the restoration of democracy in 307/6 on the proposal of Stratokles of Diomeia, is not only invaluable evidence for how his career was evaluated nearly two decades after his death, it is also of particular interest on two counts in the history of Athenian decrees: it is the earliest surviving text of a decree awarding the high honours of *sitesis* and a bronze statue to a native-born Athenian; and it is very unusual in that it exists both in a (fragmentary) inscribed version, *IG* II^2 457, and in a version preserved in a literary text, the *Life of Lykourgos* attributed to Plutarch ([Plut.] *Lives of the Ten Orators* 852). Chapter 11, also first published in 2015, examines the case, first made by the great Austrian epigraphist Adolf Wilhelm, for associating *IG* II^2 3207, the lower portion of a stele inscribed with multiple crowns, with this decree. It confirms that the crowns commemorated decrees honouring Lykourgos in his lifetime, and reviews what can be inferred about those decrees in the context of his political career and rivalry with Demades.

---

20 See chapter 9, note 69.

Bibliography and Abbreviations

Carey, C. et al. 2008: "Fragments of Hyperides' *Against Diondas* from the Archimedes palimpsest", ZPE 165, 1–19.

Csapo, E. and Wilson, P. 2014: "The finance and organisation of the Athenian theatre in the time of Eubulus and Lycurgus", in E. Csapo, H. Goette, J. R. Green and P. Wilson eds., *Greek theatre in the fourth century BC*, 393–424.

Domingo Gygax, M. 2016: *Benefaction and rewards in the Ancient Greek city. The origins of euergetism*, Cambridge.

Engen, D. T. 2010: *Honor and profit. Athenian trade policy and the economy and society of Greece, 415–307 BCE*, Ann Arbor.

Hanink, J. 2014: *Lycurgan Athens and the making of classical tragedy*, Cambridge.

Hansen, M. H. 1974: *The sovereignty of the people's court in the fourth century BC and the public action against unconstitutional proposals*, Odense.

Hansen, M. H. 1984: "The number of *rhetores* in the Athenian *ecclesia*, 355–322 BC", GRBS 25 (1984), 123–55, reprinted with addenda in Hansen 1989, 93–127.

Hansen, M. H. 1989: *The Athenian ecclesia* II, Copenhagen.

Hansen, M. H. 1991: *The Athenian democracy in the age of Demosthenes*, Oxford.

IALD: S. D. Lambert, *Inscribed Athenian laws and decrees 352/1–322/1 BC. Epigraphical essays*, Leiden, 2012.

Lambert, S. D. 2006: "Athenian state laws and decrees, 352/1–322/1: III Decrees honouring foreigners. A. Citizenship, proxeny and euergesy", ZPE 158, 115–58 (= IALD, 93–137)

Lambert, S. D. 2010: "Inscribed treaties ca. 350–321: an epigraphical perspective on Athenian foreign policy", in G. Reger, F. X. Ryan and T. F. Winters (eds.), *Studies in Greek epigraphy and history in honor of Stephen V. Tracy*, Bordeaux, 153–60 (= IALD, 377–86).

Liddel, P. 2016: "Honorific decrees of fourth-century Athens: trends, perceptions, controversies", in C. Tiersch ed., *Die Athenische Demokratie im 4. Jahrhundert. Zwischen Modernisierung und Tradition*, Berlin, 335–57.

Ober, J. 2008: *Democracy and knowledge. Innovation and learning in classical Athens*, Princeton.

Osborne, M. J. 1981–83: *Naturalization in Athens*, i–iv, Brussels.

Parker, R. 1996: *Athenian religion. A history*, Oxford.

Rhodes, P. J. 1972: *The Athenian Boule*, Oxford.

RO: P. J. Rhodes and R. Osborne, *Greek historical inscriptions 404–323 BC*, Oxford, 2003.

Whitehead, D. 2000: *Hypereides. The forensic speeches*, Oxford.

PART 1

Fundamentals

CHAPTER 1

The Locations of Inscribed Athenian Laws and Decrees in the Age of Demosthenes*

1 Introduction

An inscription is not only a text, it is also a monument, and as with any monument, understanding its location is fundamental to its interpretation. This applies rather obviously to common types of object which may carry inscribed texts such as dedications, where it is normally close to the intentional surface that the dedication is to a specific deity in a specific sanctuary, and funerary monuments, where their patently commemorative function induces reflection on the impact of the monument on the "passer-by", ancient or modern, on the context of the monument in relation to others within a funerary enclosure (*peribolos*) and on topics such as the relationship of the place of origin of the individual commemorated to the location of their monument.[1] It applies, however, no less to inscribed laws (*nomoi*) and decrees (*psephismata*), whose great value as "historical documents", much of which is admittedly unrelated to precisely where they were set up, has traditionally tended to overshadow reflection on their monumental aspects. In the last generation or so, however, work on the locations of inscribed Athenian laws and decrees, and on their monumental intention and purpose, has advanced apace. The closing years of

---

* [This paper will also be published in I. Berti, D. Marchiandi eds., *Inscribing Space: the Topography of Attic Inscriptions. Proceedings of the Conference, Heidelberg 29–30 May 2015*, Historika Suppl. 1, forthcoming]. I am grateful to Daniela Marchiandi and Irene Berti for the invitation to participate in the conference, *Inscribing Space*, and to them and other participants for their comments on the day. The paper has its origins in work done in 2012/3 while enjoying the privilege of membership of the Institute for Advanced Study, Princeton, supported by the patrons' endowment fund and the Loeb foundation, and was finalised in summer 2016 in the excellent library of the Seminar für Alte Geschichte, Heidelberg, where I am grateful to Kai Trampedach and Christian Witschel for their hospitality. I thank Peter Liddel for helpful comments on a final draft.

1 On extant Acropolis dedications see Keesling 2003, on those recorded in inventories Harris 1995 (see e.g. *IG* I^3 329 = *OR* 169). Compare, for the Asklepieion, Aleshire 1989; examples of inventories, *IG* II^3 1, 898 and 1010, cf. 1154. On Attic funerary *periboloi* of the classical period see Marchiandi 2011; relationship of place of commemoration to place of origin within Attica: Osborne 1991, 231–52 [= 2010, 139–67, at 150–57].

© KONINKLIJKE BRILL NV, LEIDEN, 2018 | DOI 10.1163/9789004352490_003

the last century saw the publication of a systematic catalogue of relief sculpture on inscribed "documents", Lawton 1995, placing on a sound basis the study of that aspect of the monumentality of Athenian inscribed laws and decrees,[2] as well as groundbreaking general papers by Detienne (1988), Hölkeskamp (1992, 1994 and 2000) and, focussing specifically on Athens, Osborne (1999). Highlights of the early years of the twenty-first century have included thought-provoking reflections on the locations of fourth-century inscribed Athenian laws by Richardson (2000), a fundamental data-gathering exercise on locations of inscribed Athenian decrees across a wide span of time by Liddel (2003), thoughtful contributions on the significance of the Athenian Agora as location of inscribed laws and decrees by Shear (2007 and 2011), and a thorough synthesis of these and many other recent contributions which also makes some telling fresh observations by Meyer (2013).[3] In this paper I aim to take this topic forward via a case study of the locations of the 281 inscribed Athenian laws and decrees of the last phase of the classical democracy (352/1–322/1 BC) which I edited for *Inscriptiones Graecae* (texts: *IG* II³ 1, 292–572; annotated translations: www.atticinscriptions.com). Though this period will be at the centre of my enquiry, for context I shall look both forwards and backwards in time. From this it will become apparent that we have to do with a pattern that displays both strong continuities and fluidities.

Most of the inscriptions I shall be reviewing carry texts of decrees of the Council of 500 (which formulated proposals, *probouleumata*, for decrees of the Assembly, as well as passing independent decrees, albeit rarely inscribed, on matters within its own competence) and of the Assembly. A small handful of them are laws, a higher form of law than decrees, passed under a cumbersome procedure by the *nomothetai*.[4] The large majority of these measures are honorific decrees, for foreigners, and from the 340s for Athenians (mostly in an official capacity). A few are treaties or other foreign policy decrees, a few (several of them laws) are religious regulations, a few are sui generis.[5]

---

2 On relief sculpture on decrees see most recently Deene 2016. The use of paint on inscribed Athenian laws and decrees would also be worth more systematic attention, albeit that it rarely survives. For some observations see Lambert 2006, 119 [= 2012b, 100–101]; Stroud 1998, 2; on reliefs, Lawton 1995, 13–14; on funerary stelai, Posamentir 2006.

3 On the significance of the Acropolis as location of inscribed decrees see now also Moroo 2016.

4 Who exactly the *nomothetai* were is unfortunately attested only opaquely in our evidence, and is the subject of continuing debate. They may have been drawn from or equivalent to the members of the Assembly sitting in special session as *nomothetai* (cf. Aeschin. 3.39). On them and in general on *nomothesia* see most recently Canevaro 2015, Canevaro 2016.

5 My figures for inscribed laws and decrees of the years 352/1–322/1 BC (excluding "dubia et incerta", *IG* II³ 1, 531–572, and those which are too fragmentary for the subject to be discern-

Exploration of this topic is facilitated by the fact that it was normal for the city at this period not only to provide financially for the inscription of a law or decree, but also to specify explicitly in the text of the decree its place of erection (*Standort*), much the most common being the Acropolis. While most decree inscriptions with an Acropolis *Standort* have also been found there, since stone was a useful building material, and since central Athens has been occupied continuously since antiquity, some had unsurprisingly wandered to other (usually central Athenian) locations prior to discovery, making places of discovery (*Fundorte*) a less reliable indicator of original location.[6]

In this paper I shall make some observations on the significance of the Acropolis as location of inscribed decrees, move on to consider the relatively small number that were placed elsewhere and the underlying drivers of location in those cases, and finally offer some reflections on the locations of inscribed laws.

2 Acropolis

Peter Liddel's 2003 analysis has demonstrated clearly the overall picture: in the 5th century BC nearly all inscribed decrees of the Council and Assembly were erected on the Acropolis. This remained the most common *Standort* throughout the classical and hellenistic periods, with some increase in numbers erected in other locations, particularly the Agora, in the hellenistic period.[7] What

---

ible, but including those dated to the middle or second half of the 4th century BC, *IG* II^{3} 1, 487–530) are: honorific, 180 (87%) (for foreigners, 116; for Athenians, 29; for Athenians or foreigners, 34; for a god, 1); treaties and foreign policy, 13 (6%); religious, 9 (4%); sui generis, 4 (2%). Overall total: 206 (100%).

6 E.g. in my corpus inscriptions originally set up on the Acropolis have been found near Lysikrates' monument (*IG* II^{3} 1, 294 fr. b), on the south slope of the Acropolis (304 fr. a, 312 fr. b, 388 fr. a), on the north slope of the Acropolis (305, 327 fr. e, 352 b, 432, 477, 481 fr. a), in the Agora (a designation which in effect overlaps with "north slope of the Acropolis", 344, 409, 426, 474 fr. a), in Athens below the Acropolis ("the lower city", 493). It was understandably less common for inscriptions to wander up to the Acropolis from other locations, but Acropolis *Fundorte* are sometimes recorded for decrees originally erected elsewhere (no clear example in my corpus, but a later case is probably *IG* II^{3} 1, 1161, a decree of 215/4 BC honouring ephebes that, like other decrees of the same type, will probably have been erected in the Agora, but whose recorded findspot is the Acropolis; cf. Lambert 2014, 26).

7 In addition to the many inscriptions found on the Acropolis that were probably set up there (cf. previous note), an Acropolis *Standort* is attested in our corpus in the following 46 decrees honouring foreigners: *IG* II^{3} 1, 294, 304, 312, 316, 317, 322, 324, 335, 342, 343, 344, 352, 367,

is it about the Acropolis that made it an appropriate location? I suggest that four aspects are relevant, of which the first has been well recognised in recent discussions, but the other three, though to a greater or lesser extent correlates of it, also repay attention in their own right.

Acropolis as Religious Space

That the Acropolis was religious space and that this is crucial to understanding it as primary location for the erection of decrees seemed to require definite assertion in 1999,[8] but has since become commonplace in discussions of this topic.[9] The Acropolis was the religious heart of the city, principal dwelling place of gods and heroes specially associated with the city, above all Athena, and focus, par excellence, of the city's religious rites and ceremonies.[10] The earliest inscriptions set up there were dedications;[11] and throughout the classical and hellenistic periods, religious content or significance was one of the drivers of a decision to inscribe a decree in the first place. Stelai inscribed with decrees were commonly headed with the invocation, "gods" (*theoi*),[12] and crowned with pediments recalling religious architecture and/or with relief sculpture which typically had a religious theme, depicting deities, heroes and personifications (e.g. an honorand being crowned by Athena). The attention paid to the aesthetic quality of the lettering on inscriptions, including use of the stoichedon style (which was a feature of inscribed laws and decrees from the start and remained the norm at this period), no less than the beauty of dedications and temples on the Acropolis, can also be articulated as an aspect of human endeavour to ensure its gifts were of a quality suitable for the gods. As Elizabeth Meyer has recently emphasised, Demosthenes could assert that "all of the Acropolis is *hiera* (sacred)",[13] and Pausanias that "on the Acropolis at Athens [in contrast to Olympia] all the statues (*andriantes*) and everything

---

375, 377?, 379, 387?, 388, 392, 398, 399, 401, 403, 411, 418, 426, 432, 434, 435, 437, 439, 452, 455, 456, 470, 474, 475, 478, 480, 485, 491, 492, 493, 499, 501, 521; the following decrees honouring Athenians: 305, 327, 400?, 469, 481?; the following laws: 445; and the following decrees of indiscernible type: 409, 477, 509, 511, 527.

8 "The importance of the Acropolis as a place of display must be related to its religious importance", Osborne 1999, 347 (= 2010, 70), arguing against the old view that decrees were inscribed because it was a "convenient central place" which facilitated their being read.

9 Most recently Meyer 2013, 457–63; Moroo 2016.

10 Cf. Liddel 2003, 80–81.

11 Now emphasised by Moroo 2016.

12 Meyer 2013, 471. William Mack will discuss the precise significance of the heading in a forthcoming paper.

13 ὅλης οὔσης ἱερᾶς τῆς ἀκροπόλεως, Dem. 19.272.

else, all are equally dedications (*anathemata*)".[14] Pausanias does not mention inscriptions specifically, and is not writing very precisely. The permanent structures of the Acropolis (did Pausanias mean to include them?) are only loosely definable as *anathemata*[15] and certainly "dedication", *anathema*, and *stele* were normally distinct terms in epigraphical language.[16] Moreover, there would seem to be a difference between the intention underlying a votive dedication, as our sources explicitly state, to honour, to give thanks or to seek favour from the gods,[17] and the somewhat vaguer, or more elusive (to us, but also not explicitly articulated in ancient sources), religiosity of the intention underlying the placement of decree stelai on the Acropolis. On the other hand there was undoubtedly a strong conceptual overlap between stelai and dedications, and sometimes a verbal one;[18] and it is helpful to conceive of decree stelai, like dedications, as having both "divine" and "human" faces, i.e. as being directed metaphorically at both gods and men.[19]

To take the three main categories of inscribed decree, the appropriateness of the Acropolis as religious space for decrees with religious content is obvious. One can easily see how this was an organic development from the practice

14 Paus. 5.21.1. Cf. Meyer 2013, 461–62. On the definition of *anathema* see also Patera 2012, 18–21 (not mentioning inscriptions).

15 They are so defined by Dem. 22.76, cf. Plut. *Per.* 14.

16 The verb normally used to express what is done to decree stelai on the Acropolis is στῆσαι (literally, "make to stand"), never in my corpus ἀνατίθημι ("put up", "dedicate", though twice κατατίθημι, "put down", IG II³ 1, 409 and 411).

17 Purpose of commerce with the gods is honouring, giving and asking, and gods receive from men gifts of honour (*time*), honorific portions (*geras*) and gratitude (*charis*), Plato *Euthyphro* 14–15; sacrifice for honour or thanks or to ask for good things, Theophrastos, *Peri Eusebeias* F12. The logic is the same whether applied to sacrifices, dedications, or other things offered to the gods, cf. Meyer 2013, 459–60 n. 29.

18 At our period decrees were usually erected on self-standing stelai erected at the initiative of the Council or Assembly, but in some cases involving Athenian honorands they were inscribed on dedications (*anathemata*), typically, but not always, bases, the most notable example being IG II³ 1, 306. See Lambert 2005, 125–29 [= 2012b, 49–55]. This induces some linguistic overlaps, e.g. IG II³ 1, 360, a base in the form of a thick stele or pillar, is referred to as a dedication in l. 1, a stele in l. 54; IG II³ 1, 417, a block from a dedication of uncertain physical type, is apparently referred to as a stele in l. 24 (unless this decree was also inscribed on a stele, separately from on 417); the dedication by the ephebes of Kekropis of 333/2, in form a stele, and inscribed also with honorific decrees, IG II² 1156 = RO 89, is apparently referred to as a stele l. 35, and a dedication at ll. 43–44, 49–51, 62–63. Compare also the mixed language used in the inscribing clause of the decree honouring Lykourgos of Boutadai, Lambert 2015, 3–5 [= this volume, chapter 11, 294–96.].

19 See e.g. in relation to votive dedications on the Acropolis, Keesling 2003, 199.

of placing inscribed dedications, and specifically, as Moroo has emphasised, inscribed dedications by public officials, there;[20] and as she and others have pointed out, a high proportion of the very earliest inscribed decrees have specifically religious content.[21] From the Acropolis there is the Hekatompedon inscription, *IG* I³ 4 (485/4 BC?), from elsewhere the inscriptions regulating the Herakleia at Marathon, *IG* I³ 2 and 3 (from the Herakleion at Marathon, the latter dating ca. 490–480?), inscriptions relating to the Eleusinian religion, *IG* I³ 5 (from Eleusis, ca. 500 BC?) and 6 (from the City Eleusinion, ca. 470–460 BC?), a decree regulating the festival of Poseidon in Sounion, *IG* I³ 8 (from Sounion, ca. 460–450?). There is a notable point in our context, however, about these very earliest extant inscribed decrees. Apart from the Hekatompedon inscription, which relates specifically to the Acropolis as well as being set up there, only one, *IG* I³ 1 (ca. 510–500 BC?), of the Athenian decrees datable with more or less confidence to before ca. 450 BC, is from the Acropolis, and it is not specifically religious in content, dealing, it seems, with arrangements for the Athenian cleruchy on Salamis. Before 450 we may certainly infer that religious content was drawing inscribed decrees to religious locations, but not mainly to the Acropolis; while it is *IG* I³ 1 alone that foreshadows the later practice of erecting decrees of a broader public character on the Acropolis.

When, after around the middle of the 5th century, the habit of inscribing on stone Athenian decrees of a broader public character on the Acropolis was established (and of inscribing them on the standard format of the essentially two-dimensional stele, rather than e.g. on pillars and other three-dimensional objects),[22] the most numerous category immediately became the honorific decree.[23] Hypereides' objection to a proposed honorific decree that

---

20 Moroo 2016, 34 notes that the earliest extant inscription erected by an official in a public capacity is *IG* I³ 590, an altar dedicated to Athena by Chairion, treasurer of Athena, commemorating his term of office, ca. 600–575 BC, and that other dedications by public officials followed, e.g. *IG* I³ 507–509bis (*hieropoioi*).

21 Moroo 2016, 37–40; Parker 1996, 123; Meyer 2013, 466–67.

22 Davies 2005, 291; Meyer 2013, 467; Meyer 2016. For the standard format of the stele in the period of my corpus see Lambert 2006, 117–19 [= 2012b, 97–101].

23 Broadly, honorific decrees form the largest single category of inscribed Athenian decree before 403/2 BC (68 of 177 of decipherable content according to Sickinger 1999a, cf. Meyer 2013, 458, 467), grow in frequency to form the large majority of all inscribed decrees by the latest phase of the classical democracy (see n. 5 above) and, by the late 3rd century to become the only category inscribed at public initiative and expense (cf. Lambert 2014, 31). Among these, decrees honouring Athenians become a significant sub-category only in the 340s (cf. Lambert 2014, 20–21; *OR* 178 = Osborne and Lambert https://www.atticinscriptions.com/inscription/OR/178, decreeing support for children of men killed under

it belonged "in the accursed rubbish dumps rather than in our sanctuaries" implicitly illustrates the high symbolic value and appropriateness assumed to inhere in placing such decrees in the pristine presence of the divine;[24] and we may conceptualise the act as commending the honorand, and indeed his honours, to the care and tutelage of the gods. It is perhaps not sensible to try to press for a more precise articulation than that; for one thing, the emphasis will be different with those cases, not infrequent in the early history of the honorific decree, less so later, in which the decree was erected at the initiative and expense of the honorands themselves. Here indeed the logical continuity with dedications is particularly apparent, as is what one might describe as a defensive logic; as Meyer puts it, "you are also letting the god know that *you* know that the gods have helped; and you thereby avoid any imputation of 'thinking big', which would bring trouble down upon you."[25] As Meyer has also recently emphasised, decrees honouring men (and implicitly also the gods) were particularly appropriate to be set up in a context where honouring the gods, with dedications and sacrifices, was already a prominent feature of the physical and ideological landscape.[26]

There are various religious factors pulling the third main category of inscribed decree to the Acropolis, namely treaties and those relating to foreign policy more broadly, two of them particularly noteworthy: the Athenian Empire exalted the goddess Athena as patron deity of the city, and from the point when, in 454 BC, the lists recording the portion of tribute set aside for Athena were first inscribed on those most massive of all inscriptions erected on the Acropolis, the tribute lists, it also became appropriate to inscribe there in Athena's honour decrees relating to the tribute, to the Athenian Empire and

---

the oligarchy, ca. 410 BC, foreshadows the genre; earliest in the regular series is *IG* II³ 1, 301 of 346/5 BC).

24 Liddel 2003, 81, commenting on Hyp. F14.79 Jensen (objecting to Demades' proposed decree for Euthykrates of Olynthos): περὶ οὗ πολλῷ ἂν δικαιότερον ἐν τοῖς ὀξυθυμίοις ἡ στήλη σταθείη ἢ ἐν τοῖς ἡμετέροις ἱεροῖς, quoted by Harpokration, commenting on the rare and, in later antiquity opaque, word ὀξυθύμια, apparently (according to Didymos, other authorities, cited by Harp., gave different explanations) the offscourings (*katharmata*) from house purifications, ritually deposited (as propitiatory offerings to Hekate?) at cross-roads (ὀξυθύμια τὰ καθάρματα λέγεται καὶ ἀπολύματα· ταῦτα γὰρ ἀποφέρεσθαι εἰς τὰς τριόδους, ὅταν τὰς οἰκίας καθαίρωσιν). Cf. Parker 1983, 30. The contrast between the ritually "positive" charge associated with the normal location of the sanctuary, and the sinister negativity of the ὀξυθύμια is clear. For a similar usage see Eupolis, *Demes* F132K-A.

25 Meyer 2013, 462–63.

26 Meyer 2013, 468 also emphasises the religiosity inherent in the protection of strangers that was part of the ideology of the honorific decree.

to Athens' foreign relations more broadly.[27] Second, the inscription of treaties was partly intended to guarantee divine sanction of the oaths which bound the parties to the treaty to observe it and which were themselves typically inscribed.[28]

I would make two further points about the religiosity of inscribing decrees on the Acropolis. First, there is an important aspect of Greek inscriptions which archaeologists and anthropologists have been quicker to recognise than many epigraphists, historians and classicists. Inscriptions have a quality of agency, are conceived of as acting independently or as extensions of human actions, in a way that is largely unfamiliar in the modern West.[29] This is manifested among other things in the phenomena of "speaking stones" (as "I am the boundary of the Agora") and the familiar conflation of the (abstract, to our minds) thing inscribed, honours or international agreements, with the physical objects on which they are inscribed, so that, for example, destroying a stele on which a treaty is inscribed is not only symbolic of or consequential on the breaking of the treaty, it actually is the breaking of the treaty.[30] A certain religious/magical quality inheres in the very written signs themselves; and that epigraphical agency has a strongly religious, even in our terms magical, quality, is demonstrated perhaps most clearly by the curse tablet, inscribed in jumbled letters on black lead, often including a magically charged depiction of the accursed, and placed down into the earth, condemning them to the maleficent attention of the infernal powers.[31] The honorific decree can be conceived of in a sense as the inverse of the curse tablet, inscribed on white marble rather than black lead, placed high in the divine space of the supernal gods, with correctly and neatly arranged lettering, and sometimes accompanied by depictions of the honorands in the beneficent presence of the gods, working, one might think, a kind of white magic.

Second, the inscribing clause normally named the Acropolis as place of erection without further specification. Occasionally, however, a specific location

---

27 First tribute list: *IG* I^3 259 = *OR* 119. Examples of decrees relating to tribute or relations with allies: *IG* I^3 14 = *OR* 121 (Erythrai); *IG* I^3 68 = *OR* 152, *IG* I^3 71 = *OR* 153, *IG* I^3 34 = *OR* 154 (tribute); *IG* I^3 40 = *OR* 131 (Chalkis).

28 Cf. Meyer 2013, 468–72.

29 See above all Gell 1998.

30 Examples are (negative) *IG* II^2 111 = *RO* 39, ll. 30–35, referring to stelai containing agreements between Athens and the cities of Keos being destroyed by rebels, and (positive) the decrees honouring Leukon of the Bosporan kingdom as interpreted by Demosthenes 20.36 (below). For a likely example in our corpus see *IG* II^3 1, 388, ll. 12–13 and see in general Culasso Gastaldi 2003 and 2010.

31 On Attic curse tablets see especially Curbera 2013, Curbera 2015 and most recently Curbera 2016.

might be added, when the subject matter of the decree made that appropriate. For example *IG* I^3 7, the decree about the privileges of the genos Praxiergidai (ca. 460–420 BC), in particular confirming its right to clothe the (old wooden) statue of Athena with the *peplos*, was to be located on the Acropolis "behind the old temple" (l. 6, probably the 6th-century temple of Athena, left in ruins after the Persian sack); and the hellenistic decrees honouring the girls who worked the wool for the *peplos* were to be set up beside the temple of Athena Polias, part of the Erechtheum complex which, not long after the passage of *IG* I^3 7, had, it seems, become home to Athena's statue.[32] The logic in such cases was normally, as in this one, religious. There is no certain case in our corpus,[33] but the existence of such cases, albeit rare, emphasises that the Acropolis was religious space in a rather generic sense; where needed, the religious context could be made more specific.

Acropolis as Public Space

The Acropolis was the city's space, its structures public structures, and it was entirely appropriate for stelai recording decisions of, and erected normally by decision and, by the period of my corpus, at the expense of, the polis, to be erected on the (Acro)polis.[34]

Was it also "public" in the sense that the public went there frequently to read the inscriptions? The old view that inscribing decrees had a specifically democratic intentionality in terms of facilitating access to information has been rather undermined by the last generation of scholarship.[35] Stone inscriptions were not always inscribed in a style that maximised legibility;[36] if information was to be communicated, ephemeral media such as wooden boards were available, and the achievement of this objective scarcely required the laborious and expensive process of inscribing a stone monument; there are gaps in the inscribed record (scarcely an inscribed decision to go to war or relating to

32 *SEG* 53.143 l. 25 (108/7 BC), cf. *IG* II^2 1034 + 1943 (103/2 BC), *IG* II^2 1942 (ca. 100 BC). On this phenomenon see Liddel 2003, 81, 86–88.

33 *IG* II^3 1, 392 is a proxeny decree which may have been required to be set up on the Acropolis in or near the Kekropion, though it is not impossible that the text should rather be read to imply erection in the prytany of Kekropis. In any case the text is too fragmentary for interpretation.

34 In the 5th century the word "polis" = Acropolis was used to express the location where stelai were to be set up, giving way in the earlier 4th century to "Acropolis". On this aspect of the Acropolis see e.g. Hölkeskamp 2000.

35 For a summary of the current position see Meyer 2013, 454–57.

36 The stoichedon style of inscribing letters in vertical columns as well as horizontal rows and the occasional inscribing of text well above eye-level, e.g. in the tribute lists (though this is exceptional), are commonly cited counterexamples.

military dispositions, no accounts of Athens' overall income and expenditure, no land or property registers) that seem inconsistent with the idea that provision of information of public interest was a straightforward driver of inscribing practice. Elements of the old position continue to be valid, however; the formulae of disclosure that sometimes occur, specifying the purpose of inscription as being e.g. "for anyone who wishes to scrutinise", *σκοπεῖν τῶι βουλομένωι*, show that one function of public written documents, including some inscriptions, particularly those of a financial character, or which made regulatory arrangements, was to enable their content to be known or scrutinised, albeit often by specific interested groups rather than the population as a whole;[37] but what about the specific point, whether placing inscribed decrees on the Acropolis helped or hindered accessibility? Osborne 1999 was surely right to emphasise as a point against the old orthodoxy that the Acropolis was a location for religious rites and no ordinary thoroughfare, as Liddel 2003 was also right to note that there were occasions when both Athenians and foreigners went up there.[38] One might add the evidence of *IG* II^2 1141, which records a decision taken by the tribe Kekropis in 376/5, "at a principal meeting of the tribesmen, voting secretly on the Acropolis";[39] even tribal Assemblies, it seems, took place on the Acropolis (in the case of Kekropis it was headquartered on the Acropolis at the Kekropion). One might also add that it is clear enough from the wording of some decrees that the inscriptions on the Acropolis were meant to be noticed by men. Note, for example *IG* II^3 1, 516, 13–19:

> … and the prytany secretary
> shall inscribe the proxeny for him on a stone
> stele and stand it on the acropolis,
> so that others may also know that
> the People knows how to give thanks
> to its benefactors.[40]

---

37 Cf. Meyer 2013, 455–56; R. Osborne and Lambert, https://www.atticinscriptions.com/inscription/IGI3/1453 note 3, https://www.atticinscriptions.com/inscription/IGI3/84 note 9. Sickinger 2009 showed that, when used in honorific decrees, the formulae ("in order than x be known" etc.) usually refer to knowledge of the fact of the honour rather than its detailed wording.

38 Liddel 2003, 80–81.

39 ἔδοξεν τῆι Κεκροπίδι φυλῆι ἐπὶ Χαρισάνδ[ρο ἄρχοντος] | τῆι κυρίαι ἀγορᾶι κρύβδην ψηφισαμένων τῶ[ν φυλετῶν] | ἐν ἀκροπόλει· (ll. 5–7).

40 ἀναγράψαι δ|ὲ] αὐτῶι τὴν προξε[ν]ί[αν τὸν γραμμα|τ]έα <τ>ὸν κατὰ πρυτανε[ίαν εἰς στήλ|ην] λιθίνην καὶ στῆσα̣[ι ἐν ἀκροπόλ|ει], ὅπως [ἄ]ν καὶ οἱ ἄλλο[ι εἰδῶσιν, ὅτ|ι ὁ] δῆμο[ς] ἐπίστατα̣ι χά[ριτας ἀποδ|ιδόναι τοῖς εὐεργε]τ[…

A further possibility is perhaps worth airing. One must concede, I think, that were the sole or main reason for inscribing a decree to encourage it to be read, the Acropolis would not be the location of choice; and perhaps, conversely, one may think of the bustling Agora, where a trickle of decrees was erected from the late-fifth century and increasing numbers from the late-fourth, as a more plausible location of choice from that point of view. Whatever reservations we may have (see below), about articulating the Agora as carrying a uniform and coherent set of connotations as location of inscribed decrees, perhaps it might be right to connect its increasing use as such in part with an increasing literateness of the public culture from the late fourth century BC; in other words one might consider the possibility that placement in the Agora reflected in part an expectation that that location would facilitate the reading of the inscriptions by a larger number of people than their placement on the Acropolis.

Acropolis as Monumental Space

Taking seriously the physical context of the Acropolis leads to a rather obvious (though until recently also somewhat overlooked) observation, namely that it is unlikely to be coincidental that the Acropolis became a common location for the city's inscribed decrees at precisely the time, after the shift of the Delian League treasury to the Acropolis in 454 and Peace with Persia after 450, that the Periclean building programme got underway. As I have noted elsewhere (if I may be forgiven for quoting myself), we may interpret "erecting inscriptions on the Acropolis … as intended … to adorn the place with fine monuments on a small scale which complemented the larger scale structures";[41] and as I pointed out above, decree inscriptions are rich in physical echoes of the architecture of the Acropolis, whether it be in the common practice of crowning them with pediments, or in depictions of Athena in the relief sculpture which echoed the form of Pheidias' statue.[42] The crucial driver behind the proliferation of decree inscriptions on the Acropolis was not, it seems, so much the ushering in of the radical democracy by Ephialtes in 462/1 and a concomitant passion for facilitating access to information, but the ushering in of the era of imperial exultation in the architecture of the Acropolis after ca. 450.

Acropolis as High Space

A final aspect of the Acropolis relevant in this context is that it was a high place. I have already noted this in the context of the contrast between honorific decrees, placed up high in the air, and curse tablets, placed down in the

41 Lambert 2011a, 201 [= this volume, chapter 3, 81]. See now also Moroo 2016.

42 Lawton 1995, 40.

earth.[43] The Acropolis was also, to use Peter Liddel's language, "conspicuous";[44] it, and by extension the structures and objects on it, were intended to be noticed. Thus Lykourgos can invoke an image of the cowardly Leokrates, mistress in tow, sailing out of the Piraeus in the aftermath of the battle of Chaironeia, feeling "no fear as he saw in the distance the Acropolis and the temple of Zeus Soter [in Piraeus]".[45] Literally or metaphorically the Acropolis loomed over Attica as a sort of physical incarnation of the moral and religious imperative to patriotic behaviour. There may perhaps also have been a symbolic significance in its being higher than the Council chamber and the Pnyx, where the decisions recorded in the inscriptions were taken. Those decisions were raised "up" from the intense contention and debate which, as the orators so often remind us, typically surrounded the proposal of an honorific decree. The final text was nearly always purified of all sign of this contention, and represents the considered, collective will of the citizens.[46]

3 Exceptions 1: Religious Driver

Where decree inscriptions in the last phase of the classical democracy are not erected on the Acropolis, I suggest that three (overlapping) drivers of location can be detected: religious; the desire to deliver a message to a particular group of viewers in a particular location; and what one might loosely term the "imperial" driver, which could draw an inscription away from Attica altogether.

We have already seen that most of the very earliest inscribed decrees were erected not on the Acropolis, but in sanctuaries appropriate to the character

43 Meyer 2013, 457–63, however, to my mind overstates in this context the significance of the *ana-* element ("up") in the word *anathema* and its cognates, which has primarily an internal, physical, reference, i.e. an *anathema* is a thing "put up" in the sense "placed upright", and this applies whether the place in which it is put is relatively high in itself, as the Acropolis, or not high at all, as with most sanctuaries at ground level in which dedications are made. As noted above, the verb κατατίθημι, "put down", occurs in relation to decree stelai placed on the Acropolis, without any implication that the Acropolis is a "low" place. Cf. Patera 2012, 19, who thinks that the *ana-* element marks "la différence de niveau entre le dédicant et la divinité".

44 Liddel 2003, 80.

45 Lyk. 1 *Against Leokrates* 17.

46 On the "de-politicised" (perhaps rather "de-controversialised") quality of texts of decrees on inscriptions see already Osborne 1999, 356–58 [= 2010, 79–81]. All the more arresting are those rare cases where the controversy creeps into the text, e.g. *IG* I^3 102 = *OR* 182, 39–47.

of their religious content (e.g. decrees relating to the Herakleia at Marathon in the Marathonian Herakleion); and that the generic religiosity of the Acropolis can, as it were, be rendered more specific such that, for example, decrees relating to Athena's *peplos* were placed explicitly next to the temple that housed her statue. This principle continues to apply throughout the history of classical and hellenistic decree inscribing, and is no less visible in the latest phase of the classical democracy. Where the content of a decree relates to a particular cult, it is set up in the sanctuary of that cult. Thus, for example, *IG* II^3 1, 292, on the sacred *orgas* (a tract of land between Eleusis and Megara) was to be inscribed, together with the previous one of Philokrates [about the sacred places], on two stone stelai, one to be set up at Eleusis by the [gateway of the sanctuary], the other in the Eleusinion in the city.[47] Thus too a set of honorific decrees relating to the sanctuary and cult of Amphiaraos was erected in the Amphiaraion after Athens had been given control over Oropos, probably by Alexander the Great after the sack of Thebes in 335;[48] and similarly decrees honouring priests and religious officials are placed in the relevant sanctuary.[49] This is an aspect of the same religio-spatial logic that normally draws decrees to the Acropolis, or occasionally to specific locations on the Acropolis. It operates in parallel with the religio-temporal logic that causes decrees honouring priests (e.g. 359) to be dated by the term of office of the priest, as well as the term of office of the archon of Athens.[50]

Normally in such cases the driver is straightforwardly religious. In one case, however, the religiosity has a markedly symbolic tinge. The Charter of the Second Athenian League (*IG* II^2 43 = *RO* 22) had famously been erected beside

47 Cf. *IG* II^3 1, 297, also on an Eleusinian matter, found in Eleusis and no doubt originally set up there.

48 *IG* II^3 1, 338 honouring Pytheas of Alopeke, superintendent of the water supply, for works on the water supply in sanctuaries of Ammon in Piraeus and Amphiaraos (a copy going also to the sanctuary of Ammon); 348 honouring Phanodemos for legislation for the Amphiaraia festival; 349 honouring Amphiaraos himself; 355 honouring the managers of the Amphiaraia festival; 360 honouring those who organised a dedication to Amphiaraos by the Council and other Athenians; 385 also probably an honorific decree. Publication in the Amphiaraion is discussed by Wilding in the *Inscribing Space* volume.

49 Thus *IG* II^3 1, 359 for Androkles priest of Asklepios goes to the Asklepieion; 365 for a priest of Asklepios or Dionysos to the Asklepieion or the theatre of Dionysos. 416 for priests in Piraeus cults led by the priest of Dionysos in Piraeus was apparently originally intended for the theatre of Dionysos in Piraeus, later changed to the theatre of Dionysos in the city (does this perhaps suggest that the right deity was more important than the right specific cult location?). 369 for *hieropoioi* also went to a sanctuary.

50 *IG* II^3 1, 359 is an example. Cf. Lambert 2012a, 73.

the statue of Zeus Eleutherios, "Zeus of Freedom" in the Agora (though the word "agora" does not occur in the text), emphasising that members of the new League were to be autonomous and free from domination by foreign powers, whether it be the Spartans, the Persians or indeed the Athenians themselves.[51] This symbolism is applied again to striking effect in *IG* II^3 1, 377 (original version) and 378 (the more fully preserved version, reinscribed under the restored democracy of 318 BC) of a decree honouring Euphron of Sikyon for supporting Athens in the struggle for Greek "freedom" from Macedonian domination that took place after the death of Alexander the Great, the Lamian War (323/2). The precise wording of the erection clause is unfortunately not recoverable, but it is clear enough, thanks to the careful work of Graham Oliver, that it was to be erected in two copies, one on the Acropolis, and one in the Agora (here the word is used) by Zeus Soter (= Zeus Eleutherios).[52]

Much has been made in recent discussions of the significance of the Agora as a space whose buildings, such as the Council chamber and law courts, housed Athens' key civic institutions, and whose monuments, such as that of the eponymous heroes of the Cleisthenic tribes, the Stoa Poikile and the altar of Zeus Soter/Eleutherios, and statues, beginning with the tyrant slayers, Harmodios and Aristogeiton, commemorated its characteristic civic values. The last decade of the fifth century, when those institutions and values became points of contention in the context of the two oligarchic revolutions, has also been emphasised as a key point in the development of the Agora as a locus for the commemoration and celebration of specifically democratic values and institutions, and as a point when inscriptions with strong associations with the democracy came to be erected there.[53] There may be something in this, but, as far as the epigraphical record is concerned, it is worth emphasising that while the Acropolis is very commonly named as such, the "Agora" is very rarely named as a location of inscribed decrees. The decree for Euphron seems indeed to be the only example of such a designation pre-dating the third century, when "the agora" without further qualification became the normal location for decrees honouring ephebes, and it is notable that, even with the decree for Euphron, the location is given a further, religiously charged specification, and

51 See most recently Meyer 2013, 491–94.

52 *IG* II^3 1, 378, 28–29 reads τὴν μὲν μίαν ἐν ἀκ̣[ροπόλει, τὴν δ'] | ἑτέραν ἐν ἀγορᾶι παρ[ὰ] τ̣[.........19.........·]. The precise wording in the lacuna is not recoverable, but, as Oliver 2003 argued, that it included a reference to Zeus Soter is suggested by the surviving wording of the same clause in what appears to be the original version of this decree, 377, ἑτέ]ραν δὲ [.........18.........]|[......11.....]ρος·

53 See especially Shear 2007 and 2011, and now also Meyer 2013, 476–86.

that it complements, but does not replace, a copy erected on the Acropolis.[54] Before the hellenistic period, therefore, we should perhaps be hesitant about conceptualising the Agora as a coherent space for the location of decrees with a unitary set of connotations.

4 Exceptions 2: Message Driver

This case of a religious driver with symbolic resonance beyond the strictly religious sphere leads nicely to cases where the message to be delivered is strong enough to drive an inscription to a specific location without religious context. A clear case in our corpus is *IG* II^3 1, 399, of 348 or 343 BC, a highly rhetorical decree proposed by the prominent, indeed virulent, anti-Macedonian and Athenian-imperialist politician, Hegesippos of Sounion,[55] and directed against those who have in the past attacked, or who might be minded in future to attack Eretria[56] or other Athenian allies. The decree is to be inscribed and set up not only on the Acropolis (there follows a lacuna which might have specified a third location, but perhaps rather the time within which it was to be erected or a specific location on the Acropolis), but also "in the port" (ἐν τῶι λιμένι, l. 20), thus sending a clear message of discouragement to those who might contemplate expeditions setting out from the Piraeus which would breach the terms of the decree.

A message to a particular audience is also implicit in the locations specified for the law against tyranny of 337/6 BC, *IG* II^3 1, 320, though, like "the port", they are not religious in character. This law, which forbade the Areopagos from sitting in the circumstances of a tyrannical coup, was to be inscribed "on two stone stelai … one at the entrance to the Areopagos as one goes into the Council chamber, the other in the Assembly."[57] Areopagites are to be dissuaded by the inscribed copy of the law, carefully and precisely located to confront them as they enter their Council chamber, from breaking it, just as potential

---

54 See Liddel 2003, 82, with table pp. 88–89.

55 He also proposed *IG* II^3 1, 316, honouring Akarnanians who had supported Athens at Chaironeia, also anti-Macedonian in implication. On him and his family see Davies 2011, 11–23.

56 The reference is apparently to a controversial expedition of 348, led by Phokion and Hegesileos, in support of Ploutarchos, tyrant of Eretria (criticised by Demosthenes 5.5, cf. schol. ad Dem. 19.290).

57 στῆσαι τὴμ μὲν ἐπὶ τ|ῆς εἰσόδου τῆς εἰς Ἄρειον πάγον τῆς εἰς τὸ βο|υλευτήριον εἰσιόντι, τὴν δὲ ἐν τῆι ἐκκλησία|ι (24–26).

attackers of allies are to be dissuaded in Hegesippos' decree, while the Assembly is presumably meant to take courage from the presence in its midst of a law entrenching its sovereignty.[58] It is the need to focus dissuasion (or encouragement) where it will be most effective that is driving these unusual locations. In other words, the location of the stone is designed to maximise its "agency", in the sense discussed above, in delivering the message it carries.

Appreciating the "hortatory intention" is, as I have emphasised elsewhere,[59] crucial to understanding many aspects of what Athens was seeking to achieve at this period with its inscribed decrees. Clauses explicitly stating that honours are awarded and inscribed to encourage the honorand and others to behave in similar honour-loving ways towards the city begin appearing regularly in inscribed honorific decrees from the 340s onwards (cf. above on *IG* II^3 1, 516); but the intention, whether encouraging, or occasionally discouraging, may also be implicit. Quite explicit is the hortatory intention underlying the location of a precursor of what was to become a common genre of inscribed decree after 307/6, *IG* II^3 1, 417 (ca. 340–325 BC), honouring the officials of the Council prytany, Leontis, to be stood "in front of the Council chamber" (ἔμπροσθεν τοῦ] βουλευτηρ̣|[ίου·), and paid for from public funds, "so that others may also [show love of honour (*philotimontai*)], in speaking and acting excellently, knowing that they will obtain due thanks from the Council and the People".[60]

It is notable that in all three of these cases of message-driven locations the law or decree is either sui generis or the first example of a new inscribed type; in such circumstances the hortatory (or dissuasory) intention has the strength to pull the stelai away from the conventional location on the Acropolis, without there being any religious aspect to the spatial logic.

58 The stele inscribed with a decree passed according to Lykourgos after the fall of the Thirty, protecting those who killed anyone who attempted to overthrow the democracy, a kind of prototype for this law, had been set up in front of the Council chamber (scil. of the 500), with, Lykourgos states, a similarly hortatory intention, i.e. to be "a reminder to those who gather each day and deliberate on behalf of the fatherland how it is necessary to behave towards such men [plotters against democracy]. And on account of this they swore to kill anyone who was perceived as even contemplating such things" (ταύτην ἔστησαν εἰς τὸ βουλευτήριον, ὑπόμνημα τοῖς καθ' ἑκάστην ἡμέραν συνιοῦσι καὶ βουλευομένοις ὑπὲρ τῆς πατρίδος, ὡς δεῖ πρὸς τοὺς τοιούτους ἔχειν. καὶ διὰ τοῦτο ἄν τις αἴσθηται μόνον μέλλοντας αὐτοὺς τούτων τι ποιεῖν, ἀποκτείνειν συνώμοσαν). Lyk. 1.124–27.

59 E.g. Lambert 2011a [= this volume, chapter 3], 2011b [= this volume, chapter 4].

60 ὅπως ἂν φιλοτιμῶνται] καὶ οἱ ἄλλοι λέγειν | [καὶ πράττειν τὰ ἄριστα εἰδότ]ε̣ς ὅτι χάρ̣ι̣τας ἀξίας ἀπολήψονται παρὰ [τῆς] βο̣[υ]λ̣[ῆ]ς καὶ τοῦ | [δήμου]. Cf. *IG* II^3 1, 391, a very fragmentary decree also erected in front of Council chamber, and above n. 58 on the hortatory significance of this location in another context.

Two further cases of Piraeus locations offer variations on the theme of message driving location. *IG* II³ 1, 298 is the great inscription of 347/6 BC honouring Spartokos and Pairisades, sons of Leukon, who had recently succeeded their father as rulers of the kingdom of the Cimmerian Bosporos on the north shore of the Black Sea, and their brother Apollonios. This stele was to be erected "near the one for Satyros [grandfather of the honorands] and Leukon" (ll. 46–47),[61] which, as we know both from Demosthenes 20.36, and from the findspot of 298, was in the Piraeus. This location was appropriate in general terms since Athens' relationship with this family was based on its great importance for Athens' grain supply, shipped into the Piraeus. Rhodes and Osborne suggest that it was designed "to impress men arriving from the Bosporos";[62] as I have noted elsewhere,[63] part of the intention underlying the inscribing of an honorific decree was to gratify the honorand; but this is not the full story. As part of the fabric of diplomatic relations between Athens and the Bosporan ruling dynasty, the latter enjoyed the unusual privilege of complete freedom from taxes (*ateleia*), principally import and export taxes, at Athens, originally awarded, it seems, to Satyros and Leukon. Was placement of 298 in the Piraeus intended to have a hortatory effect with respect to grain traders and others with an interest in the grain trade? The absence of an explicit hortatory intention clause from 298 is not a decisive counterargument, since this decree predates the earliest firmly dated occurrences of such clauses (in *IG* II³ 1, 302, of 346/5 and 306, of 343/2 BC) and hortatory intention was a factor underlying honorific practice before it came to be explicitly expressed. However, it must also be admitted that the decrees for grain traders, men of much lower social status whom Athens began to honour regularly in the years following Chaironeia, with patent hortatory intention, were erected not in the Piraeus, but on the Acropolis. In any case one can not, in this case, establish that these decrees for the Bosporan rulers were unique, or initiators of a new genre. Normal practice would have been to put them, as decrees honouring foreigners, on the Acropolis;[64] but

61 ἀναγ[ρ]|άψαι δὲ τὸ ψήφισμα τόδε τὸγ γραμματέα τῆ[ς] | βουλῆς ἐν στήλῃ λιθίνει καὶ στῆσαι πλη[σ]|ίον τῆς Σατύρου καὶ Λεύκωνος (44–47). The inscription seems to imply that there was one earlier stele, Demosthenes 20.35–36 that there were multiple decrees relating to Leukon. It seems possible that there was one stele, inscribed with multiple successive decrees for Satyros and Leukon. The decrees for Satyros and Leukon are Engen 2010, no. 7, for Spartokos and Pairisades, no. 12.

62 P. 324.

63 Lambert 2011a, 201 [= this volume, chapter 3, 78, 81].

64 The location of the decree of 285/4 BC honouring another member of the dynasty named Spartokos, *IG* II³ 1, 870. At this time, however, Athens had lost control of the Piraeus (see most recently Osborne 2016).

"normal practice", it is clear, was not an absolute rule. Our ignorance of the full details of the original decree(s) honouring Satyros and Leukon, which is the ultimate driver of the location of 298 in the Piraeus, prevents full insight into the reasons for the location; but Demosthenes informs us (20.36) that no less than three copies of the stele applying to Leukon were erected "by you and him" in the Piraeus, the Bosporan kingdom itself and at Hieron, a sanctuary on the Asiatic side of the Thracian Bosporos, past which ships trading between Athens and the Bosporan kingdom had to sail.[65] Erection of honorific decrees, or at least records of them, in honorands' home cities was not unknown in the case of honours granted by other Greek cities in the hellenistic period, but is remarkably rare for Athens.[66] It seems likely that these three locations were part of a deliberate policy by Athens and the Bosporan rulers to advertise and secure the unusual trading privileges at Athens enjoyed by the latter, perhaps with reciprocal advertisement of privileges in the Bosporan kingdom enjoyed by Athens; and that the erection of the copy at Hieron may date from a period when Athens purported to control the grain trade through the Hellespont.[67] As each ruler (or pair of rulers) succeeded his or their predecessors a new inscription was set up in the Piraeus (or in the case of Leukon perhaps a new decree added to an existing inscription honouring Satyros) guaranteeing the application to him/them of the customs privileges enjoyed by his/their predecessor(s).

This interpretation is consistent with Demosthenes' rhetorical claim in 355/4 that these stelai stood as guarantees of Athens' good faith which ought

65 στήλας ἀντιγράφους ἐστήσαθ' ὑμεῖς κἀκεινος, τὴν μὲν ἐν Βοσπόρῳ, τὴν δ' ἐν Πειραιεῖ, τὴν δ' ἐφ' Ἱερῷ. The date of the decree for Leukon can not be pinned down precisely, except that it must have been before 355 (date of Demosthenes 20); but any decree honouring Satyros must have been passed between his accession in 433/2 and death in 389/8 BC. Hieron (on which see Moreno, 2008, especially 667) was the place at which, in 340 BC, Philip II was to seize the Athenian grain-fleet, triggering war with Athens, *FGrHist* 328 Philochoros F162, cf. *FGrHist* 115 Theopompos F292. Demosthenes was later himself to propose statues in the Agora for Pairisades and his sons, Satyros and Gorgippos, Dinarchos 1.43.

66 The phenomenon is discussed in relation to proxenies by Mack 2015, 107–109. Exceptionally, in *IG* II^3 1, 1258 (196/5 BC), honouring king Pharnakes of Pontos, Athens provides for a copy of the decree to be delivered to the honorand (ll. 46–50), but this is a move with a specific diplomatic objective, namely to persuade Pharnakes to part with his money.

67 Note the Athenian "Guardians of Hellespont" (*Hellespontophylakes*) attested as exercising controls on the grain trade through the Hellespont in the 420s by the decrees relating to Methone, *IG* I^3 61 = *OR* 150 (see Rhodes and Lambert https://www.atticinscriptions.com/inscription/IGI3/61 n. 7). It is notable that there seems to be no provision to erect 298 at Hieron; a sign of the recession, by the 340s, of Athenian power in the northern Aegean. Whether the Bosporan rulers erected a copy in their kingdom, we do not know.

not, if Athens valued her reputation, to be undermined by Leptines' law revoking the privileges enjoyed by the Spartokids:

> For you should not think that you have set up these stelai other than as an agreement (*synthekas*) of all that that you have received or have given; Leukon, in adhering to them, will be seen forever to be treating you well, whereas you, while they were still standing, have made them invalid, which is much more terrible than destroying them, because for those wishing to slander the city, these stelai will stand as proof (*tekmerion*) that they speak the truth.[68]
>
> DEM. 20.37

The rhetoric of the first clause suggests that he is seeking to persuade the jurors of something that they would not otherwise have thought, i.e. that this inscription, which is after all honorific, not formally an interstate agreement (*synthekai*), in effect has the force of one. The agency he attributes to the stelai, however, whether construed as *synthekai* or honorific decree, is again striking.

One further point about 298 is noteworthy in relation to its location. The absence of religious quality to the location seems reflected in the unusual absence of divine presence in the relief, which, on the usual interpretation, depicts Spartokos and Pairisades, the new rulers of the Bosporan kingdom, and primary honorands of the decree, seated on thrones, with their younger brother, Apollonios standing by.[69] Apollonios was awarded a lesser honour in a rider to the decree, and does not seem to have been associated with his brothers in their rule. In its combination of seated and standing family members the relief recalls rather strongly the style of a relief on that other major genre of inscribed stele, the funerary monument;[70] and when we bear in mind that 298 was collocated with an earlier stele once honouring, but now in effect commemorating, the present rulers' now deceased ancestors, we have, in this combination

---

68 μὴ γὰρ οἴεσθ' ὑμῖν ἄλλο τι τὰς στήλας ἑστάναι ταύτας ἢ τούτων πάντων ὧν ἔχετ' ἢ δεδώκατε συνθήκας, αἷς ὁ μὲν Λεύκων ἐμμένων φανεῖται καὶ ποιεῖν ἀεί τι προθυμούμενος ὑμᾶς εὖ, ὑμεῖς δ' ἑστώσας ἀκύρους πεποιηκότες, ὃ πολὺ δεινότερον τοῦ καθελεῖν· αὗται γὰρ οὑτωσὶ τοῖς βουλομένοις κατὰ τῆς πόλεως βλασφημεῖν τεκμήριον ὡς ἀληθῆ λέγουσιν ἑστήξουσιν.

69 Lawton 1995, 98–99 no. 35. See figure 1.

70 Cf. Lawton's comments: "in its high relief, monumental figures disposed comfortably within the deep space of the frame, and its voluminous drapery with deeply carved folds, the relief more closely resembles the better contemporary grave reliefs than other mid-century document reliefs", comparing Diepolder 1931 plates 45.1 [= *IG* II^2 7169 for Hippon son of Agonippos of Piraeus and Philostrate], 45.2 [= *IG* II^2 11891 for Korallion wife of Agathon], and 46 [= *IG* II^2 5376] for Prokleides son of Sostratos of Aigilia and family).

FIGURE 1.1 *Decree of 347/6 honouring Spartokos and Pairisades, rulers of the Cimmerian Bosporos, and their brother, Apollonios.* IG II^3 1, 298 = NM 1471.
PHOTOGRAPH COURTESY OF NATIONAL ARCHAEOLOGICAL MUSEUM, ATHENS, © HELLENIC MINISTRY OF CULTURE AND SPORTS / ARCHAEOLOGICAL RECEIPTS FUND.

of decrees, something approaching a commemorative *peribolos*. We have observed above a certain conceptual fluidity between the inscribed decree and the dedication; this decree reminds us that there were also other fluidities: between the honorific decree and the interstate agreement, and between the kind of commemoration performed by decree stelai and funerary stelai.

A final decree erected in the Piraeus exhibits another way an inscribed decree can be used to deliver a message; and again it is sui generis, though not, in this case, placed in a location without religious connotations. *IG* II^3 1, 337 records the Assembly's decision in 333/2 BC, on the proposal of Lykourgos, to award the merchants of Kition the right to own a plot of land on which to build a temple of Aphrodite. The inscription displays a number of notable features. Unusually it records not only the Assembly's decree, but also, at first sight rather vacuously, the Council's open *probouleuma* (i.e. a *probouleuma* that contained no concrete proposal). It also contains no reference to the secretary of the Council and no clause providing for the inscription of the decree. The Kitian community in the Piraeus at this period was wholly or largely of Phoenician ethnicity and the introduction of a new cult was a sensitive matter, even where the agents were Athenian citizens. It seems clear enough that the Kitians themselves erected this decree on the site of their new temple to advertise to passers-by that their right to the site was duly founded in a decision of the People taken by the correct legal procedures. The inscription incidentally carried the further message that Athens, more than ever in the straightened circumstances of the years following Chaironeia, was willing to encourage and accommodate the foreign communities in the Piraeus on which her economic well-being relied.[71]

5 Exceptions 3: "Imperial" Driver

Since the fifth century, erection of stelai inscribed with Athenian decrees in locations outside Attica had been associated with Athenian imperialism. Such decrees expressed and embodied the reach of Athenian power in a way that complemented the imperialistic connotations, noted above, of erecting on the Athenian Acropolis tribute lists and decrees dealing with the management of the Empire and foreign relations more broadly, both at interstate level (treaties

---

71 In this respect following the advice of Xenophon, *Poroi* 3.4, cf. Lambert 2011a, 196–97 [= this volume, chapter 3, 75].

etc.) and personal level (honorific decrees).[72] The period of our corpus was one of marked transition in Athens' role in the Greek world, and the three sets of decree inscriptions it contains which were set up outside Attica express the transition rather eloquently. The corpus begins in the aftermath of the Social War which concluded in 355 BC and had weakened Athens' position within the Second League; it includes nothing to match the imperialistic tone of the inscriptions regulating the affairs of Keos, which date certainly or probably from the immediately preceding years.[73] In *IG* II^3 1, 387 (352 BC?), however, we have a last, albeit very fragmentary, epigraphic record before 338 of action taken by Athens to erect a decree overseas. The detail is not recoverable, but the decree apparently bestowed honours connected with the newly founded Athenian cleruchy in Sestos. It was to be erected both on the Athenian Acropolis (the surviving copy) and in the agora in Sestos.[74]

The other two cases belong to the years after the battle of Chaironeia, which resulted in the termination of the Second Athenian League and the accession of Athens as a subordinate member to the League of Corinth, led by the Macedonians. I have already mentioned the decrees placed in the Amphiaraion of Oropos in the years after 335 BC. On the one hand they can certainly be interpreted in part as an expression of Athenian control over the sanctuary and of Oropos more broadly, on the other the status of Oropos as border territory between Athens and Boeotia, which Athens had controlled at previous periods of its history, puts it in a rather different category from the cities and islands of her overseas Empire, and these inscriptions include no aggressive expressions of an imperialistic type. They are all probably honorific and are marked, under

72 Fifth-century examples include the decree enforcing the use of Athenian coins, weights and measures, ca. 414 BC, *IG* I^3 1453 = *OR* 155, set up systematically in the cities of the Empire, and the decree on the affairs of Karpathos and the Eteokarpathians, ca. 445–430 BC, *IG* I^3 1454 = *OR* 136, set up on the Athenian Acropolis and on Karpathos in the sanctuary of Apollo.

73 *IG* II^2 111 = *RO* 39, oaths and agreements relating to Ioulis on Keos following a rebellion, 363/2 BC, to be erected "by generals of Ioulis ... in the sanctuary of Pythian Apollo [in Ioulis], as they have been written up in Karthaia [another city of Keos] ... and ... on the [Athenian] Acropolis" (17–25); note the reference to destruction by rebels of earlier pro-Athenian stelai and murder of Athenian supporters in the same breath, ll. 30–35; *IG* II^2 1128 = *RO* 40, Athenian regulation of export of ruddle (red dye, *miltos*) from Keos, not precisely datable, set up on the Athenian Acropolis (where the stone was found), and in the cities of Keos (ll. 15–16, sanctuary of Apollo in Koresia; l. 38, port of Ioulis).

74 One should also note in this context the tiny, apparently Attic, fragment found on Thera, *IG* II^3 1, 544 (ca. 337–325 BC), which may, however, be a pierre errante.

the influence of their guiding spirit, the pious Atthidographer Phanodemos,[75] by an intense religiosity, very much concerned with honouring, celebrating and, via the hortatory intention, albeit in this case unexpressed, seeking the continuing favour of, the divine, healing, presence of Amphiaraos.[76]

More pointed is another tantalisingly fragmentary inscription set up outside Attica, *IG* II^3 1, 443, an agreement with Alexander the Great about the supply of troops on campaign, probably dating to the start of his reign (ca. 336 BC). This is most likely an Athenian copy of an agreement of the parties to the League of Corinth, which explains why it is to be erected "at Pydna in [the temple of?] Athena [and…]". The tables have been turned and, instead of providing for erection overseas of her own decrees, Athens now has to suffer the erection on the Acropolis of agreements instigated by foreign states and by alliances led by others.

6 Laws

In the fourth-century democracy, 403–322 BC, there was a distinction between laws passed by the *nomothetai*, and decrees of the Council and People.[77] The latter had henceforth to be within the law and, if they were not, were subject to attack under the procedure of *graphe paranomon*. There are upwards of 550 extant inscribed decrees of the fourth-century democracy, but only about a dozen inscribed laws.[78] The Acropolis was not the default location for

---

75 *FGrHist* 325; see https://www.atticinscriptions.com/inscription/IGII31/348, n. 2.

76 Note the inclusive expressions used by Phanodemos in his decree honouring Amphiaraos, who takes good care "of those Athenians and others who come to the sanctuary", τῶν ἀφικνουμ|ένων Ἀθηναίων καὶ τῶν ἄλλων εἰς τ|ὸ ἱερόν, *IG* II^3 1, 349, 12–14; and the crown awarded to Amphiaraos is to be dedicated to the god in his sanctuary, "for the health and preservation of the Athenian People and the children and women and everyone in the country", ἐφ' ὑγιείαι | καὶ σωτηρίαι τοῦ δήμου τοῦ Ἀθηνα|ίων καὶ παίδων καὶ γυναικῶν καὶ τ|ῶν ἐν τῆι χώραι πάντων, 28–31.

77 See now Canevaro 2015, 2016 and above n. 4. On early hellenistic lawmaking, Canevaro 2011.

78 From the earlier part of the fourth century: law on silver coinage, 375/4 BC (*SEG* 26.72 = *RO* 25); grain tax law, 374/3 BC (*SEG* 47.96 = *RO* 26); law on the Eleusinian Mysteries, 367/6–348/7 (?), *I Eleus.* 138, cf. *SEG* 30.61; unpublished law concerning Hephaistos, Athena Hephaistia and silver coinage, 354/3 BC (*SEG* 54.114; 56.26; 61.119); law on Eleusinian first-fruits, 353/2 BC (*IG* II^2 140). Note also the very fragmentary inscription apparently mentioning *nomothetai*, *SEG* 58.95, dated by the editor "before mid-iv BC". In our corpus: *IG* II^3 1, 320, law against tyranny (337/6 BC); 429, law providing for the repair of walls in Piraeus, with appended contract specifications (*syngraphai*) (ca. 337 BC); 431, provisions relating

inscribed laws in the fourth century; nor does the erection in the Stoa Basileios in the Agora of at least some of the inscribed laws produced as a consequence of the revision of the whole body of law at the end of the 5th century seem to have been regarded as establishing a precedent.[79] Instead, as Mary Richardson has established,[80] inscribed 4th-century laws were erected in places where they delivered a message to a specific viewership or which were otherwise appropriate to their content: the law on approvers of silver coinage in the Agora and the Piraeus "in the city between the tables and in Piraeus in front of the stele of Poseidon",[81] the grain tax law, which establishes grain market mechanisms, most likely also in the Agora (where it was found, though there is no inscribing clause[82]). Of those in our corpus, we have already seen one example in the anti-tyranny law, *IG* II³ 1, 320. *IG* II³ 1, 429, relating to the repair of walls in Piraeus after the battle of Chaironeia, was found in the Piraeus and was perhaps originally set up in the Piraeus theatre;[83] *IG* II³ 1, 445, laws relating to cult objects, on the Acropolis and elsewhere (ca. 335 BC), was set up on the Acropolis not by default, but because its provisions related to objects on the Acropolis and because the Acropolis, as location of the treasury of the Other Gods, had a "headquarters" function for the financial administration of other Attic sanctuaries. Since it related to the great festival of Athena, the Panathenaia, *IG* II³ 1, 447 was also probably set up on the Acropolis (findspot of fragment b; fr. a was found in the Agora).

---

to penalties and "exposure" (*phasis*) from a law whose content is otherwise unknown (ca. 337–325); 445, at least two laws relating to cult objects, on the Acropolis and elsewhere (ca. 335 BC); 447, law making provision for funding of Little Panathenaia, followed by decree providing for sacrifices at the festival (ca. 335–330 BC); and possibly also: *IG* II³ 1, 448, making provisions for an (Athenian or Macedonian) festival; 449, making provisions for a festival; 550, the end of text (of a law?) providing for liturgists to dedicate *phialai*, followed by list of liturgists (333/2 or 332/1 BC?); *SEG* 52.104, "unpublished" law found in Brauron on repair of sanctuary of Artemis at Brauron (possibly a hellenistic reinscription; original date uncertain, but possibly ca. 350 BC).

79 E.g. Draco's homicide law, *IG* I³ 104 = *OR* 183A; sacrificial calendar, *SEG* 52.48, and see Shear 2011 (cf. also the law about the trierarchy, *IG* I³ 236a). The laws on the Council, however, *IG* I³ 105 = OR 183B, were found on the Acropolis.

80 Richardson 2000; cf. Liddel 2003, 84.

81 ἐν [ἄσ]||τει μὲμ μεταξὺ τῶν τραπεζῶν, ἐμ Πειραιεῖ δὲ πρό[σ]||θεν τῆς στήλης τοῦ Ποσει[δ]ῶνος, *RO* 25, 45–47. Note that even here, though the tables in the first designation are presumably situated in the Agora, the Agora is not referred to explicitly.

82 The Aiakeion, where the grain was to be stored, and the area of the Stoa Basileios have been suggested, see Stroud 2016, 191.

83 Lambert 2007, 74–77 [= 2012b, 198–202]; cf. Richardson 2000.

There are several reasons why there are relatively few inscribed laws extant. The body of law was mostly concerned with principles and systems and could only be changed following an involved procedure; decrees were concerned mostly with specifics and were passed by a simple majority vote of the Assembly. Laws were no doubt in fact less numerous than decrees. Moreover from the start the need for durable, publicly accessible copies of laws was met by their being deposited in the city archive in the Metroon in the Agora, created at the same time as the introduction of the new law-making process at the end of fifth century.[84] Inscription on stone was always an "optional extra" for laws in the fourth-century democracy.[85] We noted above with decrees that it was those that belonged to a new inscribed category or were sui generis that tended to pull away from the traditional/normal location, the Acropolis, and indeed occasionally from religious drivers altogether, in favour of locations in which they delivered a message to a particular viewership or were otherwise appropriate to their content. With inscribed laws there was no traditional or normal default location, nor was there necessarily a religious driver. This meant that there was more freedom to erect such laws as were inscribed in locations appropriate to their content, religious or otherwise; and indeed the capacity of the inscribed copy of a law to carry a message to a particular viewership may have been an important factor in determining the decision to inscribe it in the first place.[86]

Bibliography

Aleshire, S. B. 1989: *The Athenian Asklepieion: the people, their dedications and the inventories*, Amsterdam.

Canevaro, M. 2011: "The twilight of *nomothesia*: legislation in early-hellenistic Athens", *Dike* 14, 55–85.

Canevaro, M. 2015: "Making and changing laws in ancient Athens", in E. M. Harris and M. Canevaro eds., *Oxford Handbook of Ancient Greek Law*, Oxford (forthcoming; this chapter published online, August 2015).

Canevaro, M. 2016: "The procedure of Demosthenes' *Against Leptines*: how to repeal (and replace) an existing law", *JHS* 136 (2016), 39–58.

---

84 Sickinger 1999a, 93–138. On this point see further Lambert 2017 [= this volume, chapter 2].

85 Lambert 2017 [= this volume, chapter 2] explores how far this is the case for decrees also.

86 See further Lambert 2017 [= this volume, chapter 2; for further suggestions about the pattern of law inscribing see also chapter 7 of this volume].

Culasso Gastaldi, E. 2003: "'Abbattere la stele'. Riscrittura epigrafica e revisione storica ad Atene", *Cahiers Glotz* 14 (2003), 241–62. Translated into English by C. Dickman-Wilkes, as "'To Destroy the Stele': Epigraphic Reinscription and Historical Revision in Athens", AIO *Papers* no. 2 (2014).
Culasso Gastaldi, E. 2010: "'Abbattere la stele', 'Rimanere fedeli alla stele'. Il testo epigrafico come garanzia della deliberazione politica", in A. Tamis, C. J. Mackie and S. G. Byrne eds., *Philathenaios. Studies in Honour of Michael J. Osborne*, Athens, 139–55. Translated into English by C. Dickman-Wilkes, as "'To Destroy the Stele', 'To Remain Faithful to the Stele': Epigraphic Text as Guarantee of Political Decision", AIO *Papers* no. 3 (2014).
Curbera, J. 2013: "The curse tablets of Richard Wünsch today", in M. Piranomonte and F. M. Simón eds., *Contesti Magici. Atti del Convegno Internazionale, Roma 2009*, Rome, 193–94.
Curbera, J. 2015: "From the magician's workshop: notes on the materiality of Greek curse tablets", in D. Boschung and J. N. Bremmer eds., *The Materiality of Magic*, Paderborn, 97–122.
Curbera, J. 2016: "Five curse tablets from the Athenian Kerameikos", ZPE 199, 109–18.
Davies, J. K. 2005: "The origins of the inscribed Greek stela", in P. Bienkowski, C. Mee and E. Slater eds., *Writing and Ancient Near Eastern Society. Papers in Honour of Alan R. Millard,* New York and London, 283–300.
Davies, J. K. 2011: "Hegesippos of Sounion: an underrated politician", in S. D. Lambert ed., *Sociable Man. Essays in Greek Social History in Honour of Nick Fisher*, Swansea, 11–23.
Deene, M. 2016: "Who commissioned and paid for the reliefs on honorary *stelai* in classical Athens? Some new thoughts", ZPE 198, 75–79.
Detienne, M. 1988: "L'espace de la publicité: ses operateurs intellectuels dans la cité" in M. Detienne ed., *Les savoirs de l'écriture en Grèce ancienne*, Paris, 29–81.
Diepolder, H. 1931: *Die attischen Grabreliefs des 5. und 4. Jahrhunderts v. Chr.*, Berlin.
Engen, D. T. 2010: *Honor and profit. Athenian trade policy and the economy and society of Greece, 415–307* BCE, Ann Arbor.
Gagarin, M. 2008: *Writing Greek law*, Cambridge.
Gell, A. 1998: *Art and agency: an anthropological theory*, Oxford.
Harris, D. 1995: *The treasures of the Parthenon and the Erechtheion*, Oxford.
Hölkeskamp, K.-J. 1992: "Written law in archaic Greece", *PCPhS* 38, 97–117.
Hölkeskamp, K.-J. 1994: "Tempel, Agora und Alphabet. Die Entstehungsbedingungen von Gesetzbegung in der archaischen Polis", in H.-J. Gehrke, ed., *Rechtskodifizierung und soziale Normen im interkulturellen Vergleich*, Tübingen, 135–64.
Hölkeskamp, K.-J. 2000: "(In-)Schrift und Monument. Zum Begriff des Gesetzes im archaischen und klassischen Griechenland", ZPE 132, 73–96.
Keesling, C. 2003: *The votive statues of the Athenian acropolis*, Cambridge.

Lambert, S. D. 2005: "Athenian state laws and decrees 352/1–322/1: II religious regulations", *ZPE* 154, 125–59 [= Lambert 2012b, 48–92].

Lambert, S. D. 2006: "Athenian state laws and decrees 352/1–322/1: III decrees honouring foreigners. A. Citizenship, proxeny and euergesy", *ZPE* 158, 115–58 [= Lambert 2012b, 93–137].

Lambert, S. D. 2007: "Athenian state laws and decrees 352/1–322/1: IV treaties and other texts", *ZPE* 161, 67–100 [= Lambert 2012b, 184–218].

Lambert, S. D. 2011a: "What was the point of inscribed honorific decrees in classical Athens", in S. D. Lambert ed., *Sociable Man. Essays on Ancient Greek Social Behaviour in Honour of Nick Fisher,* Swansea, 193–214 [= this volume, chapter 3].

Lambert, S. D. 2011b: "Some political shifts in Lykourgan Athens", in V. Azoulay and P. Ismard eds., *Clisthène et Lycurgue d'Athènes. Autour du politique dans la cité classique*, Paris, 175–90 [= this volume, chapter 4].

Lambert, S. D. 2012a: "The social construction of priests and priestesses in Athenian honorific decrees from the fourth century BC to the Augustan period", in M. Horster, A. Klöckner eds., *Civic Priests. Cult personnel in Athens from the hellenistic period to late antquity*, Berlin.

Lambert, S. D. 2012b: *Inscribed Athenian laws and decrees, 352/1–322/1 BC. Epigraphical essays*, Leiden.

Lambert, S. D. 2014: "Inscribed Athenian decrees of 229/8–198/7 BC (*IG* II^3 1, 1135–1255)", *AIO Papers* no. 4.

Lambert, S. D. 2015: "The inscribed version of the decree honouring Lykourgos of Boutadai (*IG* II^2 457 + 3207)", *AIO Papers* no. 6 [= this volume, chapter 11].

Lambert, S. D. 2017: "The selective inscribing of laws and decrees in late classical Athens", *Hyperboreus* 22, 2016 [2017], 217–39.

Lawton, C. L. 1995: *Attic document reliefs. Art and politics in ancient Athens*, Oxford.

Liddel, P. 2003: "The places of publication of Athenian state decrees from the 5th century BC to the 3rd century AD", *ZPE* 143, 79–93.

Mack, W. 2015: *Proxeny and polis. Institutional networks in the ancient Greek world*, Oxford.

Marchiandi, D. 2011: *I periboli funerari nell'Attica classica: lo specchio di una "borghesia"*, Paestum (Salerno).

Meyer, E. 2013: "Inscriptions as honors and the Athenian epigraphic habit", *Historia* 62, 453–505.

Meyer, E. 2016: "Posts, kurbeis, metopes. The origins of the Athenian 'documentary' stele," *Hesperia* 85, 323–83.

Moreno, A. 2008: "Hieron: the ancient sancturary at the mouth of the Black Sea," *Hesperia* 77, 655–709.

Moroo, A. 2016: "The origin and development of the acropolis as a place for erecting public decrees: the Periclean building project and its effect on the Athenian epigraphic habit", in T. Osada ed., *The Parthenon frieze. The ritual communication between the goddess and the polis*, Vienna, 31–48.

Oliver, G. J. 2003: "(Re-)locating Athenian decrees in the agora: IG II² 448", in J. Traill and D. Jordan eds., *Lettered Attica. A day of Attic epigraphy*, Publications of the Canadian Institute at Athens, no. 3, Toronto, 94–110.

OR = R. Osborne and P. J. Rhodes, *Greek historical inscriptions 478–404 BC*, Oxford, 2017.

Osborne, M. 2016: "Panathenaic fantasies", ZPE 198, 88–96.

Osborne, R. 1991: "The potential mobility of human populations", *Oxford Journal of Archaeology* 10, 231–52 [= 2010, 139–67].

Osborne, R. 1999: "Inscribing Performance", in S. Goldhill and R. Osborne eds., *Performance culture and Athenian democracy*, Cambridge, 341–58 [= 2010, 64–82].

Osborne, R. 2010: *Athens and Athenian democracy*, Cambridge.

Parker, R. 1983: *Miasma. Pollution and purification in early Greek religion*, Oxford.

Parker, R. 1996: *Athenian religion. A history*, Oxford.

Patera, I. 2012: *Offrir en Grèce ancienne. Gestes et contextes*, Stuttgart.

Posamentir, R. 2006: *Bemalte attische Grabstelen klassischer Zeit*, Munich.

Richardson, M. 2000: "The location of inscribed laws in fourth-century Athens: IG II² 244, on rebuilding the walls of the Peiraieus (337/6 BC)", in P. Flensted-Jensen et al. eds., *Polis and politics: studies in ancient Greek history presented to Mogens Herman Hansen on his sixtieth birthday, August 20, 2000*, Copenhagen, 601–15.

RO = P. J. Rhodes and Robin Osborne, *Greek historical inscriptions 404–323 BC*, Oxford, 2003.

Shear, J. 2007: "Cultural change, space and the politics of commemoration in Athens", in R. Osborne, *Debating the Athenian cultural revolution: art, literature, philosophy and politics 430–380 BC*, Cambridge, 91–115.

Shear, J. 2011: *Polis and revolution: responding to oligarchy in classical Athens*, Cambridge.

Sickinger, J. P. 1999a: *Public records and archives in classical Athens*, Chapel Hill.

Sickinger, J. P. 1999b: "Literacy, documents and archives in the ancient Athenian democracy," *American Archivist* 62, 229–46.

Sickinger, J. P. 2009: "Nothing to do with democracy: 'formulae of disclosure' and the Athenian epigraphical habit", in L. Mitchell and L. Rubinstein eds., *Greek history and epigraphy. Essays in honour of P. J. Rhodes*, Swansea, 87–102.

Stroud, R. S. 1998: *The Athenian Grain-Tax Law of 374/3 BC. Hesperia Supplement 29*, Princeton.

Stroud, R. S. 2016: "The Athenian grain-tax law of 374/3 BC", in C. Tiersch ed., *Die Athenische Demokratie im 4. Jahrhundert. Zwischen Modernisierung und Tradition*, Stuttgart, 185–93.

CHAPTER 2

The Selective Inscribing of Laws and Decrees in Late Classical Athens*

1 Introduction

In a recent paper, Michael Osborne has argued against the conventional view that only a selection of Athenian decrees was inscribed on stelai.[1] He concludes:

> … it may reasonably be suggested that the perceptibly official status of inscribed stelai of public decrees implies that all must have been inscribed …

His argument is not to my mind very persuasive;[2] but he has done a service in highlighting the need for the case for the selective publication of decrees on stone to be articulated more fully than it has been hitherto.[3] The issue is important. Inscriptions may yield certain types of specific factual historical information without our needing to understand whether all were inscribed or only a selection, but as soon as we wish to start using inscriptions, in groups or in aggregate, to address historical questions at a higher level of generality, for

---

* [This paper was first published in *Hyperboreus* 22 (2016) [2017], *Christiano Habicht Nonagenario*, 217–39]. This contribution is based on a paper I gave in the presence of Christian Habicht at the epigraphy seminar at the Institute for Advanced Study, Princeton, in February 2013, while enjoying the privilege of Membership of the Institute, supported by the Patrons' endowment fund and the Loeb foundation. I am grateful to him and the other members of the seminar on that occasion for their comments and delighted to have this opportunity to express my warm appreciation of his immense contributions to the epigraphy and history of hellenistic Athens, and for his support, behind the scenes, of the IG II[3] project. The paper was finalised in the summer of 2016 in the excellent library of the Seminar für Alte Geschichte, Heidelberg, where I am grateful to Professors Kai Trampedach and Christian Witschel for their hospitality.

1 Osborne 2012.

2 For another critique of Osborne's views see now Mack 2015, 13–17, though he does contemplate the possibility that, in fourth-century Athens, all proxeny decrees were routinely inscribed.

3 Osborne cites a number of authors who assert selectivity of inscription, without arguing for it in detail: e.g. Hansen 1984 and Hansen 1987, 123 (see also 108–118); Sickinger 1999, 91–92; Davies 2003, 328; Lambert 2011, 198–200 [= this volume, chapter 3].

© KONINKLIJKE BRILL NV, LEIDEN, 2018 | DOI 10.1163/9789004352490_004

example, "How does the corpus of inscribed decrees, taken not individually, but as a whole, suggest the direction of Athenian policy developed between date x and date y?", or "Was political influence concentrated in the hands of an elite?", questions about selectivity in the evidence base immediately arise. Understanding selectivity of inscribing – not only the fact of it, but also the reasons for it – is also crucial to understanding the fundamental question about what inscribing was for.

Osborne seeks to address the issue across a wide time span, from the fifth to the third centuries BC. This is commendable in theory, but unworkable in practice given the vast quantity of relevant evidence. Moreover, it is important to appreciate that we are not dealing with a static situation that would justify treating three centuries as a single moment, but a dynamic one that changes over time. My approach to the issue will be somewhat different from Osborne's. I shall focus mainly on the inscribed laws and decrees of the period 352/1–322/1, which I have recently edited for *IG* (*IG* II^3 1, 292–572).[4] The period has the advantage that it produced a large number of inscribed laws and decrees, and also that there is a quantity of relevant literary evidence for laws and decrees, mainly in the orators, which supplies a contrasting perspective which is illuminating.

2 Two Preliminaries

To start with an important point that Osborne overlooks: at the end of the fifth century Athens undertook a revision of its laws and thereafter made a distinction between laws and decrees. From the archonship of Eukleides (403/2), decrees of the Council and Assembly were required to be within the law.[5] About a dozen laws on stone survive from the period 403–322, and about 550 decrees. We can not address the issue of selective inscribing without thinking about this statistic: why was the number of laws that were inscribed so small when compared with the number of decrees?

Second, certainly by our period and probably from about the same time as the revision of the laws was undertaken, copies of all laws and decrees were lodged in papyrus copies in the state archive in the Metroon.[6] So for this period

4 Translated at www.atticinscriptions.com.

5 Gagarin 2008, 182–185; now Canevaro 2015.

6 Sickinger 1999, 93–138, especially 114–122. Archival copies of laws and decrees begin to be referred to in the orators only in around the period of our corpus (Aeschin. 2. 89, Dem. 19. 129; 25. 90; Lyk. 1. 66, Din. 1. 86), but it seems clear enough that the archive itself had existed

the issue is: what laws and decrees were inscribed *in addition to* being lodged in papyrus copies in the archive, and why?

3 The Epigraphical Evidence

Appendix 1 lists the inscribed laws and decrees of 352/1–322/1 by subject matter. In summary the types break down as follows:

Honorific: 180 (87%)
Religious: 9 (4%)
Treaties and other foreign policy: 13 (6%)
Other: 4 (2%)

Probably these are broadly a representative sample of all that were inscribed on stone. While we can not absolutely rule out that there are whole categories of inscribed laws and decrees that have not been discovered, it is not likely. At this period the large majority of inscribed decrees were set up on the Athenian acropolis,[7] and it and the rest of Athens and Attica have been quite thoroughly explored. Moreover, it seems that stone, of which there were plentiful local supplies, was the permanent medium of choice for Attic inscriptions. A small number of bronze inscriptions survive or are attested indirectly, and bronze

since the last decade of the fifth century, and that it, rather than inscriptions, was the normal source for texts of laws and decrees quoted by the orators. There is no direct reference to it in the inscribed laws and decrees of our period, but the prytany secretary (otherwise known as the secretary of the Council) was responsible not only for the inscribing of decrees, but also for their custody (τὰ ψηφίσματα τὰ γιγνόμενα φυλάττει), and for "making copies of everything else" (τἆλλα πάντα ἀντιγράφεται, *Ath. Pol.* 54. 3), while the secretary in charge of the laws was responsible for making copies of all laws (54. 4). Not mentioned by *Ath. Pol.* there was also a secretary called the *anagrapheus* ("recorder"), responsible "for writing up the documents" (ἐπιμεμέλητ|[α]ι τῆς ἀναγραφῆς τῶγ γραμμάτων, IG II^3 1, 469, 14–15), but this may mean documents other than laws and decrees. Similarly the archive is the most likely source not only for the texts of earlier decrees honouring Herakleides of Salamis, IG II^3 1, 367, inscribed only in 325/4 (see below), but also for most or all of the texts of decrees that had been lost and reinscribed (e.g. IG II^2 172 = SEG 32. 67, a proxeny which had disappeared and was reinscribed before 350 BC), or destroyed and reinscribed, e.g. the proxenies destroyed by the Thirty and reinscribed by the restored democracy, IG II^2 6 = SEG 29. 93, IG II^2 52, *Agora* 16. 39 etc.; and the decrees destroyed by the oligarchic regime established after the Lamian War and reinscribed by the restored democracy of 318, for Euphron of Sikyon, IG II^3 1, 377 and 378, and for Theophantos, IG II^3 1, 342 and 343.

7 Cf. Lambert (forthcoming) [= this volume, chapter 1].

may very occasionally have been used for laws and decrees, particularly those that were condemnatory or of religious significance, but there is no reason to believe its use for laws and decrees was widespread in our period.[8]

4 Literary Evidence for Laws and Decrees

It would be a major task to analyse all the literary evidence for fourth century laws and decrees,[9] and it is unnecessary for our purposes. A sample is sufficient to make my case, and as it so happens the known laws and decrees proposed by Demosthenes present quite a good sample for our purposes. All but one are known from the literary evidence and, coincidentally, they span precisely the same period as our epigraphical evidence, 352/1–322/1. 42 decrees proposed by him are known from literary evidence (about a fifth of all fourth century decrees known from the literary record), and 1 law. There is a full list at Appendix 2. Adopting the same categories as for the epigraphical record, they break down as follows:

Honorific: 11 (26%)
Religious: 1 (2%)
Treaties: 3 (7%)
Other: 28 (65%)

5 Comparison of Epigraphical and Literary Evidence: Overview

There is some degree of convergence: honorific decrees, religious measures and treaties are represented both among the inscribed record and

8 Stroud 1963, n. 1 remains the primary point of reference on bronze inscriptions in Attica; see now also the remarks of Meyer 2013, nn. 17, 51 and 53. Unlike stone the reuse of bronze usually entailed obliteration of the text and very few inscribed fragments survive. They include a record of bronze dedications from the acropolis, *IG* I³ 510, ca. 550 BC?, cf. *IG* II² 1498, 3–22 (bronze stelai dedicated by treasurers in the late 5th cent.); *IG* I³ 235, a small fragment apparently of a sacred law, ca. 450?. Several bronze stelai referred to in the literary record suggest that this material may have been used for inscriptions of a condemnatory character, e.g. the decree condemning Archeptolemos and Antiphon, [Plut.] *Lives of the Ten Orators* 834 b; the bronze stele with names of traitors next to the "old temple", *schol. Ar. Lys.* 243, Stroud 1978, 31–32, though the authenticity of many or all of these is not beyond question, cf. Habicht 1961. Further work on this topic is a desideratum.

9 For some initial findings based on such an analysis in relation to honorific decrees see now Liddel 2016.

the laws and decrees proposed by Demosthenes. However, while only a very small number of inscriptions, 2%, fall into the "other" category, 65% of Demosthenes' decrees do not belong in any of the ordinary categories represented by the inscribed record. This can naturally, I think rightly, be taken to imply that there were some types of decree proposed by Demosthenes that were not generally inscribed.

Now, one of the features of inscribing on stone was that it endowed the measure, or the message it was intended to convey, with a quality of durability or enduring validity. This is the case with all three of the main categories of extant inscribed laws and decrees in our period. In 355/4 Demosthenes was concerned to argue against Leptines that financially valuable (and to Athens costly) honours and privileges awarded to distinguished foreigners should not be revoked and that the stelai inscribed with such honours guarantee them, or ought to, in perpetuity (Demosthenes 20. 64):

> Ἠκούσατε μὲν τῶν ψηφισμάτων, ὦ ἄνδρες δικασταί. τούτων δ' ἴσως ἔνιοι τῶν ἀνδρῶν οὐκέτ' εἰσίν. ἀλλὰ τὰ ἔργα τὰ πραχθέντ' ἔστιν, ἐπειδήπερ ἅπαξ ἐπράχθη. προσήκει τοίνυν τὰς στήλας ταύτας κυρίας ἐᾶν τὸν πάντα χρόνον, ἵν', ἕως μὲν ἄν τινες ζῶσι, μηδὲν ὑφ' ὑμῶν ἀδικῶνται, ἐπειδὰν δὲ τελευτήσωσιν, ἐκεῖναι τοῦ τῆς πόλεως ἤθους μνημεῖον ὦσι, καὶ παραδείγμαθ' ἑστῶσι τοῖς βουλομένοις τι ποιεῖν ὑμᾶς ἀγαθόν, ὅσους εὖ ποιήσαντας ἡ πόλις ἀντ' εὖ πεποίηκεν.
>
> You have heard the decrees, gentlemen of the jury. Some of these men are perhaps no longer, but the works which they accomplished exist, when once they were done. It is fitting, therefore, to allow these stelai to be valid for all time, so that as long as any of these men are alive, they may suffer no wrong at your hands, and when they die, those (scil. stelai) may be a memorial of the city's character, and may stand as evidence to all those who wish to do us good, of how many benefactors the city has benefited in return.

Inscribed honorific decrees were meant to endure.

As for religious inscriptions, religion was a sphere of the city's life in which there was a particularly strong idea that arrangements should be durable. Generally one did things "according to ancestral tradition" (κατὰ τὰ πάτρια) and did not make changes; but if one did make new arrangements, they too were to endure. In our corpus *IG* II^3 1, 292, 18 requires that the sacred orgas and the other sacred precincts be cared for "for all time" (εἰς τὸν ἀεὶ χρόνον); at 447, 33 arrangements are made for the Little Panathenaia festival to be celebrated finely "for all time" (εἰς τὸν ἀεὶ χρόνον).

With treaties too it was a commonplace that they should be valid "for all time".[10]

Category VIII on the list of decrees proposed by Demosthenes lists a number that provide for meetings of public bodies on specific forthcoming dates. Now clauses providing for matters to be discussed at a forthcoming meeting occur quite commonly in the texts of inscribed Athenian decrees, but the fixing of the date of a meeting is never the decree's sole or main purpose. The sole purpose of the decree proposed by Demosthenes on 8 Elaphebolion 346 (A5) was apparently to provide for the Assembly to meet on 18 and 19 Elaphebolion. It was not a decree which had enduring validity. There would scarcely indeed be time to inscribe it before the relevant meeting took place. It is surely out of the question that this decree of Demosthenes was ever inscribed.

Category IV on the list of decrees proposed by Demosthenes are decrees providing for embassies. Again, inscribed decrees do quite frequently make provisions for embassies, but these are usually embedded in decrees with a more enduring purpose, honorific decrees or treaties. Decrees whose sole or main purpose was to despatch embassies were naturally quite common, but inscribing such decrees on stone would have served no enduring purpose.

Another ephemeral matter on which Demosthenes proposed decrees is the disposition of military forces. Most of the decrees in Category VI are of this type. They were, in a sense, very important, but they did not have the enduring qualities that would have justified inscribing them in stone. There is, in fact, only one inscribed decree of this period which provides for a military expedition: the decree of 325/4 providing for a naval expedition to found a colony in the Adriatic, *IG* II^3 1, 370; but significantly it is not a self-standing decree, erected at the initiative of the Council or Assembly, but embedded in a naval inventory. It is an exception which proves the rule that decrees making provisions for military expeditions were not generally inscribed on stelai.[11]

Category IX furnishes further examples. Decrees of a judicial character, ordering a death sentence (A10) or the arrest or imprisonment of an individual (A9, A36), or instigating processes by other institutions (A15, A37) were

---

10 That there is no such clause in the Athenian treaties of 352/1–322/1, which are mostly rather fragmentarily preserved, is due merely to accident of survival. An example from elsewhere from this period is furnished by the treaty between Miletus and Kyzikos of ca. 330, *Staatsverträge* III 409, which provides (ll. 11–12) that "the cities shall be friends for all time" (τὰς μὲν πόλεις φίλας εἶναι ἐς τὸν ἅπαντα χρόνον).

11 An exception from an earlier period is *IG* I^3 93, relating to the launch of the Sicilian expedition in 415 BC. See R. Osborne and Lambert, https://www.atticinscriptions.com/inscription/IGI3/93 n. 1.

important, but also ephemeral and not, for the most part, inviting durable commemoration.

One might select other examples, but these are enough, I think, to show that there were some categories of decree that were of an ephemeral nature which did not normally justify inscription in stone. This absence of inscription does not, of course, mean that the decrees were in some way invalid. What gave them their validity was the fact that they had been approved by the Assembly; and there were papyrus copies available in the Metroon to verify that. Texts of a number of the decrees proposed by Demosthenes that we have been discussing were read out in court. Not one of the decrees he proposed, however, is cited from an inscription. The texts that were read out had presumably been obtained from the archive.

There is another question, however: in the categories that *are* commonly represented in the inscribed record, is there reason to think that every decree was inscribed on stelai? Was every honorific decree, every treaty and every religious regulation inscribed?

6 Honorific Decrees – Not All Inscribed

Much the largest category of inscribed decree in our corpus is honorific, and since there are so many it might be tempting to suppose that all such decrees were inscribed. One has only, however, to scratch the surface of the evidence to establish that this was not the case.

(a) *Honours could be Commemorated in Ways that did not Involve Inscribing the Decree*

This is particularly clear with decrees honouring Athenians. From the 340s onwards we have a regular series of inscribed decrees honouring Athenian officials. Before that, inscribed decrees honouring Athenians are extremely rare. There is a remote theoretical possibility that, for some reason, we have simply failed to discover all decrees of this type from before the 340s;[12] but it is much more likely that these decrees were never inscribed, and that that was because, before the 340s, commemoration of the honour generally took other forms:

12 Liddel 2016, 312–313, observes that there is more evidence for Athenian honorands before the 340s in the literary than in the epigraphical record.

(i) Proclamation of the Honours in the Council, Assembly or at the City Dionysia

It is interesting that, in the debate between Demosthenes and Aeschines in the *Crown* case there is never any discussion of whether or not the decree honouring Demosthenes was, or should have been, inscribed or otherwise commemorated monumentally. Instead the dispute centres around proclamation of the honour at the City Dionysia. Aeschines (3. 32–48) alleges that this was illegal, and that honorands had normally to be content with proclamation of the honour in the Council (for decrees awarded by the Council) or Assembly (for decrees awarded by the Assembly); Demosthenes (18. 120–121) that proclamation at the City Dionysia was permitted if special provision was made for it in the decree. Apart from durability, another criterion for inscribing a decree was that it delivered a message, whether to a specific, or to a wide, group of viewers; and we may perhaps conceptualise proclamation of honours as, in this respect, an alternative to inscribing them.

(ii) Inscribed dedications

For decrees honouring Athenians, another alternative way of commemorating the honour was by an inscribed dedication. These might be inscribed with suitable commemorative wording, but did not necessarily carry the text of the decree, e.g. *IG* II³ 4, 246:[13]

> Ταξίαρχοι ἀνέθεσαν οἱ ἐπὶ Ἐλπίνο ἄρχοντο[ς] (356/5)
> στεφανωθέντες ὑπὸ τô δήμο καὶ τῆς βολῆς
> *List of taxiarchs follows*

(b) *Non-inscription of More Minor Honours*

Decrees awarding crowns of foliage rather than gold to Athenians were probably quite common. It seems that they were not, however, usually inscribed at this period.[14]

Unlike for Athenians, the city did at this period sometimes inscribe decrees awarding mere foliage crowns to foreigners, in cases where the award was accompanied by other honours, such as citizenship or proxeny or other

13 "The taxiarchs of the archonship of Elpinos (356/5) dedicated this, having been crowned by the People and the Council". One of the quite numerous dedications by Athenian officials in *IG* II³ 4 dating to before 346/5 (year of first inscribed decree in the series honouring Athenian officials, *IG* II³ 1, 301) explicitly commemorating the award of crowns by the Council and People.

14 See Lambert 2004, 88 [= 2012, 8].

privileges.[15] It is notable, however, that decrees awarding an individual foreigner a crown of any kind, and no other substantive honours, seem rarely to have been inscribed.

Again one of the few exceptions at this period is suggestive. In 325/4 Athens awarded proxeny to the grain trader Herakleides of Salamis, *IG* II³ 1, 367. Exceptionally, the decree honouring him on that occasion, the first on the stone, contained a provision requiring the secretary to inscribe not only the proxeny, but also previous decrees in his favour, and the stone is duly inscribed with a sequence of three decrees honouring him which dated up to five years earlier, 330/29 or shortly after. The natural implication is that these earlier decrees had not previously been inscribed and that copies of them had been obtained by the secretary from the archive. The character of the three decrees is indeed exceptional in several ways: the first (at ll. 47 ff.) is merely the Assembly's decree commissioning the Council to come forward with a *probouleuma* relating to Herakleides, a purely procedural decree of a type which was not normally inscribed. The second, beginning in l. 52, is the resulting *probouleuma,* which awards Herakleides a gold crown and permission to "seek from the People what good he can"; and the third, at ll. 29 ff., is the Assembly's resulting decree which confirms the award of a crown, and also makes provisions for an embassy to be sent to Dionysios, tyrant of Herakleia, to recover Herakleides' sails, which Dionysios had apparently confiscated (note that, though this was no doubt an important measure from Herakleides' point of view, it was essentially of ephemeral significance). None of this earlier series of three decrees contains an inscribing provision. Decrees awarding crowns to foreigners, but no enduring privilege, were doubtless quite common. The first decree on the list of those proposed by Demosthenes, A2, a crown for the actor Aristodemos of Metapontum, is probably an example; but they were not, it seems, normally inscribed.

There is some confirmation in the record of decrees honouring not individual foreigners, but whole cities. Such decrees did not usually make substantive awards, such as citizenship or proxeny (though there were occasionally mass citizenship grants), but they normally awarded crowns and there are several inscribed examples from this period. Interestingly, the texts seem to imply that such decrees were not necessarily inscribed. *IG* II³ 1, 304 honours the city of Pellana. The original decree is the second on the stone, at ll. 23 ff., and the provision to inscribe it is made in the first decree on the stone (see ll. 7–12), apparently passed in the following year in response to an embassy from the city. Similarly, *IG* II³ 1, 401 honouring Aratos of Tenedos and his brothers, and

---

15 For example, *IG* II³ 1, 418, which awards Asklepiodoros the right to equal taxation with Athenians (*isoteleia*) and other honours as well as a foliage crown.

the People of Tenedos, was only inscribed as a consequence of a rider to the decree, passed in the Assembly (decree 2, ll. 19–23). No provision to inscribe the decree had been included in the *probouleuma*.

How should we explain this tendency not to inscribe decrees that merely awarded crowns to foreigners? An obvious explanation is that the award of a crown, without substantive honours, was a relatively minor matter and, as such, did not usually justify an inscription. That explanation works up to a point, but it does not explain why decrees awarding gold crowns and no other substantive honours to Athenians were regularly inscribed, at least from the 340s, whereas decrees awarding only crowns to foreigners apparently were not.

Perhaps we should think here rather in terms of durability of intention. Most substantive honours, such as citizenship and proxeny, had extension in time. They conferred privileges which lasted through the lifetime of the honorand and indeed were usually hereditary. They met the durability criterion and were therefore wholly appropriate to be inscribed in stone. An award of a crown to a foreigner, on the other hand, was a momentary gesture which did not have or require the same kind of durable commemoration. For Athenians, embroiled in a fierce competition for honour, central to the public life of the city, past honours were of much greater, enduring, importance – or at least came to be, for we have here an implicit reason why decrees honouring Athenians with crowns only were not inscribed *before* the 340s.[16] One of the points indeed that Demosthenes (18. 257) makes in justification of his crown in 330 is that he was a man who had been crowned by the city on many previous occasions. Past honours, on this view, came to be of durable utility to Athenian honorands in political debate in the Assembly and in litigation in the law courts and this influenced decisions to inscribe them.

Whatever the explanations, there seem to have been some categories of honorific decree that, at this period, were not usually inscribed, including decrees awarding foliage crowns to Athenians and decrees awarding crowns of any kind but no enduring privileges to foreigners. Of those types that were commonly inscribed, we may further ask, were they all inscribed, or only a selection? With decrees awarding citizenship or proxeny, for example, can we assume that every such decree was inscribed? Here, we come to Michael Osborne's argument from "authority". As he points out, and others have pointed out before him, there is a lot of evidence to suggest that the inscribed version of a decree was or could be treated as, as he puts it, "authoritative". With honorific decrees this applies particularly to proxenies, where the identification of

16 For discussion of other reasons for this change see Lambert 2011, 197–198 [= this volume, chapter 3, 74–75].

the honour with the stele recording it is so close that the stele can be conceived of as actually being the proxeny, and where there are cases of measures being taken to re-erect, and hence re-validate, proxeny stelai that had been destroyed by the Thirty.[17] The tendency to conceptualise inscribed citizenship decrees as *being* citizenship is less strong, perhaps because citizenship consisted, to a greater extent than proxeny, of a concrete set of identifiable rights, responsibilities and privileges; but the inscription is still an important guarantee. The grant to the Akarnanians after the battle of Chaironeia is a good example.[18]

There are two general points I would make about Osborne's argument here. First, his characterisation of inscribed decrees as "authoritative" seems to me somewhat wide of the mark, insofar as it implies an actual or potential contrast or conflict between the inscribed version and the archival version of the decree. In the fourth century, and I think more generally, the primary assumption is that the archival copy and the inscribed copy of a decree will be in harmony, not that they might be inconsistent.[19] The type of "authority" that is inherent in a proxeny stele is not essentially about the detail of the text, but about the overall validity of the measure, which is conceived of as being intimately connected with the stele on which it is inscribed.

Second, there is a question of "epigraphical habit". What one might describe as this strong concept of the validity, or agency (to use the anthropological term), of stelai has its origins in the archaic period, well before the archive in the Metroon existed. The earliest inscribed proxenies and citizenship decrees date to before the foundation of the archive in the Metroon.[20] Especially in a world in which there was no public state archive, such stelai did indeed have a

17 *IG* II^2 52, cf. Lambert 2011, 209 n. 30 [= this volume, 83 n. 30].

18 *IG* II^3 1, 316, in which, in 338/7, the Athenians confirm for Akarnanian exiles the validity, in effect the practical activation, of citizenship grants that had been made to their grandfather two generations previously (ca. 400). At ll. 17–18 it is mentioned explicitly, as evidence for the honorands' entitlement to citizen rights, that the original award had been inscribed on the acropolis.

19 This is exemplified by the one clear fourth-century case of a decree of which both an inscribed version and one deriving from the archive is extant, Stratokles's decree honouring Lykourgos in 307/6, *IG* II^2 457+3207 and [Plut.] *Vit. X or.* 852. The inscribed version is fragmentary, but there is enough to see that, while the text is not precisely the same, it is consistent with the literary version, which most likely derives from the archive.

20 Precise dating is mostly difficult. Mack 2015, 81–82, discusses *IG* I^3 27 (ca. 430?) and *IG* I^3 80 (421/0) as early cases. Cf. Meyer 2013, 467–468 n. 69. The earliest extant inscribed decree awarding citizenship to an individual is *IG* I^3 102 = Osborne – Rhodes forthcoming, no. 182 of 410/9, but the mass grant of 427 to the Plataians also apparently entailed an inscription, [Dem.] 59. 105–106.

special quality of validity, or of guaranteeing or securing it; and this strong idea of their validity survived after the introduction of the archive had in fact, one might think, weakened its logic.

If we turn from generalities to the inscribed record of the honorific decrees, the actual situation is in fact, within certain parameters, clear enough. Proxeny grants, the most abundant genre of inscribed honorific decree of this period, can be probouleumatic or non-probouleumatic in form, and in either case provision for inscription may be included in the main text of the decree.[21] In other words, provision to have the decree inscribed could be included in the Council's *probouleuma,* or in the text of a proxeny grant as formulated in the Assembly on the basis of we know not what *probouleuma.* However in *IG* II^3 1, 294, for Theogenes of Naukratis, the Council's proposal to create Theogenes a proxenos is agreed by the Assembly, but it did not include a provision for inscription. Inscription and invitation to hospitality in the city hall are only included as a rider, added to the main proposal in the Assembly.[22] The impression is given that inscribing is an optional extra, not an essential element of a proxeny grant. This gains confirmation from *IG* II^3 1, 398, awarding proxeny to some Euboeans. The decree is probouleumatic, but the inscribing clause is prefaced explicitly by the qualification, "if it also seems good to the People",[23] the implication being that if it had not seemed good to the People the proxeny might have been awarded without provision to inscribe it. An uninscribed proxeny would be missing some element or aspect of traditional validity, or guarantee of validity; one suspects that most were in fact inscribed; but it is clear from these decrees that an uninscribed proxeny would not actually be invalid. Ultimately the validity depended on the vote of the People, and after the archive existed there was evidence for that in the papyrus copy lodged in the Metroon.[24]

---

21 Probouleumatic examples: *IG* II^3 1, 324 Decree 1 for Euenor of Akarnania; 426 for -machos. Non-probouleumatic: 312 for Phokinos et al.; 432 for Sopatros of Akragas.

22 The rider was proposed by Hierokleides son of Timostratos of Alopeke, the same man who had proposed the Council's *probouleuma.* One can imagine several possible reasons for this, including that Hierokleides was unable or unwilling to obtain the Council's agreement to the inscription and hospitality provisions. *IG* II^3 1, 390, for Kleomis of Methymna, also probably had the provision to inscribe added in a rider.

23 ἀ||[ναγράψαι δὲ καὶ τὴ]ν προξενίαν, ἐὰν καὶ τῶι δήμ||[ωι δοκῆι, τὸν γραμμ]ατέα τῆς βουλῆς ἐν στήληι λ||[ιθίνηι καὶ στῆσαι] ἐν ἀκροπόλει δέκα ἡμερῶν (ll. 17–20).

24 In some cities there were inscribed official lists of proxenoi, but there seems to be no evidence for one in Athens (and had there been one one might expect it to have been referred to in our abundant epigraphical and literary evidence, e.g. in relation to the proxenies destroyed by the Thirty). Cf. Mack 2015, 13–14, 286–342. Citizens by decree were usu-

Decrees awarding substantive honours to foreigners other than proxeny and citizenship would seem to belong in the same category, as regards inscription, as proxenies. We have already noted the rider adding an inscribing provision to *IG* II^3 1, 401. *IG* II^3 1, 302, Decree 1 (probouleumatic), awarding protection to Dioskourides of Abdera and his family and hospitality to Dioskourides himself also contains no inscribing clause. Provision to inscribe was presumably included in the incompletely preserved rider, Decree 2, which also granted further residence and taxation privileges.

The imperative to inscribe citizenship decrees at this period looks stronger. All the extant decrees, most of which are non-probouleumatic, include inscribing clauses in the main text;[25] there are no inscribing provisions added in riders or qualified as subject to the decision of the Assembly. A citizenship decree was such a major, and relatively unusual, award that it seems that it was natural and normal for it to be inscribed. Still we can not be certain that every citizenship decree was inscribed, or, if it was, whether this was a legal requirement of citizenship decrees or simply normal practice.

7 Treaties

The argument regarding treaties is similar to that for proxenies, in that the validity of the treaty was intimately associated with the stelai on which they were inscribed; and it is notable that treaties too are a very early species of inscription, with examples pre-dating the foundation of the archive in the Metroon.[26] In order to rescind a treaty you pull down the stele on which it is inscribed. The decree by which the Athenians declared war on Philip II (category III A17 on the list of Demosthenes' decrees) is a good example of this:

> ὁ δὲ δῆμος ... Δημοσθένους ... ψήφισμα γράψαντος, ἐχειροτόνησε τὴν μὲν στήλην καθελεῖν τὴν περὶ τῆς πρὸς Φίλιππον εἰρήνης καὶ συμμαχίας σταθεῖσαν, ναῦς δὲ πληροῦν καὶ τὰ ἄλλα ἐνεργεῖν τὰ τοῦ πολέμου.

---

ally enrolled in the lists of a deme and phratry, there being no centrally maintained list of Athenian citizens.

25 E.g. *IG* II^3 1, 333; 335; 378; 480. The same applies, however, to the probouleumatic 411 and to 452, which may or may not be probouleumatic.

26 E.g. among the more securely dated examples, *IG* I^3 48 = Osborne – Rhodes forthcoming, no. 139, treaty with Samos, 439; *IG* I^3 53 and 54 = Osborne – Rhodes forthcoming, no. 149, treaties with Rhegion and Leontinoi, 433/2.

> The People ... on the proposal of Demosthenes ... voted to destroy the stele concerning the Peace with Philip, and establishing an alliance, to fill the ships and to prosecute hostilities.

This shows, incidentally, rather clearly that not every decree resulted in a stele; a copy of the decree by which the Assembly agreed to make war on Philip was presumably lodged in the archive, but the effect on the inscribed record was to remove a stele not to put up a new one. My sense is that this association between treaties and stelai recording them is so strong that one's default expectation is that treaties would normally have been inscribed; but again, what actually makes the treaty is the decision of the Assembly and in the fourth century and later there would be a copy in the Metroon.

8 Religious Regulations

Laws and decrees with primarily religious content are more common in the epigraphical record than the literary, which consists largely of the corpus of the Attic orators. That is because, unless it involved something like making Alexander a god (category II A39 on the list of Demosthenes' decrees), the city's religion was not generally a matter of political or legal contention, whereas it was strongly appropriate for inscriptions. They were typically erected in sanctuaries; as with dedications, one face of laws and decrees erected in such locations was metaphorically directed to the gods, and epigraphical habit is relevant here too: most of the handful of inscribed Athenian decrees pre-dating the Periclean rebuilding of the acropolis were religious in content.[27] Our sources do not perhaps emphasise the sort of strong connection between the inscribing of a religious measure and its validity that we get with treaties and proxenies, but that may be because the validity of religious measures was rarely politically contentious. I think that there would be an assumption in favour of inscribing such measures, but (aside from the possibility of inscription on bronze, discussed above) I can not immediately see an argument to the effect that every one would necessarily be inscribed on a stone stele. As with other kinds of law and decree one might expect those making durable arrangements and those with a strong message to deliver (perhaps to the gods in this case as much as to men) to be inscribed.

---

27 On these points see Lambert (forthcoming) [= this volume, chapter 1].

9 Laws

We come, finally, to the issue about laws. Why are there so few inscribed laws in the fourth century in relation to the number of inscribed decrees? At 2005, 131 [= 2012, 59] I mentioned three factors that I still think are likely to be relevant:

> (a) there were simply fewer laws than decrees. Laws dealt mostly with the general, permanent and systematic, decrees with the specific and particular; decrees could be passed at every meeting of the Assembly (normally four each prytany)[28] by simple majority vote of the citizens, new laws could only be made by a cumbersome process involving multiple stages of deliberation;[29]
>
> (b) unlike decrees, the default location for inscribed laws was not the acropolis; they seem to have been spread around the city more, being erected in locations suitable to their content; and this may mean that fewer have been discovered;
>
> (c) though I do not think there is any positive evidence for this, and I do not think it very likely, more of them might have been inscribed in a medium such as bronze, or wood (as Solon's axones).

(a) seems likely to be the most important of these explanations, which may perhaps be sufficient.[30] My sense, however, is that another factor may also be

---

28 *Ath. Pol.* 43. 3 (already in the fifth century, IG I³ 40 = Osborne – Rhodes forthcoming, no. 131, 10–14).

29 That the lawmaking process in fourth-century Athens was constructed against an ideological background which emphasised the ideal immutability of the law is brought out well by Canevaro 2015, who (section 7) reconstructs the process of making new laws as follows (mainly on the basis of Dem. 20, Dem. 24, Aeschines 3. 38–40): following a preliminary vote in the Assembly permitting consideration of new laws, specific proposals were published in front of the monument of the eponymous heroes and read out in three consecutive Assemblies, in the third of which *nomothetai* might be appointed (on Canevaro's view from or equivalent to the jurors [Dem. 20. 93] or to the Assembly [Aeschin. 3. 39]); opposing laws had then first to be repealed (by a court?), with experts (*synegoroi*) appointed by the Assembly to defend them; and improper new laws were subject to being legally overturned by γραφὴ νόμων μὴ ἐπιτηδείων θεῖναι.

30 Canevaro 2015, however, section 8, notes that the relative numbers of attested γραφαὶ παρανόμων in 403–322 (35 according to Hansen 1991, 208) and γραφαὶ νόμων μὴ ἐπιτηδείων θεῖναι (6) suggests that the epigraphic record may exaggerate the imbalance between the numbers of laws and decrees. On the other hand over his whole career Demosthenes is

relevant. The small number of laws that are inscribed[31] meet rather well two of the observable criteria for inscribing a decree: they deliver a message (as for example the anti-tyranny law, *IG* II^3 1, 320, set up at the entrance to the Council chamber of the Areopagos and in the Assembly); or they have religious content (as with several inscribed laws relating to festivals). What, however, about the third criterion, durability? It was a feature of most laws that they were intended to be permanent and durable; and this makes it especially remarkable that so few are extant on stone. The archive in the Metroon, however, was created at the same time as the laws were being revised in the last decade of the fifth century.[32] Archives also preserve texts in a durable fashion. Perhaps the Metroon was designed from the start specifically to be the place where texts of laws made under the new law-making process were deposited. Whereas some types of decree had been inscribed before the creation of the archive and continued to be inscribed after it, fourth-century laws on this view were not normally inscribed precisely because they were available in the archive. They were no less valid and authoritative.

Appendix 1

Inscribed Athenian Laws and Decrees 352/1–322/1, by Subject

Inscriptions are referred to by number in *IG* II^3 1 plus a one-word title. For translations see www.atticinscriptions.com. Excluded are the "dubia et incerta", *IG* II^3 1, 531–572, and

---

known to have proposed 39 decrees of the People, 4 of the Council, but only 1 law, see Appendix 2.

31 Law on silver coinage, 375/4, *SEG* 26. 72 = Rhodes – Osborne 2003, no. 25; grain tax law, 374/3, *SEG* 47. 96 = Rhodes – Osborne 2003, no. 26; law on the Eleusinian Mysteries, 367/6–348/7 (?), *I Eleus.* 138, cf. *SEG* 30.61; unpublished law concerning Hephaistos, Athena Hephaistia and silver coinage, 354/3, *SEG* 54. 114; 56. 26; 61. 119; law on Eleusinian first-fruits, 353/2, *IG* II^2 140; law against tyranny, 337/6, *IG* II^3 1, 320; law providing for the repair of walls in Piraeus, with appended contract specifications (συγγραφαί), ca. 337 BC, *IG* II^3 1, 429; provisions relating to penalties and "exposure" (φάσις) from a law whose content is otherwise unknown, ca. 337–325, *IG* II^3 1, 431; at least two laws relating to cult objects, on the acropolis and elsewhere, ca. 335, *IG* II^3 1, 445; law making provision for funding of Little Panathenaia, followed by decree providing for sacrifices at the festival, ca. 335–330, *IG* II^3 1, 447; and possibly also: *SEG* 58. 95, fragmentary inscription apparently mentioning *nomothetai*, "before mid-IV BC"; *IG* II^3 1, 448, making provisions for an (Athenian or Macedonian) festival; *IG* II^3 1, 449, making provisions for a festival; *IG* II^3 1, 550, the end of text (of a law?) providing for liturgists to dedicate *phialai*, followed by list of liturgists; *SEG* 52. 104, "unpublished" law on repair of sanctuary of Artemis at Brauron.

32 Creation of archive: Sickinger 1999, 93–138 (cf. above n. 6); revision of laws and creation of new law-making procedure: most recently, Canevaro 2015.

decrees which are too fragmentary for the subject matter to be determined. Included, however, are those dated to the middle or second half of IV BC (IG II^3 1, 487–530).

Abbreviations
D = inscribed on a dedication made by the honorand rather than a stele erected by the city;
L = law.

1 Honorific

(a) Athenians

301; 305; 306 Council (D); 311 (D); 323 Secretary?; 325 Kalliteles; 327 Phyleus; 336 Diotimos?; 338 Pytheas; 348 Phanodemos; 355 Amphiaraia; 359 Androkles; 360 Council; 362 Epimeletai?; 365 Priest; 369 Hieropoioi (D); 389 (D); 402 Kephisophon (D); 416 Priests; 417 Leontis (D); 424; 425 Priest?; 458; 469 Kallikratides; 476 Proedroi?; 481; *IG* II^2 1155 = Lambert 2015 [= this volume, chapter 10]; *IG* II^2 1156 = Rhodes – Osborne 2003, no. 89; Lawton 1995 no. 164 = Lambert 2012, 182–183.[33] Total = 29

(b) Gods

349 Amphiaraos. Total = 1.

(c) Foreigners

293 Demokrates; 294 Theogenes; 295 Orontes;[34] 298 Spartokos; 302 Dioskourides; 303 Elaiousians?; 304 Pellanians; 307 Kephallenians or Lampsakenes; 309 Elaiousians; 310 Theoklos; 312 Phokinos; 313 Tenedos;[35] 316 Akarnanians; 317 Drakontides; 319 Alkimachos; 322 Courtier; 324 Euenor; 326?; 329?; 331 Nikostratos; 333 Archippos; 335 Amyntor; 339 Mnemon; 340 Chian; 342 Theophantos; 343 Theophantos; 344 Actor?; 345 Plataian?; 346; 347 Amphis; 351 Rheboulas; 352 Eudemos; 354 Herakleot?; 356 Larisan; 358 Eurylochos; 361 Thymondas?; 363 Phanostratos; 364; 367 Herakleides; 375 Lapyris; 376 Phokians; 377 Euphron; 378 Euphron; 379 Apollonides; 380; 383; 386; 387 Sestos; 390 Kleomis; 392; 393 Achaians; 398 Euboeans; 401 Tenedos; 403 Apelles; 404 Exiles; 405 Phaselite; 406; 411 Arybbas; 413 Chians; 414; 418 Asklepiodoros; 419 Amphipolitan; 420 Eretrian; 423 Actor; 426; 428 Philomelos; 430 Salaminian; 432 Sopatros; 434 Pydnan; 435; 436 Actor; 437; 439 Dionysios; 440 Potamon; 441 Pandios; 442; 452 Peisitheides; 453; 454 Koan; 455 Iatrokles; 456; 457 Pharsalian; 461; 462; 466; 468; 470; 473 Nikostratos; 474 Prienean; 475; 478; 479 Hestiaian; 480 Plataian; 483 Sostratos; 484 Friends; 485 Kythnos;

33 Relief from a decree (or dedication?) commemorating honours for a priestess of Athena Nike.

34 Also contains provisions relating to Orontes and grain supply.

35 Also contains provisions relating to Tenedos' financial contribution to the Second Athenian League (*syntaxis*).

490; 491; 492; 493; 495; 496 Praxias; 497 Krotoniate; 498; 501; 502; 503; 504; 505; 507; 515; 516; 517; 519; 528 Eupatas. Total = 116[36]

(d) Athenians or Foreigners?

315 Theophantos; 330; 357; 366; 371; 384; 385; 394; 395; 396; 397; 400; 421; 427; 438; 446; 450 Artikleides; 460; 463; 464; 499; 500; 506; 508; 509; 512; 513; 518; 520; 521; 522; 523; 524; 529. Total = 34.

2 Religious

292 Orgas; 297 Eleusis; 337 Kitians; 444 Nike;[37] 445 Cult (L);[38] 447 Panathenaia (L + decree);[39] 448 Festival (L?); 449 Festival (L?); 487 Lease?. Total = 9.

3 Treaties and other Foreign Policy

296 Echinaioi;[40] 299 Mytilene; 308 Messene; 318 Philip II; 370 Adriatic;[41] 381 Aitolians; 388 Akanthos;[42] 399 Attackers;[43] 412 Eretria; 443 Alexander; 482 Tenos; 488; 489 Chalkidians. Total = 13.

4 Other

320 Tyranny (L);[44] 429 Walls (L);[45] 431 Law (L);[46] 433 Sokles.[47] Total = 4

36 Note also the reliefs Lambert 2012, 181–182 nos. 1–17 and Glowacki 2003, most of which are probably from decrees honouring foreigners from this period.

37 Provides for priestess of Athena to sacrifice an *aresterion* on occasion of repair of statue of Athena Nike. Also honours the statue-maker, a Boeotian.

38 Two laws relating to cult objects.

39 Law and decree relating to Little Panathenaia.

40 Was or related to a *symbola* agreement.

41 Decree providing for a colonising expedition to the Adriatic. Inscribed not on a self-standing stele but in naval accounts.

42 Also praises the envoys from Akanthos and Dion and invites them to hospitality in the *prytaneion*.

43 Decree prohibiting military expeditions against Eretria or other allies.

44 Law against tyranny, prohibiting the Areopagos from sitting in circumstances of an anti-democratic coup.

45 Law providing for repair of walls in Piraeus and appended specifications for the work (συγγραφαί).

46 *Phasis* provisions from a law of unknown content.

47 Agreement between the city and Sokles for the exploitation of a resource and the sharing of proceeds.

Appendix 2

Laws and Decrees Proposed by Demosthenes[48]

Abbreviations
L = law, A = Assembly decree, C = Council decree or *probouleuma*.

Demosthenes' career as a proposer of laws and decrees precisely coincides with the period 352/1–322/1. Taking literary and epigraphical evidence together, he is on record as proposer of more than any other Athenian, viz. 39 decrees of the People, 4 of the Council, and 1 law. Only one of these is attested in the epigraphical record: *IG* II^3 1, 312 (= Hansen A18), honouring Phokinos, Nikandros and Dexi-. One is of unknown content (Din. F 47 Con. = Hansen A35). The remaining 42 are:

I Honorific

A2. Crown for the actor, Aristodemos of Metapontum, 347/6 (Aeschin. 2. 17).

A4. Foliage crown and invitation to dinner in the *prytaneion,* for the first embassy to Philip, 347/6 (Dem. 19. 234, Aeschin. 2. 46).

A29. Bronze statues in the Agora for Pairisades, Satyros and Gorgippos, rulers of Bosporan kingdom, ca. 330 (Din. 1. 43).

A30–31. Citizenship for Kallias of Chalkis, and his brother Taurosthenes, ca. 330 (Aeschin. 3. 85, Hyp. *Against Demosthenes* 20).

A32–34. Citizenship for Chairephilos and his sons, for Epigenes and for Konon, before 324 (Din. 1. 43).

A38. *Sitesis* in the *prytaneion* and a bronze statue in the Agora for Diphilos, 324/3 (Din. 1. 43; cf. F41 Con.).

C3. Seats in the theatre at the Dionysia for envoys from Philip II, 347/6 (Dem. 18. 28; Aeschin. 2. 55).

II Religious

A39. Prohibiting the worship of unacknowledged deities, 324/3 (Din. 1. 94).

III Treaties: Making or Abrogation

A11. Alliance with Chalkis, 342/1 (Aeschin. 3. 92–93).

A17. Declaring war on Philip II, 340/39 (*FGrHist* 328 Philochoros F55).

A20. Alliance with Thebes, 339/8 (Aeschin. 3. 142–145).

IV Providing for Embassies

A6. To the Peloponnese, 345/4 (Dem. 18. 79).

48 The list is based on Hansen 1989 (Demosthenes at pp. 41–42).

A8. To Euboea, 343/2 (Dem. 18. 79).

A13. To Eretria and Oreos, 341/0 (Aeschin. 3. 95–101)

A19. To Thebes, 339/8 (Dem. 18. 177–179).

C1. To cities to be visited by Aristodemos, 347/6 (Aeschin. 2. 19).

C4. Instructing second embassy to Philip to leave Athens immediately, 347/6 (Dem. 18. 25–29; 19. 154).

See also A26.

V Miscellaneous Foreign Policy

A3. Providing for truce and safe conduct for herald and envoys from Philip II, 347/6 (Aeschin. 2. 53–54).

A7. Relating to Ainos, member of Second Athenian League, before 342 ([Dem.] 58. 36–37, 43. Attacked by γραφὴ παρανόμων, 43).

VI Relating to Disposition of Military Forces and Defence Works

A1. Providing for an expeditionary force and a smaller permanent force to operate against Philip II, 352/1 (Dem. 4. 13–29, 30, 33. Apparently not passed).[49]

A12. Providing for expedition against Oreos, 341/0 (Dem. 18. 79).

A14. Providing for an expedition against Eretria, 341/0 (Dem. 18. 79).

A16. Providing for naval expeditions to Chersonese, Byzantium etc., 340/39 (Dem. 18. 80).

A22–24. Providing for military defence works: disposition of the guard-posts (ἡ διάταξις τῶν φυλακῶν), entrenchments (αἱ τάφροι), funding of the walls (τὰ εἰς τὰ τείχη χρήματα), 338/7 (Dem. 18. 248).

A26. Providing for a partial demobilisation and the despatch of embassies, 338/7 (Din. 1. 78–80).

A28. Providing for armed assistance to Thebes, 335/4 (Diod. 17. 8. 6).

VII On Military-Financial Matters

L1. On trierarchs, 340/39 (Dem. 18. 102–107, Din. 1. 42).

A21. Providing that "all the money should be stratiotic",[50] 339/8 (*FGrHist* 328 Philochoros F56A).

VIII Providing for Meetings of Public Bodies on Specific Forthcoming Dates

A5. Providing for an Assembly on 18–19 Elaphebolion to discuss Peace of Philokrates, 346 (Aeschin. 2. 61).

---

49 Cf. MacDowell 2009, 215.

50 τὰ δὲ χρήματα ἐψηφίσαντο πάντ' εἶναι στρατιωτικά. Hansen interprets: "transferring revenue from the theoric to the stratiotic fund".

A27. Providing for tribal Assemblies to meet on 2 and 3 Skirophorion to elect representatives responsible for repair of walls, 338/7 (Aeschin. 3. 27).

C2. Providing for an Assembly on 8 Elaphebolion to discuss Peace of Philokrates, 346 (Aeschin. 3. 67).

IX Of a Legal or Judicial Character

A9. Ordering *apophasis* against Proxenos (imprisonment), 346–343 (Din. 1. 63).

A10. Providing for death sentence on Anaxinos (?), 343 (Aeschin. 3. 224).

A15. Providing for the appointment of *nomothetai* for reform of trierarchy, 340/39 (Dem. 18. 102–107).

A25. Concerning the powers of the Areopagos, 338/7 (?) (Din. 1. 62, 82–83).

A36. Ordering the arrest of Harpalos and the confiscation of his money, 324 (Hyp. *Dem.* 8–9, Din. 1. 89).

A37. Instructing the Areopagos to investigate the Harpalos affair, 324/3 (Din. 1. 82–83).

Bibliography

Canevaro, M. 2015: "Making and changing laws in ancient Athens", in E. M. Harris and M. Canevaro eds., *Oxford handbook of ancient Greek law*, Oxford, forthcoming (this chapter published online, 2015).

Davies, J. K. 2003: "Greek archives: from record to monument", in M. Brosius ed., *Ancient archives and archival traditions*, Oxford, 323–43.

Gagarin, M. 2008: *Writing Greek law*, Cambridge.

Glowacki, K. 2003: "A personification of Demos on a new Attic document relief", *Hesperia* 72, 447–66.

Habicht, C. 1961: "Falsche Urkunden zur Geschichte Athens im Zeitalter der Perserkriege", *Hermes* 89, 1–35.

Hansen, M. H. 1984: "The number of *rhetores* in the Athenian Ecclesia, 355–322 BC", *GRBS* 25, 123–55 [reprinted with addenda in M. H. Hansen, *The Athenian Ecclesia* 2. *A collection of articles 1983–1989*, Copenhagen, 1989, 93–127].

Hansen, M. H. 1987: *The Athenian Assembly in the age of Demosthenes*, Oxford.

Hansen, M. H. 1989: "Updated Inventory of *rhetores* and *strategoi* (1988)", in M. H. Hansen, *The Athenian Ecclesia* 2. *A collection of articles 1983–1989*, Copenhagen, 34–72.

Hansen, M. H. 1991: *The Athenian democracy in the age of Demosthenes*, Oxford.

Lambert, S. D. 2004: "Athenian state laws and decrees, 352/1–322/1. I. Decrees honouring Athenians", *ZPE* 150, 85–120 [= Lambert 2012, 3–47].

Lambert, S. D. 2005: "Athenian state laws and decrees, 352/1–322/1. II. Religious regulations", *ZPE* 154, 125–59 [= Lambert 2012, 48–92].

Lambert, S. D. 2011: "What was the point of inscribed honorific decrees in classical Athens?", in S. D. Lambert ed., *Sociable man. Essays on ancient Greek social behaviour in honour of Nick Fisher*, Swansea, 193–214 [= this volume, chapter 3].

Lambert, S. D. 2012: *Inscribed Athenian Laws and Decrees, 352/1–322/1 BC. Epigraphical Essays*, Leiden.

Lambert, S. D. 2015: "Dedication and decrees commemorating military action in 339/8 BC", in A. Matthaiou and N. Papazarkadas eds., *Axon. Studies in honor of Ronald S. Stroud*, Athens, 233–46 [= this volume, chapter 10].

Lambert, S. D. forthcoming: "The locations of inscribed Athenian laws and decrees in the age of Demosthenes", in D. Marchiandi and I. Berti eds., *Inscribing space*, Turin (in series *Historika*) [= this volume, chapter 1].

Lawton, C. L. 1995: *Attic document reliefs*, Oxford.

Liddel, P. 2016: "Honorific decrees of fourth-century Athens: trends, perceptions, controversies", in C. Tiersch ed., *Die Athenische Demokratie im 4. Jahrhundert. Zwischen Modernisierung und Tradition*, Berlin, 335–57.

MacDowell, D. 2009: *Demosthenes the orator*, Oxford.

Mack, W. 2015: *Proxeny and polis. Institutional networks in the ancient Greek world*, Oxford.

Meyer, E. 2013: "Inscriptions as honors and the Athenian epigraphic habit", *Historia* 62, 453–505.

Osborne, R., Rhodes, P. J. forthcoming: *Greek historical inscriptions 478–404 BC*, Oxford.

Osborne, M. J. 2012: "Secretaries, *psephismata* and *stelai* in Athens", *Ancient Society* 42, 33–59.

Rhodes, P. J., Osborne, R. 2003: *Greek historical inscriptions 404–323 BC*, Oxford.

Sickinger, J. 1999: *Public records and archives in classical Athens*, Chapel Hill.

Stroud, R. S. 1963: "A fragment of an inscribed bronze stele from Athens", *Hesperia* 32, 138–43.

Stroud, R. S. 1978: "State documents in archaic Athens", in *Athens Comes of Age. From Solon to Salamis*, Princeton, 20–42.

PART 2

Inscribed Laws and Decrees and Athenian Policy

CHAPTER 3

What was the Point of Inscribed Honorific Decrees in Classical Athens?*

If I had to single out the academic virtue that I most admire in our honorand, it would be his capacity to identify important historical questions and to address them with rigour and good sense, but also with a clarity and directness that make his writing highly accessible to students and hugely engaging. His commentary on Aeschines' speech *Against Timarchos* is a tour de force in this respect. It is one of the best historical commentaries that have yet been produced in English on any Greek text in translation. I hope that he will accept what follows as a fitting tribute in the obvious sense that this is a paper on honorific decrees in a volume which is itself a sort of honorific decree (what they expressed in stone, we express in a printed text); but also because he has himself done so much to elucidate the central importance of *timē* as a driver of Greek social behaviour. (I shall translate *timē* conventionally in this paper as 'honour', though the Greek word encompasses a broader range in the semantic area, 'value'.) I also have our honorand's example in mind in seeking to address, with such lucidity as I can muster, a question that is in a sense quite simple, but also rather important.

All Greek inscriptions can be interpreted as social behaviour: whether it is an Assembly of citizens transmuting their decisions into public monuments, a board of officials rendering their accounts in stone, a private citizen making a dedication in a sanctuary or a dead man addressing a passer-by through the medium of an epigram on his gravestone by the wayside, inscriptions concern the communications and relations among human beings and between humans and gods. I have spent much of my time in recent years on editing inscriptions, a task which requires certain sorts of historical knowledge, but is not in itself a historical enterprise: the primary objective is to establish the best possible texts. But I am also interested in interpreting the inscriptions I work on, in using them to do history; and if we are to do that intelligently, I believe we do need to address fundamental questions about why they were inscribed, in other words to seek to understand the social behaviour of which they are an expression. The inscriptions I have mainly been working on carry

* This paper was first published in S. D. Lambert ed. *Sociable Man. Essays on Ancient Greek Social Behaviour in Honour of Nick Fisher*, (Swansea, 2011), 193–214. See also the Introduction to this volume, pp. 5–6.

© KONINKLIJKE BRILL NV, LEIDEN, 2018 DOI 10.1163/9789004352490_005

the texts of decrees of the Athenian Council and Assembly. From the earliest extant decree, dating to the end of the sixth century (*IG* I³ 1), to the end of the fourth century, about a thousand such inscriptions are extant, most to a greater or lesser extent fragmentary. Those carrying decrees which bestow honours, usually on individuals, sometimes on whole cities, are by far the most numerous, accounting for around three-quarters of this total. Apart from a handful of decrees honouring Athenian citizens, inscribed on dedications made by the honorands themselves,[1] they are all inscribed on *stēlai,* normally erected at the initiative and expense of the city. At this period over 90% of them were placed in the religious and monumental heart of the city, the acropolis.[2] Honouring people is obviously a type of social behaviour, but how should we explain it? And why is it expressed so commonly in inscribed form? What exactly was the point of inscribed honorific decrees in classical Athens?

The texts of the decrees themselves supply a ready answer. From around the middle of the fourth century the point of them is often asserted in the form of a 'hortatory intention' clause.[3] A decree of 330/29 or shortly after, honouring the grain merchant Herakleides of Salamis, will do for an example:

> To praise Herakleides son of Charikleides of Salamis and crown him with a gold crown of 500 drachmas and permit him to seek from the People what good he can, **so that others also may behave in an honour-seeking way (φιλοτιμῶνται), knowing that the Council honours and crowns those who behave in an honour-seeking way (τοὺς φιλοτιμουμένους).**
>
> RHODES AND OSBORNE 2007, NO. 95 [= IG II³ 1, 367]

The Athenians – in this case the Council, but in other contexts it is the Assembly – state that they are honouring this man in order to encourage others to behave in an honour-seeking way, in the expectation that they too will be honoured. 'Behave in an honour-seeking way' means, in practice, acting in ways that are beneficial to the city. In other words honorific decrees are levers that the city is pulling to encourage people to do things which benefit Athens.

---

1 See Lambert 2004, Lambert 2005, 125–9.

2 There is as yet no full historical study of Athenian honorific decrees. On those inscribed in 352/1–322/1 BC (which account for over a third of the number inscribed to the end of the classical democracy) see Lambert 2004, 2006, 2007a. Henry 1983 is a useful catalogue of the honours and privileges awarded, but is linguistic in focus. Over 90% on the acropolis: Liddel 2003. In general on honorific practice in Athens and elsewhere in Greece see Gauthier 1985.

3 The most recent discussion of the hortatory intention, with references to earlier bibliography, is Luraghi 2010 (see also Sickinger 2009). For an analysis of the formulae in which the intention is expressed see Henry 1996.

These levers were all the more potent in a culture in which honour was a powerful, arguably perhaps the most powerful, driver of the political actions of individuals and communities.

I want to spend most of this paper unpacking and exploring some of the implications of this, on the surface of it quite simple, explanation of the point of honorific decrees. It is, I think, the main point, but it is not the only point. There are numerous subsidiary points – subtexts we might call them – and at the end I shall briefly explore some of these.

The first question that arises about the hortatory intention is: these clauses begin appearing in honorific decrees in the 340s. Did this hortatory intentionality apply to inscribed honorific decrees passed before that? I think that it did. The hortatory clauses express a reciprocal ideology that is not only deeply embedded in Greek thought in general about proper relations between people; it is also bound closely into the fabric of honorific ideology before the 340s. It is implicit, for example, in the most common type of inscribed honorific decree in classical Athens, the proxeny.[4] When Athens appointed the citizen of another city an Athenian *proxenos,* that, in form, placed on that person a responsibility to protect Athenian interests in their home city. What justifies the person's appointment as *proxenos,* however, is that he has already been behaving in a way that is beneficial to the city. X benefits the city; city honours X; because of the honour the city expects X to continue benefiting the city. The logic, honour based on past behaviour but looking to influence future behaviour, is the same as that of the hortatory intention clause. Commonly an honorific decree represents just one point along a line of mutually beneficial exchanges that extends back generations into the past and is expected to continue long into the future, an extension in time reflected in the wording of the decrees themselves: in the frequent recognition that an honorand's benefactions continue a tradition of benefaction begun by his ancestors, and in the common extension of honours to descendants.

A good example is the decree of 347/6, renewing for Spartokos and Pairisades, newly acceded rulers of the Cimmerian Bosporos, honours and privileges, including the Athenian citizenship, explicitly stated to have been accorded to their ancestors (Rhodes and Osborne 2007, no. 64 [*IG* II³ 1, 298]). It is one of a long series of Athenian actions honouring a family whose good-will was of crucial importance for the Athenian grain supply, from the fifth century through to the third.[5] The Athenian citizenship, the highest honour normally

4 On the proxeny and other types of honorific decree honouring foreigners see Lambert 2006 and references cited there.

5 See Dem. 20 and Rhodes and Osborne 2007, notes on no. 64. Third century: *IG* II² 653 = Osborne 1981–3, T 21 [= *IG* II³ 1, 870].

awarded foreigners at this period, extended to descendants by definition; and this commonly applied also to lesser honours, such as the proxeny.

The idea often expressed in hortatory intention clauses that honorific decrees are intended to impact on the behaviour of people other than the honorands is arguably slightly different from the idea that they are intended to impact on the honorands' (and their descendants') behaviour, but I do not think it is a significant novelty. One of the arguments deployed by Demosthenes 20 *Against Leptines* in ca. 355 was that it was unwise to deprive those awarded Athenian honorific decrees of their privileges because of the negative impact that would have on other people contemplating future benefactions. I take this to be an obvious line of argument, not a novel one dreamt up by Demosthenes; and the hortatory intention clauses simply express the same basic idea in a positive rather than a negative way – *pour encourager les autres.*[6] I suggest, therefore, that the hortatory intention clauses from the 340s onwards articulate an ideology of honorific decrees that was already implicit in the system before the 340s.

The question then becomes, why is it only articulated in the 340s? At least three possible answers come to mind.

As we know from the orators, and indeed from the large numbers of surviving honorific decrees on stone from this period, such decrees were a topic high on the agenda of public debate in the mid-fourth century, both the general principles (as e.g. in Demosthenes *Against Leptines*) and individual cases. An honorific decree was, after all, the point formally at issue in the most famous speech ever delivered by a Greek orator, Demosthenes *On The Crown.* We know that there were fourth-century laws regulating the award of honours, for example the law stipulating that crowns could not be awarded to Athenian officials before they had rendered their accounts. It is not difficult to see how, in such an environment, wording which expressed a consensus view about the point of such decrees might have got into the decrees themselves. The hortatory intention clause can be read as a sort of justification for the honours; and I would guess that the prototype of such a clause was embedded originally in a law or laws of ca. 350 which regulated awards of honours.

Second answer: hortatory clauses appear at a time when the Athenians were experiencing a heightened sense of decline in the face of the rise of Macedon and the weakening of the Second Athenian League after the Social War. As

6 The thought also occurs in earlier inscriptions, e.g. the second herm commemorating the Athenian victory against the Persians at Eion in 476/5, as recorded by Aeschines (3.184, transl. Carey): 'and seeing this, men in ages to come, too, will wish the more to bear labours for the common good.' Cf. Plut. *Cimon* 7.4.

political and military power were waning, honorific decrees became relatively a more important weapon in the diplomatic armoury. The introduction of explicit hortatory intention clauses can be construed as an expression of the city's exerting itself, straining to make the decrees as efficacious as possible. Like some other features of the inscribed record at this period (e.g. decrees honouring individual grain traders, a new genre and a common one after the defeat at Chaironeia), they can be interpreted as response to decline.[7] There is some support for this line of interpretation in the way Xenophon urged the deployment of honours and rewards in the *Poroi,* his programme of measures of ca. 355 to improve the revenues of the city in the post-Social War crisis. Much of the programme, which was certainly a 'response to decline', was never implemented, but some elements, or at least its underlying principles, can be seen reflected in the real-life epigraphical record of the subsequent decades. At 3.3 he urges that market officials should be encouraged to prompt and just settlement of disputes by the award of competitive prizes. Similar in approach (albeit not specific to the economic sphere) is the award voted by the Council in the ninth prytany of 343/2 to Phanodemos of Thymaitadai for being the best and most uncorrupt speaker in the Council (*IG* II^2 223, 4–5 [*IG* II^3 1, 306]). At 3.4 Xenophon urges that preferential seating (*proedria*) in the theatre and hospitality (*xenia*) should be awarded to beneficent merchants and shippers (*emporoi* and *nauklēroi*), 'so that, being honoured, not only for the sake of profit, but also of honour, they might behave towards us as friends.'[8] There is a striking example of precisely this policy in the decree of ca. 337–325 proposed by Lykourgos for the grain-trader, Sopatros of Akragas, which awarded him both *xenia* and a seat at the forthcoming City Dionysia (Lambert 2006, no. 37 = *SEG* 54.170 [= *IG* II^3 1, 432]). Finally, at 3.11 Xenophon urges that foreigners should be encouraged to contribute to his proposed capital fund by the prospect of being inscribed as benefactors for all time.[9] Xenophon's capital fund was never introduced, but we might take as an example of this general policy towards encouraging benefaction the decree of 330/29, also proposed by Lykourgos, and nominating Eudemos of Plataia among the benefactors of the Athenian People for his offer of financial support 'for the war', if needed (probably the revolt of Agis against Macedon in 331 is meant), and his provision of oxen to help with the construction of 'the stadium and the Panathenaic theatre' (Rhodes and Osborne 2007, no. 94 = Lambert 2006, no. 42 = *SEG* 55.173 [= *IG* II^3 1, 352]).

7 Response to decline: cf. Lambert 2012.

8 ταῦτα γὰρ τιμώμενοι οὐ μόνον τοῦ κέρδους ἀλλὰ καὶ τῆς τιμῆς ἕνεκεν ὡς πρὸς φίλους ἐπισπεύδοιεν ἄν.

9 εἰ μέλλοιεν ἀναγραφήσεσθαι εὐεργέται εἰς τὸν ἅπαντα χρόνον.

Third answer: the key is in the language. Hortatory intention clauses promote *philotimia;* they start appearing at the same time as *philotimia* begins to be praised as a positive value in Athenian decrees. In the radical democracy there had been a reluctance explicitly to promote *philotimia* because it sat uneasily with an egalitarian, collectivist ideology, but by the mid-fourth century the advantages of promoting *philotimia* had come to be seen as outweighing the drawbacks, whether because that ideological consensus was softening, because the democracy was more mature and stable and so able to accommodate less anxiously the promotion of such a value, or simply because, as its power and wealth declined, the city was under increasing pressure to secure the benefactions of the wealthy and powerful by any means available.[10]

Another important development in inscribed honorific decrees took place in the 340s. Before that, generally speaking, only foreigners were honoured by such decrees. It is only in the 340s that Athenian citizens began regularly to be so honoured – ordinary Athenian officials more commonly than prominent politicians.[11] With some adaptation, each of the three explanations I have just given for the appearance of the hortatory intention clause can be applied also to the new practice of regularly inscribing decrees honouring Athenians.[12]

Firstly, the prominence of honours on the political agenda, as well as encouraging explicit articulation of their purpose, may also have heightened an awareness that they could be as useful in encouraging Athenian officials to behave well towards the city as they were in encouraging foreigners to behave well; and it is perhaps relevant here to note that it must have been very difficult to find enough good people to fill competently the vast number of annual offices that existed in fourth-century Athens. Positive incentives could clearly be very useful, especially in a political culture in which, while breadth of political participation had, since the time of Pericles, increasingly been facilitated by

10 Cf. Whitehead 1983 and 1993. *Philotimia* appears to emerge first as a praiseworthy virtue in deme decrees, shortly before 350. Rhodes and Osborne 2007, 233, and Osborne forthcoming suggest that this is because, as small communities, demes were, or sooner became, more dependent on the benefactions of individuals than larger ones such as the polis. Whitehead 2009, 53–4, explains the emergence of *aretē* as a praiseworthy virtue (first in a decree honouring the Mytilenaeans of 368/7, *IG* II^2 107 = Rhodes and Osborne no. 31, 14) in similar terms: '… can perhaps be put down to the changed (more moderate, less aggressively egalitarian) ethos of the city in the fourth century.'

11 See Lambert 2004; 2005, 125–9.

12 At 2004, 86–7, I suggested that other factors may have been: (a) an increasingly developed epigraphic and bureaucratic culture; (b) tribes had long been honouring Athenians with inscribed decrees, and this may have generated pressure for the city to follow suit.

payment of relatively small *per diem* allowances and expenses (usually of a few obols), officials did not receive salaries in anything like the modern sense.[13]

Second, as hortatory intention clauses can be interpreted as response to decline in the face of the rise of Macedonian power, so one might offer a similar explanation for the introduction of inscribed honours for Athenians. I tend to agree with Nick Fisher that the reason why Aeschines won his patently weak case against Timarchos in 346/5 (the same year as the earliest dated example in the regular series of inscribed decrees honouring Athenian officials, *IG* II² 215 = Lambert 2004, no. 18 with n. 3 [= *IG* II³ 1, 301]), was that it plugged into a general anxiety about the calibre and performance of city officials, which was generated primarily by a sense of decline. If Aeschines (and later that famous harrier of miscreants, Lykourgos) were wielding the stick to punish the badly behaved official, inscriptions honouring officials on the acropolis can be seen as the carrot to encourage the well-behaved.[14]

Thirdly, explicitly encouraging *philotimia* may be contentious when it relates to foreigners; it is potentially even more problematic and divisive when applied to Athenians. Such decrees involve, in a sense, promoting one Athenian above another; it was only in the settled domestic political circumstances of the mid-fourth century (or, conversely, one might argue, against the background of the unsettling dynamics of power within the Greek world as a whole), that this came to be perceived as tolerable.

I should not want to press the significance of this new genre of inscribed decree too far, however, because, as we know not least from the Leptines speech, Athenians had certainly been honoured in decrees before the 340s.[15] It is just that the decrees were not inscribed; and this raises an important point, which is the distinction between decrees that were and were not inscribed, or to put the question in the terms of this paper, what was the point not just of *passing but* specifically of *inscribing an* honorific decree?

A key text here is two decrees of the 340s inscribed on the same stone and honouring the city Pellana in the Peloponnese (*IG* II² 220 = Lambert 2007a, no. 66 [= *IG* II³ 1, 304]). As usual with inscriptions, they are not fully preserved; the surviving text reads as follows:

---

13 Numerous offices: Hansen 1980. Payments to officials: Loomis 1998, 9–31.

14 Fisher 2001. On this see also Lambert 2012. Perceived need to offer incentives for good behaviour to officials: Xen. *Poroi* 3.3 (above).

15 Cf. Lambert 2004, 85–7. Apart from references in the orators to decrees honouring Athenians before the 340s (e.g. Dem. 20.86), we know this from dedications made by those who had been honoured by the Council and/or People (see e.g. the first 30 or so inscriptions in *Agora* XV, *SEG* 21.668).

(344/3) ... was secretary ... of the prytany. Of the presiding committee Hippoch[-] of [*deme*] was putting to the vote. [*name*] son of Oinobios of Rhamnous (5) proposed:

concerning what the ambassadors of the Pellanians reported, the People shall resolve that the secretary of the Council shall inscribe the decree which Aristo[-] proposed about the Pellanians last year on a (11) stone *stēlē* and stand it on the acropolis; and the treasurer of the People shall give towards the inscribing 30 drachmas from the People's fund for expenditure on decrees, (15) **so that the city of the Pellanians shall continue always to be friendly and well-disposed towards the Athenian People, as in previous times;** and to praise the (20) ambassadors of the Pellanians and invite them to hospitality in the *prytaneion* tomorrow.

In the archonship of Euboulos (345/4), in the ninth prytany, of [*tribe name*], for which (25) [-]enos son of I[-] of Oion was secretary. On the tenth of the prytany. Of the presiding committee [*name*] of Eitea was putting to the vote. Aristo[-] son of [-]tonikos of [*deme*] proposed:

(30) ... report ... sent ...

In 345/4 there was diplomacy between Pellana and Athens. Exactly what was discussed and agreed is quite obscure, except that the upshot was an Athenian decree honouring Pellana which was not at that time inscribed (the second decree on the stone). The following year an embassy came from Pellana to Athens. Again we do not know what it was about, but the upshot was that the Athenians passed and inscribed a decree, the sole provision of which was that the decree honouring Pellana passed the previous year was to be inscribed; and it is notable that it is specifically the inscribing of the decree that is endowed with hortatory intention.[16] Clearly, there was more to all this than meets the eye. Perhaps the decision to do no more than inscribe the previous year's decree is a consolation prize, in effect the outcome of a failed negotiation; but prize it still is. The inscription would make no sense unless having an inscription honouring you set up on the Athenian acropolis was something that was genuinely desirable to potential honorands (or, if one took a cynical view, something that Athens wanted potential honorands to find desirable), and such I think we can take honorific inscriptions on the acropolis to be. It was very rare, however, that the inscription was the only object of the honorific exercise: we should, I suggest, normally interpret the act of inscribing an honorific decree as an *enhancement* of the substantive honours, such as the

16 This is fairly unusual (cf. Sickinger 2009, 93–4).

crown, proxeny, citizenship, or whatever other honours and privileges were being awarded.

So, what did this enhancement consist of? Was it about communicating knowledge of the honour? Some honours were concrete (such as a crown, the award of which was typically the central honour) or substantive (e.g. citizenship), but insofar as honour is an abstract quality to do with the opinion of others it cannot exist in a vacuum; by definition it depends to an extent on people knowing about it. Yes, the debate on a proposal for honours in the Athenian Council and Assembly communicated knowledge of the honour, at least to an Athenian audience; yes, sometimes (though this is rare in fourth-century decrees) there was provision for announcement of the honours before the crowds massed at a suitable festival;[17] but it seems reasonable to suppose that part of the intention of inscribing honorific decrees on the acropolis was so that the honour should be enhanced by being widely known about, and indeed that is arguably implicit in the language of hortatory intention clauses like those in the inscriptions quoted above, in the passage of Demosthenes, *Against Leptines,* cited below, and in other types of decree where provision is explicitly made that it should be inscribed, 'so that everyone may know'.[18] It is well-known that Greek inscriptions were commonly conceived of as 'oggetti parlanti', as speaking the words inscribed on them (e.g. 'I am the boundary marker of the Agora'), and this idea can also be applied to the texts of honorific (and indeed other types of) decrees, which are normally introduced by the words: 'x spoke' (εἶπεν), x being the name of the proposer of the decree in the Council or Assembly. The inscription elevates (from Pnyx or Council-chamber to the acropolis), petrifies and perpetuates in the name of the Athenians collectively the performance of an honorific utterance, originally an actual speech of an individual citizen in Assembly or Council.[19]

---

17 There is an example in the decree honouring the rulers of the Bosporan kingdom, referred to above, ll. 29–33 (announcement of crowns by the *athlothetai* at every Great Panathenaia).

18 Cf. Hedrick 1999; Sickinger 2009. Anton Powell suggests to me that part of the dynamic here may have been a realisation that 'good news' of the type contained in honorific decrees would not be transmitted and remembered as easily as bad; an inscription gave it an extra push.

19 This can be seen as an aspect of the phenomenon known by anthropologists as 'agency', whereby there was a tendency in ancient Greece (as in some other cultures) to conceptualise inanimate objects as if they were agents of change, like persons, or extensions of the 'agency' of persons or groups. See Gell 1998; Whitley 2007; and James Whitley's paper in this volume.

I should not, however, wish to push this line of explanation too far. When honorific decrees express an intention that something be known by inscribing it, it is not usually the detailed content of the decree, but rather its very existence. It is the fact of the inscribed decree, and many others like it, that generates the hortatory effect, not detailed knowledge of the contents.[20] Moreover, although both Athenians and foreigners undoubtedly went up to the acropolis on high days and holidays, it was no ordinary thoroughfare; and whether it was foreigners or Athenians, we cannot tell how many of those who went up there would have had the capability or interest to read the inscriptions. Certainly I think that honorific inscriptions should be conceptualised as monuments to be seen and not merely as texts to be read (or indeed simply as speaking texts);[21] and certainly one should think in terms of the monument as a whole, and not merely the text, as carriers of the honorific intention. This should include the relief sculpture which adorned some honorific decrees and typically (not always) depicted the honorand being crowned by Athena, together with the patron deity or other symbol of the honorand's city. Lawton 1995 has given us an excellent catalogue of such sculpture. Clearly its function, simply stated, was to convey in visual terms key features of the import of the text. There is much to be done, however, to elucidate its intentionality more fully, and indeed that of other physical features of inscribed decrees (on paint, see Lambert 2006, 119), and their relationship to the text of the monument and its physical context.[22]

---

20 Compare the provision at Rhodes and Osborne 2007, no. 64 [*IG* II^3 1, 298], 46–7, that the *stēlē* be set up (in the Piraeus) 'near the one of Satyros and Leukon.' The '*stēlē* of Satyros and Leukon' (one of the '*stēlai* for Leucon' in various places referred to by Dem. 20.36) was apparently a well-known landmark: a monument named for its honorands, and so, by its very existence, enhancing their honour and fame.

21 On inscriptions (including their texts) as artefacts see especially Stoddart and Whitley 1988, Whitley 1997, Whitley 2006.

22 Recent studies which show the way forward include Blanshard 2004 (on the relief on the Athenian law against tyranny of 337/6, Rhodes and Osborne 2007, no. 79 [*IG* II^3 1, 320]) and 2007; Moreno 2007, 260–9 (on the relief on the decree for the rulers of the Bosporan kingdom, referred to above); Scafuro 2009, 75–6 (on the absence of relief on the decree crowning Amphiaraos, on which see further below). As for other physical features, the most remarkable perhaps is the variability that was achieved within the scope of what was an essentially simple format. The decrees are individualised such that every one is different, whether in dimensions, or in detail such as mouldings, decoration, arrangement of the lettering. This in itself can be seen as an enhancement of the honour. In general on the format of the decree *stēlē* and its origin (perhaps linked to the funerary *stēlē*), see Davies 2005.

The character of the place where it was set up – usually (but not always) the sacred heart of the city, the acropolis – was also a carrier of an inscribed decree's intentionality.[23] Though there are a few early fifth-century inscriptions from the acropolis, Athenians started regularly setting up inscribed decrees there around the middle of the century. This is conventionally explained in terms of an ideological link with the radical democracy, with ideas of accountability, and of spreading knowledge and information, and there may be something in that;[24] but in my view a major incentive is likely to have been the Periclean building programme. Erecting inscriptions on the acropolis was intended, I suggest, to adorn the place with fine monuments on a small scale which complemented the larger scale structures;[25] and which incidentally also celebrated the city as a place of verbal culture as well as a place of architectural and sculptural culture. It was no doubt the fact that an inscribed monument honouring you had been erected on the acropolis, alongside the finest monumental architecture in the world, that would primarily have delighted the honorands (many of whom, in the case of foreign rulers and such like, never came to Athens and will never have seen the monuments honouring them), to an extent independently of any thought about how many people would see it or read it.

Was the point of inscribing honorific decrees different from the point of inscribing other types of decree? The other two main categories of inscribed decree in the classical period were religious regulations and interstate treaties.[26] I agree with Cathy Keesling that dedications on the acropolis had two faces – one

---

23 On the character of the acropolis as locus of inscriptions see Osborne 1999, 346–7; Liddel 2003, 80–1 (who also catalogues the few honorific decrees set up in other locations in the classical period). On the Agora as a developing locus of commemoration, including inscriptions, in and around the last decade of the fifth century, see Shear 2007. Only a very small proportion of extant honorific decrees were set up in the Agora before the hellenistic period. [On this topic see now also this volume, chapter 1].

24 See e.g. Meritt 1940, 89–93; Hedrick 1999; and most recently Osborne 2009, 104–5. Sickinger 2009, however, rightly points out that the so-called 'formulae of disclosure' in Athenian inscriptions, 'in order that x may be known' vel sim., including some types of hortatory intention clause, rarely have the specifically democratic objective of informing citizens (as in *IG* I^3 84.26, where regulations for the leasing of the sanctuary of Kodros, Neleus and Basile are inscribed 'so that it may be possible for anyone who wishes to know them') and are more commonly couched 'in terms of honour, competitive display and emulation.'

25 Cf. the suggestive remarks of Liddel 2003, 80–1. There are a number of design features of inscriptions which resonate with the monumental context, e.g. the crowning pediments echoing temple architecture and perhaps signifying that an inscription could be viewed in a way as a little shrine of its own (cf. Davies 2005, 294, and below on the common superscription, 'gods').

26 Cf. Lambert 2005, 2007b.

looking towards men and one looking towards the gods;[27] and I think the same thing applies to decree inscriptions, which, like dedications, were typically located in or close to religious sanctuaries (usually the acropolis) and share some of the character of dedications (e.g. frequently carrying the superscription, θεοί – 'gods'). To put it another way, inscribed decrees were intended to engage both men and gods in a nexus of relations and intercommunication.[28] One can certainly see how the solemn presentation of an honorand to the city's gods could itself be conceptualised as an honour, a guarantee of the future good-will of the city (implied by Dem. 20.64, quoted below), and a recommendation of the honorand to the gods' benign attention. This is emphasised by the presence of deities in the relief sculpture, including the common transmutation of the agent of the honour from the Athenian People (as expressed in the text) to Athena herself (as expressed in the relief). Arguably, however, the face of honorific decrees was turned more towards men: they were primarily about gratifying the honorand, who was nearly always human,[29] and about the effects of that gratification on the behaviour of the honorand and other humans. And arguably the face of religious regulations and treaties was turned more towards the gods. Both of these types of decree communicated and demonstrated solemn commitments to human viewers, whether Athenians or foreigners; but the divine aspect is closer to the intentional surface. The gods could be expected to take a particularly close interest in inscriptions regulating divine matters, and the solemn placement of treaties on the acropolis complemented and expressed the religious sanction that attended the oaths by which the parties to the treaty bound themselves to adhere to it, oaths which were typically part of the treaty text.

---

27 Keesling 2003, 199.

28 The religious connotations of setting up inscribed decrees on the acropolis are well brought out by Osborne 1999, 346–7, and Liddel 2003, 80–1.

29 A striking exception is the decree from the Amphiaraion proposed in 332/1 by a man of strong religious sensibilities, the Atthidographer Phanodemos (*FGrH* 325), honouring the god Amphiaraos, *IG* VII 4252 = Lambert 2004, 87 and 107 with n. 75 [= *IG* II^3 1, 349], passed on the same day as a decree honouring Phanodemos himself for his legislation for the Great Amphiaraia festival (*IG* VII 4253 = Lambert 2004, no. 16 [= *IG* II^3 1, 348]). One way of viewing this pair of decrees is precisely as a meditation on the human and divine orientations of honorific decrees; another as a meditation, in this foreign-but-Athenian territory of Oropos, on the duality of the Athenian honorific system (Athenians and foreigners) and the unifying power of Amphiaraos, whose crown is to be dedicated 'for the health and preservation of the Athenian People and of their children and wives and of everyone in the land', ll. 27–31. Cf. Scafuro 2009, 75 (a suggestive discussion which, however, needs adjustment on some points, e.g. in the distinction she draws between 'cultic' and 'civic' crowning. All the crownings she discusses had a religious aspect).

If I had to express in a sentence the point of inscribing any decree, it would be that it was to endow it with enhanced, solemn, significance and validity as expression of the collective Athenian will. It is this which helps explain how inscribed decrees can be so intimately connected with what they record that destroying an inscription recording something is often conceptualised as destroying the thing recorded.[30] It also has implications for how we can use inscribed decrees as historical evidence. Combined with the fact that we have a large and probably fairly random sample of all decrees inscribed on the acropolis in the classical period, and that the acropolis was the principal site for erecting honorific decrees, it enables us to examine extant decrees honouring foreigners as a group and to draw legitimate inferences from them as to the development of the city's foreign policy priorities over time. This is an approach to these decrees that I have begun to explore elsewhere.[31]

The hortatory intention clause is the stated point of honorific decrees and expresses, I think, the main point; but it is not the only point. There are numerous subsidiary points or subtexts, of which I mention here a few of the more important. It is a feature of these subtexts that they seem to come into play more with some honorific inscriptions than with others.

First, how far was it the point of honorific decrees to express or assert the power or prestige of persons other than the honorand? I do not think there is much, as regards classical Athens, in Paul Veyne's contention in relation to later, less democratic, Greek polities, that the honorific system was intended to express the superior status and distinction of the elite as a class.[32] The 'elite' of the classical Athenian democracy did not articulate itself as a separate class; indeed the very term 'elite' is of questionable applicability in a society in which

30 Thus we have a series of six *stēlai* from the early fourth century inscribed with decrees restoring proxenies which had been rescinded under the Thirty. On some of them the proxeny is described as being 'on' the *stēlē* (as *IG* II^2 6 + *SEG* 29.83, 'since the *stēlē* on which was their proxeny was destroyed under the Thirty'), on others as actually being the *stēlē* (as *IG* II^2 52, 'since his [grandfather?] Xanthippos was *proxenos* and the Thirty destroyed the proxeny, the secretary of the Council shall inscribe them as *proxenoi* and benefactors of the Athenians'). Destroying the *stēlē* is conceptualised as destroying the proxeny and setting up a new *stēlē* as restoring it. In relation to inscribed treaties and other formal decrees relating to foreign relations this elision of inscription and substance of what was inscribed is very common. E.g. in the Prospectus of the Second Athenian League (*IG* II^2 43 = Rhodes and Osborne 2007, no. 22), '... for whichever of the cities making the alliance there happen to be unfavourable *stēlai in* Athens, the Council ... shall be empowered to destroy them ...'.

31 Lambert 2008, 2010b, 2012.

32 Veyne 1976, 264–71. See on this most recently Luraghi 2010 (with references to previous discussions of Veyne's theory).

there was genuine breadth of political participation. With such an 'elitist' ideology, the system would simply not have achieved the widespread popular support that was necessary to sustain it in a city which was not only democratic but in important ways collectivist in outlook. Moreover, as a matter of fact, a good proportion of the Athenian honorands on inscribed decrees under the classical democracy were ordinary Athenian officials, most of them appointed by lot and serving their turn in office in the democratic way; they were not, for the most part, men of high political distinction.[33]

I think there is more in the idea that honorific decrees were intended in part to express the power and prestige of Athens. The highest honour normally awarded a foreigner – deployed sparingly and usually for very prominent individuals – was the Athenian citizenship, membership of the body which granted the honour – and this fact no doubt boosted the Athenians' own self-importance at times when they were strong, and bolstered a flagging self-confidence as power ebbed away after 360.[34] If the larger Periclean monuments on the acropolis expressed Athens' imperial self-confidence, the honorific inscriptions erected alongside them and intended (if I am right) to complement them monumentally can be seen as also complementing them ideologically: look, they said, how influential we are; look at the vast network of cities and eminent individuals who are our friends. It does seem to me appropriate to interpret those most massive of epigraphical monuments on the acropolis, the Athenian Tribute Lists, as carrying a clear message of the power of Athens, and I think it enhances honour if the honorand is persuaded of the power of the city that grants the honour. I should hesitate, however, to push this line of interpretation very far. For an honorific act to be fully effective the prime focus normally has to be the qualities of the honorand and that arguably implies a certain reticence on the part of the body bestowing the honour; if the *point* of honouring someone were felt to be the assertion of the qualities of the bestower of the honour, that would obscure and detract from the attention paid to the qualities of the honorand. So I think this is a subtext, but I do not think it is the point of honorific decrees.

Polly Low has pointed to an apparent imbalance as regards the Athenian Empire of the fifth century: Athens honours its allies, but they do not seem to have reciprocated in kind; the reciprocal of the honours was perhaps rather the allies' tribute.[35] One might infer that the awarding of honour was, at least in these circumstances, an expression of the city's superior power over the

33 See Lambert 2004.

34 On Athenian decrees granting citizenship see Osborne 1981–83, Lambert 2006.

35 Low 2007, 242–8.

honorands. There may be something in this, though we should tread cautiously. As Low points out, the situation in the Second Athenian League was very different. An example of a reciprocated honorific relationship with another city at the later period is Athens' relationship with Elaious, consistently loyal member of the Second Athenian League (Dem. 23.158), which honoured Athens in 346/5 (*IG* II^2 1443, 93–5), and was itself honoured by Athens on several occasions.[36] Is one more or less liable to honour those who are more powerful than oneself? The logic seems to work in contradictory directions. On the one hand we might think that a certain minimum of sovereignty, or at least freedom of manoeuvre in foreign affairs, is necessary for the passing of such decrees to be meaningful or even possible. Apart from decrees honouring individual foreigners, Athens also passed decrees honouring whole cities (those relating to Elaious are examples), decrees which have as much in common with other decrees concerning interstate relations (such as treaties), as they do with decrees honouring individuals. It is noteworthy that Athens herself abruptly ceased inscribing decrees honouring other cities after the battle of Chaironeia.[37] On the other hand the much weaker Athens of that later epoch, transformed overnight from leader of the Second Athenian League to subordinate member of the alliance system led by the Macedonian king, did not hesitate to inscribe decrees currying favour with individual leading figures of the Macedonian regime.[38] Perhaps the phenomenon Low identifies for the fifth century can partly be explained on the basis not that the Athenians were quicker to *pass* decrees honouring allies, but more specifically quicker to *inscribe* them in significant numbers than the allies were their decrees honouring Athens – in other words it may in part be a feature of the precocious Athenian 'epigraphic habit' (and therefore, if I am right, of the architectural development of the acropolis in the Periclean period), rather than of the substance of honorific practice (i.e. the number of decrees actually passed).

In addition to asserting the power of Athens, I think inscribed honorific decrees can, or can sometimes, be interpreted as assertions of the power of the proposers of the decrees, in other words as instruments of competitive display by political leaders. This seems to work particularly well in the case of the two most prolific proposers of inscribed decrees in classical Athens, Lykourgos and

---

36 *Agora* XVI 53, of 357/6; probably *IG* II^2 219 = Lambert 2007a, no. 65 [*IG* II^3 1, 303], of 345/4; Rhodes and Osborne 2007, no. 71 = Lambert 2007a, no. 70 [= *IG* II^3 1, 309], of 341/0.

37 Lambert 2010b.

38 E.g. *IG* II^2 240 = Lambert 2006, no. 33 [= *IG* II^3 1, 322] (337/6) for a man who had looked after Athenians visiting Philip II, *IG* II^2 402 + *SEG* 42.91 = Lambert 2007a, no. 105 [= *IG* II^3 1, 484] (ca. 324–322/1) for friends of the (Macedonian) king and Antipater.

Demades. The number of extant inscribed decrees proposed by these two men exceeds by a wide margin the numbers proposed by anyone else before 321.[39] I doubt that it is coincidental that they were not only contemporaries, but rivals for influence, Demades vigorous and effective in promoting Athenian interests by pursuing positive relations with the Macedonians, Lykourgos implicitly, if not overtly, hostile to the Macedonians, but vigorous and effective in promoting domestic regeneration, and arguing (unsuccessfully) against awarding Demades a statue and other high honours (the so-called *megistai timai*).[40] They are the only leading politicians in classical Athens who are attested in the epigraphical record as having proposed inscribed decrees at the same meeting of the Assembly on multiple occasions;[41] and I do not think it coincidental that several of these decrees belong to a sphere of politics that had specifically to do with display, i.e. the theatre, and were proposed at the special meeting of the Assembly which took place in the theatre of Dionysos after the City Dionysia, a meeting which may have been attended by foreigners, an occasion when the city and its institutions was on display in a rather strong sense.[42] In this context inscribed decrees demonstrated the power and influence of their proposers with or on behalf of this or that prominent honorand or celebrity poet, actor or theatrical benefactor; and it is undoubtedly relevant here that it was precisely at this period that it became common practice to highlight the names of decree proposers, for example by inscribing them in a line by themselves, even though this breached the normal *stoichedon* arrangement of the letters.[43]

Written texts can look backwards in time and they can look forwards in time, and intentionally so. Herodotos wrote so that the deeds of men should not be forgotten with the passage of time (1.1); Thucydides intended what he wrote to be a possession for all time (1.22); and there is a passage of Demosthenes 20

39 Fifteen self-standing inscribed decrees proposed by Demades are conveniently listed by Brun 2000, 177–8 (to which add *IG* II^2 713 [*IG* II^3 1, 929], persuasively ascribed to the fourth-century Demades rather than a putative homonymous grandson by Byrne 2010, though inscribed in the third century). There are eight self-standing inscribed laws and decrees proposed by Lykourgos (Lambert 2007a, 120–1). No other Athenian politician proposed more than three or four extant inscribed decrees (cf. Hansen 1984).

40 Lyk. F9 *Against Kephisodotos Concerning the Honours for Demades*. The most recent substantial treatments of these politicians are Brun 2000 on Demades, Humphreys 2004, chapter 3, on Lykourgos. On the latter see now also Brun 2005, Rhodes 2010, Faraguna 2012, and on his family Blok and Lambert 2009. On the *megistai timai* see further below.

41 See Habicht 1989.

42 See Lambert 2008. *IG* II^2 713 [*IG* II^3 1, 929] (on which see above) also had a theatrical context.

43 See especially Henry 1977, 63–6; cf. (focusing on the period 307–302) Tracy 2000.

which indicates that one might, in inscribing honorific decrees, intentionally have a view to a more distant future:

> It is fitting, therefore, to permit these *stēlai* to be valid for all time, so that as long as any of these men [sc. honorands] are alive, they may suffer no wrong at your hands, and when they die, those inscriptions may be a memorial of the city's character, and may stand as evidence to all those who wish to do us good, of how many benefactors the city has benefited in return.
>
> DEMOSTHENES 20, *Against Leptines*, 64

However, there is no romantic sense here of perpetuating the honorand's memory for its own sake. Demosthenes is striving to emphasise the value of the 'honours system', and in particular of not rescinding honours once granted, and he does so in terms which emphasise their utility to both parties: during the honorand's lifetime the inscription functions as tangible guarantee of the city's good-will, and after his death it is the city that will benefit from the hortatory effect. There are suggestions here of the inscription's function as a memory aid in a world where, as Thucydides famously pointed out, citizens' knowledge of their own city's past could be rather weak (6.56–9). In this context Demosthenes is thinking of foreign honorands rather than Athenians, but the 'guarantee of the city's goodwill' he mentions would also be an attractive incentive to honour-seeking behaviour by Athenian officials, who, under the democracy, and especially if they were wealthy, were always at risk of malicious prosecution from the so-called 'sykophants'; and this may be a further factor in the emergence of the new genre of inscribed decree honouring Athenians a decade after this speech was made (cf. Aeschin. 3.10).

Alongside the routine inscriptions recording the fairly modest honours awarded to ordinary Athenian officials from the 340s onwards, there was a much more exclusive type which awarded the highest honours to political leaders – including a bronze statue and meals at public expense (*sitēsis*) in the prytaneion, the so-called *megistai timai*.[44] There is literary evidence for such awards in the classical period,[45] but the earliest surviving inscription of this type – the only one dating to the fourth century – is the decree of 307/6 proposed by the leading politician, Stratokles, posthumously honouring the orator

44 Cf. Gauthier 1985, 24–8 and 92–103; Rhodes and Osborne 2007, notes to no. 8 and no. 22; Lambert 2004, Luraghi 2010.

45 E.g. Demosthenes 20.69 quotes from 'the *stēlē*' honouring Konon. On the decree honouring Demades see above.

Lykourgos and, typically of this genre, it gives an extensive eulogistic account of the politician's career and achievements (*IG* II² 457+513 and [Plut.] *X Orat. Vit.* 852a–e [see now this volume chapter 11]). Nino Luraghi has recently pointed out that this tendency to include more wordy accounts of an honorand's achievements is observable in a period when collections of inscriptions were being published,[46] and biographies of statesmen were being written,[47] and has suggested that there may have been a deliberate intention for the narrative, usually 'spun' in a particular direction,[48] to impact not only on the contemporary political environment, but also on the honorand's reputation in the written historical record.[49]

In the fourth century one Athenian reaction to decline, beginning in the earlier part of the century, but intensifying in the period after the defeat at Chaironeia in 338, was to improve the present by looking to the past for lessons and inspiration. This played an important role in the development of a documentary approach to history, because to learn from the past you have to know about it, and there were fifth-century documents, not least inscriptions, which were relevant. So intense was this focus on inscriptions as sources of past *exempla* that a culture developed of re-inscribing, elaborating and indeed inventing old inscriptions and deploying them for instructional purposes.[50] Part of the point of some genuine honorific decrees of this period was also to articulate this aspiration to connect with and learn from the past, especially the fifth-century glory days. The clearest example is an inscribed decree of, probably, the post-Chaironeia period, honouring the craftsman who had raised and restored a statue of Athena Nike which had been dedicated originally from spoils of successful campaigns of the Archidamian War, specified in detail on the inscription and verifiable from Thucydides (*IG* II² 403 + Lambert 2005, no. 3 [*IG* II³ 1, 444]. Cf. Thuc. 3.85, 106–12, 114; 4.2–3, 46, 49). The intention was

46 E.g. *FGrH* 342 Krateros and, apparently, *FGrH* 328 Philochoros (see Jacoby *ad* Philochoros, p. 375) both produced collections of Athenian inscriptions.

47 E.g. there was a biography of Lykourgos by his contemporary, Philiskos (Olympiodoros ad Plato, *Gorgias* 515c, sect. 10).

48 There is a good deal of 'spin' in the account Stratokles gives of Lykourgos' career, e.g. making him out to be more overtly hostile to Alexander than was actually the case, cf. Brun 2005, Rhodes 2010, Faraguna 2012.

49 Luraghi 2010. See also Rosen 1987.

50 An example is Rhodes and Osborne 2007, no. 88, an inscription from the deme Acharnai dating from around the third quarter of the fourth century and purporting to record the 'ancestral oath of the ephebes' and the oath which the Athenians swore before the battle of Plataia. On this phenomenon see Habicht 1961 and especially Davies 1996.

to express, at a time of defeat, an aspiration to Victory, an aspiration to emulate those glory days of the earlier phase of the Peloponnesian War.

Another example is a decree honouring the Akarnanians, Phormio and Karphinas, who had supported the Athenians at Chaironeia and were now, in 337, in exile at Athens. Proposed by the fiercely patriotic anti-Macedonian politician Hegesippos of Sounion, nicknamed 'Topknot' (*Krobylos*) for his 'past-connective' habit of wearing his hair long and in a bun, this decree, with its deliberate references to the honorands' grandfather Phormio, named, it seems clear, after the famous Athenian general of the Archidamian War, and himself made an Athenian citizen at the end of the fifth century, was also undoubtedly intended to project a political message about how the past could be used to inform present aspirations (Rhodes and Osborne 2007, no. 77 [*IG* II^3 1, 316]).[51] I explore these cases, and other aspects of the deployment of the past in fourth-century inscribed laws and decrees, more fully elsewhere.[52]

Acknowledgements

A version of this paper was delivered at the Classical Association annual meeting in Glasgow, 5 April 2009, in a panel on 'Discourses of Honour in Fourth-Century Athens'. I am grateful to the panel organiser, Benjamin Keim, for inviting me to participate, to those who contributed to the discussion on that day, and to Robin Osborne, Anton Powell and James Whitley for very helpful comments on a written draft.

Bibliography

Azoulay, V., Ismard, P. eds. 2012: *Clisthène et Lycurgue d'Athènes. Autour du politique dans la cité classique*, Paris.

Blanshard, A. J. L. 2004: "Depicting democracy. An exploration of art and text in the law of Eukrates", *JHS* 124, 1–15.

Blanshard, A. J. L. 2007: "The problems with honouring Samos: An Athenian document relief and its interpretation", in Z. Newby and R. Leader-Newby eds., *Art and inscriptions in the ancient world*, Cambridge, 19–37.

Blok, J. H., Lambert, S. D. 2009: "The appointment of priests in Attic *gene*", *ZPE* 169, 95–121.

51 On Hegesippos see John Davies' paper in this volume.

52 Lambert 2010a, 2012.

Brun, P. 2000: *L'orateur Démade*, Bordeaux.
Brun, P. 2005: "Lycurgue d'Athènes: un législateur?", in P. Sineux ed., *Le législateur et la loi dans l'antiquité: hommage à F. Ruzé*, Caen, 187–200.
Byrne, S. G. 2010: "Some people in third-century Athenian decrees", in R. Catling and F. Marchand eds., *Onomatologos. Studies in greek onomastics and prosopography presented to Elaine Matthews*, Oxford, 122–31.
Davies, J. K. 1996: "Documents and 'documents' in fourth-century historiography", in P. Carlier ed., *Le IVe siècle av. J.-C. Approches historiographiques*, Nancy, 29–39.
Davies, J. K. 2005: "The origins of the inscribed Greek stela", in P. Bienkowski, C. Mee and E. Slater eds., *Writing and ancient Near Eastern society: Papers in honour of Alan R. Millard*, New York, 283–300.
Faraguna, M. 2012: "Lykourgan Athens?", in V. Azoulay and P. Ismard eds., *Clisthène et Lycurgue d'Athènes. Autour du politique dans la cité classique*, Paris, 67–88.
Fisher, N. R. E. 2001: *Aeschines. Against Timarchos*, Oxford.
Gauthier, P. 1985: *Les cités grecques et leurs bienfaiteurs*, Paris.
Gehrke, H.-J., Luraghi, N., Foxhall, L. eds. 2010: *Intentional history. Spinning time in ancient Greece*, Stuttgart.
Gell, A. 1998: *Art and agency: An anthropological theory*, Oxford.
Goldhill, S., Osborne, R. eds. 1999: *Performance culture and Athenian democracy*, Cambridge.
Greco, E., Lombardo, M. eds. 2006: *La grande iscrizione di Gortyna: centoventi anni dopo la scoperta*, Athens.
Habicht, C. 1961: "Falsche Urkunden zur Geschichte Athens im Zeitalter der Perserkriege", *Hermes* 89, 1–35.
Habicht, C. 1989: "Zwei Athenische Volksbeschlüsse", *Chiron* 19, 1–5.
Hansen, M. H. 1980: "Seven Hundred *archai* in Classical Athens", *GRBS* 21, 151–73.
Hansen, M. H. 1984: "The Number of *rhetores* in the Athenian *Ecclesia*, 355–322 BC", *GRBS* 25, 123–55, reprinted with addenda in Hansen 1989, 93–127.
Hansen, M. H. 1989: *The Athenian Ecclesia II. A collection of articles 1983–89*, Copenhagen.
Hedrick, C. W. 1999: "Democracy and the Athenian epigraphical habit", *Hesperia* 68, 387–439.
Henry, A. S. 1977: *The Prescripts of Athenian decrees*, *Mnemosyne* Suppl. 49, Leiden.
Henry, A. S. 1983: *Honours and privileges in Athenian decrees*, Hildesheim.
Henry, A. S. 1996: "The hortatory intention in Athenian state decrees", *ZPE* 112, 105–17.
Humphreys, S. C. 2004: *The strangeness of gods*, Oxford.
IALD: S. D. Lambert, *Inscribed Athenian laws and decrees, 352/1–322/1 BC. Epigraphical essays*, Leiden, 2012.
Keesling, C. 2003: *The votive statues of the Athenian acropolis*, Cambridge.
Lambert, S. D. 2004: "Athenian state laws and decrees, 352/1–322/1: I Decrees honouring Athenians", *ZPE* 150, 85–120 [= *IALD*, 3–47].

Lambert, S. D. 2005: "Athenian state laws and decrees, 352/1–322/1: II Religious regulations", ZPE 154, 125–59 [= IALD, 48–92].

Lambert, S. D. 2006: "Athenian state laws and decrees, 352/1–322/1: III Decrees honouring foreigners. A. Citizenship, proxeny and euergesy", ZPE 158, 115–58 [= IALD, 93–137].

Lambert, S. D. 2007a: "Athenian state laws and decrees, 352/1–322/1: III Decrees honouring foreigners. B. Other awards", ZPE 159, 101–54 [= IALD, 138–83].

Lambert, S. D. 2007b: "Athenian state laws and decrees, 352/1–322/1: IV Treaties and other texts", ZPE 161, 67–100 [= IALD, 184–218].

Lambert, S. D. 2008: "Polis and theatre in Lykourgan Athens: the honorific decrees", in A. P. Matthaiou and I. Polinskaya eds., *Mikros hieromnemon. Meletes eis mnemen Michael H. Jameson*, Athens, 53–85 [= IALD, 337–62].

Lambert, S. D. 2010a: "Connecting with the past in Lykourgan Athens: an epigraphical perspective", in H.-J. Gehrke, N. Luraghi and L. Foxhall eds., *Intentionale Geschichte. Spinning time in ancient Greece*, Stuttgart, 225–38 [= this volume, chapter 5].

Lambert, S. D. 2010b: "Inscribed treaties ca. 350–321 BC: an epigraphical perspective on Athenian foreign policy", in G. Reger, F. X. Ryan and T. F. Winters eds., *Studies in Greek epigraphy and history in honor of Stephen V. Tracy*, Bordeaux, 153–60 [= IALD, 377–86].

Lambert, S. D. 2012: "Some political shifts in Lykourgan Athens", in V. Azoulay and P. Ismard eds., *Clisthène et Lycurgue d'Athènes. Autour du politique dans la cité classique*, Paris, 175–90 [= this volume, chapter 4].

Lawton, C. L. 1995: *Attic document reliefs*, Oxford.

Liddel, P. 2003: "The places of publication of Athenian state decrees from the fifth century BC to the third century AD", ZPE 143, 79–93.

Loomis, W. T. 1998: *Wages, welfare costs and inflation in classical Athens*, Ann Arbor.

Low, P. 2007: *Interstate relations in classical Greece. Morality and power*, Cambridge.

Luraghi, N. 2010: "The Demos as narrator: public honours and the construction of future and past", in H.-J. Gehrke, N. Luraghi and L. Foxhall eds., *Intentionale Geschichte. Spinning time in ancient Greece*, Stuttgart, 247–64.

Meritt, B. D. 1940: *Epigraphica Attica* (*Martin classical lectures* 9), Cambridge, Mass.

Mitchell, L., Rubinstein, L. eds. 2009: *Greek history and epigraphy. Essays in honour of P. J. Rhodes*, Swansea.

Moreno, A. 2007: *Feeding the democracy. The Athenian grain supply in the fifth and fourth centuries BC*, Oxford.

Osborne, M. J. 1981–1983: *Naturalization in Athens*, Brussels.

Osborne, R. 1999: "Inscribing performance", in S. Goldhill and R. Osborne eds., *Performance culture and Athenian democracy*, Cambridge, 341–58.

Osborne, R. 2009: "The politics of an epigraphic habit: the case of Thasos", in L. Mitchell and L. Rubinstein eds., *Greek history and epigraphy. Essays in honour of P. J. Rhodes*, Swansea, 103–14.

Osborne, R. forthcoming: "Euergetism and the public economy of classical Athens", in G. J. Oliver and Z. Archibald eds., *The power of the individual in ancient Greece. Essays in honour of J. K. Davies.*
Rhodes, P. J. 2010: "'Lycurgan' Athens", in A. Tamis, C. J. Mackie and S. Byrne eds., *Philathenaios. Studies in honour of Michael J. Osborne*, Athens, 81–90.
Rhodes, P. J., Osborne, R. 2007: *Greek Historical Inscriptions 404–323 BC*, Oxford [1st ed. 2003].
Rosen, K. 1987: "Ehrendekrete, Biographie und Geschichtsschreibung. Zum Wandel der griechischen Polis im frühen Hellenismus", *Chiron* 17, 277–92.
Scafuro, A. C. 2009: "The crowning of Amphiaraos", in L. Mitchell and L. Rubinstein eds., *Greek history and epigraphy. Essays in honour of P. J. Rhodes*, Swansea, 59–86.
Shear, J. 2007: "Cultural change, space and the politics of commemoration", in R. Osborne ed., *Debating the Athenian cultural revolution,* Cambridge, 91–115.
Sickinger, J. P. 2009: "Nothing to do with democracy: 'Formulae of disclosure' and the Athenian epigraphical habit", in L. Mitchell and L. Rubinstein eds., *Greek history and epigraphy. Essays in honour of P. J. Rhodes*, Swansea, 87–102.
Stoddart, S., Whitley, J. 1988: "The social context of literacy in archaic Greece and Etruria", *Antiquity* 62, 761–72.
Tracy, S. V. 2000: "Athenian politicians and inscriptions of the years 307 to 302", *Hesperia* 69, 227–33.
Veyne, P. 1976: *Le pain et le cirque*, Paris.
Whitehead, D. 1983: "Competitive outlay and community profit: *Philotimia* in democratic Athens", *Classica et Mediaevalia* 34, 55–74.
Whitehead, D. 1993: "Cardinal virtues: the language of public approbation in democratic Athens", *Classica et Mediaevalia* 44, 37–75.
Whitehead, D. 2009: "*Andragathia* and *arete*", in L. Mitchell and L. Rubinstein eds., *Greek history and epigraphy. Essays in honour of P. J. Rhodes*, Swansea, 47–58.
Whitley, J. 1997: "Cretan Laws and Cretan Literacy", *AJA* 101, 635–61.
Whitley, J. 2006: "Before the Great Code: public inscriptions and material practice in archaic Crete", in E. Greco and M. Lombardo eds., *La grande iscrizione di Gortyna: centoventi anni dopo la scoperta*, Athens, 41–56.
Whitley, J. 2007: "Letting the stones in on the act: statues as social agents in archaic and classical Greece", *Kodai: Journal of Ancient History 13/14. Proceedings of the international symposium on the ancient Mediterranean world*, 185–98.

CHAPTER 4

Some Political Shifts in Lykourgan Athens[1]

Since 2000 I have been working on a volume in the series *Inscriptiones Graecae*, which will include all the inscribed state laws and decrees of Lykourgan Athens. Drafts of the *lemmata* are complete and revisions are in progress. In the meantime I have published a series of *prolegomena*. Their purpose is primarily epigraphical, but not exclusively so, and they may be helpful to historians seeking to orientate themselves in this material.[2] I mention this because in part it explains why inscriptions will figure rather prominently in this paper. I also think, however, that there are good methodological reasons for a focus on the inscribed laws and decrees of the *polis* when one is seeking to address questions about developments in "the political" in Lykourgan Athens. For the laws passed by Athenian citizens sitting as *nomothetai* and the decrees passed by Athenian citizens sitting as the Assembly, or – in committee as it were – as the Council, supply an insight of unique quality into the preoccupations and priorities of the city at this period. The record is of course selective: not all laws and decrees were inscribed; those which were inscribed were those to which the majority of Athenians present and voting for the measure in question on the day decided to give special significance by transforming them into enduring monumental form, in most cases by erecting them in the central, sacred space of the city, the acropolis – those which carried meanings and messages that the citizens especially wished to convey to and about themselves, to

1 [This paper was first published in V. Azoulay, P. Ismard, eds. *Clisthène et Lycurgue d'Athènes. Autour du politique dans la cité classique.* (Paris, 2011), 175–190. See also the Introduction to this volume, pp. 7–8.] I am grateful to the organisers of this colloquium for inviting me to participate, and to them and the other participants, from whose papers and comments on the day I learnt much. The bibliography on Lykourgan Athens is immense and I shall not attempt in this paper to refer systematically even to the most important work. Noteworthy among the many excellent previous contributions of fellow participants is Faraguna 1992.

2 The main series of *prolegomena*, through which others can be traced, is an annotated catalogue: Lambert 2004, 2005, 2006, 2007a and b. This covers all the self-standing laws and decrees and also notes the few that are incorporated in other types of inscription (*e.g.* Rhodes & Osborne 2007, n° 100 [*IG* II^3 1 370], the decree for a colony in the Adriatic incorporated in the naval lists, and discussed in this volume by Ober [2011], is Lambert 2004, n° 29; 2007b, p. 74). This paper is one of a second connected series in which I seek to explore the historical implications of this material. Others in this series include Lambert 2008, 2010a, 2010c and forthcoming b [= 2010d].

© KONINKLIJKE BRILL NV, LEIDEN, 2018 | DOI 10.1163/9789004352490_006

and about non-citizens and outsiders and to and about the gods. Not all survive, but the number that do – about 270 from the period 352–322 – is a large enough and probably a random enough sample to be treated for our purposes as representative.

The question, therefore, that I propose to address in this paper is: what changes are observable in Lykourgan Athens in the political priorities and preoccupations of the Athenians as reflected in the laws and decrees which they inscribed at this period? And I shall address the question at a reasonably high level of generality, not looking so much at the specific provisions and circumstances of individual decrees, which inevitably show great variability from case to case, but at the shape of the overall picture: at changes in the types of messages the Athenians were seeking to project, changes which give an insight into developments in the city's political priorities and identity. I shall argue that a key factor running through several of these developments is a strengthening of the emphasis given to the city's dialogue with its own past: an increasing sense of decline in comparison to that past and a concomitant desire to connect with and learn from it.

Honorific Decrees

The large majority of inscribed decrees at this and all periods were honorific, and such decrees had a rather specific purpose, which is revealed to us by the so-called hortatory intention clauses that begin to appear in them in the 340s. The precise wording varies, but in essence these are clauses which state that the purpose of passing the decree – sometimes explicitly the purpose of inscribing the decree – is, by honouring those who have displayed *philotimia* towards the city, to encourage the future display of *philotimia* towards the city by the honorand and/or others in the expectation that they will receive similar honours.[3] In other words the decrees not only recognise past services to the city, they are an attempt to manipulate future behaviour and to embrace as

3 On these clauses, see Henry 1996. Hortatory clauses are usually attached to the granting of the honours as a whole, but are occasionally connected specifically to the inscribing of the decree, *e.g.* *IG* II^2 220 [*IG* II^3 1 304], of 344/3, the sole provision of which is that a decree passed the previous year honouring the city of Pellana in the Peloponnese, but not inscribed at the time, should now be inscribed on the acropolis "so that the city of the Pellanians shall continue always to be friendly and well-disposed towards the Athenian People, as in previous times". See my discussion in Lambert 2006, p. 116; and in general now also Sickinger 2009.

many as possible in the web of beneficent reciprocal exchange binding Athens to individuals and communities throughout the Greek world.

Until the 340s inscribed decrees of this type nearly always honoured foreigners; it was only in the 340s that the Athenians began regularly to inscribe decrees honouring their own fellow-citizens, not, for the most part, prominent generals and leading politicians, but ordinary Athenian officials: state secretaries, priests, superintendents of the water supply, members of the Council, that sort of thing.[4] This development is, I think, best understood in conjunction with the emergence of the hortatory intention clauses at precisely the same time: essentially these inscriptions are levers designed to make ordinary Athenian officials behave well; and why is there a perceived need for this specifically in the 340s? Because, I suggest, it is in the 340s that the Athenians are gripped by an intensified sense of the decline of their *polis*, decline in comparison with the glory days of the fifth century, decline in the face of the rise of Macedon, and by an acute sense that the performance of the *polis* is crucially dependent on the performance of its officials. It is part of the same urgent sense of the need to encourage and maintain standards in public life which is also detectable, for example, in the success of Aeschines' case against Timarchos in 346, and which, after Chaironeia, produced the frenetic reforming zeal of Lykourgos and his like-minded colleagues across the range of "the political", from finance to religion to military education, a movement in which the recognition and award of outstanding contributions to the well-being of the *polis* by individuals was a key weapon in the reformer's armoury, a "carrot" to complement the "sticks" wielded against those who failed to make the grade, by Aeschines in the *Timarchos* case, and later most famously in several cases prosecuted by Lykourgos.[5] *Philotimia* was a problematic (aristocratic/elitist/contention-encouraging) virtue which the city was notably reluctant to

---

4 See Lambert 2004. The award was typically of a crown of gold or foliage, sometimes with money for a sacrifice and dedication. Decrees were also passed awarding much higher honours (*e.g.* bronze statue and *sitesis* in the prytaneion) to major political figures (*e.g.* Demades, Brun 2000, p. 78–83), but they were either not inscribed or they have not survived. The earliest extant inscribed decree of this type is that awarding posthumous honours to Lykourgos, in 307/6, *IG* II^2 457 = [Plut.], *Mor.* 851F–852E.

5 I agree here with Fisher's analysis of the reason for Aeschines' victory, Fisher 2001. 346, the year of the Peace of Philokrates, was later perceived as a critical point in Athens' downward trajectory; it was also the year of the Timarchos case and of the earliest dated surviving inscribed decree honouring an Athenian official, *IG* II^2 215 = Lambert 2004, n° 18 with n. 3 [= *IG* II^3 1 301]. Lykourgos 1, *Against Leokrates*, directed against a man who had fled Attica in the aftermath of Chaironeia, is the *locus classicus* of Lykourgan stick-wielding. Note also Lykourgos' extension of the use of treason trials (*eisangelia*) and his prosecution of the case

recognise formally in the language and practice of its decrees before the 340s,[6] and in the longer perspective the introduction of inscribed decrees honouring Athenian citizens marks a significant staging post on the road from the democratic collectivism of the high classical *polis* to the emphasis and reliance on individual euergetism which is such a marked feature of hellenistic political culture.[7] At first the decrees are a little reticent about the detail of the financial contributions made by citizen honorands, though such contributions are often implied;[8] later hellenistic decrees tend to be more explicit.[9]

Foreign Relations

Chaironeia marked a watershed in Athenian external relations, as the city was transformed from proud leader of the Second Athenian League to subordinate member of the panhellenic alliance led by Philip of Macedon. This too occasioned a profound political shift which is observable in the epigraphic record. Treaties are one of the major categories of inscribed Athenian decree. There

in which Dem. 25 *Against Aristogeiton* is a supporting speech, discussed in this volume by Faraguna [2011] and Azoulay [2011].

6 Cf. Whitehead 1983 and 1993; Rhodes & Osborne 2007, n° 46, with commentary.

7 On this topic see also Faraguna's paper in this volume, and Azoulay's analysis of ways that some at least, Lykourgos among them, sought to propagate at this time a stronger idea of the collective of the *polis*. This development can perhaps be interpreted as in tension with, and to an extent intended to control, the increasing *de facto* dependency of the city on voluntary euergetism. Also relevant here is the major programme, perhaps starting in the late-40s (though the date is uncertain), under which extensive tracts of public land were sold off to (most wealthy) private individuals (Lambert 1997).

8 As, for example, when Pytheas of Alopeke, superintendent of the water-supply, is praised for "constructing a new fountain by the sanctuary of Ammon and repairing the fountain in the Amphiaraion", IG II^2 338 = Lambert 2004, n° 15 [= IG II^3 1 338], of 333/2; or when Phanodemos of Thymaitadai "has legislated well and in an honour-loving way about the sanctuary of Amphiaraos, so that the quadrennial festival and the other sacrifices to the gods in the sanctuary of Amphiaraos may be as fine as possible, *and he has supplied the means for these things (porous peporiken) and for the repair of the sanctuary*", IG VII 4253 = Lambert 2004, n° 16 [= IG II^3 1 348], of 332/1.

9 *E.g.* IG II^2 776 [= IG II^3 1 1026], of 237/6?, where the priestess of Athena Polias is praised *inter alia* because "she contributed a hundred drachmas from her own resources to the Praxiergidai for their ancestral sacrifice" (l. 18–20). The key turning point in this public-to-private shift was the abolition of the liturgy system by Demetrios of Phaleron after 317; but this was the culmination of a trend of development which can be traced to the 340s. Cf. my remarks, Lambert 1997, chapter 8.

are eight treaties (or similar) in the Athenian epigraphical record of the decade and a half before Chaironeia, most of them bilateral. In the equivalent post-Chaironeia period, the years between Chaironeia and the death of Alexander, there are no bilateral treaties involving Athens and another city. Only two inscribed treaties from this period of Athenian history are extant: the fragments of the Peace of Corinth itself[10] and a very fragmentary treaty with Alexander about the supply of troops on campaign:[11] both are Athenian copies of multilateral agreements of the Hellenic League under Macedonian leadership. This epigraphical silence speaks eloquently of the extent to which Athens' international freedom of manoeuvre was constrained in the years after Chaironeia. Here we have a whole sphere of "the political" – a central feature of the "freedom and autonomy" to which, to use the contemporary diplomatic language, every Greek *polis* aspired, namely the power to make and break treaties, from which Athens seems now to have been excluded.[12]

A comparable shift is detectable in the inscribed decrees honouring foreigners. There was less of a problem with the "political correctness" of encouraging *philotimia* when it came to these decrees: foreigners were outsiders to the Athenian polity; inscribing decrees for them was not relevant to issues of how citizens should treat each other, and they had always been the most common type of inscribed decree. These decrees too, however, witness the introduction of explicit references to *philotimia* and of hortatory intention clauses in the 340s, and this makes them more transparently instruments of foreign policy, levers which could be pulled to encourage outsiders to serve Athenian interests, a form of monumentalised diplomacy.

In addition to decrees honouring individual foreigners, in the fourth century before Chaironeia Athens also passed decrees honouring whole cities – usually but not always members of the Second Athenian League. Directed at states rather than individuals, such decrees can be seen as instruments of inter-state diplomacy, more comparable in this sense to treaties than to decrees honouring individuals; and a corollary of Athens' withdrawal from bilateral treaty-making after Chaironeia was that she also withdrew from inscribing decrees honouring whole cities: no such decree is datable to the period between Chaironeia and the Lamian War.[13]

10 *IG* II^2 236 = Rhodes & Osborne 2007, n° 76 = Lambert 2007b, n° 9 [= *IG* II^3 1 318].

11 *IG* II^2 329 = Lambert 2007b, n° 10 [= *IG* II^3 1 443].

12 For a catalogue of inscribed treaties of this period see Lambert 2007b; for discussion, Lambert 2010a.

13 On decrees honouring whole cities, see Lambert 2010a.

This withdrawal from formal interstate diplomacy did not, of course, mean a complete withdrawal from active participation in foreign relations. The city continued busy and active in pursuing her interests on the international scene. The standard narrative account of Athenian history at this period, based primarily on literary sources (Diodoros, Plutarch, the orators) in which the exploits of Philip and Alexander take centre stage after 338, shows this clearly enough, though the general impression those sources convey is more of a re-active policy, whether to Philip and Alexander themselves or to the anti-Macedonian initiatives of Thebes, of an Agis or a Harpalos, or to the threat to the cleruchy on Samos posed by Alexander's exiles decree, than a pro-active one.[14] A striking example of an independent initiative documented in the epigraphical record is the colony which Athens sent to the Adriatic in 325/4, an initiative for which our sole evidence is the decree preserved in the naval lists, Rhodes & Osborne 2007, n° 100 [*IG* II^{3} 1 370], discussed in this volume by Ober. Our most abundant epigraphical evidence for the development of Athenian foreign relations at this period, however, is the large corpus of inscribed, self-standing, Athenian decrees honouring individual foreigners. The statistics are not very firm or decisive, but the number of such decrees certainly shows no decline after Chaironeia and may show a slight increase over the preceding period.[15] In the absence of bilateral interstate relations, it was these decrees that now carried the thrust and burden of the formal side of Athens' foreign relations. What do they tell us about the spheres of foreign policy to which Athens was giving priority between Chaironeia and the Lamian War and how did these differ from what went before? What policy levers was she trying to pull? To what ends was she seeking to direct her influence? The large majority of decrees honouring foreigners at this period fall into three broad categories: unsurprisingly perhaps, easily the most numerous are decrees which, directly or indirectly, concern relations with Macedon. Unsurprisingly

14 For a recent political narrative of the period from an Athenian point of view, see Habicht 1997, chapter 1.

15 See the catalogue of 162 inscribed decrees honouring foreigners dating to 352/1–322/1, Lambert 2006, 2007a. A complex range of awards were made, ranging from the highest honour normally awarded foreigners at this period, the Athenian citizenship, through the common award of proxeny (notionally placing an obligation on the honorand to protect Athenian interests in his home city), to substantive privileges, major (*e.g.* the right to own land and property in Attica, *enktesis*) and minor (*e.g.* right of preferential access to the Council or Assembly, hospitality at the *prytaneion* on the day after the decree was passed, tickets for a performance in the theatre), and more symbolic ones (e.g. the ubiquitous crowns and the title "*euergetēs*"). A full historical analysis of Athenian honorific decrees is a scholarly desideratum (Henry 1983 is linguistic in focus). See Lambert 2006, p. 115–119.

too they display a shift of direction after Chaironeia: before it such decrees are aimed at encouraging and supporting enemies of Philip,[16] while those aimed at maintaining good relations with the Macedonian regime and its friends put in an appearance only in the years after the battle.[17] Interestingly, however, Athens does not hesitate to inscribe decrees after Chaironeia which show her giving a warm welcome to enemies of Philip who had supported Athens but were now in exile from their home cities.[18] The importance of sending to the world (and to itself, no doubt) the message that Athens was loyal to friends in adversity could override, it seems, the danger that the news of such loyalty might not be welcome to the new Hegemon of Greece; and later in the 30s and early 20s there are other decrees which arguably express muted or suppressed resistance,[19] or an aspiration to resist.[20]

The other two main categories of decree honouring foreigners are in a sense more interesting when it comes to thinking about significant shifts in Athens' political priorities, for both are new after Chaironeia and, in their preoccupations and implications, they both show the way forward: they are characteristically hellenistic.

16 *E.g.* IG II^2 226 = Rhodes & Osborne 2007, n° 70 = Lambert 2006, n° 4 [= IG II^3 1 411], providing refuge at Athens to Arybbas, former king of Molossia, who had been expelled from his kingdom by Philip, probably in 342. Cf. Lambert 2010a, n. 17 and 18.

17 *E.g.* IG II^2 240 = Lambert 2006, n° 33 [= IG II^3 1 322], of 337/6, proposed by Demades, for a man (son of Andromenes) who "takes care now of Athenians visiting Philip, doing all the good he can with Philip for the Athenians". Cf. Lambert 2010a, n. 19.

18 *E.g.* IG II^2 237 = Rhodes & Osborne 2007, n° 77 = Lambert 2006, n° 5 [= IG II^3 1 316], proposed by the vigorous anti-Macedonian politician Hegesippos of Sounion, for Akarnanians who had supported the Athenians at Chaironeia. Cf. Lambert 2010a, n. 18.

19 *E.g.* IG II^2 351 = Rhodes & Osborne 2007, n° 94 = Lambert 2006, n° 42 = Lambert 2008, n° 5 [= IG II^3 1 352], of 330/29, proposed by Lykourgos and honouring Eudemos of Plataia, who, among other things, had promised to donate 4,000 drachmas "for the war" (= the rebellion of Agis in 331/0?), had it been needed.

20 *E.g.* this is implicit in the attention paid to the cult of Athena Nike at this time, which can be seen essentially as a transmutation into religious terms of a deeply felt desire which could not otherwise be openly expressed. See IG II^2 403 = Lambert 2005, n° 3 [= IG II^3 1 444] (decree about repair of a statue of Athena Nike); [Plut.], *Mor.* 852B, cf. Paus. 1.29, 16 (Lykourgos' replacement of the golden Nikai on the acropolis, melted down for coin in the later stages of the Peloponnesian War); IG II^2 334 = Lambert 2005, n° 7 = Rhodes & Osborne 2007, n° 81 [= IG II^3 1 447], l.20–22 (sacrifice to Athena Nike in the new provisions for sacrifices at the Little Panathenaia); Lambert 2007a, p. 130 (honorific decree for priestess of Athena Nike).

Grain Supply

The first of these is decrees honouring grain traders. A preoccupation with grain supply was, of course, nothing new for Athens: it was natural in a populous city which was not endowed with the qualities of land and climate necessary to produce significant quantities of bread-wheat; it can be traced as a major preoccupation throughout the classical period and it was a fixed item on the agenda of the Assembly. Nor is the topic new to Athenian inscriptions after Chaironeia. In the fourth century one of Athens' most important diplomatic relations was with the rulers of the kingdom of the Bosporos, from which, so Demosthenes claims in *Against Leptines*, Athens imported more grain than from all other sources combined;[21] and there was a series of inscribed decrees honouring these rulers before 338, including a much anthologised decree for the sons of Leukon, shortly after they had succeeded their father in 347/6.[22] We now also have the striking grain tax law of 374/3, which casts a bright ray of light on the importance for Athens of the supply of grain from her Aegean island possessions, Lemnos, Imbros and Skyros.[23] What is new, however, after Chaironeia, is that Athens begins systematically and quite frequently to inscribe decrees honouring individual foreign grain traders, men who were actually involved in shipping grain around the Mediterranean.[24] What are we to make of this shift? As the hortatory intention clauses again make clear, the main object of the exercise was to encourage traders to ship their grain to Athens rather than somewhere else. To an extent this is a product of circumstances specific to the grain supply in the 30s and 20s: there is good evidence for shortages in Greece as a whole at this period, whether caused by crop failures or disruption and diversion of supply to meet Macedonian priorities;[25] but the underlying anxieties are also very clearly a response to political decline. For Athens one of the

21 Dem. 20.31–32.

22 *IG* II^2 212 = Rhodes & Osborne 2007, n° 64 [= *IG* II^3 1 298].

23 *SEG* 47.96 = Rhodes & Osborne 2007, n° 26.

24 The relevant decrees can be found in Lambert 2006 and 2007a, items marked [G], with Lambert 2007b, p. 81–84.

25 See, for example, the inscription of ca. 330–326 from Cyrene listing contributions made by that city "during the grain shortage in Greece", Rhodes & Osborne 2007, n° 96, and the decrees for Herakleides of Salamis of 330/29–328/7 and 325/4, *IG* II^2 360 = Lambert 2006, n° 43 = Rhodes & Osborne 2007, n° 95 [= *IG* II^3 1 367], with the commentaries of Rhodes & Osborne. Athens tops the list of contributions from Cyrene with 100,000 medimnoi. The Adriatic colony founded in 325/4 was, among other things, "in order that the People may control their own trade and transport in grain" (Rhodes & Osborne 2007, n° 100, [*IG* II^3 1 370] 217–220).

advantages of Empire, in the fourth century as in the fifth, had been the control it gave her over trade routes and sources of supply of economic commodities. In the fourth century, in addition to the grain tax law, we have, most strikingly, the inscription dating to the period of the Second Athenian League (*ca.* 350?), Rhodes & Osborne 2007, n° 40, which shows the cities of Keos being required by Athens to ship their entire production of red dye – *miltos* – to Athens and nowhere else, and only on ships specified by Athens. (Keos produced the best *miltos* in Greece according to Theophrastos, *On Stones* 8.51–54, and it was used amongst other things for staining pottery). In the immediate aftermath of the defeat at Chaironeia Athenian anxieties ran immediately to the security of the grain supply;[26] and it is not, I think, coincidental, that it is precisely at the point that Athens loses control of the Second Athenian League that she begins systematically to honour grain traders, for a consequence of the loss of Empire was a radical reduction in Athens' power to manipulate the supply and traffic of grain in and through the Eastern Mediterranean. She could no longer rely on the exercise of imperial persuasion to secure supplies;[27] nor, it seems, were there options open to her at the level of interstate diplomacy.[28] It was on individual grain traders that she was obliged to focus her diplomatic attention and effort. This new genre of decree set a pattern: the decrees of the Lykourgan period honouring grain traders stand at the head of a series which continued through later decades; and the grain supply was to continue to be of high long

---

26 In 330, at a time of shortage, Demosthenes reminded the Athenians that he had been appointed commissioner for grain purchase in the aftermath of Chaironeia and travelled overseas to secure supplies (Dem. 18.171, 248), and Lykourgos alleged against Leokrates that he went to Rhodes after the battle and spread rumours of Athens' defeat, with the consequence that grain traders who had intended to ship cargoes to Athens unloaded them in Rhodes, depriving Athens of crucial supplies (Lyk. 1.18, 42).

27 Cf. the point well made by Mossé 1973, p. 92, in relation to the accusations against Lampis in Dem. 34.36 (327/6) and Parmeniskos in [Dem.] 56.10 (*ca.* 322), that, although they had started from Athens and should therefore, according to Athenian law (see Dem. 34.37, 35.51, Lyk. 1.27), have transported the grain they collected in Egypt and the Bosporan kingdom to Athens, they had been induced to offload it in other places (Akanthos and Rhodes): "furthermore, these two examples bear witness to the unquestionable decline of Athenian power, for it is obvious that, in the days when Athens dominated the Aegean, traders sailing from Athens would not have dared infringe the law which ordered them to bring back the whole or part of their cargo to that city".

28 See above on the absence of bilateral treaties between Athens and other states at this period.

term priority and concern in hellenistic Athens, a topic which Graham Oliver has illuminated in his recent book.[29]

Theatre

The second new category of decree honouring foreigners which emerges after Chaironeia are decrees honouring men for services connected with the Athenian theatre. I have published elsewhere fresh texts and some discussion of this set of decrees.[30] Some of them honour men who made financial contributions to two of the great public building projects of the Lykourgan period: the theatre of Dionysos and the Panathenaic stadium;[31] others honoured foreign poets, actors and others who had contributed to the great Athenian dramatic festivals.[32] Some were passed at the special Assembly in the theatre of Dionysos which the city held each year in Elaphebolion after the celebration of the City Dionysia. An active engagement by the *polis* with its theatrical life was, of course, no more a new thing after the battle of Chaironeia than an active engagement with its food supply, but the regular, systematic honouring with inscribed decrees of men who had contributed to this aspect of the life of the *polis* was an innovation. It should undoubtedly be connected with the policy of promotion of the City Dionysia and other aspects of Athenian theatre, and of the city's festival and cultural life more broadly, which is a familiar feature of Lykourgan Athens, most famously in the canonisation of Aeschylus, Sophocles and Euripides and the building works at the theatre of Dionysos.[33]

29 Oliver 2007a.

30 Lambert 2008. On the theatrical politics of the Lykourgan period see also Azoulay's paper in this volume [Azoulay 2011].

31 The pair of decrees probably for members of the same Plataian family: *IG* II² 345 = Lambert 2008, n° 4 [= *IG* II³ 1 345] and *IG* II² 351 = Lambert 2008, n° 5 = Rhodes & Osborne 2007, n° 94 [= *IG* II³ 1 352]; and *SEG* 36.149 = Lambert 2008, n° 6 [= *IG* II³ 1 470].

32 Agora XVI 79 = Lambert 2008, n° 1 [= *IG* II³ 1 344] (actor?); *IG* II² 347 = Lambert 2008, n° 2 [= *IG* II³ 1 347] (poet, Amphis of Andros); *IG* II² 429 = Lambert 2008, n° 8 [= *IG* II³ 1 423] (actor); *IG* II² 348 = Lambert 2008, n° 9 [= *IG* II³ 1 436] (actor); *IG* II² 551 = Lambert 2008, n° 10 [= *IG* II³ 1 473] (someone who had "served enthusiastically a succession of chorēgoi"). Add now *IG* II² 713 [= *IG* II³ 1 929], for a Theban (pipe-player?), on which see further below.

33 In addition to the inscriptions mentioned above, note also [Plut.], *Mor.* 841F, 851F–852E; *IG* II² 457; and e.g. *SEG* 33.143, *IG* II² 1157 and *IG* II² 1198. Building works: Hintzen-Bohlen 1997, p. 21–31. See Lambert 2008, p. 58. The inscribing in the early 320s of the list of vic-

There is also here, I suggest, a similar motivation and dynamic to the one we observed in relation to the grain supply decrees. In a world where the city's political and military capacity to secure its food supply was much diminished, it was obliged to rely to an extent on the good will of grain traders, to be secured in part by the prospect of honours. By the Lykourgan period the Greek theatre had acquired many of the attributes of an entertainment "industry" with fierce competition to attract international "star" poets and actors, by financial and other incentives. Alexander is said to have paid off a fine imposed on one actor for failing to appear at the City Dionysia in order to appear instead at one of his own festivals and to have paid 10 talents to another.[34] Lykourgos himself proposed a decree offering large cash prizes (600 to 1000 drachmas) for dithyrambic poets at a festival in the Piraeus.[35] Rather like modern celebrities, "star" performers could acquire elite levels of wealth. There is no decree of this period honouring an *Athenian* poet or dramatist. If Athens wished to showcase itself as the leading city of Greek drama, there was patently a realisation that this was to be achieved not only by building splendid theatres and erecting statues of the best Athenian dramatists of the past. The city also needed to exert itself to attract international "star" performers, and it did so by offering both financial incentives and, as our decrees indicate, the less tangible, but no less real, incentive of honour.

If one can legitimately measure influence by the number of extant inscribed decrees that a man proposed, far and away the most influential Athenian politicians of Lykourgan Athens (indeed of the whole of Athenian history before 322) were Lykourgos and Demades.[36] One generally thinks of them as on opposite sides of a fence constructed to divide so-called "pro-Macedonian" from "anti-Macedonian" politicians; and their rivalry is clear enough. Lykourgos vigorously opposed the proposal to award extravagant honours to Demades (see further below). We should probably interpret the number of inscribed decrees they proposed as an aspect of this rivalry. An inscribed decree proposed by you on the acropolis displayed to contemporaries, no less than it displays to us,

---

tors at the City Dionysia since the early fifth century, IG II^2 2318, is also relevant in this context.

34 Plut., *Alex*. 29.

35 [Plut.], *Mor*. 842A.

36 Fifteen self-standing inscribed decrees proposed by Demades are conveniently listed by Brun 2000, p. 177–178 (to which add IG II^2 713 [IG II^3 1 929], but that was inscribed in the third century); there are eight self-standing inscribed laws and decrees proposed by Lykourgos: see Lambert 2007a, p. 120–121. No other Athenian politician of this, or any period before 322, proposed more than three or four extant inscribed decrees.

your influence in the Assembly. This is one policy sphere, however, where both politicians were active: Lykourgos proposed two of the extant decrees in this theatrical genre;[37] in my article I identified Demades also as proposer of two,[38] but that number should be increased to three if we accept Sean Byrne's persuasive argument that a decree of this type previously dated to the third century and attributed to an otherwise unattested homonymous grandson of Demades, *IG* II^2 713 (+ Add.) [*IG* II^3 1 929], was actually proposed by the famous Demades himself.[39] This evidence for Demades' involvement in theatrical politics adds a further aspect to Patrice Brun's attempt to give us a more rounded impression of Demades' political contribution than has generally been inferred from the negative spin of the very limited literary record for this politician.[40]

The other proposers of these theatrical decrees whose names are preserved are all different men. We may infer, I think, that there was a fair degree of consensus about this theatre policy in Athens across the political spectrum; and that, as far as Lykourgos and Demades were concerned, this was a sphere of policy in which they were rivals not in the sense that they were seeking to drive policy in different directions, but in the sense that they were competing to attract popular support for differing specific measures which had essentially the same objectives.[41]

As with the decrees honouring grain traders, this new genre of decree honouring contributors to the Athenian theatre also set a pattern for the political priorities that were to preoccupy Athens in the hellenistic period. As a genre of inscribed decree it was quite short-lived; there are sporadic later examples, but they tend to be for theatrical people who were also prominent on the broader political scene;[42] and in general future generations did not maintain quite the

37 *IG* II^2 345 = Lambert 2008, n° 4 [= *IG* II^3 1 345]; *IG* II^2 351 = Lambert 2008, n° 5 = Rhodes & Osborne 2007, n° 94 [= *IG* II^3 1 352].

38 *IG* II^2 346 = Lambert 2008, n° 3 [= *IG* II^3 1 346]; *IG* II^2 372 = Lambert 2008, n° 7 [= *IG* II^3 1 384].

39 Byrne 2010. The honorand, [Arist?]on son of Echthatios of The[bes] had performed services (as pipe-player in Wilhelm's somewhat adventurous restoration) in respect of the agones [at the Dionysia?]. The decree is inscribed below another, which, in the third century, provided for it to be inscribed.

40 Brun 2000.

41 One notes in this respect also their service together on a Pythais, *Syll.*^{3} 296 = *FD* III 1.511 [= *IG* II^3 4 18], and on the board of *epimeletai* of the Amphiaraia in 329/8, *IG* VII 4254 = *Syll.*^{3} 298 = Lambert 2004, n° 17 [= *IG* II^3 1 355].

42 *E.g.* *IG* II^2 657 [*IG* II^3 1 877] for the poet Philippides, an influential figure at the court of Lysimachos (Plut., *Demetr.* 12).

intensity of political concentration on theatrical and cultural regeneration which is such a marked feature of Lykourgan Athens; but the new genre looked to the future in another important respect: it represented a shift away from a *polis* whose identity was grounded primarily in its political and military power and influence, towards a *polis* whose identity was grounded primarily in its cultural power and influence; and from a *polis* whose identity was grounded primarily in its role in the contemporary world to one whose identity was grounded primarily in its past achievements.

Religion and Festivals

Another notable aspect of Lykourgan Athens was an intense engagement of the *polis* with the regeneration of its religious and festival life and this too is a prominent feature of the inscribed laws and decrees of the period, catalogued, with brief discussion, in Lambert 2005. We have, for example, the famous law and decree introducing enhancements to the sacrifices at the annual celebration of the Panathenaia, to be funded from the proceeds of rental of land called the "Nea";[43] the law of Phanodemos providing for the celebration of a new festival, the Great Amphiaraia, in the newly acquired territory of Oropos (Phanodemos is known to us primarily as an Atthidographer, *FGrHist* 325, but he is also the most prominent Athenian in the epigraphical record of Lykourgan Athens, after Lykourgos and Demades);[44] and there are several more fragmentary inscriptions.[45] This is not a new genre – we have inscribed festival regulations dating to before Chaironeia[46] – but we have more dating to the years *ca.* 335–330 than we do from the whole of the period 403–338;[47]

43 *IG* II^2 334 + *SEG* 18.13 = Rhodes & Osborne 2007, n° 81 = Lambert 2005, n° 7 [= *IG* II^3 1 447].

44 *IG* VII 4253 = *Syll.*^{3} 287 = Lambert 2004, n° 16 [= *IG* II^3 1 348].

45 Lambert 2005, p. 144–49.

46 A fifth-century example is *IG* I^3 82, of 421/0, about the Hephaisteia.

47 The period 403–338 shows two examples: *Agora* XVI 56, of 367–348, regulating the Eleusinian Mysteries; *IG* II^2 47 (*SEG* 21.233, 47.122), of 370–350, establishing sacrifices at the Asklepieion at Zea and providing money for construction of a temple. Lambert 2005, p. 144–145 lists four, all dating to *ca.* 335–330. Apart from the Panathenaia these relate to a festival linked with the Peace of Corinth, *SEG* 16.55 = Lambert 2005, n° 8 [= *IG* II^3 1 448]; an unidentifiable festival (Amphiaraia or Epitaphia?), *SEG* 32.86 = Lambert 2005, n° 9 [= *IG* II^3 1 449]; and (probably) the great festival of Zeus on the acropolis, the Dipolieia, *Agora* XVI 67 = Lambert 2005, n° 10 [= *IG* II^3 1 551]. Note also the very fragmentary *IG* II^2 310 = Lambert 2005, n° 11 [= *IG* II^3 1 540].

and, interestingly, the genre is entirely absent from the epigraphical record of fourth century Athens after Alexander's death. Religion is a complex phenomenon and there is no simple explanation of this development. Partly it is about cultural display, about the city's desire to present itself, to itself and to the outside world, with the maximum of splendour.[48] Partly it has to do with the paideutic qualities of religion. *Paideusis* is a key theme of the Lykourgan period,[49] perceived as vital to the well-being of the city, apparent most obviously in the great ephebic reform of the mid-330s.[50] Its connection with religion is manifest in the ephebic oath, inscribed at this period in the sanctuary of Ares and Athena Areia in Acharnai, in which a very earthy religion, grounded in the fatherland and its crops, is powerfully deployed to inculcate patriotic values: "I shall not disgrace the sacred weapons ... I shall defend the *hiera* and *hosia* ... I shall honour the ancestral *hiera*. Witnesses: the gods Aglauros, Hestia, Enyo, Enyalios, Ares and Athena Areia, Zeus, Thallo, Auxo, Hegemone, Herakles, the boundaries of the fatherland, wheat, barley, vines, olives, figs.[51]" And as Lykourgos' speech against Leokrates makes clear, the myths that were associated with religion, for example those relating to the sacrifice of Erechtheus and the daughters of Kekrops, could also be felt to have powerful paideutic value. Partly I think it is also legitimate to adduce here the personality of Lykourgos himself, who as member of the *genos* Eteoboutadai, responsible for supplying the two major priesthoods on the acropolis, Athena Polias and Poseidon Erechtheus, inherited an intense personal sense of religious engagement.[52] But partly too we should not underestimate the power in the Greek mind of the simple idea that a city that was on good terms with the gods was a healthy city and likely to be a successful one. As Josine Blok points out in her paper for this colloquium, what made a citizen in classical Athens, as ordinary Athenians themselves perceived it, was, above all, participation in those same *hiera* and *hosia* which the ephebes swore to defend, both of them categories defined in relation to the gods.

48 Cf. Humphreys 2004, p. 87.

49 On this, see above all Humphreys' analysis of Lykourgos, 2004, p. 77–129, especially p. 120, and Azoulay's paper in this volume.

50 On this reform, see Rhodes & Osborne 2007, n° 89 with their commentary; on the date and on the short-lived *eutaxia* liturgy, which is perhaps to be associated with it, see Lambert 2001b, p. 56–57; 2002b, p. 122–124 [*IG* II^3 1 550].

51 Rhodes & Osborne 2007, n° 88.

52 On Lykourgos and the Eteoboutadai see most recently Blok and Lambert 2009, *s.v.* Priest of Poseidon Erechtheus. Two of Lykourgos' sons held this priesthood, though it is not clear that he did so himself. Among other prominent figures of this period this religious engagement is especially notable in Phanodemos, cf. Lambert 2004, p. 87 with n. 12.

Relationship to the Past

There is also another factor that is relevant here and I leave it to last because it can, I suggest, be seen as a sort of golden thread linking a number of the developments that I have been discussing and is, I believe, of fundamental importance in any attempt to grasp the nature of developments in "the political" in Lykourgan Athens, namely, an intense preoccupation with, engagement and focus on the city's own past, particularly, but not only, the glory days of the fifth century. I have suggested that a sense of the city's decline in relation to that past is a driver of several of the political shifts observable at this period: that it generated a desire to improve the performance of city officials by honouring them with inscribed decrees, and that it generated anxieties about the grain supply that resulted in the new policy of inscribing decrees honouring grain traders. It was an awareness of the towering achievements of fifth century Athenian drama that caused the city to emphasise and seek to enhance its role and status as leading city of Greek culture at a time when its political and military status were ebbing away; and, I suggest, it is in part the commemorative aspects of religion – the way that the practice of *polis* religion connected citizens with the city's past in ways which spoke to present needs and anxieties – which caused the city to focus its attention on this aspect of the city's activities at this period. This topic requires a paper of its own and I can not do it justice here. As in Christianity the eucharist commemorates paideutically the last supper, death and resurrection of Jesus Christ, so the enhanced practice of religious rituals in Lykourgan Athens strengthened the paideutic commemoration of "myths" of the city, both distant and more recent in time, creating a rich tapestry of resonance and connection. For example in the Little Panathenaia as enhanced by the law and decree of the late 330s mentioned above, one of the most beautiful cows bought with the proceeds of the lease of the *Nea* is to be sacrificed to Athena Nike.[53] I have remarked above on the way the attention paid to this cult at this period is an expression of a suppressed Will to Victory; but the significance is much richer and more complex than this. This ritual, as enacted on the acropolis, not only linked to the foundation of the temple of Athena Nike in the glory days of the fifth century and to the dedication of gold and bronze *Nikai* at that period (cf. below on *IG* II^2 403 [*IG* II^3 1 444]), it was presided over by the priestess of Athena Nike, tenant of a priesthood established at that period as (perhaps) the first "democratic" *polis* priesthood, selected not from the *genē* but from the Athenian People as a whole;[54] and

53 Rhodes & Osborne 2007, n° 81, l. 20–21 [*IG* II^3 1 447].

54 *IG* I^3 35 and *IG* I^3 1330; Lambert 2010b.

was enacted at a festival which was the context for the tyrannicide,[55] a heroic deed referred to by Lykourgos *Against Leokrates* 51, and which finds an echo in the famous law of 337/6 condoning the murder of anyone who sought to overthrow the democracy and replace it with a tyranny, and placing restrictions on the Areopagos in such circumstances.[56] Thus this new ritual of the Panathenaia subtly asserts and confirms Athens' democratic heritage, a response on the religious plane to perceived threats to the ancestral democracy, which were another aspect of the Post-Chaironeia Anxiety.

If we look briefly outside the epigraphical sphere, this focus on the past and its paideutic value also links the two great political speeches of the year 330. Lykourgos' speech *Against Leokrates* is packed with paideutic stories about the past, designed to impress on the jury the value of self-sacrifice in the interests of the wider community; and a major theme of Demosthenes' speech *On the Crown* is that Athenians owed it to their own past, to the heroic deeds of their ancestors, to resist Philip, and that was true even though resistance turned out in the end to be futile.

This intense focus on the past, particularly the fifth-century glory days, is also a marked feature of the inscriptions of this period, a topic I explore more fully elsewhere.[57] A decree I have already mentioned, IG II^2 403 = Lambert 2005, n° 3 [= IG II^3 1 444], is the *locus classicus*. It is about the repair and "raising" of a statue of Athena Nike on the acropolis (apparently by increasing the height of the base), which, as the text spells out in detail, had originally been dedicated from the spoils of campaigns in Western Greece during the 420s. The action resonates with, and was perhaps a prelude to, one of Lykourgos' proud achievements: the replacement of the golden *Nikai* on the acropolis which had been melted down for coin in the later stages of the Peloponnesian War.[58] In this decree the Athenians are reaching back at a time of national crisis to connect with a period when the Athenian Empire was at its strongest, "raising" literally and symbolically the goddess of Athena Victory at a time of defeat.

Another striking, if more subtle, example is the decree of 338/7, proposed by the fiercely anti-Macedonian politician, Hegesippos of Sounion, which provided a refuge in Athens for Phormio and Karphinas, Akarnanians exiled from their home city in the aftermath of the allied defeat at Chaironeia.[59] The decree refers explicitly to the citizenship grant made to their grandfather, also called

55 Thuc. 6.56–58.

56 Rhodes & Osborne 2007, n° 79 = Lambert 2007b, n° 14 [IG II^3 1 320].

57 Lambert 2010c.

58 [Plut.], *Mor.* 852B, cf. Paus. 1.29.16.

59 IG II^2 237 = Rhodes & Osborne 2007, n° 77 = Lambert 2006, n° 5 [= IG II^3 1 316].

Phormio, who was probably named for the Athenian general Phormio, active in western Greece in the 420s, and whose citizenship, it can be calculated, may well have been granted *ca.* 400, i.e. in the aftermath of the Peloponnesian War. This was a situation which had special resonance in the post-Chaironeia years and Lykourgos alludes to it in his extant speech as holding lessons for the present situation: "Our city was a slave [...] to the Thirty when its walls were torn down by the Lakedaimonians [...] yet [...] we won back our freedom and earned the right to be guardians of Greek prosperity".[60] The past could inform the present in all sorts of ways.

A feature common to both these inscriptions is a focus on the acropolis, the sacred heart of the city, as locus of past-connectivity. In *IG* II^2 403 [*IG* II^3 1 444] it is the inscription on the acropolis which makes the connection, against the backdrop of the famous 5th century temple, between the newly "raised" *Nike* on the acropolis and the circumstances in which the original statue was dedicated. The text of the decree for the Akarnanians, inscribed on the acropolis, mentions explicitly that the decree for the elder Phormio was also "inscribed on the acropolis", thus creating a monumental "paideutic" link between the present situation and the past moments in history alluded to in the text of the inscription. This, I think, gives us a helpful perspective on a point touched on by some other speakers at the colloquium: the scarcity of new architectural and sculptural works on the acropolis in the Lykourgan period, in contrast to the frenetic activity elsewhere in the city.[61] Inscriptions are monuments and Athenians inscribed more laws and decrees in the Lykourgan period than during any other comparable length of time. The large majority of them were set up on the acropolis; and what did the acropolis signify to an Athenian of the 30s and 20s of the fourth century? One of the most significant pronouncements of the great inscriber Lykourgos is from his speech opposing the award of high honours to his great rival, Demades. He is comparing the small achievements and extravagant honours proposed for Demades with the massive achievements and modest honours of Pericles:

> Pericles, after capturing Samos and Euboea and Aegina, building the Propylaia, the Odeion and the Hekatompedon [all on or around the acropolis] and depositing 10,000 talents of gold on the acropolis, was crowned with a crown of foliage.[62]

---

60 Lyk. 1.61.

61 See the paper of Monaco [2011].

62 Lyk., *Against Kephisodotos Concerning the Honours for Demades*, fr. 9.2 Conomis.

To a Lykourgan Athenian the acropolis was, I suggest, the monumental expression of the city's glorious fifth-century past; and by setting up their inscriptions there the Athenian People were expressing in monumental form a respect for, and a desire to connect with and be educated by, that past.

If it was in the Lykourgan period that Athens became a "Hellenistic" city, it was also arguably at this period that fifth-century Athens became "classical" Athens.

Bibliography

Azoulay, V. 2011: "Les métamorphoses du *koinon* athénien: autour du *Contre Léocrate* de Lycurgue", in V. Azoulay and P. Ismard eds., *Clisthène et Lycurgue d'Athènes. Autour du politique dans la cité classique*, Paris, 191–217.

Blok, J., Lambert, S. D. 2009: "The appointment of priests in Attic *gene*", ZPE 169, 95–121.

Brun, P. 2000: *L'orateur Démade. Essai d'histoire et d'historiographie*, Bordeaux.

Byrne, S. G. 2010: "Some people in third-century Athenian decrees", in R. Catling ed., *Onomatologos. Studies in Greek onomastics and prosopography presented to Elaine Matthews,* Oxford, 122–33.

Faraguna, M. 1992: *Atene nell'età di Alessandro: problemi politici, economici, finanziari*, Roma.

Faraguna, M. 2011: "Lykourgan Athens?", in V. Azoulay and P. Ismard eds., *Clisthène et Lycurgue d'Athènes. Autour du politique dans la cité classique*, Paris, 67–86.

Fisher, N. R. E. 2001: *Aeschines. Against Timarchos*, Oxford.

Habicht, Chr. 1988: "Die beiden Xenokles von Sphettos", *Hesperia* 57, 323–27.

Habicht, Chr. 1997: *Athens from Alexander to Antony,* Cambridge Mass. [1st ed. 1995].

Henry, A. S. 1996: "The hortatory intention in Athenian state decrees", ZPE 112, 105–19.

Hintzen-Bohlen, B. 1997: *Die Kulturpolitik des Eubulos und des Lykurg. Die Denkmäler- und Bauprojekte in Athen zwischen 355 und 322 v.Chr.*, Berlin.

Humphreys, S. C. 2004: "Lycurgus of Boutadai: an Athenian aristocrat", in S. C. Humphreys, *The strangeness of gods. Historical perspectives on the interpretation of Athenian Religion*, Oxford, 77–129 (*Afterword*: 110–29) [1st ed. 1985].

IALD: S. D. Lambert, *Inscribed Athenian laws and decrees, 352/1–322/1* BC. *Epigraphical essays*, Leiden, 2012.

Lambert, S. D. 1997: *Rationes Centesimarum. Sales of public land in Lykourgan Athens*, Amsterdam.

Lambert, S. D. 2001b: "Ten notes on Attic inscriptions", ZPE 135, 51–62 [= IALD, 221–39].

Lambert, S. D. 2004: "Athenian state laws and decrees, 352/1–322/1: I Decrees honouring Athenians", ZPE 150, 85–120 [= IALD, 3–47].

Lambert, S. D. 2005: "Athenian state laws and decrees, 352/1–322/1: II Religious regulations", ZPE 154, 125–59 [= IALD, 48–92].

Lambert, S. D. 2006: "Athenian state laws and decrees, 352/1–322/1: III Decrees honouringforeigners. A. Citizenship, proxeny and euergesy", *ZPE* 158, 115–58 [= *IALD*, 93–137].

Lambert, S. D. 2007a: "Athenian state laws and decrees, 352/1–322/1: III Decrees honouring foreigners. B. Other awards", *ZPE* 159, 101–54 [= *IALD*, 138–83].

Lambert, S. D. 2007b: "Athenian state laws and decrees, 352/1–322/1: IV Treaties and other texts", *ZPE* 161, 67–100 [= *IALD*, 184–218].

Lambert, S. D. 2008: "Polis and theatre in Lykourgan Athens: the honorific decrees", in A. P. Matthaiou and I. Polinskaya eds., *Mikros hieromnemon. Meletes eis mnemen Michael H. Jameson,* Athens, 53–85 [= *IALD*, 337–62].

Lambert, S. D. 2010a: "Inscribed treaties ca. 350–321 BC: an epigraphical perspective on Athenian foreign policy", in G. Reger, F. X. Ryan and T. F. Winters eds., *Studies in Greek epigraphy and history in honor of Stephen V. Tracy*, Bordeaux, 153–60 [= *IALD*, 377–86].

Lambert, S. D. 2010b: "A polis and its priests: Athenian priesthoods before and after Pericles' citizenship law", *Historia* 59, 143–75.

Lambert, S. D. 2010c: "Connecting with the past in Lykourgan Athens: an epigraphical perspective", in H.-J. Gehrke, N. Luraghi and L. Foxhall eds., *Intentionale Geschichte. Spinning time in ancient Greece*, Stuttgart, 225–38 [= this volume, chapter 5].

Lambert, S. D. 2010d: "Athenian chronology, 352/1–322/1 B.C.", in A. Tamis, C. J. Mackie and S. Byrne eds., *Philathenaios. Studies in honour of Michael J. Osborne,* Athens, 91–102 [= *IALD*, 389–400].

Monaco, M. C. 2011: "Offrandes publiques et privées sur l'Acropole et l'Agora d'Athènes à l'époque lycurguéenne (340–320 av. J.-C.)", in V. Azoulay ans P. Ismard eds., *Clisthène et Lycurgue d'Athènes. Autour du politique dans la cité classique*, Paris, 219–30.

Mossé, Cl. 1973: *Athens in decline 404–86 B.C.*, London.

Ober, J. 2011: "Comparing democracies. A spatial method with application to ancient Athens", in V. Azoulay and P. Ismard eds., *Clisthène et Lycurgue d'Athènes. Autour du politique dans la cité classique*, Paris, 307–324.

Oliver, G. J. 2007a: *War, food, and politics in early hellenistic Athens*, Oxford.

Rhodes & Osborne: P. J. Rhodes and R. Osborne, *Greek historical inscriptions 404–323 B.C.,* Oxford, 2007 [1st ed. 2003].

Sickinger, J. P. 2009: "Nothing to do with democracy: 'Formulae of disclosure' and the Athenian epigraphical habit", in L. Mitchell and L. Rubinstein eds., *Greek history and epigraphy. Essays in honour of P. J. Rhodes*, Swansea, 87–102.

Whitehead, D. 1983: "Competitive outlay and community profit: *Philotimia* in democratic Athens", *Classica et Mediaevalia* 34, 55–74.

Whitehead, D. 1986: *The demes of Attica, 508/7-ca. 250 B.C. A political and social study*, Princeton.

Whitehead, D. 1993: "Cardinal virtues: the language of public approbation in democratic Athens", *Classica et Mediaevalia* 44, 37–75.

PART 3

Inscribed Laws and Decrees and the Past

CHAPTER 5

Connecting with the Past in Lykourgan Athens: An Epigraphical Perspective

The story a historian would tell about the relationship of Lykourgan Athens to the past might run along the following lines.[1] Situation: crisis of confidence undermined by failure to stem the Macedonian tide at Chaironeia; reaction: paideutic connection to Athens' past (that is, a process of intense engagement with the past with a view to improving the present); agents: a group of "conservative" politicians (by "conservative" I mean in this context men with a strong sense of the past and of its potential for informing the present), Lykourgos the most prominent. One result: impetus given to the construction in the Western mind of classical Athens as creator of models of behaviour to be emulated as morally exemplary and cultural artefacts to be revered as "classics." Examples: the heroisation of Perikles[2] and the canonisation of Aeschylus, Sophocles and Euripides.[3]

1 [This paper was first published in L. Foxhall, H.J. Gehrke and N. Luraghi eds., *Intentional History: Spinning Time in Ancient Greece* (Stuttgart, 2010), 225–38. See also the Introduction to this volume, pp. 8–9.] I am very grateful to those who contributed to the discussion in Freiburg and particularly to Josine Blok, Nick Fisher, Nino Luraghi and Robin Osborne for comments on drafts. By "Lykourgan Athens" I mean the period between the establishment of the Macedonian hegemony at the battle of Chaironeia in 338 and the failure of the Athenian-led rebellion against Macedon after Alexander's death (the Lamian War, 323–2). At this time Athens was largely free in the conduct of its domestic affairs, but constrained in its foreign policy (on the constraints from an epigraphical perspective see Lambert 2010. The most influential politicians of the period were Lykourgos (until his death in 325) and Demades, who pursued a policy of more active co-operation with the Macedonians. Recent synoptic accounts include: Tracy 1995, 1–51; Habicht 1997, 6–35; Humphreys 2004. On Demades see Brun 2000.

2 Lyk. F 9.2, see further below. Admiration for Perikles was not of course invented by Lykourgos, but Lykourgos' Perikles is much closer to the Perikles of later tradition (e.g. Plutarch's *Life*, note especially the emphasis on the building programme) than the Perikles of Thucydides.

3 Paus. 1.21, 1–3; [Plut.] *Lyc.* 841f. The emphasis on theatrical culture is reflected in the emergence at this time of a new genre of inscribed decrees: those honouring foreign actors and other foreign contributors to the theatrical life of the city. See Lambert 2008. On *paideusis* as a policy theme at this period see Humphreys 2004, 120–1, rightly emphasising in this context the major reform of the ephebate introduced by Epikrates in or shortly before 334/3. On this

© KONINKLIJKE BRILL NV, LEIDEN, 2018 | DOI 10.1163/9789004352490_007

It has been recognised that the development of a documentary culture has a significant contribution to make to this story. "Documents" of the past were elaborated, manufactured and deployed to serve contemporary purposes, often paideutic, a practice which can probably be traced back at least to the constitutional upheavals and associated revision/recreation of the "Solonian" corpus of law at the end of the fifth century, but which reaches a sort of climax in the numerous stories about the past contained in Lykourgos' speech *Against Leokrates*, some of them "documented" and all of them designed to impress on the jury, by examples taken from "history," the rightness of a type of courageous patriotic behaviour and the wrongness of its converse in the context of a speech aiming at the conviction of a man alleged to have fled Attica in the aftermath of the Athenian defeat at Chaironeia.[4]

Inscriptions have not been neglected in the scholarly literature on this topic. A good example is Rhodes – Osborne 2007, no. 88, an inscription of about this period from the Attic deme Acharnai recording what purports to be the "ancestral oath of the ephebes" and "the oath which the Athenians swore when they were about to fight against the barbarians" (i.e., at Plataia). These are characteristic examples of paideutic deployment of 'documents.' The resurrection, elaboration and inscribing of the oath of Plataia in particular demonstrates a remarkable, and quite typical, passion for connecting not just with a generalised past, but with a specific glorious moment; and the commentary of Rhodes – Osborne is full and informative. Undoubtedly much of the original stimulus for anthologising this inscription, however – it was inherited by Rhodes – Osborne from its predecessor volume, Tod 1947[5] – was that these are both "documents" which also turn up in our literary sources, including Lykourgos' speech against Leokrates,[6] and the focus of attention has therefore been on addressing the questions this raises about the relationship of the literary and epigraphical versions of the texts. In this paper I should like to shift the perspective somewhat: to consider what light inscriptions can cast *in their own right* on the city's process of "past-re-creation," focusing on the inscribed

reform see also Rhodes – Osborne 2007, 453; Lambert 2002, 122–3. A concern with *paideusis* (as with many of the phenomena discussed in this paper) was not, of course, wholly new after 338. Fisher 2001, 53–66, for example, persuasively identifies a general anxiety about the moral well-being of the citizens, and the young in particular, as an important factor in the success of Aeschines' speech *Against Timarchos*, delivered in 346/5, and as foreshadowing "Lykourgan" policy preoccupations.

4 Lyk. 1, delivered in 331/0. Cf. Davies 1996.

5 Tod 1947 no. 204.

6 Lyk. 1.76–8 and 80–2.

laws and decrees of the Athenian state (i.e., decrees passed by the Council and/or Assembly and laws passed by the *nomothetai*) of which, in recent years, I have been preparing a new edition for *Inscriptiones Graecae* (*IG* II^3 fascicle 2).[7] Among other things this will entail reflection on the significance of the physical context in which the inscriptions were placed: on their monumental intentionality.

I take as my starting point the inscribed state decree which is, I think, the most eloquent about Lykourgan deployment of the past, *IG* II^2 403 = Lambert 2005, no. 3 [= *IG* II^3 1 444]:

> .... of the *proedroi* – of Kerameis was putting to the vote. – son of – of Lakiadai proposed: concerning the report of those who were elected by the People to oversee the repair of the statue of Athena Nike which the Athenians dedicated from the Ambrakiots and (10) the army in Olpai and those who rose against the People of Corcyra and from Anaktorion, the Council shall decide: ... to bring them before the People.... at the next Assembly and (15) to place this matter on the agenda and to put the opinion of the Council before the People that it seems good to the Council, concerning the sacrifice to the goddess, that the priestess of Athena sacrifice a propitiatory sacrifice (*aresterion*) on behalf of the People, since the exegete (20) advises it ... money ... of the People shall give ... since the statue-maker ... made [the base?] higher...(25).... (30) praise the statue-maker – of Boeotia because....

Script and orthography suggest the 40s, 30s or 20s of the fourth century, and as we shall see, the measure is definitely "Lykourgan" in character. The proposer, interestingly, is not Lykourgos himself (who was a demesman of Boutadai), but an unidentifiable man from Lakiadai.[8] The decree concerns the repair of

7 Lambert 2004, 2005, 2006 and 2007a and b contain groundwork for this edition.

8 "Although we tend to speak of the period as 'the Lycurgan age,' its reforms were carried through by the energetic cooperation of an appreciable segment of the upper class," Humphreys 2004, 84. We are not, however, in Augustan Rome, but in fourth-century Athens – Athens of the mature democracy – and it was not a matter of one man leading and the rest of the "upper class" following, but rather a collective movement in which many participated. Cf. Brun 2005; Rhodes forthcoming [2010]. It is characteristic of the period that the most prominent Athenian in the epigraphical record, after Lykourgos and Demades, was Phanodemos of Thymaitadai, a man who engaged intensely with the past (author of an Atthis, *FGrHist* 325) and with religion (e.g., legislator for the Amphiaraia festival, *IG* VII 4253 = Lambert 2004 no. 16 [= *IG* II^3 1 348], proposer of the only Athenian inscribed decree honouring a divine figure, Amphiaraos, *IG* VII 4252 = Lambert 2004, 107 [= *IG* II^3 1 349]). Cf. Lambert 2004, 87.

a statue of Athena Nike, a subject about which a committee of the Assembly has made a report to the Council. The Council in turn has made a proposal to the Assembly, which the Assembly has agreed. The statue was originally dedicated from spoils of campaigns in western Greece during the Peloponnesian War: from Demosthenes' victory over a Peloponnesian-Ambrakiot army at Olpai in the winter of 426/5 and from the defeat, in the following summer, of Corcyraean exiles on Mt. Istone by Sophokles and Eurymedon and a successful campaign in alliance with the Akarnanians against Anaktorion. The campaigns are described in detail by Thucydides in books 3 and 4,[9] but, while quite possible, it is uncertain whether we should be right to infer a knowledge of Thucydides on the part of the drafter of this decree. Thucydides does not refer to our statue in his account and the wording in ll. 8–12 might have been copied from the original statue base. The first recommendation of the committee seems to have concerned a sacrifice: having consulted an exegete it is recommended that the priestess of Athena[10] sacrifice an *aresterion*, a propitiatory sacrifice following work on sacred property.[11] Then we hear something about money – presumably financial provision was made for the sacrifice. The text then becomes largely illegible, but there is enough to see that the statue-maker had apparently made the statue higher (perhaps by increasing the size of the base) and in ll. 30–1 we see that he was praised for his work and that he was a Boeotian.

The project recorded by this inscription undoubtedly resonates with one of Lykourgos' proud achievements, the replacement of the golden Nikai on the acropolis which had been melted down for coin towards the end of the Peloponnesian War, in 406/5.[12] This statue had clearly not been melted down and was perhaps in bronze.[13] Pausanias apparently saw another bronze Nike on the acropolis, dedicated to commemorate the Sphakteria campaign of 425.[14]

9 Thuc. 3.85, 106–12 and 114; 4.2–3, 46 and 49.

10 Presumably the priestess of Athena Nike, who was selected by lot from all Athenian women (*IG* I^3 35, 36 and 1330, cf. Parker 1996, 125–6), rather than the priestess of Athena Polias, who was appointed from the genos Eteoboutadai (Aeschin. 2.147, cf. Parker 1996, 290–3).

11 Cf. Hesych. s.v. *aresasthai*; *IG* II^2 204 [*IG* II^3 1 292], 58; 1672, 302–3.

12 [Plut.] *Lyc.* 852b, cf. Paus. 1.29, 16 (Lykourgos responsible for golden Nikai and *kosmos* for 100 maidens); *IG* II^2 1493 with Lambert 2005, 138–9.

13 One might expect *andriantopoios*, the term used here, to refer to the maker of a human statue. *Agalmatopoios* is normal for a statue of a deity. However, *andriantopoios* seems also to be used for a worker in metal rather than stone at Arist. *Eth. Nic.* 1141a 10–11.

14 Paus. 4.36, 6. Whether this Nike and ours were contemporary in origin with the foundation of the temple of Athena Nike is uncertain. *IG* I^3 35 provided for the temple and its

It would seem reasonable to suppose that the "raising" of our bronze Nike was a prelude to the more ambitious re-creation of the golden ones, but we cannot date either action precisely.

This decree is typical of the way that Lykourgan Athens deployed the past: reaching back at a time of national crisis to connect with a period when the Athenian empire was at its strongest; "raising" literally and doubtless symbolically the goddess of Athena Victory at a time of defeat.

If the time-to-connect-with is significant, so is the location of the connection. The cult of Athena Nike was on the acropolis, the bronze statue of Athena Nike to which our inscription refers was on the acropolis and the inscription itself was found on the acropolis and no doubt, like most inscriptions found there, it was also set up there (one imagines next to the repaired statue, though we can not be certain of that). Now one certainly thinks of the Lykourgan period as one of vigorous building activity, much of it associated with institutions characteristic of the fifth century democracy and empire – the theatre of Dionysos, the Panathenaic stadium, the Pnyx, the Lyceum, naval buildings in the Piraeus, the temple of Apollo Patroos in the agora,[15] and so on – but the acropolis itself does not immediately come to mind as a focus of attention and indeed there seems to be no record of major building works there at this period.[16] I wish to suggest, however, that it is, or should be, central to any account of Lykourgan past-connectivity.[17]

---

priestess. It has conventionally been dated to the 440s but Mattingly 2000 and Gill 2001 (cf. *SEG* 50.36) make a case for the 420s, shortly before *IG* I³ 36, of 424/3, which makes detailed provision for the priestess' salary. The balance of argument now perhaps favours the 420s, but it is doubtful whether our statue is strictly relevant to this debate. It seems that a number of metallic Nikai were dedicated during the Archidamian War; but they were not necessarily connected directly with the foundation of the temple. In general on the sanctuary of Athena Nike see Mark 1993; most recently on the date of *IG* I³ 35, Lougovaya-Ast 2006 (favouring the 440s).

15 This, of course, is an instance of monumental connectivity with Athens' more distant past, celebrating Apollo as father of Ion. Apparently associated with this was the "gilding of the altar of Apollo in the agora" undertaken by Neoptolemos of Melite, for which he was rewarded, on Lykourgos' proposal, with a statue ([Plut.] *Lyc.* 843f). Significantly in our context, Neoptolemos was also responsible for restoring the temple of Artemis Aristoboule in Melite founded by Themistokles to commemorate the "good counsel" which won the Persian Wars. See Parker 1996, 155 and 245–6.

16 Humphreys 2004, 87 and 120–1. See also Hintzen-Bohlen 1997.

17 I sketch here an outline approach to "interpreting" the acropolis in Lykourgan Athens. A much fuller account is desirable. For a full account of the acropolis in the period after the death of Alexander see von den Hoff 2003. The acropolis was at the centre of things,

It is mentioned just once by Lykourgos in his surviving speech: fairly near the beginning he presents us with a vivid image of Leokrates fleeing Attica, slaves and mistress in tow, in a boat from the Piraeus. Lykourgos tells us that, as Leokrates slipped out, he "felt no fear as he saw in the distance the acropolis and the temple of Zeus Soter and Athena Soteira which he was betraying."[18] The cult of Zeus Soter and Athena Soteira was one of the most popular in Attica in the Lykourgan period and their sanctuary in the Piraeus the thing most worth seeing in the port in Pausanias' day.[19] Their mention here connects with the soteriological theme which runs through the speech: Leokrates has failed in his duty to save his country; the jury should feel no obligation to save him from the executioner. He has failed to "save" Zeus Soter and Athena Soteira; they can not be expected to save him. But Leokrates has also failed to save the acropolis; and the polis can not be expected to save him. Acropolis = polis.

At one level the acropolis was a suitable focus for Lykourgan past-connectivity because it was the location of the buildings which, more than any other, expressed the imperial self-confidence of fifth-century Athens: Parthenon and Propylaia, Erechtheum and temple of Athena Nike. It was also a place with which Lykourgos himself had a special relationship as member of the Eteoboutadai, the *genos* which traced its descent from Erechtheus and Boutes and supplied the two most important acropolis priesthoods: the priestess of Athena Polias and the priest of Poseidon Erechtheus. It is not clear whether Lykourgos held the latter priesthood in person, but two of his sons certainly did.[20] Erechtheus was the Ur-Athenian who, in sacrificing his daughter for the good of the city (in myths located on or around the acropolis), provided a model of Athenian patriotic behaviour. Significantly, the story features as one of the examples of such behaviour recounted by Lykourgos in his speech against Leokrates;[21] and also significantly, among the few new "Lykourgan" monuments on the acropolis were thrones for the priests of Boutes and Hephaistos, both perhaps also Eteoboutad priesthoods.[22]

---

but past-connectivity was of course also expressed epigraphically in other locations. The Acharnai stele, Rhodes – Osborne no. 88, mentioned above, is a good example.

18 Lyk. 1.17.

19 Paus. 1.1, 3. Cf. Parker 1996, 238–41; 2005, 466–7.

20 See [Plut.] *Lyc.* 843e–f (misleadingly translated in the Loeb). Cf. Lambert forthcoming.

21 Lyk. 1.98–101.

22 In addition "the priestess of Athena" (apparently Polias) was the subject of a lost speech of Lykourgos (Lyk. F 6). Thrones: *IG* II^2 4982 (Hephaistos), 5166 (Boutes). Cf. Paton 1927, 484 with fig. 206; Brommer 1978, 109 and 251 no. 1 with Taf. 40, 3; Humphreys 2004, 119. Eteoboutad priests: see Lambert forthcoming. The *gene*, with their connotations of "straight descent" from Ur-Athenians (see e.g., *Ath. Pol.* F 3 and on Hesychius' description

As we can see from the reference to Erechtheus and indeed several other myth-historical paideutic anecdotes in Lykourgos' speech, variously located in space and time,[23] "classical" Athens was by no means the only time-and-place-to-be-connected-with in Lykourgan ideology, but there is confirmation that the period of construction of the major monuments of the acropolis was a focus of attention in a fragment of the speech in which he argued against the proposal to honour his contemporary and political rival, Demades. The context seems to have been a comparison of the modest awards and magnificent achievements of Perikles with the undeserving performance and exaggerated honours claimed by Demades:

> Perikles, after capturing Samos and Euboea and Aegina, building the Propylaia, the Odeion and the Hekatompedon [all on or around the acropolis], and depositing 10,000 talents of gold on the acropolis, was crowned with an olive crown.[24]

I should like to reflect a little more on how inscriptions fit into this picture. Inscribed Athenian decrees of this period often have an explicit intentionality: the most common type of decree is honorific and, from the mid-fourth century onwards, they frequently contain wording which expresses the thought: "these honours are awarded and this decree is inscribed to encourage the honorand to continue to behave in ways which favour the city and to encourage others to emulate him in the hope of future honours." I have briefly treated this type of epigraphic intentionality elsewhere;[25] and Nino Luraghi discusses it more fully in his paper in this volume. My interest here is in a somewhat different aspect of epigraphic intentionality, more strongly physical and more specifically located on the acropolis. My suggestion is that inscriptions provide evidence for attention being paid to the [physical] acropolis by the [abstract] polis where, implicitly or explicitly, the paideutic quality of the acropolis' past seems to be a focus of attention. This is most obvious in the Athena Nike inscription that I

---

genos ithagenon, commonly applied to his entries for Attic *gene*, Parker 1996, 284–5) embodied precisely the sort of connectivity with the past which was emphasised in Lykourgan culture and it is unsurprising that they were a focus of attention at this period (cf. Humphreys 2004, 99–100).

23 It was not only Athens that provided the exempla. On Sparta in Lykourgan ideology see Fisher 2007.

24 Lyk. F 9.2.

25 Lambert 2006, 116–17.

have already discussed, but one can identify it in other inscriptions too. I give three further examples.

The first does not seem to carry an explicit paideutic intention, but it does show us the acropolis as an explicit focus of the city's attention at this period. *IG* II^2 333 [*IG* II^3 1 445] is our only Attic inscription inscribed with two laws; the second, certainly proposed by Lykourgos, relates to *exetasmos*, special examinations of valuable objects in temples; the first is more fragmentary. Probably it was also proposed by Lykourgos, but we cannot be certain. The surviving text relates to dedications and movement of objects, including processional vessels, on or down from the acropolis, with penalties for breaches imposed on public slaves. It was characteristic of Lykourgan culture that it was focused not only on the macro-scale of things, but on the micro-level as well: not only on big things like temples, but on the smaller objects associated with them.[26]

The second inscription that I want to mention contains, I think, a clearer acropolis-related paideutic subtext: Rhodes – Osborne no. 81 [*IG* II^3 1 447], a law and decree about the Little Panathenaia.[27] Again, though not proposed by Lykourgos himself (the proposer was probably the minor politician Aristonikos of Marathon)[28] it is definitely Lykourgan in character and date. It provides for leasing of land referred to as "New" (*Nea*) and for the application of the resulting funds for the enhancement of the programme of sacrifices at the festival.

It goes without saying that the Panathenaia is the prime festival of Athenianness and entirely appropriate as a focus of attention at a period of civic regeneration. In addition to this festival measure the new Panathenaic stadium was one of the major Lykourgan construction projects.[29] It is also clear enough that the festival had historic paideutic value, both in the sense that the festival itself had a history associating it with moments of Athenian glory (e.g., the

26 Note for example the *dermatikon* accounts, which detail receipts from the sale of skins of animals from state sacrifices from 334/3–331/0, *IG* II^2 1496; accounts of the making of new processional vessels and golden Nikai, *IG* II^2 1493; Lambert 2005, 138–9; accounts of bronze statues and other objects on the acropolis (including bronze stelai), perhaps to be melted down in the context of a *kathairesis*, *IG* II^2 1498–1501a, Harris 1992. All these accounts were set up on the acropolis.

27 = Lambert 2005 no. 7. The "Little Panathenaia" was the elements of the festival which recurred every year, in contrast to the "Great Panathenaia," the enhancements (competitions, etc.) which occurred every four years.

28 See Rhodes – Osborne 2007, 400.

29 *IG* II^2 351 = Rhodes – Osborne no. 94 = Lambert 2006 no. 42, 15–20 [= *IG* II^3 1 352]; [Plut.] *Lyc.* 841d. See Rhodes – Osborne's note and Lambert 2008.

tyrannicide in the sixth century,[30] focus for imperial celebration in the fifth)[31] which were doubtless more or less present to the mind of participants in the 30s and 20s of the fourth century, and in the sense that festival mythology emphasising Athenian-ness – whether to do with Erichthonius and autochthony or Theseus and synoecism – was recalled in the festival rituals.[32] But the point I particularly want to emphasise in this context – and it is one that we can fail to register if we conceptualise the construction of the Panathenaic stadium outside the city as at the centre of Panathenaic attention in the Lykourgan period – is that again the prime focus of these regulations for the Little Panathenaia is the acropolis. Most of the cattle bought with the new money raised from the *Nea* are to be sacrificed to Athena Polias, the primary goddess of the acropolis, except, the text carefully specifies, for "one, to be selected from the most beautiful of the cows, to be sacrificed to Athena Nike."[33] The resonance with the remaking of the golden Nikai melted down in the Peloponnesian War and the repair of the bronze Nike dedicated in the Peloponnesian War and commemorated in *IG* II^2 403 [*IG* II^3 1 444] seems quite clear, and that inscription shows us that we are right to interpret this ritual innovation as containing retrospective paideutic intentionality: it is meant to recall to the mind of participants in the ritual – that is to say notionally the entire population of Athens – an Athens in its period of greatest power and victory: the mid-fifth century and the early years of the Peloponnesian War. And we must envisage this not only abstractly/conceptually, but in a monumental context; and not only statically,

30 Thuc. 6.56–8, another heroic deed referred to by Lykourgos (1.51). It finds an echo in the law of 337/6 condoning the murder of anyone who sought to overthrow the democracy and replace it with a tyranny, Rhodes – Osborne no. 79 = Lambert 2007b no. 14 [= *IG* II^3 1 320]. This law was not set up on the acropolis (one copy was placed in the Assembly and one at the entrance to the Council-chamber of the Areopagos), but it is replete with points of past-connectivity, with its anxieties about the Areopagos and echoes of earlier Athenian anti-tyranny laws. See Rhodes – Osborne's note.

31 E.g., Athenian allies were required to send a "cow and a panoply" and escort them in the procession. *IG* I^3 34, 41–2; 71, 56–8; 46, 15–17; Schol. Ar. *Nub.* 386; Parker 1996, 142 and 2005, 254.

32 Festival founded by Erichthonios (= Erechtheus) son of Hephaistos, symbol of Athenian autochthony and inventor of the chariot. He was recalled by the Panathenaic competition involving leaping on and off horses/chariots (*apobasis*): Hellanikos *FGrHist* 323A F 2, [Eratosth.] *Cat.* 13, etc. See Parker 2005, 254. Founded by Theseus: Paus. 8.2, 1, cf. Istros *FGrHist* 334 F 4; Parker 2005, 255. The association with synoecism is perhaps to be connected with the prominence of the city's subdivisions (demes, etc.) in the festival organisation and in the careful articulation of the different social groups that made up Athenian civic society in the procession (Parker 2005, 258–9).

33 Rhodes – Osborne no. 81 B [*IG* II^3 1 447], 20–1.

but dynamically. We need, I suggest, to imagine the gaze of Mr, Miss (even Mrs)[34] Athenian Citizen, metic and colonist, participant in the Panathenaia in the 320s, shifting from the beautiful cow about to be sacrificed to Athena Nike, to the splendid newly "raised" and restored bronze statue of the goddess dedicated (as *IG* II^2 403 [*IG* II^3 1 444] would remind him or her) from the spoils of victories in the Peloponnesian War, to the glistening golden Nikai, symbolising the Athenian capacity to leap back over the military failure of 404 and the more recent failure at Chaironeia to recapture the golden age of the mid-fifth century. And out of the corner of his or her eye, he or she would also perhaps have caught a glimpse of the Parthenon frieze....[35]

The Lykourgan period was a particularly active one in the sphere of festival reform and enhancement[36] and this past-as-*paideusis* aspect of festivals, their rituals, myths and monuments, should feature prominently in any attempt to explain this activity.

The third inscription I wish to mention in this connection belongs in a comparable context: *Agora* XVI 67 = Lambert 2005, no. 10 [= *IG* II^3 1 551]. It is very fragmentary, but it is definitely Lykourgan in date and we can be fairly confident that it related to the other great Athenian festival of the acropolis, the Dipolieia. This was the premier Athenian festival of Zeus, its centrepiece an ox-killing ritual, the Bouphonia, whose thematic material seems to have been the proper relations of agricultural man to his working animals, and which was so venerable and obscure that it connoted archaism even in the fifth century.[37] The past that "Lykourgan" Athenians wish to connect with has a fifth-century focus, but also a focus in the heroic and mythical time: as noted above, Lykourgos mixes

---

34 The procession included maiden basket-bearers. Mature/married women were not among the groups who participated formally in the procession, but they were represented strikingly by the leading actors in the ritual, the priestesses of Athena Polias and Athena Nike. It is difficult to say whether they were also present as onlookers/followers of the procession. Cf. Jameson, 1999; Parker 2005, 218.

35 If our Citizen were standing in the right place and attending to smaller items as well as the wider scene, he (and/or his wife/daughter?) might also have noticed not only *IG* II^2 403 [*IG* II^3 1 444], but a relief commemorating the honorific crown he had recently voted in the assembly for the priestess of Athena Nike and depicting the crowning of the priestess by a Nike held by Athena, Lawton no. 164 = Lambert 2007b, 130. We do not know whether the decree awarding the crown mentioned her services in relation to the *aresterion* she sacrificed for the raised statue of Athena Nike or the beautiful cow whose sacrifice she now supervised every year at the Panathenaia; but it is clear enough that, in the Lykourgan period, this priestess was kept busy carrying out the people's instructions.

36 Cf. Lambert 2005, 131; Parker 1996, 242–55.

37 Ar. *Nub*. 984.

anecdotes from both indiscriminately in his oratory. For the purposes of Lykourgan past-connectivity both the (to our minds "real") fifth century and the (to our minds "unreal") time of myths and heroes are equally valid.

I said in relation to *IG* II^2 333 [= *IG* II^3 1 445] that, as far as the monumental aspects of Lykourgan policy were concerned, it was right to attend to small things as well as big things: that was in relation to dedications, processional vessels and such like. One might add that another class of small object that is relevant in this context is the inscriptions themselves, for their significance lies not only in the policy decisions that they record, but in their very existence, in other words in the fact that a decision was taken to inscribe them. In all three of the cases I have just mentioned, not only does the content of the inscription relate to the acropolis, the inscription was itself set up there. Throughout the classical period (and indeed beyond) the acropolis was overwhelmingly the most common site for the placement of state laws and decrees[38] (and it was a very common site for the placement of accounts inscriptions and dedications). By the Lykourgan period the acropolis was home to over two centuries' worth of inscribed dedications and nearly two centuries' worth of state decrees inscribed on stone:[39] hundreds, perhaps thousands, of inscriptions. An inscription placed on the acropolis in the Lykourgan period resonated architecturally with other acropolis monuments, most of them products of Athens' fifth-century glory days, even at the level of detail: temples had pedimerits; so did many inscribed decrees.[40] Temples contained and were decorated with figurative sculpture; some inscribed decrees were decorated with figurative reliefs.[41] Temples were dedicated to gods; state decrees erected there were commonly headed with the invocation "gods" (*theoi*), whether or not their content was explicitly religious. Inscriptions set up on the acropolis at this period also resonated with other inscriptions set up there in earlier times. It is not perhaps coincidental that the practice of setting up large numbers of state laws and decrees on the acropolis originated at about the same time as the

38 See Liddel 2003. See also Osborne 1999 and other discussions referred to by Liddel n. 3.

39 The earliest inscribed state decree, *IG* I^3 1, perhaps dates to the end of the sixth century.

40 Cf. Davies 2005, 294.

41 Relief sculpture on Attic documentary inscriptions is catalogued by Lawton 1995. In state laws and decrees of this period it appears mainly on decrees honouring foreigners (see Lambert 2007a, 129–30). Much remains to be done to elucidate the relationship between text and relief sculpture and the wider environment of the acropolis. On the interplay of text and relief see recently Blanshard 2004 (on the law against tyranny, cf. above n. 30) and 2007 (on *IG* I^3 127). Cf. above n. 35.

great fifth-century temples were constructed;[42] and that the many account-bearing inscriptions set up on the acropolis in the Lykourgan period jostled, as it were, with the Athenian Tribute Lists. This connecting-with-the-past aspect of inscriptions on the acropolis in a monumental perspective is also a theme which can be traced at the level of the texts. And I do not only mean here that epigraphical language and formulae developed organically over time such that the way things were expressed on Lykourgan inscriptions connects with the way they were expressed on inscriptions of the fifth century, though that is perhaps part of the picture. The connection to the fifth century operates also at the level of the *content* of the texts. We might take as an example one of the most anthologised inscriptions of this period: the decree of 338/7, Rhodes – Osborne no. 77 [*IG* II³ 1 316],[43] one of the earliest decrees to be passed after the battle of Chaironeia. It honours Akarnanians who had supported the allies against Philip and came to Athens as exiles in the aftermath of the allied failure. In l. 8 we read that the principal honorands, Phormio and Karphinas of Akarnania, were ancestral friends (*patrothen philoi*) of the Athenian people, and we learn more about this background in ll. 15–21:

> Since the Athenian People made Phormío the grandfather of Phormio and Karphinas an Athenian, and his descendants, and the decree which effected this was inscribed on the acropolis, the grant which the People made to their grandfather Phormio shall be valid for Phormio and Karphinas and their descendants.

One may calculate that Phormio, the grandfather of Phormio and Karphinas, must have been awarded his Athenian citizenship in about 400.[44] It would be nice to think, though we cannot be certain, that this was in the aftermath of the Athenian failure to win the Peloponnesian War, an event which recalls the circumstances of Athens post-Chaironeia and has a particular resonance in Lykourgan ideology. In a striking passage of his speech against Leokrates,

---

42 The increase in the numbers of state inscriptions placed on the acropolis from around the mid-fifth century is conventionally linked with increased openness and accountability associated with the radical democracy post-Ephialtes, but I am inclined to think that it has as much to do with the stimulus of a monumental context which was being enhanced by the Periklean building programme. In general the character of the acropolis as sacred space is as important to understanding why inscriptions were placed there as its character as public space (cf. Hölkeskamp 1994; Hedrick 1999; Samons 2000, 312–17).

43 = Lambert 2006 no. 5.

44 Cf. M. Osborne 1981–1983 vol. III–IV T 25.

Lykourgos reflects on the difference between a city which has been totally destroyed, from which there is no recovery, and a city which has been subject to an enslavement from which it may still aspire to set itself free:

> If one must speak the truth, destruction is the death of a city. This is the greatest proof: a long time ago our city was a slave to tyrants, *later to the Thirty when its walls were torn down by the Lakedaimonians*. Yet after both of these, we won back our freedom and earned the right to be guardians of Greek prosperity.[45]

Another striking aspect is the name Phormio, borne both by one of the two honorands of 338/7 and by their grandfather. The grandfather was almost certainly named for Phormio the famous Athenian general of the Peloponnesian War, who made an alliance with Akarnania before the war, was much liked there according to Thucydides and was active in western Greece in the 420s:[46] in fact precisely the same time and region that was alluded to quite explicitly in the decree about the Athena Nike statue with which I began this paper.

As with the activity relating to that statue the past is connected with not only conceptually, but physically and monumentally, for the proposer of our inscription, the wild anti-Macedonian patriot Hegesippos of Sounion, here showing himself as a true "Lykourgan,"[47] takes the trouble to draw attention to the fact that the "decree which effected this [i.e., the award of citizenship to the first Phormio of Akarnania] was inscribed on the acropolis." Rhodes – Osborne no. 77 [*IG* II^3 1 316] was also set up on the acropolis. So again a conceptual (in this case one might say subliminal) message about how the past may inform the present finds expression in monumental form. We do not know for certain that Rhodes – Osborne no. 77 [*IG* II^3 1 316] was set up next to the older inscription, but it would be quite characteristic if it had been (sometimes in this sort of case explicit provision is made for a decree to be placed next to another one, but not here). Our Athenian-on-the-acropolis-looking-at-the-monuments would be invited by our inscription to reflect on the Peloponnesian War: the glory days of the 420s and the lessons about failure overcome implicit in the

45 Lyk. 1.61.

46 Thuc. 2.68, 6–7; 3.7, 1. Rhodes – Osborne 2007, 382.

47 Also proposer of the emphatically worded (and non-formulaic) decree, *IG* II^2 125 = Rhodes – Osborne no. 69 (with note p. 349) = Lambert 2007b no. 6 [= *IG* II^3 1 399] and probable author of [Dem.] 7. He was known as "Krobylos" for his "past-connective" habit of wearing his hair in a bun (Aeschin. *Tim.* 64, with the note of Fisher 2001; Diog. Laert. 3.24, etc.).

denouement; and all around him (or her) the monuments would be conveying, as it were, the same message.

I should like to finish with a wider reflection about epigraphical practice, for looking at inscriptions in the sort of way that I have been attempting here may suggest a possible approach to answering the rather elusive question: why was a particular decree or class of decree of the Athenian Council and/or Assembly inscribed and not another particular decree or class of decree of those bodies (most decrees, of course, were never inscribed). Part of the answer to this question must, I think, lie in the direction of the decree's monumental potential: its capacity to convey a strong message *qua* monument. Honorific decrees are surely the commonest type of inscribed decree because their character as public monuments is intimately connected with their honorific – and hortatory – intentionality.[48] This in turn may suggest a partial answer to another intriguing question about the Athenian epigraphical record: why did the Lykourgan period produce so many inscriptions, more than from any other period of comparable length? And why is Lykourgos himself so prominent in them – in the epigraphical record of classical Athens second only to Demades as decree proposer[49] and connectable, directly, indirectly or at least ideologically, with much of the rest of the epigraphical output of the period. Several factors must, I think, be relevant. They will include the natural trajectory of the epigraphical habit – a snowball tendency for ever more decrees to be inscribed; and the development of a more literate and bureaucratic administrative culture as the fourth century progressed. But part of the explanation, I suggest, is the character of the Lykourgan period as one which displays a particularly heightened sense of the need for a paideutic engagement with the past and the capacity of inscriptions, particularly (though not only) inscriptions placed on the acropolis, to contribute to the fulfilment of that need at both monumental and textual levels. And why is Lykourgos so prominent in the epigraphical record? Part of the answer must surely again lead us back to the acropolis: as member of the

48 Thus in *IG* II^2 220 = Lambert 2007a no. 66 [= *IG* II^3 1 304], of 344/3, it is not the awarding of honours to the city of Pellana (which took place the previous year), but specifically the erection of the decree recording their award, that is conceived of as manufacturing the hortatory intention. See Lambert 2006, 116.

49 It seems to have been primarily the proposer of a decree who determined whether or not it was to be inscribed (in inscribed decrees a clause providing for inscription was normally included in the record of the proposer's motion), though he was subject to legal constraints of various kinds, the details of which are largely obscure (see, e.g., Lambert 2004, 87 with n. 9).

Eteoboutadai with a strong sense of engagement with his religious heritage this, the city's place of inscriptions, was his spiritual home.

Bibliography

Blanshard, A. J. L. 2004: "Depicting democracy. An exploration of art and text in the law of Eukrates", *JHS* 124, 1–15.

Blanshard, A. J. L. 2007: "The problems with honouring Samos: An Athenian document relief and its interpretation", in Z. Newby and R. Leader-Newby eds., *Art and inscriptions in the ancient world*, Cambridge, 19–37.

Brommer, F. 1978: *Hephaistos*, Mainz.

Brun, P. 2000: *L'orateur Démade*, Bordeaux.

Brun, P. 2005: "Lycurge d'Athènes: un législateur?", in P. Sineux ed., *Le législateur et la loi dans l'antiquité: hommage à F. Ruzé*, Caen, 187–200.

Davies, J. K. 1996: "Documents and 'documents' in fourth-century historiography", in P. Carlier ed., *Le IVe siècle av. J.-C. Approches historiographiques*, Nancy, 29–39.

Davies, J. K. 2005: "The origins of the inscribed Greek stela", in P. Bienkowski, C. Mee and E. Slater eds., *Writing and ancient Near Eastern society: Papers in honour of Alan R. Millard*, New York, 283–300.

Fisher, N. R. E. 2001: *Aeschines. Against Timarchos*, Oxford.

Fisher, N. R. E. 2007: "Lykourgos of Athens: Lakonian by name, Lakoniser by policy?", in N. Birgalias, K. Buraselis and P. Cartledge eds., *The contribution of ancient Sparta to political thought and practice*, Athens.

Gill, D. W. J. 2001: "The decrees to build the temple of Athena Nike (IG I^3 35)", *Historia* 50, 257–78.

Goldhill, S., Osborne, R. eds. 1999: *Performance culture and Athenian democracy*, Cambridge.

Habicht, C. 1997: *Athens from Alexander to Antony*, Cambridge, MA.

Harris, D. 1992: "Bronze statues on the Athenian acropolis: the evidence of a Lykourgan inventory", *AJA* 96, 637–52.

Hedrick, C. 1999: "Democracy and the Athenian epigraphical habit", *Hesperia* 68, 387–439.

Hintzen-Bohlen, B. 1997: *Die Kulturpolitik des Euboulos und des Lykurg*, Berlin.

Hölkeskamp, K.-J. 1994: "Tempel, Agora und Alphabet. Die Entstehungsbedingungen von Gesetzgebung in der archaischen Polis", in H. J. Gehrke ed., *Rechtskodifizierung und soziale Normen im interkulturellen Vergleich*, Tübingen, 135–64.

Hoff, R. von den 2003: "Tradition and innovation: portraits and dedications on the early hellenistic acropolis", in O. Palagia and S. V. Tracy eds., *The Macedonians in Athens 322–229 BC*, Oxford.

Humphreys, S. C. 2004: "Lycurgus of Boutadai: an Athenian aristocrat, with Afterword", in S. C. Humphreys, *The strangeness of gods. Historical perspectives on the interpretation of Athenian Religion*, Oxford, 77–129.

IALD: S. D. Lambert, *Inscribed Athenian laws and decrees, 352/1–322/1 BC. Epigraphicalessays*, Leiden, 2012.

Jameson, M. H. 1999: "The spectacular and the obscure in Athenian Religion", in S. Goldhill and R. Osborne eds., *Performance culture and Athenian democracy*, Cambridge, 321–40.

Lambert, S. D. 2002: "Afterwords. 1. *IG* II^2 417, the Eutaxia liturgy and the relief, Lawton no. 150", *ZPE* 141, 122–23 [= *IALD*, 294–96].

Lambert, S. D. 2004: "Athenian state laws and decrees, 352/1–322/1: I Decrees honouring Athenians", *ZPE* 150, 85–120 [= *IALD*, 3–47].

Lambert, S. D. 2005: "Athenian state laws and decrees, 352/1–322/1: II Religious regulations", *ZPE* 154, 125–59 [= *IALD*, 48–92].

Lambert, S. D. 2006: "Athenian state laws and decrees, 352/1–322/1: III Decrees honouring foreigners. A. Citizenship, proxeny and euergesy", *ZPE* 158, 115–58 [= *IALD*, 93–137].

Lambert, S. D. 2007a: "Athenian state laws and decrees, 352/1–322/1: III Decrees honouring foreigners. B. Other awards", *ZPE* 159, 101–54 [= *IALD*, 138–83].

Lambert, S. D. 2007b: "Athenian state laws and decrees, 352/1–322/1: IV Treaties and other texts", *ZPE* 161, 67–100 [= *IALD*, 184–218].

Lambert, S. D. 2008: "Polis and theatre in Lykourgan Athens: the honorific decrees", in A. P. Matthaiou and I. Polinskaya eds., *Mikros hieromnemon. Meletes eis mnemen Michael H. Jameson*, Athens, 53–85 [= *IALD*, 337–62].

Lambert, S. D. 2010: "Inscribed treaties 350–321: an epigraphical perspective on Athenian foreign policy", in G. Reger, F. X. Ryan and T. Winters eds., *Studies in Greek epigraphy in honor of Stephen V. Tracy*, Bordeaux, 153–60 [= *IALD*, 377–86].

Lambert, S. D. forthcoming: *The priesthoods of the Eteoboutadai*.

Lawton, C. 1995: *Attic document reliefs*, Oxford.

Liddel, P. 2003: "The places of publication of Athenian state decrees from the fifth century BC to the third century AD", *ZPE* 143, 79–93.

Lougovaya-Ast, J. 2006: "Myrrhine, the first priestess of Athena Nike", *Phoenix* 60, 211–25.

Mark, I. S. 1993: *The sanctuary of Athena Nike in Athens: architectural stages and chronology*, *Hesperia* Suppl. 26, Princeton.

Mattingly, H. B. 2000: "The Athena Nike dossier: *IG* I^3 35/36 and 64A-B", *CQ* 50, 604–606.

Osborne, M. J. 1981–1983: *Naturalization in Athens*, Brussels.

Osborne, R. 1999: "Inscribing performance", in S. Goldhill and R. Osborne eds., *Performance culture and Athenian democracy*, Cambridge, 341–58.

Parker, R. C. T. 1996: *Athenian religion. A history*, Oxford.

Parker, R. C. T. 2005: *Polytheism and society at Athens*, Oxford.

Paton, J. M. ed. 1927: *The Erechtheum*, Cambridge, MA.
Rhodes, P. J. 2010: "'Lycurgan' Athens", in A. Tamis, C. J. Mackie and S. Byrne eds., *Philathenaios. Studies in honour of Michael J. Osborne*, Athens, 81–90.
Rhodes, P. J., Osborne, R. 2007: *Greek historical inscriptions 404–323 BC*, Oxford [1st ed. 2003].
Samons, L. J. 2000: *Empire of the owl. Athenian imperial finance*, Stuttgart.
Tod, M. N. 1947: *Greek historical inscriptions. Vol. II (403–323 BC)*, Oxford.
Tracy, S. V. 1995: *Athenian democracy in transition*, Berkeley.

CHAPTER 6

Inscribing the Past in Fourth-Century Athens*

The Past in the History of Fourth-Century Athens

The past might feature rather prominently in the narrative that a modern historian would construct of the history of Athens in the fourth century BC. From an external perspective, that of Athens' role and status in the Greek world, the dominant feature before 338 was arguably the Second Athenian League – a deliberate attempt to resurrect Athens' fifth-century maritime empire, to make the past present. After 359 the main story was the astonishing growth of the power of Macedon under Philip II and Alexander, of Athens' vigorous attempts to resist, culminating in a decisive defeat at Chaironeia in 338 and a subsequent process of adaptation to a new world order in which the city's political status was radically reduced. I have argued elsewhere that an intense engagement and preoccupation with the city's past, particularly, but not only, the glory days of the fifth century, runs as a golden thread through a number of the key developments in the city's policy-making through this traumatic later phase.[1] For example, an impetus to connect with the past through the myth and ritual of religious practice contributed to a surge in the attention being directed by the city to its religious life in the Lykourgan period, to its sacrifices, festivals and theatre. The last of these highlights that this was a phenomenon that operated at more than one level: the events played out on the tragic stage connected the audience with a heroic and mythical past; but the political focus on the theatre as cultural institution – the building works, the statues of Aeschylus, Sophocles and Euripides, and so on – also served to connect the city with a period of its own history that was acquiring heroic and mythical qualities: the glory days of the fifth century. The city was seeking to emphasise and enhance its role and status as leading centre of Greek culture, a role that was rooted in the fifth century, at a time when its political power and military status were ebbing away. In a longer perspective, one which arguably runs to

---

* [This paper was first published in J. Marincola, L. Llewellyn-Jones, and C. Maciver eds., *Greek Notions of the Past in the Archaic and Classical Eras: History without Historians*. Edinburgh Leventis Studies 6 (Edinburgh, 2012), 253–75. See also the Introduction to this volume, pp. 8–9.]

1 S. D. Lambert, 'Some political shifts in Lykourgan Athens', in V. Azoulay and P. Ismard (eds), *Clisthène et Lycurgue d'Athènes: Autour du politique dans la cité classique* (Paris: Publications de la Sorbonne, 2011), pp. 175–90 [= this volume, chapter 4].

© KONINKLIJKE BRILL NV, LEIDEN, 2018 | DOI 10.1163/9789004352490_008

the present day, this second phase was much more important than the first: it marked the secular transition of Athens from a city whose external identity resided primarily in its contemporary political and military power, to one whose external identity resided primarily in its cultural heritage and prestige; a city, in other words, defined more by its past than its present.

From an internal perspective too the past loomed over Athens' fourth-century present. The prevailing democratic system and culture, in fourth-century Athenian minds, were those created by the political heroes of the past – Solon, Cleisthenes, Pericles – and inherited in their main features from the fifth century. What was new was that, outside the philosophical schools, this system and culture were no longer contentious, and that was in part because the traumatic experience of the regime of the Thirty, the narrow and brutal oligarchy imposed on Athens by the Spartans at the end of the Peloponnesian War, had made everyone a democrat. But as the growth in Macedonian power had a traumatic effect on Athens' external identity, so it transformed the city's internal political landscape. Following the failure of Athens' rebellion against Macedon after the death of Alexander in 323, Antipater had the leaders of the resistance executed, abolished the ancestral democracy and replaced it with an oligarchy in which possession of wealth was a prerequisite for political participation. The long-term effect, however, was not to uproot and destroy democracy as an aspect of Athens' distinctive identity, but to embed it as part of the city's 'heritage' from the past, to be self-consciously reactivated and reintroduced, with greater or lesser cynicism and artificiality, on several occasions over the following century, usually at the instigation or at least with the co-operation of a dominant external power.

Inscriptions as Sources for Study of Developing Attitudes to the Past

So, my thesis is that the past played an important role in fourth-century Athenian history and that the development of collective Athenian attitudes to it is accordingly an interesting and worthwhile topic of investigation. One can of course pursue it in many media, including monuments and physical artefacts of many kinds, as well as written sources.[2] I propose in this chapter

---

2 For a recent survey of appeals to the past in the fourth century, mostly in the orators, see P.J. Rhodes, 'Appeals to the past in classical Athens', in G. Herman (ed.), *Stability and Crisis in the Athenian Democracy: Proceedings of a Conference in Jerusalem, 2009, in memory of A. Fuks* (Stuttgart: Steiner, 2011), pp. 13–30.

to pursue it in a medium which is both a physical artefact and a written text: inscriptions, specifically inscribed laws and decrees. They are a type of written evidence which has some advantages, for example over the works of historians and philosophers, which reflect individual authorial or elite perspectives. Inscribed laws and decrees, I would contend, reveal much more clearly the collective attitudes of the citizens. Admittedly they were proposed by individual politicians; but they were also agreed by a majority of the citizens present and voting. And those citizens not only voted them into law, they also gave them a special significance (by no means accorded to all) by having them inscribed and set up as monuments – mostly on the Acropolis, the sacred space at the heart of the city. They are a deliberate and significant expression of the collective Athenian mind.[3]

The importance of inscriptions as a source for developing attitudes to the past is also apparent from the way that they impinge on other contemporary written sources. Beginning probably in the context of the revision and reinscribing of Athenian law in the last decade of the fifth century, a culture developed of searching out, discovering and indeed inventing 'documents' of the past, many of them inscriptions. It is a culture which develops and intensifies over the course of the fourth century, reaching a climax in Lykourgos' *Against Leokrates*. This speech contains a remarkable catalogue of examples from 'history', several of them 'documented' by inscriptions, designed to impress on the jury the importance of patriotic behaviour, with the objective of convicting a man accused of fleeing Attica in the aftermath of the battle of Chaironeia. We can also observe this development in the epigraphical record. Two of the documents referred to by Lykourgos are the 'ancestral oath of the ephebes' and the 'oath which the Greeks swore before the battle of Plataia'; and we also have inscribed versions of these two supposed 'documents', set up in the temple of Ares in Acharnai at around the same period.[4]

---

3 The weight of this significance is illustrated by the first six inscriptions listed in the Appendix, which all restore the title of *proxenos* to men whose awards are said to have been annulled by or under the Thirty; in no. 2 the proxeny actually *is* the stele. The city expresses its collective will by erecting inscriptions which express it or pulling down earlier inscriptions which contradict it; e.g. in the Prospectus of the Second Athenian League (no. 10), any stelai at Athens unfavourable to any city that joins will be torn down. See also no. 11, no. 16.

4 P. J. Rhodes and Robin Osborne, *Greek Historical Inscriptions 404–323* bc (Oxford: Oxford University Press, 2007; 1st pub. 2003), no. 88. On the discovery, invention and fabrication of inscriptions of the past at this period see especially J. K. Davies, 'Documents and "documents" in fourth century historiography', in P. Carlier (ed.), *Le IVe siècle av. J.-C.: Approches historiographiques* (Nancy: de Boccard, 1996), pp. 29–39; also C. Habicht, 'Falsche Urkunden zur Geschichte Athens im Zeitalter der Perserkriege', *Hermes* 89 (1961), pp. 1–35.

This phenomenon is eloquent witness to an increasing intensity of interest in the past as the fourth century progressed; and to a focus on inscriptions, authentic or otherwise, as sources of knowledge of the past; but the inscriptions I am going to discuss do not belong to this category of discovered or invented 'documents' of the past. They are all genuine contemporary laws and decrees, proposed by individual politicians and passed by the collective of Athenian citizens sitting in plenary as the Assembly or in committee, as the Council or as *nomothetai*. Over 750 such inscriptions survive from the fourth century. Most of them belong to one of three categories: inter-state treaties, religious regulations and, easily the most numerous, honorific decrees.

Honorific decrees are not only the most numerous category, they are also the most liable to include explicit references to the past, because the honours are invariably justified in terms of past actions. Sometimes these are simply the past actions of the honorand, but quite frequently they include the actions of his ancestors. The highest honour Athens normally bestowed on foreigners was the Athenian citizenship, by definition a hereditary status, and other honours were also often hereditary, including the most common awarded in inscribed decrees, the proxeny, which formally bestowed on the honorand the duty of representing Athenian interests in his home city. This hereditary tendency meant that honorific decrees supplied a natural peg on which to hang references to the past, and this retrospective aspect can be expressed in the physical arrangements for inscribing them: it is not uncommon for the text of a decree to refer to an earlier one in the same location honouring an ancestor, and for the later decree to specify that it be inscribed on or next to the earlier one.

I made a start on this topic elsewhere, where my focus was specifically on the Lykourgan period.[5] This chapter reports the results of a survey I have now carried out of all the c. 550 inscribed Athenian laws and decrees of 403–321. The Appendix lists the thirty-three which I have identified as of interest. I have *not* strictly listed every reference to the past in every inscription – that would include every justification clause for every honorific decree and would not have yielded very interesting results. What I have done is to identify those which contain references not only to the immediate past circumstances of the decree, but to a more distant past, or which are otherwise interesting or significant. I have covered systematically only the period to 321, a restriction driven by practical limitations on what can realistically be covered in a single chapter,

5 S. D. Lambert, 'Connecting with the past in Lykourgan Athens: An epigraphical perspective', in H.-J. Gehrke, N. Luraghi and L. Foxhall (eds), *Intentional History: Spinning Time in Ancient Greece* (Stuttgart: Steiner, 2010), pp. 225–38 [= this volume, chapter 5].

but I have included as the last item on the list one rather significant and illuminating case from the last decade of the century.

Developing Attitudes to the Past in Inscribed Fourth-Century Laws and Decrees

We may establish immediately that, before about 350, there is virtually no specific or explicit reference to any past event beyond the immediate context or rationale for the decree.

No. 7 nicely illustrates the potential for references to the past that the hereditary nature of honours created. It honours Sthorys of Thasos for his services as a seer at the battle of Knidos in 394, awarding him the Athenian citizenship. The wording of the decree makes clear that the service at Knidos was the culmination of a series of good deeds not only by himself but also by his ancestors, who were Athenian *proxenoi*, and it is specified explicitly that the new decree is to be set up next to previous decrees that honoured him, but nothing specific is said about his previous services or those of his ancestors. The focus is on the immediate context.

The main – practically the only – exception to this general silence about the past is references to the Thirty. The first six inscriptions on the list are all renewals of proxenies stated to have been destroyed by the Thirty.[6] This is consonant with other indications of the power of the memory of the Thirty in the early years of the fourth century, and of the tendency for people to define themselves and to be defined by others with reference to their relations to that regime.[7] In a remarkable number of the extant speeches of Lysias of the 390s and 380s the speaker is concerned to attack or defend actions and attitudes in relation to the Thirty; and it is an impression also conveyed by the rest of the

6 Whether no. 18 should be added to this list is unclear, as the circumstances in which this proxeny stele had 'disappeared' are not made explicit.

7 See for example A. Wolpert, *Remembering Defeat: Civil War and Civic Memory in Ancient Athens* (Baltimore: Johns Hopkins University Press, 2002), in relation to the orators; J. L. Shear, 'Cultural change, space and the politics of commemoration', in R. Osborne (ed.), *Debating the Athenian Cultural Revolution* (Cambridge: Cambridge University Press, 2007), pp. 91–115, on the significance of the regime in the development of the monumental topography of the Agora; P. J. Rhodes, 'Stability in the Athenian democracy after 403 BC', in B. Linke, M. Meier and M. Strothmann (eds), *Zwischen Monarchie und Republik: Gesellschaftliche Stabilisierungsleistungen und politische Transformationspotentiale in den antiken Stadtstaaten* (Stuttgart: Steiner, 2010), pp. 67–75, on the contribution made by the memory of the Thirty to the stability of the fourth-century democracy.

epigraphical record. The most notable set of inscriptions from the decade following the restoration of democracy in 403 is a group specifically honouring the heroes of the restoration.[8] One of them (*SEG* 28.45 [= *SEG* 52.45]) includes an epigram celebrating the collective efforts of those patriots who risked their lives by opposing the Thirty, or rather 'those who had sought to rule with unjust laws', and the extent to which these inscriptions entered popular consciousness is shown by Aeschines, who in 330, and intent on contrasting these heroes of democracy with the cowards of Chaironeia, cites this very epigram from this very inscription (Aeschin. 3.187–90).

These proxeny renewals show that in the 390s and 380s Athenians were defining not only their relations with each other in terms of attitudes to the Thirty, but also their relations with foreigners. Interestingly in at least two of the six it is (unusually) the honorands themselves who pay for the reinscription of the proxenies; it is as if they have something to prove to a new democracy still preoccupied with defining people by their attitudes to the hated regime. It may also be relevant here that, as Julia Shear has emphasised, although the Thirty were Athenians, they were not only installed with Spartan support, they were articulated in commemorative terms as if they were foreign, external enemies of the city – enemies from whom foreigners wishing to cultivate Athenian good will would, it seems, need to be careful to distance themselves.

The enduring importance of the memory of the Thirty in the first half of the fourth century is confirmed by the decrees for Eukles and Philokles, no. 17 on the list, inscribed at the same time on the same stone at some date in the decade or so before 356. Philokles has just been appointed herald of the Council and People in succession to his father, Eukles, and has had not only the decree recording his own appointment inscribed, but also the earlier decree, dating a generation earlier, which had originally appointed his father. The earlier decree justifies Eukles' appointment on the grounds of services performed by him in relation to the restoration of the democracy in 403, and the later decree includes a reference to the earlier appointment and its rationale in wording which echoes the earlier one. Your or your father's participation in the restoration of the democracy was something that was patently still guaranteed to make you popular in Athens a generation after the events. Interestingly, there are (uncertain) indications that Eukles may originally have been a foreigner who was awarded the citizenship for his services; and interestingly too, like the restored proxenies, it seems that the decrees were inscribed at the honorand's own initiative and expense. This is not so much the city making a statement

8 Well discussed by Shear, 'Cultural change'.

about the democratic credentials of Philokles and his family as Philokles making a statement about his family's own democratic credentials.[9]

Before 350 the only other specific references to a past that is at all distant from the immediate context occurs in decrees concerning relations between states, and the reference is invariably to the King's Peace, made in 386 (and subsequently renewed), or to events in the Greek world that have taken place since the King's Peace. In no. 9, of 384/3, Athens is very anxious to put across the message that its alliance with Chios is not intended in any way to threaten or undermine the King's Peace made two years earlier, and the decree refers explicitly to that Peace, and in quite a wordy fashion. In no. 10, the Prospectus of the Second Athenian League in 378/7, eight years after the Peace, the Athenians state explicitly that one of the purposes of the new League is 'so that the peace and friendship sworn by the Greeks and the King in accordance with the agreements may be in force and endure'; and the collective weight and significance of these inscribed words is confirmed by the fact that, at some subsequent point in the history of the League, they were deliberately erased from the stone. Ten years later, after the Spartan defeat at Leuktra had shaken up the balance of power, pushing Athens into alliance with Sparta against Thebes and raising questions in people's minds about the continuing relevance of the Second Athenian League, the King's Peace is still being referred to as the setter of the diplomatic framework. When envoys from Dionysios of Syracuse come to Athens in 369/8 (no. 13) they are praised not only because they are good men with regard to the people of Athens and the allies, but because they 'come in support of the King's Peace, which was made by the Athenians and the Spartans and the other Greeks'; and when, in the same year, envoys from Mytilene come to Athens inquiring about the future of the Second Athenian League (no. 14), Athens carefully spells out in its reply that it had led the league against Sparta 'when the Spartans were campaigning against the Greeks, contrary to the oaths and the agreement [= King's Peace]'.

After 386 Greek cities were operating quite consciously and deliberately within the diplomatic framework of the King's Peace: it set the parameters of Athenian inter-state relations just as the United Nations Charter, the North Atlantic Treaty and the European Union treaties set the parameters of the inter-state relations of western European states in the modern world; and it was natural for international actions to be justified with reference to it – especially perhaps international actions that might otherwise be vulnerable to criticism.

---

9 The monuments erected on public initiative in the immediate aftermath of the Thirty had, as far as Athenians were concerned, carefully emphasised collective resistance to the Thirty, not the actions of specific individuals.

There are some apparent allusions to practices common in Athens' fifth-century empire in decrees relating to the Second League: e.g. in the prohibition on Athenians owning property in member states in the Prospectus (no. 10) and in the provision in no. 12, of 373/2, that the Parians should send offerings to the City Dionysia and the Panathenaia; but the fifth-century empire is never explicitly mentioned.

After c. 350 we begin to get more explicit references to a more distant past in honorific decrees. As we have seen, in earlier decrees there are vague references to the services of ancestors. After mid-century these begin to become more specific.

The path-breaker is no. 19, of 347/6, honouring Spartokos and Pairisades, brothers who had recently succeeded their father, Leukon, as rulers of the Bosporan kingdom, a crucial source of supply of Athenian grain. The decree not only names the honorands' father, but also their grandfather, Satyros, who had ruled the kingdom between 433/2 and 389/8 – more than forty years previously. A number of factors are relevant here: the references to this ruling family in Demosthenes 20, *Against Leptines*, show that their crucial role in Athens' food supply gave their names currency in the Assembly and law-courts. Moreover the effect of this decree is to confirm for the new rulers honours, including the Athenian citizenship, which had originally been granted to Satyros and Leukon; and the text of the new inscription provides explicitly that it is to be inscribed (in fact in Piraeus) on a stele and set up 'near the one of Satyros and Leukon'. Not very many state decrees were set up in the Piraeus and it sounds as if the 'stele of Satyros and Leukon' was something of a Piraeus landmark. One wonders whether it might also be relevant that the proposer of this decree with its quiet historical allusions was Androtion the historian of Attica.[10]

This is the earliest fourth-century inscription to mention by name a foreigner whose services to Athens extended back beyond what one may perhaps characterise as the psychological hurdle of the regime of the Thirty and into the Peloponnesian War period, and it does so very unobtrusively. The defeat by Philip at Chaironeia nine years after Androtion's decree and its profound consequences in terms of the reduction of Athens' status and power – including the loss of the Second Athenian League – intensified the backward-looking tendency in the collective Athenian mind: the past – in particular the glory days of the fifth century – were a better time than the present and held powerful lessons for present conduct. This is illustrated very well by two inscriptions

---

10 It is not coincidental in relation to the topic of this chapter that another historian of Attica, Phanodemos, was to be one of the most prominent Athenians in the epigraphical record of the Lykourgan period (e.g. proposer of no. 27).

which go much further than any earlier inscribed decree, not only in that they allude in a more detailed way to events located in a more distant past, but also in that there is a clear agenda and purpose in terms of the politics of the present. The inscriptions are no. 21, a decree providing for the repair of a statue of Athena Nike originally dedicated from the spoils of Athenian victories in western Greece in the 420s, and no. 22, honouring two brothers, Phormio and Karphinas of Akarnania. I shall deal with these decrees quite briefly here.[11]

I have included a full translation of no. 21 in the Appendix. It sets out in detail the precise circumstances in which the statue was originally dedicated, mentioning specific campaigns that can be verified from Thucydides. This Nike was probably in bronze, but the measure is of a piece with one of Lykourgos' proud achievements: the restoration of the golden Nikai on the Acropolis which had been melted down for coin towards the end of the Peloponnesian War.[12] One of the elements of restoration was apparently the 'raising' of the statue (probably by increasing the height of its base). This is not only a textbook case of the use of a religious vehicle or cover to express collective national aspiration at a time when explicit expression of such aspirations was difficult – raising Victory at a time of defeat; it is also characteristic of the Lykourgan period that it does so in a way that reaches back to the past for inspiration and example, and not just to a vague, generalised past, but to a specific, 'documented' episode.

No. 22 is a more subtle case, and the past-connective agenda is less explicit, but in essence it is doing much the same thing. The two brothers being honoured in this case were leaders of a small Akarnanian contingent that had fought with the Athenians at Chaironeia and they are now being welcomed as exiles, in effect activating the honorary Athenian citizenship that had originally been awarded to their grandfather. One of the pair is named Phormio and the grandfather who had originally been granted Athenian citizenship was also Phormio. This elder Phormio was undoubtedly named for the Athenian general Phormio who campaigned successfully in western Greece during the Archidamian War – precisely the same area and period as the one alluded to by the decree about the statue of Athena Nike. And again the text of the decree refers explicitly to the earlier decree which had awarded the elder Phormio the citizenship (which must have been passed in c. 400) and which, the decree

11 I have previously discussed the decrees in Lambert, 'Connecting with the past' [= this volume, chapter 5], and returned to them in Lambert, 'Some political shifts' [= this volume, chapter 4]. On no. 22 see also J. K. Davies, 'Hegesippos of Sounion: An underrated politician', in S. D. Lambert (ed.), *Sociable Man: Essays in Greek Social History in Honour of Nick Fisher* (Swansea: Classical Press of Wales, 2011), pp. 11–24.

12 [Plut.] *Lives of Ten Orators* 852b, cf. Paus. 1.29.16.

states, was 'inscribed on the Acropolis'. The past-connective agenda here is confirmed by the identity of the proposer, the forceful anti-Macedonian politician Hegesippos of Sounion, probable author of [Demosthenes] 7, and known by the nickname 'Topknot' (*Krobylos*) for the archaic fashion in which he wore his hair. As John Davies has emphasised,[13] this should not be seen as a mere sartorial affectation, but as an eloquent symbol of a political agenda. Hairstyles, like religious statues, could be potent signifiers.

My survey has yielded just one other significant case of a historical reference in the decrees of the Lykourgan period. Again it occurs in an honorific decree and again it relates to ancestors of the honorand. It is no. 30, of 327/6, which honours a member of a famous Rhodian family of mercenary commanders, which had married into the Persian aristocracy, and one of whose members, Barsine, bore a son, Herakles, to Alexander the Great. The identity of the honorand is uncertain, but the wording of lines 29–34, in which Mentor is described as 'the father of Thymondas', suggests that it may have been this Thymondas, who is best known for commanding the Greek mercenaries for Darius against Alexander at Issos in 333. Thymondas' father was well remembered for his favourable treatment of Greek mercenaries in Egypt in the 340s, some of whom one can perhaps imagine among the Athenians who voted for this decree; but the decree also mentions two other ancestors of the honorand: Pharnabazos, satrap of Daskylion 413–387, who had co-operated with Athens in the 390s when Sparta was fighting Persia; and his son Artabazos, who had co-operated with Athenian general Chares in the 350s, when Artabazos was in revolt from the Persian king.

There does not seem here to be a deliberate attempt to connect with the fifth-century glory days: the historical points of reference all seem to be post-403. The context is military and one might perhaps construct this as, in a way, the linear descendant of those passages in Homer in which two heroes on the battlefield stand and recite their ancestry and discover their family connections. But still we have the specificity – the named ancestors – which, as we have seen, is absent from decrees of the earlier part of the century. There was a clear fashion for connecting with specific past events and people in the post-Chaironeia world, and this decree should be seen as part of that trend. One might suspect that there is also intended to be a reassuring comfort-value in these particular references. In the real world, following first Chaironeia and now Alexander's conquest of the east, Athens had in ten years been reduced from big fish in the Greek pond to political minnow in the vast new eastern Mediterranean world created and dominated by the Macedonians.

13 Davies, 'Hegesippos of Sounion'.

But Pharnabazos and Artabazos were big names to conjure with: they were indeed classic names of powerful Persian satraps, borne not only by the two specific individuals referred to here, but by a succession of Persians stretching back for as long as Greeks had had to do with Persians. The world may have changed very fast, but this decree surely projected a nostalgic reassurance – in truth perhaps an illusion – that actually it had stayed the same: there was still a Pharna- or an Arta- – or at least a descendant of one – out there; the Persian Empire had, in a sense, not disappeared after all; and Athens could still deal with its potentates on equal terms. The parallels between this decree and the one honouring the Akarnanians are rather striking, and there is perhaps another connection: Hegesippos, proposer of that decree, is best known as a virulent anti-Macedonian. The proposer of our decree is unfortunately unknown, but it is unlikely to be irrelevant that Thymondas was best known for leading the Greek mercenaries against Alexander at Issos. If connecting-with-the-past implied an aspiration to restore the Athens of its glory days, that also had implications for current attitudes and policies towards the Macedonians, a subject which divided Athenians after Chaironeia no less than it had before.

Though I do not have the space in this chapter to extend my systematic survey of historical references in Athenian laws and decrees beyond 321, I have included, as no. 33, what is, I think, the most striking example of past-referencing in the inscribed decrees of the final decades of the century. It is a decree of 307/6, proposed by the leading politician Stratokles shortly after the ousting of Demetrios of Phaleron and the so-called restoration of democracy under the aegis of Antigonos and Demetrios Poliorketes. It honours posthumously the politician Lykourgos, who had died in 325. Athens had started regularly honouring its own citizens with inscribed decrees in the 340s, but there is not one such decree among items 1–32 in the Appendix. That is because they do not mention past events, ancestors and such-like: such subject matter was part of the culture of relations with outsiders, not of relations between the equal citizens of a democracy. In contrast no. 33, the earliest extant decree awarding the so-called 'highest honours' to an Athenian (including a statue and *sitesis* in the *prytaneion*), does refer to the honorand's ancestors, Lykomedes (his great-grandfather) and Lykourgos (his grandfather), commemorating their public burial in the Kerameikos and their manly virtue (*andragathia*). This is significant in a 'democratic' context, because we are told that Lykourgos' grandfather was killed by the Thirty,[14] though, interestingly, this is not explicitly asserted in the text of the decree itself; and because the family belonged to the distinguished

14 [Plut.] *Lives of Ten Orators* 841a–b.

genos Eteoboutadai, though this too is not explicitly asserted, a perhaps more readily understandable reticence.[15] This decree, however, is past-connective in the more radical sense that it is wholly about a dead man, a figure of the past, and makes a series of striking statements about him and his achievements, asserting a heroic role for him not only on the domestic Athenian scene, but as a major figure in the wider world. The decree panders to Athenian aspirations to freedom and autonomy and to be a big player on the international stage, all of it to an extent a mirage in the world of 307/6; and there is also an element of mirage in the assertions made about Lykourgos. Consistently with the other post-Chaironeia decrees we have been considering, there is a strongly anti-Macedonian flavour about this past-connective decree; but there is little sign that, in reality, Lykourgos had pursued the openly confrontational approach to Alexander that the decree implies. There are no statements of defiance in his extant speech or in his inscribed laws and decrees; his opposition to Alexander was more subdued and implicit.[16] But the most significant point for our purposes is that it was Lykourgos who, more than anyone, was responsible for the backward-looking culture of Athens in the post-Chaironeia era; he who established authoritative texts of Aeschylus, Sophocles and Euripides and had their statues erected in the theatre; and his speech against Leokrates that marks the high-water mark for the practice of adducing documented, historical examples to inform the present. Lykourgos the great citer of historical examples has now himself become one big historical example, a role he was to continue to

---

15 Contrast the *pinax* set up by Lykourgos' son, Habron, in the Erechtheum, and illustrating the succession of priests of Poseidon Erechtheus in the *genos* (including himself) back to Boutes and Erechtheus the son of Earth and Hephaistos ([Plut.] *Lives of Ten Orators* 843e–f, cf. J. Blok and S. D. Lambert, 'The appointment of priests in Attic *gene*', *ZPE* 169 (2009), pp. 109–14). Reticence about *genos* membership is a marked feature of Athenian decrees honouring Athenians, even those which honoured priests who were appointed from *gene* (cf. S. D. Lambert, 'The social construction of priests and priestesses in Athenian honorific decrees from the fourth century BC to the Augustan period', in M. Horster and A. Klöckner (eds), *Civic Priests* (Berlin: de Gruyter, 2012), pp. 67–134).

16 On the extent to which this decree distorted historical reality see the recent papers of P. Brun, 'Lycurgue d'Athènes: Un législateur?', in P. Sineux (ed.), *Le législateur et la loi dans l'antiquité: Hommage à F. Ruzé* (Caen: Presses Universitaires de Caen, 2005), pp. 187–200; P.J. Rhodes, '"Lycurgan" Athens', in A. Tamis, C.J. Mackie and S. Byrne (eds), *Philathenaios: Studies in Honour of Michael J. Osborne* (Athens: Greek Epigraphical Society, 2010), pp. 81–90; and M. Faraguna, '"Lykourgan" Athens?', in Azoulay and Ismard, *Clisthène et Lycurgue d'Athènes*, pp. 67–88.

perform in Hellenistic Athens.[17] Stratokles' decree honouring Lykourgos is the clearest possible sign that Athens would, for the future, be living off its past.

Appendix: References to the Past in Inscribed Athenian Laws and Decrees, 403–321 BC

Abbreviations

Ag. 16: A. G. Woodhead, *The Athenian Agora. Vol. XVI: Inscriptions. The Decrees* (Princeton: American School of Classical Studies at Athens, 1997).

Davies (2011): J. K. Davies, 'Hegesippos of Sounion: An underrated politician', in S. D. Lambert (ed.), *Sociable Man: Essays in Greek Social History in Honour of Nick Fisher* (Swansea: Classical Press of Wales, 2011).

Lambert (2004): S. D. Lambert, 'Athenian state laws and decrees, 352/1–322/1: I Decrees honouring Athenians', *ZPE* 150 (2004), pp. 85–120 = Lambert (2012), pp. 3–47.

Lambert (2005): S. D. Lambert, 'Athenian state laws and decrees, 352/1–322/1: II Religious regulations', *ZPE* 154 (2005), pp. 125–59 = Lambert (2012) pp. 48–92.

Lambert (2006–7): S. D. Lambert, 'Athenian state laws and decrees, 352/1–322/1: III Decrees honouring foreigners. A. Citizenship, proxeny and euergesy'. *ZPE* 158 (2006), pp. 115–58, and 'B. Other awards', *ZPE* 159 (2007), pp. 101–54 = Lambert (2012), pp. 93–183.

Lambert (2007): S. D. Lambert, 'Athenian state laws and decrees, 352/1–322/1: IV Treaties and other texts', *ZPE* 161 (2007), pp. 67–100 = Lambert (2012), pp. 184–218.

Lambert (2010): S. D. Lambert, 'Connecting with the past in Lykourgan Athens: An epigraphical perspective', in H.-J. Gehrke, N. Luraghi and L. Foxhall (eds), *Intentional History: Spinning Time in Ancient Greece* (Stuttgart: Steiner, 2010), pp. 225–38. [= this volume, chapter 5]

Moreno (2007): A. Moreno, *Feeding the Democracy: The Athenian Grain Supply in the Fifth and Fourth Centuries BC* (Oxford: Oxford University Press, 2007).

Nat.: M. Osborne, *Naturalization in Athens* (Brussels: Koninklijke Academie voor Wetenschappen, Letteren en Schone Kunsten van België, 1981–3).

RO: P. J. Rhodes and Robin Osborne, *Greek Historical Inscriptions 404–323 BC* (Oxford: Oxford University Press, 2007; 1st pub. 2003).

Scafuro (2009): A. C. Scafuro, 'The crowning of Amphiaraos', in L. Mitchell and L. Rubinstein (eds), *Greek History and Epigraphy: Essays in Honour of P. J. Rhodes* (Swansea: Classical Press of Wales, 2009), pp. 59–86.

17 As emphasised most recently by Eric Perrin (E. Perrin-Saminadayar, *Éducation, culture et société à Athènes: Les acteurs de la vie culturelle athénienne (229–88). Un tout petit monde* (Paris: de Boccard, 2007)).

Whitehead (2008): D. Whitehead, 'Athenians in Sicily in the fourth century BC', in C. Cooper (ed.), *Epigraphy and the Greek Historian* (Toronto: University of Toronto Press, 2008), pp. 57–67.

1. *IG* II^2 6; *SEG* 29.83
Date: After 403
Description: Restoration of proxeny for Eurypylos and four brothers [from Thasos?]
Proposer: Monippides (not otherwise known)
Text: ... since the stele on which was their proxeny was destroyed under the Thirty, the secretary of the Council shall inscribe the stele at the expense of Eurypylos ...

2. *IG* II^2 52
Date: After 403
Description: Restoration of proxeny for grandson of Xanthippos
Proposer: –
Text: ... since his [grandfather?] Xanthippos was *proxenos* and the Thirty destroyed the proxeny, the secretary of the Council shall inscribe them as *proxenoi* and benefactors of the Athenians ...
Comment: The original stele for Xanthippos may be *IG* I^3 177.

3. Ag. 16.39
Date: After 403
Description: Restoration of proxeny
Proposer: –
Text: ... the secretary of the Council shall inscribe the decree on a stone stele on the acropolis, since the stele set up for them previously was destroyed under the Thirty ...

4. *IG* II^2 9; *SEG* 14.35; 32.41
Date: After 403
Description: Restoration of proxeny
Proposer: –
Text: ... since the stele set up for them previously was destroyed under the Thirty, the secretary of the Council shall inscribe ...
Comment: The original decree (of 410/9?) was perhaps inscribed below this decree.

5. *IG* II^2 66c; *SEG* 14.40; 15.83
Date: After 403
Description: Restoration of proxeny for a Kaphyan
Proposer: –
Text: ... from Kaphyai [*in Arcadia*] and ... since the stele was destroyed under the Thirty ...

6. Ag. 16.37
Date: After 403
Description: Restoration of proxeny for family from Ialysos [Rhodes]
Proposer: –
Text: … since their [father?] was *proxenos* and benefactor and the stele was destroyed under the Thirty, the secretary of the Council shall inscribe him and his brothers *proxenoi* and benefactors at the expense of …

7. Ag. 16.36; Nat. D8
Date: 394/3
Description: Citizenship grant to the *mantis* Sthorys of Thasos, for services at sea-battle (= Knidos)
Proposer: –
Text: … since his ancestors were *proxenoi* and benefactors … since Sthorys has continued his previous enthusiasm for the Athenians … he is a good man … and his ancestors previously … inscribe this decree at the expense of Sthorys on a stele where the previous decrees for him have been inscribed …
Comment: Sthorys is mentioned c. 389 in decree honouring Thasians, *IG* II^2 24.14–15.

8. *IG* II^2 31; Nat. PT 31
Date: 386/5
Description: Decree honouring Hebryzelmis, king of Odrysian Thrace
Proposer: –
Text: … he shall have everything granted to his ancestors [*? citizenship*] …

9. *IG* II^2 34; RO 20
Date: 384/3
Description: Alliance with Chios
Proposer: –
Text: … the common discussions which took place among the Greeks, have been mindful to preserve, like the Athenians, the peace and friendship and the oaths and the existing agreement which the king and the Athenians and the Spartans and the other Greeks swore [= King's Peace, 386] … there shall remain in force the peace and the oaths and the agreement … make the Chians allies on a basis of freedom and autonomy, not contravening any of the things written on the stelai about the Peace …

10. *IG* II^2 43; RO 22
Date: 378/7
Description: Prospectus of the Second Athenian League

Proposer: Aristoteles (minor politician)

Text: … so that the Spartans shall allow the Greeks to be free and autonomous, and to live at peace occupying their own territory in security [[and so that the peace and friendship sworn by the Greeks and the King in accordance with the agreements may be in force and endure]] … for those who make alliance with Athenians and the allies, the people shall renounce whatever Athenian possessions there happen to be, private or public, in the territory of those who make the alliance … for whichever of the cities making the alliance there happen to be unfavourable stelai in Athens, the Council … shall be empowered to destroy them …

11. Ag. 16.46

Date: 375?

Description: Alliance with Kephallenia

Proposer: –

Text: … *anti-Athenian laws in Kephallenia to be destroyed and erased …*

12. RO 29

Date: 373/2

Description: Decree relating to Paros

Proposer: –

Text: … in accordance with tradition (*kata ta patria*) and (the Parians shall) send for the Panathenaia a cow and panoply and for the Dionysia a cow and phallus as a commemoration (*mnemeion*) since they happen to be colonists of the Athenian people …

13. *IG* II^2 103; Nat. D 10; RO 33

Date: 369/8

Description: Decree relating to Dionysios of Syracuse

Proposer: Pandios (minor politician)

Text: … praise Dionysios the archon of Sicily, and the sons of Dionysios, Dionysios and Hermokritos, because they are good men with regard to the people of Athens and the allies, and come in support of the King's Peace, which was made by the Athenians and the Spartans and the other Greeks …

14. *IG* II^2 107; RO 31

Date: 369/8

Description: Decree relating to Mytilene

Proposer: Kallistratos (politician)

Text: … reply to the envoys who have come that the Athenians fought the war for the freedom of the Greeks and when the Spartans were campaigning against the

Greeks, contrary to the oaths and the agreement [= King's Peace], they themselves went in support, and they called on the other allies to go and render the support due to the Athenians, abiding by the oaths, against those contravening the treaty …

Comment: Context is that Mytilenean envoys have come to Athens with questions about future of the Second Athenian League following Sparta's defeat at the battle of Leuktra.

15. *IG* II^2 216 + 261 = *SEG* 14.47

Date: 365/4?

Description: Decree about *paradosis* (formal handover by treasurers to their successors) of sacred objects on Acropolis

Proposer: –

Comment: Decree refers to archonship of Kalleas (377/6) in context of *paradosis* of the statue (*agalma*) and processional vessels (*pompeia*) and everything else on the Acropolis from one year's treasurers of Athena to the next. Also refers to a decree proposed by Androtion which dealt with these matters.

16. *IG* II^2 111; RO 39

Date: 363/2

Description: Decree concerning Ioulis on Keos

Proposer: Aristophon (general who had imposed settlement on Ioulis after revolt)

Comment: Text contains extensive detail about background to decree: Chabrias had settled the island after initial revolt; then there had been a counter-revolution by men who had thrown over the stelai (i.e. those recording the settlement imposed by Chabrias), killed members of pro-Athenian party etc.

17. *IG* II^2 145; Nat. T20; Ag. 16.52

Date: 1. 402–399 2. before 356/5

Description: 1. Decree of 402–399 appointing Eukles herald of the Council and people – inscribed on same stele as no. 2 and at same time

2. Decree of before 356/5 appointing his son Philokles to same post

Proposers: 1. Eurippides (politician)

2. Melanopos (politician)

Text: 1. … since Eukles was a good man concerning the Athenian people and the return (*kathodos* – i.e. in 403/2) and the freedom of the Athenian people, he shall be herald …

2. … since Eukles the father of Philokles was a good man concerning the Athenian people and the return and the freedom of the Athenian people … and since he seems to be suitable and orderly … *he shall be herald like his father …*

Comment: This succession of heralds continued in the same family to 140/39.

18. *IG* II^2 172; *SEG* 32.67
Date: Shortly before 350
Description: Decree honouring Democharis of N-
Proposer: Kratinos (minor politician?)
Text: Since Democharis son of Nymphaios of N- is renewing the proxeny which he shows was granted to his ancestors, be it decreed by the Council, since his stele has disappeared (ἠφάνισται αὐτῶ[ι ἡ στήλη]) ...[*proposal*] ... to praise Democharis son of Nymphaios because he is a good man concerning the Athenian people, both himself and his ancestors ...

19. *IG* II^2 212; RO 64; Lambert (2006–7) no. 3; Moreno (2007) 260–79 [= *IG* II^3 1 298]
Date: 347/6
Description: Decree honouring Spartokos and Pairisades sons of Leukon, rulers of Bosporan kingdom (shortly after they succeeded their father)
Proposer: Androtion of Gargettos (historian of Attica, *FGrHist* 324)
Text: *Decree maintains reciprocal relations between Athens and the ruling dynasty of the Bosporan kingdom. Mentions Satyros (ruler 433/2–389/8, grandfather of honorands) and Leukon (ruler 389/8–349/8, father). Stele to be set up near stele of Satyros and Leukon (in Piraeus).*
Comment: Dem. 20 *Against Leptines* confirms relations with this dynasty were crucial for Athenian grain supply.

20. *IG* II^2 283; Lambert (2006–7) no. 85; Lambert (2007) 83–4; Whitehead (2008) [= *IG* II^3 1 430]
Date: c. 337?
Description: Decree honouring Ph- of Salamis
Proposer: –
Text: Honorand had brought grain cheaply from Egypt, ransomed citizens from Sicily and sent them home at his own expense, and donated a talent for the *phylake* (protection of the city).
Comment: The donation for the *phylake* is perhaps a reference to the *epidosis* following the battle of Chaironeia in 338. The context in which citizens had been ransomed from Sicily is obscure (cf. Whitehead).

21. *IG* II^2 403; Lambert (2005) no. 3; Lambert (2010) 226–8, 232 [= *IG* II^3 1 444].
Date: 340–330
Description: Decree on repair of statue of Athena Nike
Proposer: – of Lakiadai (unidentifiable)

Text: ... concerning the statement of those who were appointed by the people about the repair of the statue of Athena Nike **which the Athenians dedicated from the Ambrakiots and the (10) army at Olpai and those who stood against the Corcyraean people and from the Anaktorians**, that the Council shall decide: that the – shall bring them before the people [-] at the next Assembly (15) and put the matter on the agenda, and submit the opinion of the Council to the people, that it seems good to the Council both concerning the sacrifice to the goddess that the priestess of Athena should perform the propitiatory sacrifice on behalf of the people, since the exegete (20) requires it ... the money ... that – of the people shall give ... since the statue-maker ... made ... higher...(25) ... of the Athenians the...(30) [to praise] the statue-maker, – of Boeotia because ... of the city...[just as?] in the ...

Comment: The statue was originally dedicated from spoils of victorious campaigns in western Greece during the Archidamian War (420s) (Thuc. 3.85, 106–12, 114; 4.2–3, 46, 49).

The wording was perhaps taken from that on the original statue base. For this type of wording cf. *IG* I^{3} 522 (inscribed shield dedicated in Agora c. 425):

Ἀθηναῖοι	The Athenians [dedicated this]
ἀπὸ Λακεδ-	from the Laked-
αιμ[ο]νίων	aimonians
ἐκ [Πύ]λο	from Pylos

22. *IG* II^{2} 237; RO 77; Lambert (2006–7) no. 5; Lambert (2010) 234–5; Davies (2011) [= *IG* II^{3} 1 316]

Date: 338/7

Description: Decree honouring Phormio and Karphinas and other Akarnanian exiles

Proposer: Hegesippos of Sounion (leading anti-Macedonian politician, probable author of [Demosthenes] 7, known as 'Topknot' (*Krobylos*) for the archaic fashion in which he wore his hair

Text: ... since Phormio and Karphinas are ancestral friends of the Athenian people and preserve the good will towards the Athenian people which their forefathers handed on to them ... since the Athenian people made Phormio the grandfather of Phormio and Karphinas an Athenian, and his descendants, and the decree which did this was inscribed on the Acropolis ...

Comment: The honorands had fought with the Athenians against Philip of Macedon at Chaironeia.

23. *SEG* 12.87; Ag. 16.73; RO 79; Lambert (2007) no. 14 [= *IG* II^{3} 1 320]

Date: 337/6

Description: Law permitting the killing of anyone attempting to overthrow democracy and set up a tyranny

Proposer: Eukrates of Piraeus (executed when Macedonians abolished the Athenian democracy in 322/1)

Comment: This law seems to re-enact earlier anti-tyranny laws (e.g. law attributed to Solon by *Ath. Pol.* 8.4) and adds a prohibition on sessions of Areopagos during a revolution. However, there is no explicit reference to earlier laws.

24. *SEG* 16.55; Lambert (2005) no. 8 [= *IG* II^3 1 448]

Date: Shortly after 338/7?

Description: Makes arrangements for a festival (*to celebrate Peace of Corinth?*)

Proposer: –

Comment: Refers to 'the stele about the Peace', i.e. the Peace of Corinth with Philip II, 338/7.

25. *IG* II^2 373 + 242; Lambert (2006–7) no. 34 [= *IG* II^3 1 324]

Date: 337/6 and 322/1

Description: Decrees honouring Euenor of Akarnania (a doctor)

Proposer: Diophantos of Myrrhinous (politician)

Comment: The later decree is inscribed in a different hand but on the same stone as earlier one. Euenor was later awarded citizenship, *IG* II^2 374.

26. *IG* II^2 337; RO 91; Lambert (2005) no. 4 [= *IG* II^3 1 337]

Date: 333/2

Description: Decree granting Kitians from Cyprus right of ownership of a plot of land to build a temple of Aphrodite

Proposer: Lykourgos of Boutadai (leading politician)

Text: … about what is decided to have been the lawful (35) supplication of the Kitian merchants who are asking the people for right of ownership of a plot of land on which to found a sanctuary of Aphrodite, that the people shall decide to give the merchants (40) of the Kitians the right to own a plot of land on which to found the sanctuary of Aphrodite, **as the Egyptians have founded the sanctuary of Isis.**

Comment: The reference is probably to a recent foundation of a temple of Isis and not to a measure of Lykourgos' fifth-century BC ancestor, nicknamed 'the Egyptian' (Aristophanes, *Birds* 1296, *PCG* Kratinos F32, Pherekrates F11).

27. *IG* II^2 VII 4252; Lambert (2004) 107; Scafuro (2009) [= *IG* II^3 1 349]

Date: 332/1

Description: Decree honouring the god Amphiaraos

Proposer: Phanodemos of Thymaitadai (historian of Attica, *FGrHist* 325)

Text: … since he takes good care of those Athenians and others who come to the sanctuary …

Comment: This wording is normally used for (human) foreign honorands who have been hospitable to Athenian visitors.

28. *IG* II^2 351 + 624; RO 94; Lambert (2006–7) no. 42 [= *IG* II^3 1 352]
Date: 330/29
Description: Decree honouring Eudemos of Plataia for contributions to building of Panathenaic stadium and theatre
Proposer: Lykourgos of Boutadai (leading politician)
Text: … previously offered to the people a donation of 4,000 drachmas 'towards the war', had it been needed …
Comment: The reference is perhaps to the failed revolt against Macedon led by king Agis of Sparta in 331.

29. *IG* II^2 399; Lambert (2006–7) no. 56 [= *IG* II^3 1 358]
Date: 328/7?
Description: Decree honouring Eurylochos of Kydonia
Proposer: Demades of Paiania (leading politician)
Comment: Names [father] as earlier benefactor.

30. *IG* II^2 356; RO 98; Lambert (2006–7) no. 103 [= *IG* II^3 1 361]
Date: 327/6
Description: Honorific decree; honorand's name not preserved (Thymondas?)[18]
Proposer: –
Text: … previously his ancestors Pharnabazos and Artabazos continued to benefit the Athenian people and were useful to the people in the wars and Mentor the father of Thymondas rescued the Greeks who were campaigning in Egypt, when Egypt was taken by the Persians [in 343/2] …
Comment: Pharnabazos: Persian satrap of Daskylion 413–387. Had co-operated with Athens against Sparta in 390s (see RO no. 9, no. 10 and no. 12, with notes)
Artabazos: co-operated with Athenian general Chares in 350s (Diod. 16.22.1).
Mentor: mercenary commander for Persians in Egypt, winning over Greek mercenaries fighting for Egypt, 343/2; fled with Darius after Gaugamela, 331; went over to Alexander, with most of his sons, 330; satrap of Bactria, 329; governor of rock of Arimazes, 327 (Diod. 16.42–51 etc.)
Thymondas: commanded Greek mercenaries for Darius against Alexander the Great at Issos, 333 (Arr. *Anab.* 2.13.2, Curt. 3.3.1 etc.)

---

18 The usual identification of the honorand as an (otherwise unattested) Memnon should be rejected. The traces once visible in l. 11, and taken by Kirchner in *IG* II^2 to be from that name, were probably from the name of the proposer of the decree. See *IG* II^3.

31. *IG* II^2 360; RO 95; Lambert (2006–7) no. 43 [= *IG* II^3 1 367]
Date: 325/4
Description: Decree honouring Herakleides of Salamis
Proposer: Demosthenes of Lamptrai (minor politician)
Text: … the secretary … shall inscribe this decree and the other praises which there have been for him on stone stele and stand it on the Acropolis
Comment: The decree of 325/4 is duly followed on the stone by four earlier decrees honouring Herakleides, dating back to 330/29, which had not been inscribed at the time they were passed and had apparently been retrieved by the secretary from the state archive.

32. *IG* II^2 365; Lambert (2006–7) no. 107 [= *IG* II^3 1 375]
Date: 323/2
Description: Decree honouring Lapyris of Kleonai
Proposer: Epiteles of Pergase (minor politician)
Text: … the secretary of the Council shall inscribe this decree on the stele on the Acropolis on which is inscribed the proxeny for Echenbrotos of Kleonai the ancestor of Lapyris.
Comment: The earlier stele referred to is extant (*IG* II^2 63), inscribed in 402–377, and this decree is inscribed not on it, but on a separate stone.

33. *IG* II^2 457 (= [Plut.] *Lives of Ten Orators* 852) [See now this volume, chapter 11.]
Date: 307/6
Description: Decree honouring Lykourgos of Boutadai (who had died in 325)
Proposer: Stratokles of Diomeia (leading politician)
Text: … and Lykourgos' ancestors, Lykomedes and Lykourgos, both while living were honoured by the people, and on their deaths the people granted them public burial in the Kerameikos on account of their manly virtue… [Lykourgos] built the arsenal and the theatre of Dionysos and the Panathenaic stadium and repaired the gymnasium at the Lyceum and adorned the whole city with many other buildings, and when the Greeks were beset by fears and great dangers when Alexander overpowered Thebes [in 335] and conquered the whole of Asia and the other parts of the inhabited world, he continued implacably to oppose him on behalf of the people and showed himself unimpeachable on behalf of the fatherland and the salvation of all the Greeks throughout his life, striving for the freedom and autonomy of the city by every means … etc.

PART 4

Inscribed Laws and Decrees and Democracy

CHAPTER 7

The Rule of Law in Practice in Late Classical Athens: An Epigraphical Perspective

For it is necessary for happiness to be ruled not by the threats of a man, but by the voice of the law.[1]

HYPEREIDES, *Funerary Oration* 25

∴

1 Introduction

Belief in the rule of law was a cornerstone of Athenian democratic ideology, as it is of modern Western democratic ideology; and, as Edward Harris has persuasively argued, it was an ideal which can be observed in action in the city's institutions, systems and structures, and in the behaviours and attitudes of individual citizens of the classical Athenian democracy of the 5th and 4th centuries BC.[2] In the fourth-century democracy the rule of law was asserted in a way it had not been in the fifth by means of a formal hierarchy of legislation. The Assembly was no longer wholly unconstrained in its decision-making powers. Its decrees had henceforth to be within the law, i.e. the corpus of Athenian law as revised between 410/9 and 400/399,[3] and supplemented from time to time

1 οὐ γὰρ ἀνδρὸς ἀπειλὴν ἀλλὰ νόμου φωνὴν κυριεύειν δεῖ τῶν εὐδαιμόνων. From the swansong of the classical Athenian democracy, delivered over the dead of the first, successful, year's fighting against the Macedonians in the Lamian War in 323/2. Cited by Harris 2013, 3, along with several other expressions of the ideal, e.g. in the funerary orations by Lysias 2.19 (Corinthian War), and Pericles, Thuc. 2.37 (Peloponnesian War). Democracy and the rule of law are connected with eachother e.g. by Aeschin. 3.6 (democratic cities governed by the established laws, τοῖς νόμοις τοῖς κειμένοις, tyrannies and oligarchies by the dispositions of those in power, τοῖς τρόποις τῶν ἐφεστηκότων, cf. 1.4). This and similar ideas are a *topos* in the orators at this period, cf. e.g. Aeschin. 1.4–5, 3.169, 196; Dem. 22.46, 24.5 and 75–76, 25.20–21; Lyk. 1.3–4, cf. 20, 79, 138; Hyp. *Eux.* 5; Din. 3.16.

2 Most recently in Harris 2013. See also Harris 2006.

3 On the revision see Canevaro 2015, sect. 6; cf. Shear 2011, 70–111, 227–62. It took place in two stages: before the Thirty, 410–404 BC; and after the restoration of democracy,

© KONINKLIJKE BRILL NV, LEIDEN, 2018 | DOI 10.1163/9789004352490_009

by new laws passed under a deliberately cumbersome procedure by the whole citizen body, or a subset thereof, sitting as *nomothetai*.[4] The tension created by the requirement that decrees be within the law is vividly documented in the orators, from whom it is apparent that the *graphe paranomon*, the procedure for challenging a decree of the Council or Assembly in the courts for illegality, was a major political weapon. Over 35 *graphai paranomon* are attested in the literary record of the period 403–322;[5] and, given the prevalence of honorific decrees in the inscribed record,[6] it is worth noting that over half of these were against honorific decrees.[7] It was under this procedure, for example, that, in 330, Aeschines prosecuted Ktesiphon for proposing that Demosthenes be

403/2–400/399 BC. The following laws inscribed in Attic script as part of the first stage of this revision process are extant: *IG* I³ 104 = *OR* 183A (Draco's homicide law, 409/8 BC); *IG* I³ 105 = *OR* 183B (laws about the Council); *IG* I³ 236a (law about the trierarchy); *IG* I³ 237 (law about assessment for taxes or contributions); *IG* I³ 236b + *SEG* 39.18 + *SEG* 54.54 (law fragment, uncertainly attributed to the same law as IG I³ 236a); *SEG* 52.48B + *SEG* 57.64B + https://www.atticinscriptions.com/inscription/SEG/5248b (sacrificial calendar, 410–404 BC). From the second stage, inscribed in Ionic script, only the second revision of the sacrificial calendar is extant: *SEG* 52.48A + *SEG* 57.64A + https://www.atticinscriptions.com/inscription/SEG/5248a.

4 On the procedure and the compostion of the *nomothetai* see Canevaro 2015, sect. 7 (cf. this volume, chapter 1 n. 4, chapter 2 n. 29, chapter 9 n. 24). Aristotle *Pol.* 1292a distinguishes types of democracy governed by the rule of law from more despotic types in which the mass of the People is unconstrained by the law in its making of decrees and demagogues flourish, cf. Liddel 2016, 311.

5 Hansen 1991, 205–12, cf. Hansen 1974. The earliest attested cases in fact pre-date the revision of the laws at the end of the fifth century. Earliest is Andoc. 1.17, 22, a successful *graphe paranomon* brought in 415 (cf. Canevaro 2015, sect. 5). To Hansen's figures need to be added the *graphai* (at least some of which were *graphai paranomon*) referred to in Hyp., *Diondas* (below n. 7).

6 87% of extant inscribed laws and decrees of 352/1–322/1 BC of discernible content are honorific. Cf. chapter 2.3 with Appendix 1.

7 The figures given by Hansen 1991, 211 are, from a total of 38 *graphai paranomon* (including the small number from before 403/2 BC), 19 are against honorific decrees, 13 against decrees of other sorts, 6 against decrees of unknown type. In Hyp., *Against Diondas*, first published by Carey et al. 2008, Hypereides alleges (sect. 3) that Diondas brought fifty *graphai* against opponents of Philip II. Of these, apart from the *graphe paranomon* against Hypereides' and Demomeles' award of a crown to Demosthenes (which was already known, cf. Hansen 1974, 36 no. 26), he mentions specifically *graphai* against Charidemos (3.15–17, perhaps a *graphe paranomon* against the decree honouring him, though Hypereides' language is opaque), Lykourgos (3.19–20, an unspecified *graphe paranomon* and a *graphe asebeias* before the *basileus*), fifteen against Demosthenes (3.20–21, unspecified for what), and three on the same day against Hypereides himself (3.22, unspecified for what).

awarded a crown. It is clear from Aeschines' speech in the case how deeply embedded the *graphe paranomon* was in fourth-century Athenian political culture: the famous, long-lived politician, Aristophon of Azenia, boasted that he had been acquitted in no less than seventy-five *graphai paranomon*, while Kephalos was proud never to have been prosecuted for any of his proposals. Aeschines implies that it was not only a weapon to be used against political enemies; friends sometimes found themselves in court against friends, so common was this type of prosecution.[8] In this paper I shall explore some of the ways that commitment to the "rule of law" in general and anxiety about potential *graphai paranomon* in particular are evident in the corpus of inscribed laws and decrees of 352/1–322/1 BC; and I shall argue that there are indications in this body of evidence that this preoccupation with legality reached a peak of intensity in the very last years of the classical democracy, in the period after the battle of Chaironeia.

2 Corrections and Supplements

A preoccupation with legality (among other considerations) is apparent, first of all, in "corrections", a type of amendment in inscribed decrees similar in effect to the "rider" (i.e. an amendment to a decree proposed in the Assembly), but apparently introduced as an afterthought, it seems after the "final" text of the decree had been committed to writing; and in the related phenomenon, clauses permitting the Council to make provisions supplementary to or amending the Assembly's decree. The earliest of these in this corpus combines both. A correction tacked onto the end of the decree of 352/1 relating to the sacred tract (*hiera orgas*) on the borders of Athens and Megara, it empowers the Council to make supplementary provisions:

> The following correction is made:
> if this decree is lacking in any respect, the Council shall be empowered to vote whatever seems to it to be best.[9]

---

8 Aeschin. 3.194–195. Penalties for the proposer ranged from none at all in the case of an action brought after more than a year, through to a fine, small or large, to permanent deprivation of citizen rights, *atimia*, in the case of a third offence (Hansen 1991, 207; Demades fell foul of the last rule, Diod. 18.18.2, and Philippides was at risk of doing so in the case brought against him by Hypereides, see *Phil.* 11).

9 [τ]άδε ἐπαν[ο]ρθοῦται· | [ἐὰν δέ του προσδέηι τόδ]ε τὸ ψήφισμα, τὴν βουλὴν κυρίαν εἶνα|[ι ψηφίζεσθαι, ὅ τι ἂν αὐτῆι δ]οκῆι ἄριστον εἶναι. *IG* II³ 1, 292, 84–86.

The decree in question is long and complex, establishing an elaborate procedure for consulting the Delphic oracle about whether or not the sacred tract should be cultivated, and while the anxiety generating this correction may have to do in part with concern about the legality of the decree, it may also be driven more broadly by concern for propriety on what was a sensitive topic, both from a religious point of view, and in terms of relations with Megara,[10] and a straightforward recognition that there were detailed points on which the Council was going to need to amplify and adjust what the Assembly had agreed.

A similar provision is included, not as a correction, but embedded in the body of the decree providing in 325/4 BC for the despatch of a colony to the Adriatic, *IG* II^3 1, 370. Again it empowers the Council to make supplementary provisions relating to the despatch of the colony, though in this case the proviso is added that the Council should not undo anything decreed by the People.[11] Again this is a major decree providing for a complex operation and the concern is perhaps more likely to be a straightforward, realistic, recognition that the Council will need to work through and fill in some of the detail of the arrangements. It is less easy to see the reason for the inclusion of a similar clause empowering the Council to make supplementary provisions in the decree of ca. 345–320, providing for exiles, *IG* II^3 1, 404, 7–9.[12] The decree is fragmentary and there may have been some complex, innovative or unusual feature that generated administrative anxiety on the part of the proposer, for example in relation to the provision for travel expenses in ll. 3–5, which might (the text is too fragmentary to be certain) have applied to the exiles rather than, as was much more common, to Athenian officials; but the clause is inserted between two quite formulaic provisions: a "protection" clause (5–7) requiring the Council and the generals to take care of the exiles, and a clause stipulating the application of the decree until the exiles' return home (9–10). In any case, concern about the legality of the decree, while a possible factor, may again not be the main driver here.

Such a concern is much more apparent in the second explicit "correction" clause in this corpus. In 323 BC Athens awarded the citizenship to its close ally and leader of the pro-Athenian party in Sikyon during the Lamian War,

10 A context of difficult relations with Megara is implied by *FGH* 324 Androtion F30 and *FGH* 328 Philochoros F155. Cf. https://www.atticinscriptions.com/inscription/IGII31/292.

11 ἐὰν δέ τοῦ προσδέει τόδε | τὸ ψήφισμα τῶν περὶ τὸν | ἀπόστολον, τὴν βουλὴν | κυρίαν εἶναι ψηφίζεσθαι | μὴ λύουσαν μηθὲν τῶν | ἐψηφισμένων τῶι δήμωι. (95–100).

12 εἰὰν δέ του π|ροσδέηι τόδ]ε τὸ ψήφισμα, τὴν β[ουλὴν κυρίαν εἶναι ψηφίζ|εσθαι, ὅ τι ἂν α]ὐτῆι δοκῆι ἄριστ[ον εἶναι.

Euphron. The decree exists in a very fragmentary original version, as inscribed during the war, *IG* II^3 1, 377 (323/2) and in a much better preserved reinscription by the briefly restored democracy of 318/7, *IG* II^3 1, 378.[13] A correction (so expressed in the original version of the decree, 377, 5[14]), proposed by Pamphilos son of Euphiletos (so expressed at 378, 32[15]), rectifies the omission, apparently by pure oversight, from the original text of the decree, of the provision for the Assembly to take a second vote on Euphron's citizenship. This second vote was a legal requirement at this period,[16] and the correction makes the concern with procedural legality quite explicit in providing that the vote was to be put to the next Assembly "in accordance with the law" (κατὰ τὸν νόμον, 377, 8 and 378, 34–5).[17] In the euphoric atmosphere at Athens in the winter of 323/2 following the initial Athenian successes against Macedon (the decree was passed in the fifth prytany) it does not seem likely that this "correction" was driven by specific anxiety about a potential, politically motivated, *graphe paranomon* so much as by a genuine, principled, concern for, and for displaying a commitment to, legality. As Hypereides had just recently emphasised at the time this decree was passed, it was "necessary for the happy to be ruled ... by the voice of the law". It was, after all, one of the ideals for which the war was being fought.

13 As we learn from the second decree inscribed on the stone in 318/7 BC Euphron had in the meantime been killed resisting the reimposition of the Macedonian garrison on Sikyon after the defeat of the allies in the Lamian War (*IG* II^2 448, 54) and the original version of the decree honouring him in 323/2 BC had been destroyed.

14 τάδε ἐπανορθοῦτ[αι·...... 12...... δοῦ|να]ι δὲ τὴν ψῆφον κτλ. The lacuna might perhaps have contained a reference to the proposer.

15 τάδε Πανφίλου τοῦ Εὐφιλήτο⟨υ⟩· [δοῦναι δὲ τὴν ψῆ]|φον κτλ.

16 A requirement since perhaps 385/4 BC or soon after, it is first attested in *IG* II^2 103 = *RO* 33, 33–36 (369/8 for Dionysios of Syracuse and his sons, see notes in *RO*). Other cases of omission of the provision are known, including *IG* II^3 1, 335, of 334/3 BC, for Amyntor, but the bottom of the decree is not preserved and as M. Osborne 2010–2013, 67 n. 23, observes, it could have been recorded later in the text (as in M. Osborne 1981–1983, D64), or added as an amendment or correction, as with the decrees for Euphron.

17 An explicit reference to the law is not usual in this context, missing e.g. from *IG* II^3 1, 452, 24–25 (for Peisitheides of Delos, ca. 334 BC); 480, 13–16 (for a Plataian, 325–322/1). It does, however, apparently occur in the very fragmentary grant of mid-iv BC, 490, 5–10: "... and the prytany of the tribe Pandionis shall put the vote about – at the next Assembly according to the law ([κατὰ τὸν ν]όμο[ν])".

3 Incidental References to the Law in Decrees

A preoccupation with legality is also reflected in numerous incidental general references to the law in decree texts. While these occur before 338, as will be seen from the following discussion, they are more numerous in decrees dating after the battle of Chaironeia. Decrees may place specific obligations on those officials whom the laws make responsible for certain matters;[18] and officials are commonly honoured for performing their duties "according to the law(s)".[19] Moreover, if an official is adjudged at his *euthynai* to have fulfilled his office justly, he may "seek benefits from the People", as the law encourages him to do (*IG* II^3 1, 469, 28–31, of ca. 330). Foreigners do not escape the warm embrace of the law when they reside at Athens or otherwise come into contact with the city. A foreign honorand may be praised because he and his ancestors, "paid all the capital taxes (*eisphorai*), which the laws required of them" (*IG* II^3 1, 419, 9–11, of ca. 340–320). Foreigners could also petition the Council or People, and if their request was granted, they were deemed to have made a lawful petition

18 E.g. ἐπι]μελεῖσθαι [δ]ὲ τῆς ἱερᾶς ὀργάδος καὶ τῶν ἄλλω|[ν ἱερῶν τεμεν]ῶν τῶν Ἀθήνησιν ἀπὸ τῆσδε τῆς ἡμέρας εἰς τὸν | [ἀεὶ χρόνον οὕ]ς τε ὁ νόμος κελεύει περὶ ἑκάστου αὐτῶν καὶ…("there shall have oversight of the sacred tract and the other [sacred precincts] at Athens from this day for all time both those whom the law requires for each of them, and…", *IG* II^3 1, 292, 18, of 352/1); δοῦναι δὲ αὐτίκα εἰς] θυσίαν 𐅄 δραχμὰς τοὺς ταμίας, οὓς εἴρηται ἐκ τοῦ νόμου ("and the treasurers specified in the law shall immediately give 50 drachmas…", 306, 25–26, of 343/2).

19 Officials were required when rendering their accounts of their period of office (*euthynai*) to demonstrate that they had performed their office according to the laws. Thus, before his *euthynai* (pryt. 9 of his year of office, 336/5) Phyleus of Oinoe τὴν ἀρχὴν ἄρχει δικαίως καὶ κατὰ | τοὺς ν]όμους ("is performing his office justly and according to the laws", *IG* II^3 1, 327, 34–35, cf. 60 for his colleagues in office), and after his *euthynai* (pryt. 3 or 8 of 335/4), ἦρξεν καλ[ῶς κ]αὶ κ[ατὰ τοὺς νόμους ("he performed his office well and according to the laws", 327, 8), and the payment for his crown is to be legalised, ὅπως | ἂ]ν καὶ οἱ ἄλλοι οἱ καθιστάμε[νοι γραμματεῖς φιλοτιμῶντα]|ι πρός τε τὴν βουλὴν καὶ τὸν δ[ῆμον, ἄρχειν κατὰ τοὺς νόμου]|ς καὶ εἶναι χρήσιμοι τῶι δήμ[ωι τῶι Ἀθηναίων· ("so that others who are appointed [secretaries] may [show love of honour] towards the Council and the People, [in performing their office according to the law]s", 327, 20–23). In *IG* II^3 1, 323, 14 (337/6?) the crown is to be awarded to the official, probably the secretary of the Council, ἐπειδὰν τὰς εὐθύνας] δῶι, δόξ|[αντ' ἄρξαι τὴν ἀρχὴν δικαίως ? καὶ κατὰ τοὺς] νόμους ("when, having passed his *euthynai*, he is deemed to have performed his office justly and according to the laws", cf. 417, 21–2). In *IG* II^3 1, 359 (of 328/7) Androkles, priest of Asklepios, ἐπιμελεῖται το[ῦ] | τε ἱεροῦ καὶ [τῶν] ἄλλων, ὧν αὐτῶι οἱ νόμοι πρ|οστάττουσιν, κα̣λ̣ῶς καὶ εὐσεβῶς ("is managing both the sanctuary and the other things which the laws require of him well and piously, 13–15, cf. 402, 11, ca. 345–35; 476, 21, 326/5–324/3).

(ἔννομα ἱκετεύειν).[20] Miscreants meanwhile (it is mainly Athenians that are at issue in such contexts) are to be faced with the full force of the law. *IG* II³ 1, 399, 10 (of 348 or 343) instructs the Council to bring forward a proposal to the Assembly to ensure the punishment, "according to the laws", of those who had invaded Eretria; *IG* II³ 1, 431, 3–4 (of 337–325), is a fragment of a law providing for application of penalties prescribed indeed "in the law"; and *IG* II³ 1, 447, 61 (of 335–330), requires the sacred officials (*hieropoioi*) in charge of the Panathenaia to organise the procession and "punish those who are disobedient with the punishments from the laws" (this the only instance where foreigners seem also be in view). Finally, *IG* II³ 1, 370, 77 (of 325/4), requires the Council to oversee the despatch of the colony to the Adriatic, punishing disorderly trierarchs "according to the laws".

One of the most familiar formulae in decree texts of this period is that providing for the public funding of a decree stele "from the People's fund for expenditure on decrees", ἐκ τῶν εἰς τὰ κατὰ ψηφίσματα ἀναλισκομένων τῶι δήμωι. This matter too, however, was in fact regulated by law, as we learn from *IG* II³ 1, 322, 25, of 337/6, where it is specified that the treasurer of the People is to pay 30 drachmas for inscribing a decree "according to the law" (κατὰ τὸν νόμον), while in *IG* II³ 1, 359, 31, of 328/7 payment for the stele is to made "from whatever source the laws ordain" (ὅθεν οἱ νόμοι κελεύουσι[ν]). We can not rule out that there were specific reasons for these references to the law, for example that a law on this topic had just been passed in 337/6, but it seems more likely that it is not coincidental that both these references occur in the post-Chaironeia period and that we should take them as an indicator of an intensified preoccupation in that period not only with actually complying with the law, but with displaying that compliance on the surface of the text. *IG* II³ 1, 359 honoured a priest of Asklepios and might be supposed not to have been hugely contentious;[21] *IG* II³ 1, 322, however, was proposed by Demades, honoured a courtier of Philip II and is likely to have been highly contentious, with a *graphe*

---

20 Thus for the merchants of Kition, granted their petition to found a sanctuary of Aphrodite (337, 34–35, of 333/2); or for Asklepiodoros, who had petitioned the Council for honours, including *isoteleia*, in recognition of his exploits "fighting against the enemy on the trireme of Chares of Aixone" (418, 5–9, of ca. 340–320).

21 That decrees honouring priests, though quite common in the epigraphical record, were not generally contentious, is suggested by the fact that references to such decrees are lacking in the literary record of this period, largely the orators (see Liddel 2016, 319).

paranomon not only a possibility, but quite likely.[22] The reference to the law here looks to be a quite deliberate pre-emptive strike against such an attack.

4 Reference to Specific Laws

Apart from these general references to "the law(s)", two specific laws, passed in the post-Chaironeia period, are referred to quite frequently in inscribed decrees. Both of them involve the imposition of limitations on foreigners with special privileges. In 334/3 a law was apparently introduced which restricted the phratries to which foreigners granted the Athenian citizenship by decree could be admitted, and thereafter it is referred to in decrees bestowing citizenship as limiting the new citizen's choice of phratry.[23] This limitation was perhaps similar in character to the limitations imposed on newly enfranchised Plataians in 427, preventing them from being candidates for an archonship or priesthood, and patently motivated by a concern that those eligible for the city's most sensitive offices be of pure blood.[24] We do not know of any phratries membership of which conferred eligibility for city priesthoods – this was

---

22 Hypereides brought a *graphe paranomon* against Demades at this time (338–336) for proposing a proxeny for another ally of Philip II, Euthykrates of Olynthos (Hyp. F14.76–86 Jensen = Hansen 1974, 37 no. 28) and against Philippides for proposing an honorary decree for the presiding committee (*proedroi*) who chaired the Assembly when honours for Philip II and/or other leading Macedonians were carried (Hyp. *Phil.* = Hansen 1974, 39 no. 32, cf. Whitehead 2000, 31–32). Particularly relevant to the sensitivity of inscribing such decrees is Hypereides' remark in relation (it seems) to the former (F14.79) that "it would be much more just for the stele to have been placed in the accursed refuse dumps (ἐν τοῖς ὀξυθυμίοις) than in our sanctuaries (ἢ ἐν τοῖς ἡμετέροις ἱεροῖς)." In F14.76 Hypereides parodies the decree: Δημάδης Δημέου Παιανιεὺς εἶπεν· ἐπειδὴ Εὐθυκράτης προὔδωκε τὴν ἑαυτοῦ πατρίδα Ὄλυνθον καὶ αἴτιος ἐγένετο τὰς πόλεις τῶν Χαλκιδέων οὔσας τετταράκοντα ἀναστάτους γενέσθαι … ("Demades son of Demeas of Paiania proposed: since Euthykrates betrayed his own fatherland, Olynthos, and caused the cities of the Chalkidians, being forty, to be laid waste …"). This may betray a sensitivity to Demades' decree-drafting style. At least, it is perhaps not coincidence that the only other instance of the expression, αἴτιος ἐγένετο, in this corpus is (restored, but persuasively) in the decree proposed by Demades for Eurylochos of Kydonia, who had ransomed Athenian captives in Crete and sent them home at his own expense and "was responsible for their having been saved", [αἴτιος | ἐ]γένετο τοῦ σωθῆναι, *IG* II^3 1, 358, 17–18.

23 *IG* II^3 1, 333, 29; 335, 15–16; 378, 22–23; 452, 22–23; 453, 3–4; 480, 12–13.

24 [Dem.] 59.106.

generally a function of *gene* within them – but it is not implausible that there were phratries which had such, or other religiously sensitive, functions.[25]

Second, at some point between 329 and 325 a law appears to have been passed which prevented foreigners awarded the right to own land in Attica (*enktesis*) from acquiring public or sacred land. The restriction is referred to explicitly in the grant to the doctor, Euenor, in 322/1,[26] but this may also be the significance of the phrase, "according to the law", with which *enktesis* grants are qualified from 325/4 onwards.[27]

5 Provision for Passage of Laws to Legalise Decrees

There is another indication of an intensified preoccupation with the legality of decrees in the latest phase of the classical democracy. In a manner unprecedented in earlier Athenian decrees, three decrees of the post-Chaironeia period actually make provision for laws to be introduced to legalise specific actions that the Assembly wished to take by decree, all of them, characteristically of the period, in the financial sphere. In 329/8 the Assembly decided to award 100 drachmas to the managers of the Amphiaraia festival for a sacrifice and dedication, but this financial allocation was outside the law, and so the treasurer of the People was required to "advance" (προδανεῖσαι) the money, and an amendment to the law was to be put to the next meeting of the *nomothetai* to legalise the arrangement (*IG* II^3 1, 355).[28] Comparable arrangements were made in 335/4 to legalise the award of a 1,000 drachma crown to Phyleus of Oinoe (*IG* II^3 1, 327, 15–20) and in ca. 334 to legalise payment of 1 drachma a

---

25 Cf. Lambert 1993, 53.

26 εἶναι ... ἔγκτησιν ἀπέχοντι τῶν [κ]ọị[νῶν καὶ τῶν ἱε|ρῶ]ṿ (*IG* II^3 1, 324, 44–46).

27 First at *IG* II^3 1, 367, 20, of 325/4. Also at 379, 12 (323/2?), 468, 16–17 (after 329?), 473, 12 (329–322?), 474, 8–9 (ca. 329–322), 475, 8–9 (ca. 329–322), 478, 4 (ca. 325?), 479, 14 (after 329?). The phrase does not appear in *IG* II^3 1, 352, 29, of 330/29. For a different interpretation see Pečirka 1966, 144–45; Henry 1983, 214–15.

28 This is followed on the stone by the most obscure clause in the corpus of decrees of this period (ll. 41–5): δοῦναι δὲ καὶ τὰς τριάκοντα δ|[ρ]αχμὰς τὸν ταμίαν τοῦ δήμου τοῖς | ạἱρεθεῖσιν ἐπὶ τὸν ἀγῶνα, ἃς εἴρη|ται διδόναι ἐν τῶι νόμωι τῶι αἱρε|θέντι ἐπὶ τὴν εὐταξίαν· "and the treasurer of the People shall give to those elected to manage the competition (scil. at the Amphiaraia) the thirty drachmas which are specified in the law to be given to the man elected to be in charge of good order". The specific context and significance of this accounting adjustment is wholly obscure; but the broader preoccupation with displaying careful attention to financial legality, even in relation to the relatively paltry sum of 30 dr., is clear enough.

day subsistence to Peisitheides of Delos (*IG* II³ 1, 452, 41–46). In general terms the reason why an amendment to the law was required in these cases is clear enough: the *merismos*, the system by which money was allocated to different funds, was governed by law, and these arrangements clearly breached that law in some way. The specific reasons for the breach in these three cases are unclear, however. One can see that the arrangement for Peisitheides might have been novel enough to require legislation, but it is obscure why it was needed in the other two cases, which do not appear on the surface to be different from many other honorific awards. In a broader perspective, however, we should surely interpret these instances as evidence not only for a real concern with the legality of decrees, but for displaying that concern on the surface of the decree, against the background of a culture in which the *graphe paranomon* was an ever-present threat.

6 Chronological Distribution of Inscribed Laws

There are ca. 570 extant inscribed decrees of 403/2–322/1, but only a handful of inscribed laws. As we saw in chapter 2.9 the main reasons for this disparity are likely to be that new laws were in reality passed much less frequently than decrees, and also perhaps that, after the revision of the laws at the end of the fifth century, texts of the laws passed under the new system were deposited in the new archive in the Metroon, which was perhaps intended specifically for that purpose, and had removed some of the impetus for inscribing them on stone. Though there are very few inscribed fourth-century laws extant, their distribution in time does display a discernible acceleration. There are none at all dating to between 403 and 376; ca. six from the 36 years, 375/4–339/8;[29] and probably a little more than that from the 17 years, 338/7–322/1, viz.:[30]

---

29 Law on silver coinage, 375/4 (*SEG* 26.72 = *RO* 25); grain tax law, 374/3 (*SEG* 47.96 = *RO* 26); unpublished law concerning Hephaistos, Athena Hephaistia and silver coinage, 354/3 (*SEG* 54.114; 56.26); law on Eleusinian first-fruits, 353/2 (*IG* II² 140 = *I Eleus.* 142). To these four should probably be added: the regulations of the Eleusinian Mysteries, 367/6–348/7 (*I Eleus.* 138, cf. *SEG* 30.61); and the "unpublished" law on the repair of the sanctuary of Artemis at Brauron (*SEG* 52.104), which may have been reinscribed ca. 200 BC (Lambert 2007, 80 = *IALD*, 208), but is perhaps to be dated originally ca. 354/3–343 (Rhodes 2013, 215 with n. 85 argues for a date before 343; unless it is a product of reinscription from an archival copy, the inclusion of father's name and demotic of the proposer would indicate a date after 354/3). Note also the very fragmentary inscription apparently mentioning *nomothetai*, Walbank 2008, 10–11 no. 7 (*SEG* 58.95, dated by the editor "before mid-iv BC").

30 Those marked * are either opisthographic or have smooth backs, which, at this period, is almost exclusively a feature of inscribed laws rather than decrees. Cf. Lambert 2005,

IG II^3 1, 320. Law against tyranny (337/6).
IG II^3 1, 429. Law providing for the repair of walls in Piraeus, with appended contract specifications (*syngraphai*) (ca. 337).*
IG II^3 1, 431. Provisions relating to penalties and "exposure" (*phasis*) from a law whose content is otherwise unknown (ca. 337–325).[31]*
IG II^3 1, 445. Two laws relating to cult objects, on the acropolis and elsewhere (ca. 335).*
IG II^3 1, 447. Law making provision for funding of Little Panathenaia, followed by decree providing for sacrifices at the festival (ca. 335–330).

and perhaps also:

IG II^3 1, 448. Makes provisions for an (Athenian or Macedonian) festival.*[32]
IG II^3 1, 449. Makes provisions for a festival.*[33]
IG II^3 1, 550. End of text (law?) providing for liturgists to dedicate *phialai*, followed by list of liturgists (333/2 or 332/1?).[34]

The number of inscribed laws increases, therefore, as time progresses. We can not necessarily infer from this that laws were *passed* more frequently over time; but it does seem that laws were *inscribed* more frequently over time. This may to an extent be a product of a general snowballing of the epigraphical habit;[35] and it may also be relevant that the religious and financial regeneration of the city were at the top of the policy agenda after 338, and these were spheres of policy which were heavily regulated by law; but against the background of the

---

129–30 = *IALD*, 56–58. Laws were required for these measures because they impacted on matters governed by existing laws, in particular the city's constitution, or its religious (including the sacrificial calendar, cf. above n. 3) and financial systems. *IG* II^3 1, 429, for example, is concerned to a large extent with the financial system for funding wall repairs, and refers (l. 12) to a "previous law" on the subject. Why the arrangements for the sacrifices at the Little Panathenaia (*IG* II^3 1, 447 II) are made by Assembly decree is unclear; but the decree makes provisions for the application of funding raised under the provisions of the law which is preserved on the upper part of the inscription (447 I), so perhaps the Assembly had been commissioned to act by the *nomothetai* (cf. Lambert 2005, 144 = *IALD*, 79–80).

31 For comparable provisions cf. the silver coinage law, *RO* 25, 23–28.

32 Cf. Lambert 2005, 129–30, 145 no. 8, 146–48 = *IALD*, 56–58, 81 no. 8, 85–88.

33 Cf. Lambert 2005, 129–30, 145 no. 9, 148–49 = *IALD*, 56–58, 81 no. 9, 88–89.

34 For the case for interpreting the text as from a law see Lambert 2000, 56 = *IALD*, 228.

35 Approximately the same number of laws and decrees will be included in *IG* II^3 1 fasc. 1, covering the 51 years 403/2–353/2 as were included in fasc. 2, covering the 31 years 352/1–322/1.

rest of this paper one might suggest that a further relevant factor was an intensified preoccupation in the period after Chaironeia with displaying the rule of law through the inscribed record.

7 Conclusion

This paper has sought to demonstrate that a commitment to the rule of law is manifest in a number of ways in the inscribed laws and decrees of 352/1–322/1. It can be seen as being motivated by a general, principled, commitment to legality, by a self-conscious desire to display that commitment as part of Athens' democratic identity and heritage, and more specifically by a self-interested concern on the part of proposers to protect decrees from being attacked as illegal by *graphe paranomon*. It has also argued that there are indications of an intensified preoccupation with the rule of law in the very last phase of the classical democracy after 338: explicit "corrections" to decrees, and provisions for the Council to supplement decrees, occur throughout the corpus, but the one correction that is most clearly motivated by concern for the legality of a decree, that in the decree for Euphron of Sikyon, occurs in 323/2. Again, there are references to, and stipulations requiring conduct to be in accordance with, the law, throughout the period, but these occur more frequently in decree texts after 338. The only reference requiring public provision for payment for a stele to be "according to the law" occurs in Demades' decree of 336 honouring a courtier of Philip II that was certain to be controversial and very likely to be attacked by *graphe paranomon*. Two specific laws, both restricting privileges awarded to foreigners, are referred to frequently in decrees post-dating 338, and it is only between 338 and 322 that decrees provide explicitly for laws to be passed legalising what would otherwise be illegal proposals. Finally, though there are also other possible explanations for the phenomenon, it may also be relevant that new laws were more frequently inscribed after 338. There was, in a sense, no better way to display a commitment to the rule of law than to inscribe more laws on stone.

How are we to explain this intensified preoccupation with the rule of law after Chaironeia? It is, I suggest, a reaction to defeat comparable to others that are detectable in the epigraphical record, including an intensified preoccupation with religious observance, and a concern to connect with the city's past and promote its cultural heritage.[36] It is part of a self-conscious attempt to embed and promote Athens' distinctive democratic identity, apparent for

36 See chapters 4, 5 and 6.

example in the law against attempts to undermine democracy,[37] and the attention directed to the cult of Demokratia.[38] Athenians at this period were attempting to recapture, emphasise and reinforce the distinctive features that made Athens the greatest city of Greece, and one of those features was a commitment to the rule of law.

Bibliography and Abbreviations

Canevaro, M. 2015: "Making and changing laws in ancient Athens", in E. M. Harris and M. Canevaro eds., *Oxford handbook of ancient Greek law*, Oxford forthcoming, this chapter published online 2015.

Carey, C. et al. 2008: "Fragments of Hyperides' *Against Diondas* from the Archimedes palimpsest", ZPE 165, 1–19.

Hansen, M. H. 1974: *The sovereignty of the people's court in the fourth century* BC *and the public action against unconstitutional proposals*, Odense.

Hansen, M. H. 1991: *The Athenian democracy in the age of Demosthenes*, Oxford, Blackwell.

Harris, E. M. 2006: *Democracy and the rule of law in classical Athens: essays on law, society and politics*, Cambridge.

Harris, E. M. 2013: *The rule of law in action in democratic Athens*, Oxford.

Henry, A. S. 1983: *Honours and privileges in Athenian decrees: the principal formulae of Athenian honorific decrees*, Hildesheim.

IALD: *Inscribed Athenian laws and decrees 352/1–322/1* BC. *Epigraphical essays*, Leiden, 2012.

Lambert, S. D. 1993: *The phratries of Attica* (^{2} 1998), Ann Arbor.

Lambert, S. D. 2000: "Ten notes on Attic inscriptions", *ZPE* 135, 51–62 [= *IALD*, 221–39].

Lambert, S. D. 2005: "Athenian state laws and decrees, 352/1–322/1: II Religious regulations", *ZPE* 154, 125–59 [= *IALD*, 48–92].

Lambert, S. D. 2007: "Athenian state laws and decrees, 352/1–322/1: IV Treaties and other texts", *ZPE* 161, 67–100 [= *IALD*, 184–218].

Liddel, P. 2016: "Honorific decrees of fourth-century Athens: trends, perceptions, controversies", in C. Tiersch (ed.), *Die Athenische Demokratie im 4. Jahrhundert. Zwischen Modernisierung und Tradition*, Berlin, 335–57.

OR: R. Osborne and P. J. Rhodes, *Greek historical inscriptions 478–404 BC*, Oxford, forthcoming.

Osborne, M. J. 1981–1983: *Naturalization in Athens*, Brussels.

37 *IG* II^3 1, 320 of 337/6.

38 See Introduction, n. 15.

Osborne, M. J. 2010–2013: "Additions (real and imagined) to the corpus of Athenian citizenship decrees", *Horos* 22–25, 53–78.

Parker, R. 1996: *Athenian religion. A history*, Oxford.

Pečirka, J. 1966: *The formula for the grant of enktesis in Attic inscriptions*, Prague.

Rhodes, P. J. 2013: "The organization of Athenian public finance", *Greece and Rome* 60, 203–23.

RO: P. J. Rhodes and R. Osborne, *Greek historical inscriptions 404–323 BC*, Oxford, 2003.

Shear, J. L. 2011: *Polis and revolution. Responding to oligarchy in classical Athens*, Cambridge.

Walbank, M. B. 2008: *Fragmentary decrees from the Athenian Agora*, *Hesperia* Supplement 38, Princeton.

Whitehead, D. 2000: *Hypereides. The forensic speeches*, Oxford.

CHAPTER 8

Proposers of Inscribed Laws and Decrees and the Distribution of Political Influence in Late Classical Athens*

> And you [i.e. Demosthenes] blame me if I come before the People, not continuously, but at intervals, and you think that no-one notices that you have derived this expectation, not from democracy, but another form of government. For in oligarchies it is not he who wishes, but the man in power who addresses the people; but in democracies it is he who wishes, and whenever it seems good to him. And speaking from time to time is the sign of a man who engages in politics because of the call of the hour and for the common good; but letting no day go by, of the man who is making a trade of it and speaking for hire.[1]
>
> AESCHINES 3 *Against Ktesiphon* 220

1 Introduction

Aeschines' implication that, in contrast to oligarchies – and one might add, modern representative forms of democracy – in the direct Athenian democracy it was merely by "addressing the People", and not by tenure of office (or "power"),

* This paper was largely written at the Institute for Advanced Study, Princeton, where I enjoyed the privilege of Membership in 2012/13. I am very grateful to audiences that year at the Institute, at the University of Pennsylvania and at Princeton University for helping me to improve it. It was revised in the excellent library of the British School at Athens in the autumn of 2016. I thank James Kierstead for comments on a late draft.

1 ἐπιτιμᾷς δέ μοι, εἰ μὴ συνεχῶς, ἀλλὰ διαλείπων, πρὸς τὸν δῆμον προσέρχομαι, καὶ τὴν ἀξίωσιν ταύτην οἴει λανθάνειν μεταφέρων οὐκ ἐκ δημοκρατίας, ἀλλ᾽ ἐξ ἑτέρας πολιτείας. ἐν μὲν γὰρ ταῖς ὀλιγαρχίαις οὐχ ὁ βουλόμενος, ἀλλ᾽ ὁ δυναστεύων δημηγορεῖ, ἐν δὲ ταῖς δημοκρατίαις ὁ βουλόμενος, καὶ ὅταν αὐτῷ δοκῇ. καὶ τὸ μὲν διὰ χρόνου λέγειν σημεῖόν ἐστιν ἐπὶ τῶν καιρῶν καὶ τοῦ συμφέροντος ἀνδρὸς πολιτευομένου, τὸ δὲ μηδεμίαν παραλείπειν ἡμέραν ἐργαζομένου καὶ μισθαρνοῦντος.

© KONINKLIJKE BRILL NV, LEIDEN, 2018 | DOI 10.1163/9789004352490_010

that a politician exercised influence, seems true and is uncontroversial.[2] His remarks, however, raise another question the answer to which is less clear cut. How far was politics – that is to say, above all decision-making in the Council and Assembly – dominated by the type of man who "let no day go by without making a speech" – in other words by an elite group of what one might describe as "professional politicians"? How far was it the man who spoke from time to time because of the call of the hour and for the common good, as it were the ordinary Athenian?

A strong body of opinion has sought to downplay Aeschines' amateur idea, emphasising the influence wielded by the elite politicians, among whom, and despite his protestations to the contrary, this body of opinion would place Aeschines himself. The view has been expressed perhaps most authoritatively in the last generation by M. H. Hansen:

> To make a speech in the Assembly demanded some eloquence and rhetorical training, which not every citizen possessed. That is why debate was dominated by a small group of half- or fully-professional orators ... The Athenians' ideal speaker was, it is true, the plain man who spoke his honest mind with modest infrequency and without circumlocution: the fourth-century orators [and here Hansen cites the passage above] liked to praise that ideal, but with a rhetorical dexterity that gives away the professional ... At any Assembly meeting there were, say, several hundred *rhetores* in the formal sense, i.e. people who might on occasion pluck up courage to come forward and propose something; but of *rhetores* in the political sense there can never have been more than a score or so – fewer than a hundred in the whole period from 403 to 322.
>
> HANSEN 1991, 144

Recently, however, the idea that political influence was primarily exercised by an elite has been subject to some welcome critical reappraisal, most influentially

2 The tendency, as the fourth century progressed, for elective offices to gain influence over the city's finances, the theoric board or controller (deployed effectively by Euboulos after 355, and by Demosthenes after 338), the treasurer of the military fund, and the controller of the financial administration (*epi tei dioikesei*, post held by Lykourgos in person probably for the quadrennium 336/5–333/2 and subsequently for two quadrennia by surrogates) does nothing to gainsay this. Like the generalship in the fourth century, such offices were regarded as requiring technical expertise, but they did not bestow political power, in the sense of overriding the normal procedures of political decision-taking by Council and Assembly, and were subject to the same accountability as any other office. Cf. Hansen 1991, 160, 263–64; Rhodes 2013, 219–24. On Lykourgos' office and accountability cf. Lambert 2015, 8–12 (= this volume, chapter 11).

by Josiah Ober in his 2008 book, *Democracy and Knowledge*, in which he argued that Athenian democracy, via mechanisms such as the Cleisthenic tribal system, was a uniquely well-networked polity, optimally adapted to the transfer of political expertise between its citizens:

> If the argument developed in this chapter is correct, this elite domination argument is fundamentally flawed in its assumption of radical informational asymmetry between elite speaker and mass audience (p. 162)

> It seems unlikely that any Athenian had the sort of general political mastery that Thucydides attributed to Pericles, much less that of Plato's philosopher-kings. The single most noteworthy aspect of Athenian government may be its capacity to operate in the absence of system-level grand-masters (p. 123)

In particular Ober argues that his theory about the transfer of political skills in the Athenian democracy should have operated progressively, such that:

> … over time, the population of 'politically active citizens' should be increasingly representative of, and indeed functionally co-extensive with, the citizen population as whole. The obvious advantages enjoyed by wealthy citizens, and by those with easy geographical access to the city centre, should lessen (p. 166)

and he finds support for this in Claire Taylor's work, which has demonstrated that wealth and proximity to the city centre were less strongly associated with political activity in the fourth century than in the fifth.[3]

In this paper I propose to explore the extent to which the data on proposers of inscribed laws and decrees in the latest phase of the Athenian democracy, i.e. 354/3–322/1 BC, support the proposition that political influence was in fact wielded to a significant degree by ordinary individual Athenians.[4] 322/1 marks

---

3 Taylor 2008.

4 I am not, in this paper, concerned with the extent to which ordinary Athenians participated in debate in the Assembly, a topic on which the epigraphical record is silent. Note, however, Socrates' comment that it is remarkable how, when in the Athenian Assembly, the administration (*dioikesis*) of the city is on the agenda, "he who rises to give advice may equally be a carpenter, bronzesmith, cobbler, merchant, shipper, rich, poor, well-bred, ill-bred…" (Plato, *Protagoras* 319d); and often rather noisy audience participation in Assembly debates was common (cf. Hansen 1991, 146; most recently Thomas 2016; Rhodes 2016, 248–50, with bibliography, n. 22).

the end of the classical democracy, following the defeat of Athens' attempt to reassert its independence from Macedon after the death of Alexander, the Lamian War. The start-date of the analysis is determined by the fact that it is only from 354/3 that proposers begin to be identified on inscriptions by all three name-elements, name, father's name and demotic, information crucial for identification. Before 354/3 proposers were referred to by name only; occasionally the names are distinctive enough to enable identification, but often they are not, and the overall picture generated by the epigraphical evidence is rather sketchy as regards generating meaningful statistics.

There are about 79 extant inscribed laws and decrees of the period 354/3–322/1 which preserve all three elements of the proposer's name (or at least enough of them to enable identification).[5] There is also a quantity of evidence on decree proposers in literary sources, mainly the orators.[6] Hansen conducted an analysis of the attested proposers of this period in an article first published in 1984, and reprinted with addenda in 1989;[7] and summarised his findings in the 1991 book from which I have already quoted.[8] His results showed that there was a remarkably large number of different proposers; in fact, the large majority of proposers are attested as proposers of only one law or decree; and this would seem at first sight to lend support to Ober's argument that at this period political expertise was rather broadly spread. As we shall see shortly, however, Hansen thought that the data could be explained consistently with his view that the political process was dominated by an elite. Hansen's analysis was ground-breaking, but there is scope to improve on it. That is not so much because of any fundamental changes in the data. There has indeed been significant progress since 1984, in readings, and datings and interpretation of individual inscriptions; but with one or two exceptions that we shall explore below, that progress has not changed the overall picture. As we shall see, however, Hansen's interpretation of the data is open to question at several points. Moreover, in compiling his statistics, Hansen combined data obtained from literary and epigraphical sources (more or less) indiscriminately. This is unfortunate as it obscures the perspectives, or distortions, inherent in the two types of evidence, especially in the literary sources. We can also enhance the analysis by attending to two factors that Hansen did not explicitly consider: the socio-economic status of proposers; and patterns in the distribution of the data over time.

5 Catalogued at Appendix 1.

6 Hansen 1984, 132, counted 98 decrees in literary sources proposed by a named Athenian in the period 355–322, and a total of 181 decrees in both kinds of evidence moved by 82 citizens.

7 Hansen 1984.

8 Hansen 1991, 143–46 and 271–72. See also Hansen 1987, 108–18.

2 Is Successful Decree Proposing a Good Indicator of Political Influence?

First, we must think about whether successful proposing of laws and decrees is actually a good indicator of political influence. A key issue here is how far the proposer of a decree was the real man behind it. Hansen argues that often he was not, and that that explains why there are so many decree proposers. He writes:

> Many of the proposers of decrees are mere names, never heard of again in any other context. There are at least two good explanations ... in the first place, every other decree passed by the Assembly was probouleumatic [i.e. ratification of a proposal from the Council]. Even a political leader could only be a councillor twice in his life ... so if he wanted to have a motion passed by the Assembly he usually had to find a councillor to collaborate with him; the councillor would be the formal, answerable proposer and put the motion to the Council and then to the Assembly. The probouleumatic procedure thus entailed that many decrees were put up by an ordinary councillor, whose name can be read today in the preamble to the decree ... while the real initiator was a political leader who supported the motion ... in the Assembly.
>
> HANSEN 1991, 145

Second, Hansen argues, minor figures might be prevailed upon by major politicians to lend their names to proposals. That way the major politician avoided being attacked in the courts for having made an illegal proposal (*graphe paranomon*).[9]

One must concede a degree of force to these arguments, but the analysis is also open to challenge at a number of points. Hansen's claim that "every other decree passed by the Assembly was probouleumatic" was based on P.J. Rhodes' analysis, in his 1972 book on the Athenian Boule, of the relative numbers of probouleumatic and non-probouleumatic decrees across the fourth century as a whole. My own analysis, set out in chapter 9, suggests that, in the last phase of the classical democracy, the large majority of decrees was in fact non-probouleumatic, and that all but a small handful of those that were probouleumatic were debated in the Assembly. This reduces the extent to which one can reasonably attribute the large numbers of decree proposers to the fact that they were ordinary Athenians speaking, as councillors, on behalf of the "big men" who were really responsible for the proposals they sponsored.

9 On the *graphe paranomon* see further below and chapter 7.

We might also take a closer look at the three major items of evidence for the patterns of behaviour that Hansen refers to. In [Dem.] 59.43 (343–340 BC) Apollodoros alleges that his opponent Stephanos, the husband of Neaira, at an early stage of his career (early-360s) was "still only a sykophant, one of those men who stand around the podium shouting, and is paid to indict people and bring *phasis* actions and put their name on other people's motions, until he fell under the influence of Kallistratos of Aphidna".[10] The other two are both from Aeschines 3: at 125 he alleges that Demosthenes pressurised a councillor to make a proposal in the Council on his behalf, "taking advantage of the proposer's inexperience" (προσλαβὼν τὴν τοῦ γράψαντος ἀπειρίαν), while at 159 the claim seems to be that, for a spell after the battle of Chaironeia, Demosthenes' position was so weak that Nausikles' name appeared on decrees in place of Demosthenes: "and in the initial period [scil. after battle of Chaironeia] the man was all a-tremble, and coming half-dead to the rostrum, he urged you to elect him Guardian of the Peace, but you didn't allow Demosthenes' name to be written on the decrees, but assigned this to Nausikles; and now he expects to be crowned."[11] This, together with Demosthenes' own statements about his weak position after Chaironeia,[12] is perhaps the basis for the more general claim of Plutarch, *Dem.* 21 (in any case of no independent historical value) that, between Chaironeia and Philip's death in 336 Demosthenes had his friends propose decrees for him (implying fear of a successful *graphe pranomon*).[13]

What are we to make of these cases? Hansen infers that they represent normal patterns of behaviour, but this is questionable. It is not so much that Aeschines presents such name-substitutions as exceptional and deviant practice that arouses scepticism, but that they amount to no more than contentious allegations by an opposing orator. As with all statements in the orators

10 ἀλλ' ἔτι συκοφάντης τῶν παραβοώντων παρὰ τὸ βῆμα καὶ γραφομένων μισθοῦ καὶ φαινόντων καὶ ἐπιγραφομένων ταῖς ἀλλοτρίαις γνώμαις, ἕως ὑπέπεσε Καλλιστράτῳ τῷ Ἀφιδναίῳ.

11 τοὺς μὲν πρώτους χρόνους ὑπότρομος ἦν ἄνθρωπος, καὶ παριὼν ἡμιθνὴς ἐπὶ τὸ βῆμα, εἰρηνοφύλακα ὑμᾶς αὐτὸν ἐκέλευε χειροτονεῖν. ὑμεῖς δὲ οὐδ' ἐπὶ τὰ ψηφίσματα εἰᾶτε τὸ Δημοσθένους ἐπιγράφειν ὄνομα, ἀλλὰ Ναυσικλεῖ τοῦτο προσετάττετε: νυνὶ δ' ἤδη καὶ στεφανοῦσθαι ἀξιοῖ. This is rather opaque; the implication seems to be, however, that in some way decrees with Demosthenes' name on them (i.e. proposed by him?) were deemed unacceptable. Harris 1994 suggests that it implies not that Nausikles' name replaced Demosthenes' as decree proposer, but that Nausikles was appointed "Guardian of the Peace" (i.e. Athenian delegate to the League of Corinth) in place of Demosthenes.

12 Dem. 18.249.

13 τοῖς δὲ ψηφίσμασιν οὐχ ἑαυτόν, ἀλλ' ἐν μέρει τῶν φίλων ἕκαστον ἐπέγραφεν ... ἕως αὖθις ἀνεθάρρησε Φιλίππου τελευτήσαντος. On the likely dependence of this statement on Aeschines' passage cf. Harris 1994, 380.

implying political corruption, there was doubtless some underlying reality, but there was also exaggeration and distortion. Taken in the round, we should expect, and the sources tend to confirm, that there was a wide variety in the dynamics impelling a councillor to make a proposal; for some, in this well-networked city, it was indeed an opportunity to propose honours, or to formulate other types of proposals on behalf of others, who might include family, friends and fellow deme members; for others it was an opportunity to pursue areas of public policy in which they had a particular interest, whether or not in collaboration with more or less powerful individuals. It is in the nature of the inscribed record that this kind of background to decree formulation is not made explicit, but there is not infrequently circumstantial evidence that is suggestive of some of the factors driving a councillor to make a proposal.

IG II^3 1, 359, honouring Androkles son of Kleinias of Kerameis, priest of Asklepios for the year 328/7 BC, and otherwise unknown, is a case in point. Of the two decrees on the stone the second was proposed in the Council by a Euetion son of Autokleides of Sphettos, a man of the liturgical class, aged just over 60 (*APF* 5463), with no obvious connection to the honorand except that he contributed in the same year as a councillor to a public dedication to another healing deity, Amphiaraos (360, 12). It seems not impossible that a common interest in health and healing cults supplied a link between these men. The first decree on the stone, which is non-probouleumatic, was proposed in the Assembly by Prokleides son of Panta- of Kerameis, also just over 60, who was not only from the same deme as the priest, but is also on record as dedicator to Asklepios, supplying two potential points of contact.[14]

A clear example of a term on the Council being used to pursue policy spheres in which the councillor was particularly interested is presented by the term of office of the religious specialist and historian of Attica, Phanodemos of Thymaitadai (*FGH* 325). Abundantly documented in the epigraphical record, Phanodemos played a leading role in the religion and festival life of the major cult site of Oropos, the Amphiaraion, after its acquisition by Athens, probably after the sack of Thebes in 335.[15] His term of office on the Council some years

14 *IG* II^2 4404. A rather different, it seems looser, dynamic binding proposer with those interested in the proposal is implied in Xenophon's account (*Hell.* 1.7.1–9) of the Assembly's famous decision to condemn the generals to death for their failure to pick up Athenian survivors of the naval battle of Arginousai in 406. The proposer of the decree was a Kallixenos, who was "persuaded", by means and for motives that are left unclear, by the relatives of those who had died to make his proposal in the Council.

15 Honoured for that role, including proposing the legislation for the Great Amphiaraia festival, in 332/1 by *IG* II^3 1, 348, he proposed honours for Amphiaraos on the same day, *IG* II^3

earlier, in 343/2, is documented by *IG* II[3] 1, 306, a dedication to Hephaistos instigated by Phanodemos (decree 2). On it was inscribed the decree by which the Council had been praised by the Assembly for its conduct of the City Dionysia (decree 1), two decrees honouring the Council's administrator (decrees 4 and 5), and a decree honouring Phanodemos himself as victor in the competition held among those speaking in the ninth prytany for being the best and most incorruptible speaker throughout the year. The text does not make it explicit, but most likely decree 2 was proposed by Phanodemos in the ninth prytany and was the occasion for his winning the competition. 343/2 was a year full of contentious business in Athenian foreign policy, as the Peace of Philokrates unravelled; but there is no indication that Phanodemos embroiled himself in any of that. Instead he stood out for his contributions to the much less contentious sphere of religious policy, and in particular, it seems, for proposals to commemorate the Council's own fine work in administering the City Dionysia.

Another example is the series of five decrees honouring the (otherwise unknown) grain trader, Herakleides of Salamis, *IG* II[3] 1, 367. Here the links between the proposers and the honorand are entirely obscure. The links between the Athenians involved in the award of the honours, however, are clear enough, particularly in the case of decrees 1–3. The initiative to honour Herakleides for the first time, sometime between 330/29 and 328/7, was taken by Telemachos son of Theangelos of Acharnai, who proposed in the Assembly both the decree commissioning from the Council a proposal to honour Herakleides (decree 1), and the eventual Assembly decree that resulted from that proposal (decree 3). We know nothing about Telemachos' economic circumstances, but he was a busy decree proposer, as we know from both the literary and epigraphical records.[16] The proposer of the Council's *probouleuma* commissioned on Telemachos' motion was Kephisodotos son of Euarchides of Acharnai. A generation later, in 298/7, a man of the same name was honoured by the soldiers stationed at Sounion for his work as inspector (*exetastes*), *IG* II[2] 1270. This may have been the same man, or a descendant, but there is no obvious connection to the circumstances of the decree for Herakleides and nothing else is known about him. The key point here however is likely to be that Kephisodotos was from the same deme as Telemachos, Acharnai. What we have here is a man wishing to put a measure through the Assembly persuading one of the representatives of his deme on the Council that year to pass a *probouleuma*

1, 349, headed the list of managers for the first celebration of the Great Amphiaraia in 329/8 (IG II[3] 1, 355, 22, cf. *Ath. Pol.* 54.7) and contributed to a dedication to Amphiaraos in 328/7 (IG II[3] 1, 360, 31).

16 For details see Lambert 2015, 10–11 (= this volume, chapter 11, 301–302), and further below.

through the Council, as a basis for his own proposal in the Assembly. The initiative lies with Telemachos, who was, it seems, somewhat more prominent than Kephisodotos. This might be construed by a hostile orator as Telemachos prevailing upon the less experienced Kephisodotos to do his dirty work for him in the Council, but one could equally well, and perhaps more plausibly, interpret it as the Cleisthenic system of deme representation on the Council working in the way that was intended.[17]

Even if he was proposing a measure in some sense on behalf of someone else, a councillor still had to persuade a majority of 500 of his fellow citizens to vote for his proposal,[18] and he had to take the proposal forward to the Assembly, where he would normally, one might think, expect to speak in its defence. Hansen suggests that proposing a decree in the Assembly did not necessarily require you to speak for it, and could therefore, he implies, be done by anyone without rhetorical skill.[19] It is true that, despite the use of the term εἶπεν ("spoke") of proposers in decree prescripts, it is unclear whether, at this time, decree proposals were actually still read out by their proposers, or rather by the secretary of the Council and People;[20] and some proposals coming up from the Council may have been nodded through at the *procheirotonia*. The Assembly's time was limited and not all proposals were selected for debate.[21] But, not least given what we understand about the fundamentally oral character of the Athenian democracy,[22] one's expectation would be that the man

17 Another example of implied collaboration between a more prominent and a less prominent citizen, albeit not one that involves the Council, is *IG* II^3 1, 298, for the Bosporan rulers, proposed by Androtion (in the Assembly), but with a (perhaps pre-arranged) rider drawing the youngest of the brothers of the ruling family into the scope of the decree, proposed by the son of Androtion's old associate in battles against Demosthenes, Timokrates. This is a case where, as typically with non-probouleumatic decrees, the original proposer of the Council's *probouleuma*, far from muddying the proposer statistics, is not mentioned at all in the inscribed record.

18 The detail of this, e.g. how many councillors normally participated in debates and votes in the Council, is admittedly obscure. It is unsurprising to learn from Dem. 22.36 that not every councillor turned up to every meeting.

19 Hansen 1984, 127.

20 He was responsible for reading out documents at Council and Assembly meetings (*Ath. Pol.* 54.5, cf. *IG* II^3 1, 327 and 306, 10), but it is unclear if that included texts of proposals.

21 On the *procheirotonia*, the detailed operation of which is obscure, see chapter 9.5. There are only two likely candidates for inclusion in the *procheirotonia* among the inscribed decrees of this period.

22 On written documentation in the courts, which only slowly in the course of the fourth century became an acceptable substitute for oral representation in person in contexts such as witness statements, see Thomas 1989, 42–44. The principle that adult male

who proposed a decree would normally speak in support of it.[23] Any proposal successfully carried in the Council, and on through the Assembly would seem to indicate possession of a fairly significant degree of political expertise. Moreover, while there are indeed decrees proposed by relatively obscure individuals, there are also plenty of cases of leading politicians making proposals in their own name, which casts doubt on the extent to which it was normal practice for leading figures to suborn nonentities to propose their decrees for them, whether councillors or not. Such an interpretation is more suggestive of the patron-client system that operated in Roman politics than that of the equal, fiercely independent, citizenry that comprised the fourth-century Athenian democracy.

We might also pause for a moment over the case in Demosthenes 59. Stephanos, the supposedly minor figure alleged to have corruptly lent his name to the proposals of others, was someone who was actually, at the time of the speech against him making this allegation, quite a successful politician – he appears in the epigraphical record, for example, as proposer of a treaty with

citizens represented themselves in court was strong and persistent, however, and one would expect the same kind of attitude to apply in the Assembly. It is partly this kind of cultural attitude that underlies the distaste for the use of substitute names for "real" proposers implicit in the orators.

23 Demonstrable instances are fewer than one might expect. Demosthenes is the only orator whose Assembly speeches survive, but if Hansen's analysis of them is correct (1989b, 283–86), there is only one, the *First Philippic* (Dem. 4, 352/1 BC), that was delivered in support of a decree proposed by the speaker (not as a councillor; he was on the Council in 347/6, Dem. 19.154 etc., Aeschin 2.17 etc., and possibly 337/6, Aeschin. 3.160, cf. Rhodes 1972, 4 n. 8). For what it is worth, there is support for the proposition that councillors induced (so the author would have us believe), into making proposals on behalf of others would expect to have to defend them in the Assembly in Xenophon's account of the decision to condemn the generals after Arginousai (above n. 14). During the debate in the Assembly Kallixenos' proposal is attacked for being illegal and some of the *prytaneis* (famously including Socrates) accordingly decline to put the proposal to the vote. At this point, Xenophon writes, Kallixenos "again mounted the platform, and urged that they should be condemned in the same terms (scil. as the generals)" (αὖθις Καλλίξεινος ἀναβὰς κατηγόρει αὐτῶν τὰ αὐτά). The key word here is "again", for it implies that Kallixenos had mounted the Assembly platform before to speak in support of his original proposal. Rhodes 2016, 248, notes a possible exception at *Ath. Pol.* 29.1, reporting that, in the context of the appointment of the 400 in 411, the decree to appoint thirty *syngrapheis* was proposed by Pythodoros, but the speech "before" the decree (πρὸ τοῦ ψηφίσματος) was made by Melobios (later a member of the Thirty). This may, however, be no more than a slightly loose way of describing what was on any account a common phenomenon, namely a probouleumatic decree proposed by x, relatively obscure councillor, supported in a speech made by y, more prominent politician.

Mytilene (*IG* II^3 1, 299) – and the allegation related to the early stages of his career, more than twenty years previously, a time when Stephanos was taken under the wing of a more senior politician, Kallistratos of Aphidna. Seen in a less contentious light, this, one might think, was how the system was supposed to operate – the less experienced developing their political expertise, including in the drafting and supporting of decree proposals, under the aegis of a more senior figure.[24] This is surely Ober's well-connected, tightly networked, polis in action.

I suggest that, taken in the round, making a successful proposal, whether in the Assembly or the Council, is a reasonably good indicator that you were a man of some political expertise and influence.

3 Qualities of the Epigraphical Data

The literary evidence is arguably quite misleading, therefore. It is important to penetrate beyond the negative construction given to certain patterns of behaviour by protagonists in the orators seeking by rhetorical means to blacken the name of their opponents. It is also important to recognise that, in some areas, one of which we shall review shortly, statistics derived from the orators on proposers of laws and decrees are based on anything but a random sample. Before seeking to draw general conclusions on this topic from the epigraphical data, however, we must also review issues to do with its quality. The number of inscriptions that survive from this period with names of proposers preserved is about 79; very small, of course, in proportion to the total number passed, but large enough to be indicative at least of some broad patterns.

In contrast to the literary evidence, the sample is probably of quite good quality as far its randomness is concerned: we know that the large majority of decree inscriptions were set up on the Acropolis,[25] a quite limited physical space, and it and its immediately surrounding area, including the Agora, have been quite thoroughly explored and excavated in the years since Greek independence.

Another factor that might at first sight seem to have the potential to distort the picture presented by our sample is the practice of "destroying" inscriptions for political reasons. This happened after Athens' defeat by Macedon in the Lamian War in 322 and the imposition by Antipater of an oligarchic regime. We know of two decrees honouring Athens' allies in the war that were destroyed at

24 Androtion and Polyeuktos son of Timokrates in *IG* II^3 1, 298 (n. 17) again present a suggestive parallel. Diondas similarly comes across in Hypereides' speech against him as a young man (under 25, *Against Diondas* 8.5) out to make his mark (Carey et al. 2008).

25 See chapter 1.

this time, later to be re-inscribed by the restored democracy in 318;[26] and the famous law against tyranny, *IG* II^3 1, 320, passed in 336, seems also to have been torn down at this period. However, stone is a rather durable material; destroying an inscription may mean that it is smashed up, but it doesn't necessarily mean that it is obliterated off the face of the earth.[27] The fragments endure and remain available to be discovered by archaeologists, and as a matter of fact fragments of what are probably the original, "destroyed" versions of the two honorific decrees have been discovered; and the law against tyranny was re-used in the foundations of an early hellenistic building in the Agora, where again it remained to be rediscovered by modern archaeologists.

I suggest, therefore, that it is a reasonable working hypothesis that the surviving decrees are broadly representative of all that were inscribed. Are they representative of all the laws and decrees that were passed? By this period all decrees, including, it seems, the texts of inscribed ones, were deposited in papyrus copies in the Metroon in the Agora, and it is clear that not all laws and decrees were inscribed on stone.[28] The analysis of decrees attested in the literary record carried out in chapter 2 shows that there were many types that were not usually inscribed: they range widely in subject matter; they are not necessarily unimportant, but they are mostly on matters of a more ephemeral character for which permanent commemoration in stone was inappropriate: decrees relating to dispositions of military forces, for example, and judicial processes. What types of decree were inscribed? Inscribed laws and decrees at this period belong to four types:[29]

(a) honorific (for foreigners, and from the 340s regularly for Athenians). They represent the large majority (87%). They award a wide range of different

---

26 Decrees honouring Euphron of Sikyon, as re-erected on restoration of democracy in 318/7: *IG* II^3 1, 378. Fragment of original version of 323/2, destroyed after Lamian War: 377. Decrees honouring Theophantos, most likely also as re-erected on restoration of democracy in 318/7: *IG* II^3 1, 343. Fragment of original version of 332/1, destroyed after Lamian War: *IG* II^3 1, 342.

27 Admittedly the *stelai* recording the conviction and punishments meted out to Alcibiades are said to have been cast into the sea when Alcibiades was restored to favour in 407 (Diod. 13.69), but whether or not this is authentic (and stone stelai at any rate did not normally record convictions and punishments), it may have seemed appropriate given the religious context of Alcibiades' offences and punishments. Such connotations were lacking in the destruction of stelai that seems to have taken place in 322. Cf. Meyer 2013, 492.

28 On this topic cf. chapter 2.

29 See chapter 2, section 3.

honours, from the Athenian citizenship for prominent foreigners, to gold crowns for Athenian officials.

(b) on religious subjects, including for example provisions relating to festivals (4%).

(c) treaties with foreign states and other decrees dealing with foreign policy (6%).

(d) "other" topics (e.g. the law against tyranny, *IG* II^3 1, 320) (2%).

These have three common features in their intentionality which set them apart from the types that were not inscribed, and which come into focus in different ways with the different types: durability, general applicability (i.e. they are not, or not only, relevant to an individual, but intended to deliver a message of some kind to a wide public), and a religious aspect, reflecting the fact that religious sanctuaries were the default location for decrees and that, metaphorically, one face of them was directed at the gods as well as at men.[30] As these qualities suggest, the types of law and decree that were inscribed were, by definition, generally on matters of importance. Nothing was more important to the well-being of an ancient city than its religious observances; treaties with other states are major instruments of foreign policy. I will pause a moment on honorific decrees, as this is by such a long way the most common inscribed category (and indeed the most common category in the literary and epigraphical evidence taken together),[31] and it might be tempting to view them as minor matters that (perhaps) could suitably be delegated to minor political figures.[32] This is not a view that I share. *Timē* was of central importance to the functioning of the Greek city.[33] In the Greek value system it is what drove men to act in the public good. The manipulation of it by Greek cities – the awarding of honours in recognition of past benefactions and to encourage future benefactions, as part of a reciprocal system of exchange of benefits – was a powerful instrument of foreign policy in the case of honours for foreigners – and supplied an important

30 See chapter 1.

31 Hansen 1991, 156–57; cf. Liddel 2016.

32 Hansen 1991, 211, of *graphai paranomon* against honorific decrees: "in most cases the attack was against a pretty trivial honorary decree", though he also comments aptly that "such matters had a greater significance for the democracy, and for Athenian society as a whole, than a modern European might expect".

33 Cf. Lambert 2011 (= chapter 3). For a recent succinct statement of the importance of the "honours system" to the functioning of the city of Athens, with references to older bibliography, see Kremmydas 2012, 8–11, commenting on a speech which illustrates its central role with great clarity, Dem. 20 *Against Leptines*; and most recently the more extensive discussion of the issues in relation to the same speech by Canevaro 2016, 77–97.

incentive to a city's officials to perform their duties well in the case of honours for its own citizens. It is abundantly clear from the Attic orators that the issue of honour was very high on the agenda of the Assembly in this period, both in relation to specific individuals and broader policy.[34] It produced the most highly rated speech in the history of Greek oratory, Demosthenes *On the Crown*; and of the ca. 38 known prosecutions for proposing illegal decrees, *graphai paranomon*, no less than ca. 19 were against proposals that were honorific.[35]

Major politicians certainly were closely involved in proposing honorific decrees. Over a quarter – 10 of the 39 – Assembly decrees on record as proposed by Demosthenes were honorific.[36] All the inscribed decrees proposed by the consummate diplomat, Demades, and most of those proposed by Lykourgos were also honorific.[37] Honour was the life-blood of the city's internal operation and of its international relations; honorific decrees were often highly contentious; and proposing a decree of this kind was far from a formality. It certainly required social and political expertise and standing to do so successfully. Let us move on to consider the relevant data.

4 Findings

A *Numbers of Proposers/Measures Proposed in Inscribed Laws and Decrees of 354/3–322/1*[38]

43 proposers: 1 measure (including Demosthenes son of Demosthenes of Paiania)
8 proposers: 2 measures
1 proposer: 3 measures (Diophantos son of Phrasykleides of Myrrhinous)
1 proposer: 8 measures (Lykourgos son of Lykophron of Boutadai)
1 proposer: 10 measures (Demades son of Demeas of Paiania)

---

34 Rewarding and punishing are two of the most important duties of the city according to Dem. 20.154, 24.215. Of these two it was primarily rewarding that was the Assembly's domain (cf. Hansen 1991, 157).

35 13 were against decrees of other kinds, 6 against decrees of unknown type, Hansen 1991, 211, cf. Hansen 1974. The publication of Hypereides *Against Diondas* (Carey et. al. 2008) has not significantly affected the picture (cf. chapter 7 n. 7).

36 See the table of laws and decrees proposed by Demosthenes, chapter 2, Appendix 2. The evidence for several of these is Din. 1 *Against Demosthenes* 43 (323 BC), where Demosthenes is alleged to have been bribed to propose honours for a long list of both Athenians and foreigners.

37 See chapter 11 section 2 and further below.

38 These figures summarise Appendix 1 and do not include decrees proposed outside the timespan of this study, i.e. 354/3–322/1.

These figures from the inscriptions, based on the table at Appendix 1, would seem to indicate that the capacity to exercise political influence and expertise was indeed spread remarkably widely in late classical Athens as regards the numbers of individuals attested as proposers. In this respect the picture conveyed by the epigraphical data is not significantly different from that implied by the literary evidence. The message they convey is the same, and mutually supportive.[39] We shall return to the interpretation of this multiplicity of proposers below, though I note in passing that these data do not appear to support the dichotomy Hansen draws, surely overschematically, between professional politician and occasional proposer. One respect, however, in which the literary evidence shows a markedly different picture from the epigraphical data is in the distribution of decrees among major politicians. Taking the literary record and the epigraphical record together, Demosthenes is on record as proposing 39 decrees, 38 of them in the literary record, 1 in the epigraphical.[40] Demades comes next, with 10 decrees in the literary record and 11 in the epigraphical on Hansen's figures; and Lykourgos next, with 10 in epigraphical, 1 in literary sources.[41] How are we to explain the small number of inscribed decrees proposed by Demosthenes, and conversely, the large number proposed by Demades and Lykourgos? Sample size is certainly an issue here, particularly, as we shall see, for the period before Chaironeia; we can not press the statistics very hard; but if we can find substantive explanations of the pattern, particularly for the post-Chaironeia period, when the numbers are larger, we should do so.

In Demosthenes' case the meagre epigraphical record of decree proposing is not perhaps so difficult to explain, as we shall see below;[42] but the contrast with the literary record does stimulate reflection on the extent to which the literary evidence is biased towards this politician, in the sense that it conveys an exaggerated impression of his influence. Why is Demosthenes so prominent as decree proposer in the literary record? Partly it is surely because he was indeed an influential figure, especially in the years leading up to Chaironeia. This was conceded by his enemies at home, Aeschines above all; and recognised by contemporary external observers, such as Theopompos of Chios.[43] But the evidence for Demosthenes as decree-proposer derives largely from the orators;

39 Hansen 1984, 132–34; 1984, 155: "The number of citizens involved in politics as proposers … was much larger than usually believed".

40 Hansen 1984, 133. See also chapter 2, Appendix 2.

41 Hansen 1984, 132–33. Detail at 1989a, 40 (Demades), 53–54 (Lykourgos). His figures include non-self-standing decrees referred to in other inscriptions.

42 This discussion of the relatively small number of Demosthenes' inscribed decrees supersedes the views I expressed in Lambert 2001.

43 Flower 1994, 136–47. Cf. MacDowell 2009, 9–13.

and it is scarcely coincidental here that, of the seventy-four extant Assembly or forensic speeches dating to this period, no less than sixty are ascribed to Demosthenes himself (admittedly some of them falsely), and eight are by other orators but relate to cases in which Demosthenes was involved.[44] In fact, if we exclude the speeches of Hypereides, preserved only on papyrus, there is only one which survived through antiquity and the Middle Ages complete and in continuous manuscript tradition, and which has nothing to do with Demosthenes, Lykourgos 1 *Against Leokrates*. Now the reason for this is not solely or even mainly that Demosthenes dominated the politics of his time; it is, in the first place, that he had a nephew, Demochares, who was an influential politician in the restored democracy, after the "liberation" of Athens from Macedonian control in 307/6, and who vigorously promoted his uncle's reputation as a patriotic politician;[45] and in the second place that, long after his political reputation had ceased to be relevant to the current political scene, he became the exemplary Greek orator (and the exemplary writer of Attic Greek), whose speeches dominated the curriculum of the rhetorical schools.[46] This posthumous reputation impacted on the biographical and narrative historical record, in which the story of Athens in this period became to a marked degree the story of Demosthenes;[47] and it surely played a big role in the selection of speeches by other orators on the curriculum. By and large those that were relevant to the story of Demosthenes survived; those that were not, did not.

I suggest, therefore, that, while the epigraphical statistics perhaps underrate Demosthenes' political influence, the literary record of his activity as decree

44 Aeschines 1–3, Dinarchos 1–3, Hypereides *Against Demosthenes* and *Against Diondas* (Carey et al. 2008).

45 Partly no doubt to boost his own standing, but partly also as a counter to the much more sceptical view of Demosthenes propounded by the Peripatetics in general, and Demetrios of Phaleron in particular. See Cooper 2000. Demochares proposed a decree honouring his uncle in 280/79 (archon Gorgias), [Plut.] *Lives of the Ten Orators* 847d, 850f–851c (see most recently MacDowell 2009, 424–26). He also wrote a history, more rhetorical than historical according to Cicero, *Brutus* 286, in which he attacked Demetrios of Phaleron (Polyb. 12.13.7–8).

46 See Cooper 2000, and most recently Kremmydas 2012, 62–64. Cooper stresses (p. 224), that in the hellenistic period "the real story" was "Demosthenes the orator" and biographies were concerned less with his political achievements and more with the incidental details of his life as background to his literary accomplishments. "It was not until Plutarch … that Demosthenes was treated as a real political figure", but Plutarch's own purpose was moral rather than historical (MacDowell 2009, 11).

47 It may not be irrelevant that this story was created in the hellenistic period, when the Greek political world was in reality dominated by "big men".

proposer probably exaggerates it. As Ober notes, the Athenian democratic system had a notable capacity to operate in the absence of "system-level grand masters". We should not make the mistake of seeing Demosthenes as such a "grand master".[48]

Why are Lykourgos and Demades so prominent in the epigraphical record of decree proposers? Both these two politicians were active as proposers only after the battle of Chaironeia, in other words the second half of our period; and here another statistic is relevant:

B *Chronological Distribution of Datable Inscribed Laws and Decrees with Identifiable Proposers*

354/3–339/8 BC (16 years): 26 (35%)
338/7–322/1 BC (17 years): 49 (65%)

In other words, the number of inscribed decrees with identifiable proposers datable to the 16 years before the battle of Chaironeia is only about half that datable to the roughly equivalent number of years after Chaironeia. This is certainly relevant to understanding why Demosthenes features so slightly in the epigraphical record, as on any account he was politically active primarily in the years before Chaironeia. Similarly, as the two most influential politicians of the post-Chaironeia period, both of them active as proposers of measures, predominantly honorific decrees, it is to an extent not surprising that Lykourgos and Demades are relatively well-represented. Two significant longer-term trends, however, would seem also to be relevant.

First, if we take the whole span of decree inscribing at Athens from the fifth century to the end of the fourth, the number of honorific decrees increases steadily over time, both in absolute terms, and relative to other types of decree. In the fifth century, though honorific decrees were the largest single inscribed category, the majority, ca. 60%, were not honorific; by the last quarter of the fourth century 80–90% were honorific; and by the end of the third century honorific decrees had become the only category inscribed at public initiative and expense.[49] One factor driving this trend, I suggest, is that, as Athens declined in power, the range of measures available in the foreign policy sphere became more limited and the relative importance of the honorific decree as a

48 Cf. Rhodes 2016, 262: "If there was a period when 'everything was administered by [Demosthenes'] decrees and laws and embassies' (Dem. 18.320, cf. 218–21, 302), it was only in the short period leading up to Chaironeia".

49 Cf. chapter 1 n. 23.

foreign policy lever became greater. This is apparent, for example, in the regular appearance, from the 340s onwards, of the "hortatory intention" clause in the texts of honorific decrees. This was a clause which stated explicitly that the purpose of the decree – sometimes specifically the purpose of inscribing it – was to encourage others to behave towards Athens in an honour-loving way, in other words to benefit the city. The more Athens' power declines, the more she strains to make these decrees as effective as she can, seeking to use each individual decree as a lever to influence the behaviour towards her of, the implication is, any foreigner who might potentially benefit the city.[50] Though some of these developments, such as the hortatory intention clauses, begin in the 340s, it is natural enough that the battle of Chaironeia, the point at which Athens lost her status as leader of the Second Athenian League and ceased to be a fully independent city in the conduct of her foreign policy, should be a significant staging post along this trend of development. As I pointed out in 2010,[51] the epigraphical record suggests that, after Chaironeia, Athens appears radically to reduce its engagement in independent diplomacy at the interstate level: there are no inscribed bilateral treaties, for example, between Athens and any other city, dating from the period between Chaironeia and the Lamian War. I suggest, therefore, that one reason why Lykourgos and Demades are so prominent among decree proposers in the epigraphical record is that, as the leading figures of the post-Chaironeia years the thrust of their – and Athens' – efforts in the foreign policy sphere have become channelled in a more concentrated way into influencing the world through the honorific system.[52]

---

50 On this see also Lambert 2011 and 2012a (= this volume, chapters 3 and 4).

51 Lambert 2010a.

52 An interesting fact about Lykourgos is that he is said to have employed an expert, Eukleides of Olynthos (otherwise unknown), to help him with his decrees: εἰσήνεγκε δὲ καὶ ψηφίσματα, Εὐκλείδῃ τινὶ Ὀλυνθίῳ χρώμενος ἱκανωτάτῳ περὶ τὰ ψηφίσματα ("and he introduced decrees, making use of an Olynthian, Eukleides, who was an expert in decrees", [Plut.] *Lives of Ten Orators* 842c). Since Eukleides was not an Athenian, this can not refer to a practice of substituting Eukleides' name for Lykourgos' as decree proposer, in the manner discussed in section 2. Unless this is a distortion with its roots in comedy or anti-Lykourgan rhetoric, Eukleides, it seems, helped Lykourgos with the drafting of decrees (not, it seems, laws, which are discussed by [Plut.] in the previous section, and for which Lykourgos perhaps took personal responsibility), and perhaps too with other aspects of the process of getting them passed through the Council and Assembly. One suspects that it may have been his (presumably rather heavy) duties as *epi dioikesei*, on top of his work in the courts, that generated a need for support with decrees. In any case his employment by someone who was himself, one would think, an expert, suggests an increasing professionalisation of the skills necessary to be a successful decree proposer in the final years of

Second, the culture of inscribing, the so-called "epigraphical habit" was also gaining in intensity at this period. This applies across the range of the city's epigraphical output, which reaches an overall peak of production in the 330s and 320s, but it applies also specifically to the honorific decree; one of the factors boosting the number of honorific decrees at this period is that, beginning in the 340s, Athens began regularly inscribing decrees honouring its own citizens. Not only are more decrees being inscribed, they are also becoming more wordy – and, perhaps, more attention is being invited to the detail of the inscribed words. This includes the beginnings of a tendency to highlight the names of decree proposers on the stone, for example by inscribing them in a line by themselves, even though this breached the normal stoichedon arrangement of the texts.[53] The proposer wants his name to be noticed. The potential for this development had been there since 354/3, when decree proposers had begun to be fully identified by father's name and demotic, but it is only realised after Chaironeia, when inscribed decrees have become, I suggest, instruments of competitive display by political leaders. It is surely relevant here that Lykourgos and Demades were not only contemporaries, but rivals for political influence. Some of the inscribed decrees proposed by these two men were actually proposed at the very same meeting of the Assembly,[54] and several belong to a sphere of politics that has specifically to do with display, namely

the classical democracy and also reminds us that those decrees of Lykourgos (or anyone else) for which we have evidence, whether literary or epigraphical, are the small tip of a large iceberg. Quite possibly Lykourgos was responsible for hundreds of decrees (including some that he presumably failed to get passed) over the course of his (relatively short) career at the top in Athenian politics (Hansen 1991, 156, calculates that there were perhaps ca. 30,000 decrees passed by the Assembly in the fourth-century democracy).

53 For this development, which becomes a more common feature after 307/6, see Tracy 2000; Henry 1977, 63–66; chapter 11 section 2. Among the decrees proposed by Demades it is a feature of *IG* II³ 1, 322 (337/6 BC), for a courtier of Philip II; 330 (335/4 BC)?; 358 (328/7 BC, same day as 357, proposed by Lykourgos); 384 (322/1 BC) honours connected with the theatre; and it is a feature of 357 (328/7 BC) proposed by Lykourgos. It is also a feature of honorific decrees proposed by Demetrios son of Euktemon of Aphidna, 348 (332/1 BC); Euphiletos son of Euphiletos of Kephisia or Kikynna, 378 (323/2 BC, as reinscribed 318/7); Kallisthenes son of Charmylos of Trinemeia, 360 (328/7 BC) ?; Polyeuktos son of Sostratos of Sphettos, 343 (332/1 BC, as reinscribed 318/7); Telemachos son of Theangelos of Acharnai, 315 (339/8 BC. A notoriously active decree-proposer, see Athen. 9.407e, Lambert 2015 = chapter 11 at n. 33, and above, one wonders if it is coincidental that this decree is the earliest to show this feature). All these decrees are certainly or probably honorific.

54 Chapter 11 n. 18; Appendix 1. This includes a case where decrees proposed by Demades and Lykourgos on the same day have the proposer's name highlighted (see previous note).

the theatre, and were proposed at the special meeting of the Assembly which took place in the theatre of Dionysos after the City Dionysia, a meeting which may have been attended by foreigners, an occasion when the city, its institutions and its leading politicians, were on display in a rather strong sense.[55] So explanations are, I suggest, available for the relatively high number of decrees proposed by Lykourgos and Demades in the epigraphical record.

What, however, about the social status of the decree proposers? There might have been many of them, but to what extent were they wealthy and prominent individuals? We must look at our third set of statistics:

C *Relative Status of Decree Proposers 354/3–322/1*

TABLE 1[56]

Political Role	% Class A	% Class B1	% Class B2	% Class C
Proposer of law or decree[a]	38	21	22	19
Liturgist (= class A by definition)[b]	59	14	14	14
Secretary of the Council[c]	11	26	22	41
Member of presiding committee (*proedros*)[d]	1	6	38	55

a The numbers are: class A, 19; B1, 10.5; B2, 11; C, 9.5.

b 7 of the 8 liturgists in classes B2 and C are attested by name and demotic only. If we had fuller onomastic information about these men more of them would be assignable to classes A or B1.

c Since all the secretaries are attested with father's name and demotic, these statistics will slightly overstate the difference in status between secretaries and *proedroi*, none of whose father's names are attested.

d Since none of the fathers' names of *proedroi* are attested these statistics will slightly exaggerate their obscurity in comparison with liturgists and secretaries.

I have divided Athenian citizens for this purpose into four classes:

55 Cf. Lambert 2012a (= chapter 4).

56 For a breakdown of the data in this table see Appendices 1–4.

Class A: member of family of liturgical class (*APF*) or otherwise attested as very wealthy and/or prominent
Class B1: attested in contexts suggestive of wealth or prominence
Class B2: attested in contexts not suggestive of wealth or prominence (e.g. on a funerary monument, service in the democracy as councillor or public arbitrator)
Class C: completely unknown.

The table shows the proportion of members of four groups attested in each class. Given the relatively patchy state of our evidence, even in this, the best documented period of Athenian history, we can not equate attestation in a lower class with actual membership of that class. Some men attested in class C will actually have been wealthy and/or prominent individuals. We can, however, obtain an idea of relative wealth and prominence of men in different groups by aggregating the data for the group as a whole and comparing them with the data for the other groups. For comparison, therefore, and to enable us to pitch the relative level of wealth and prominence of the average proposer, I have included statistics relating to liturgists, the small elite of wealth who were liable to undertake costly public obligations such as the trierarchy, to secretaries of the Council, who held office for a year, and who were relatively ordinary Athenians,[57] and to members of the presiding committee of the Council (*proedroi*), who held office for a day and were in effect random Council members.[58]

We have two inscribed lists of liturgists from this period and the figures show the proportion of the men on these two lists who are attested in other evidence as belonging to the classes shown.[59] 73% of men on the two lists are identifiable from other evidence as belonging in classes A or B1. These figures demonstrate that, at this period, our evidence for the highest classes in terms of wealth and prominence is very good: most of those who performed liturgies are attested as belonging to wealthy or prominent families. Row 1 shows that 59% of proposers are attested as belonging to classes A and B1, less than the proportion of liturgists. Proposers were on average, therefore, rather less prominent and wealthy than members of the liturgical class.

The fourth row shows that members of the presiding committee of the Council are almost entirely attested in the lower two classes, with only 7% attested in classes A and B1. The statistic confirms that the Council at this period

57 Previously elected and filled by "distinguished" men, in the time of *Ath. Pol.* (54.3) this secretaryship was appointed by lot (scil. from qualified men who put themselves forward).
58 *Ath. Pol.* 44.2.
59 *IG* II³ 1, 550 (333/2 or 332/1 BC) and *SEG* 25.177 (331/0 BC).

was not dominated by the prominent and wealthy, but, as was predictable from the restriction of tenure to twice in a lifetime, was broadly representative of the Athenian population as a whole.[60] It also shows that the wealth and prominence of the average proposer of an inscribed law or decree was significantly higher than the wealth and prominence of the average councillor.

In comparison, 37% of secretaries of the Council (row 3) are attested in classes A and B1, showing that they were significantly more wealthy and prominent than the average councillor (7%), but less wealthy and prominent than the average proposer (58%).

What we have shown, therefore, is that there was an upward progression in wealth and prominence from councillor (7%), to secretary of the Council (37%), to proposer (58%) to liturgist (73%).[61] Proposers of inscribed laws and decrees were, on average, wealthier and more prominent than secretaries of the Council or councillors, but less wealthy and prominent than members of the liturgical class.

D *Average Status of Proposer by Type of Measure*

We can fill out the picture by looking at the statistics for class of proposer, broken down by type of measure.

TABLE 2

Type of measure	Honours Athenian	Honours God	Honours foreigner	Religious	Treaty/ foreign
Number of cases/ proposers[a]	17/17	1/1	37/31	7 (including 4 laws)/6	4/4
Proposed in Council[b]	75%	0%	24%	-	-
% class A or B1 proposers	32%[c]	100%	78%[d]	86%[e]	75%

a The first figure is the number of decrees, the second the number of different proposers. In other words, every decree honouring an Athenian was proposed by a different man.

60 Cf. chapter 9, p. 229.

61 For reasons noted above, because of the relative quality of the onomastic data, these figures probably exaggerate somewhat the obscurity both of the *proedroi* and liturgists relative to proposers and secretaries of the Council; but this will not affect the overall picture.

b This includes decrees of the Council, *probouleumata* and probouleumatic decrees, and excludes non-probouleumatic decrees and riders.
c A: 5. B1: 0.5. B2: 4.5. C: 6.
d A: 23. B1: 6. B2: 4.5. C: 3.5
e A/B1: 6. B2/C: 1.

The numbers in each sample are in most cases rather small, and in those cases we cannot press the statistics. On treaties see briefly below. It may well be significant that nearly all the proposers of religious measures are in classes A or B1, but that may be because most of them are laws. The proposer of the law against tyranny, Eukrates, was also a prominent individual, among those executed on Antipater's orders after the Lamian War. It may be that wealth and prominence were commonly adjuncts of the authority and skill needed successfully to undertake the cumbersome and weighty process of sponsoring a new law.[62] What clearly is significant, however, is the difference between proposers of honours for Athenians and honours for foreigners, the latter being on average very much more wealthy and prominent than the former. In fact the percentage of proposers of decrees honouring foreigners attested in classes A and B1, 78%, is closely comparable with the percentage of liturgists attested in those classes, 75%. The corollary here is that these proposers predominantly made their proposals in the Assembly (76%), while the proposers of decrees for Athenians were predominantly councillors, i.e. proposers of Council decrees, *probouleumata* and probouleumatic decrees.

The highest honours awarded to Athenians, which might include a bronze statue, permanent dining rights in the *prytaneion*, and preferential seating (*proedria*) in the theatre, were awarded only rarely in the fourth-century democracy and there are no extant inscribed examples of the decrees from our period.[63] The inscribed decrees for Athenians in our period all honour

62 On which see Canevaro 2015 (cf. chapter 2, n. 29). *FGH* 325 Phanodemos of Thymaitadai, proposer of the law on the Amphiaraia festival (*IG* II^3 1, 348) was also wealthy and prominent. The proposers of the earlier fourth century inscribed laws are unidentifiable, with the exception of the grain-tax law (*RO* 26), proposed by the prominent politician, Agyrrhios (*APF* 8157).

63 The earliest well-preserved inscribed decree awarding the highest honours is *IG* II^2 450 = *ABSA* 95, 2000, 486–89 E1, for Asandros of Macedon in 314/3, though the fragmentary *SEG* 29.86 = RO 11 (cf. Rhodes and Lambert on AIO) for Euagoras of Salamis in 394/3 is perhaps an earlier instance. The earliest extant decree awarding such honours to a native-born Athenian is the posthumous decree for Lykourgos of Boutadai of 307/6, *IG* II^2 457 + 3207, with [Plut.] *Lives of the Ten Orators* 852 (see AIO). On the highest honours at Athens see now M. Domingo Gygax 2016: 192–99 on awards to the "great benefactors" of the

Athenians for the performance of democratic offices (including priesthoods);[64] typically they are annual officials appointed by lot, though terms of office were on occasion longer,[65] or even shorter or ad hoc.[66] Usually the offices filled by the honorands (e.g. Council members, officials, secretaries) did not obviously entail financial contributions; the honorands were not uncommonly more or less ordinary Athenians;[67] and even where they were wealthy and

---

early fourth century, Konon in 394/3, first to be awarded a bronze statue since Harmodios and Aristogeiton (Dem. 20.70), Euagoras, Iphikrates, Chabrias and Timotheos; 227–29 on awards in our period, including to Demades in 335 BC, the first known civilian recipient.

64 Listed in Lambert 2004 (= *IALD*, 3–47). The decree for Phanodemos of Thymaitadai, *IG* II³ 1, 348, is a marginal case, but his service as proposer of a law for the Amphiaraion (νενομοθέτηκεν περὶ τὸ ἱερὸν τοῦ Ἀμφιαράου) is constructed in it as performance of a quasi-office.

65 Pytheas of Alopeke, honoured by *IG* II³ 1, 338, held the probably quadrennial elective office in charge of the water supply (ἐπὶ τὰς κρήνας, cf. *Ath. Pol.* 43.1). As a general, Diotimos, perhaps honoured by *IG* II³ 1, 336 (n. 71 below) also held elective office, though annual. The priest of Zeus Soter, one of four priests in Piraeus cults honoured by *IG* II³ 1, 416, was perhaps a "democratic" priest, appointed annually by lot from the tribes in rotation, like the priest of Asklepios (Lambert 2010b, 171; 2012b, 70). The three others, Dionysos in Piraeus (2010b, 170), Poseidon Pelagios (2010b, 171) and Ammon, might also have been "democratic" priests, or *genos* priests (or in the case of Ammon, a priest appointed from a group of *orgeones*, 2010b, 163–64) in office for life (cf. 2012b, 70–71).

66 Strictly speaking the presiding committee of the Assembly (*proedroi*), probably honoured by *IG* II³ 1, 476 (and in another instance in the case at issue in Hyp. *Phil.* 4, where the proposed honours are attacked on the grounds that the *proedroi* put to the vote a proposal to honour one or more leading Macedonians), were in office only for a day, but one might conceptualise this as an aspect of their annual term on the Council. Similarly for other honours awarded to councillors for specific actions qua councillors, e.g. the councillors honoured *IG* II³ 1, 360, 41–57, for organising a dedication to Amphiaraos. *IG* II³ 1, 348 honours Phanodemos for proposing a law, a function without specific duration, so far as we know (cf. n. 64).

67 The clearest case of honours for an office entailing no financial cost and filled by ordinary Athenians (cf. table 1 above) is that of the *proedroi, IG* II³ 1, 476 (previous note). Eudoxos son of Theangelos of Sypalettos, whose performance as Council administrator in 343/2 (a busy year) was so outstanding that he was awarded not only a 500 dr. crown on the Council's expense account, proposed by [Kallipho?]n son of Antikrates of Pambotadai (perhaps class B2 or C), but a second 500 dr. crown funded by personal contributions from individual councillors (average 1 dr. each), proposed by Brachyllos of Erchia (B2), *IG* II³ 1, 306 decrees 4 and 5, seems unlikely to have been expected to spend his own money in the exercise of his duties, and he is otherwise completely unknown in person or by family. Kallikratides son of Kallikrates of Steiria is honoured by *IG* II³ 1, 469, on the proposal of the unknown Hieronymos of Rhamnous, for the efficient performance of his duties as recorder (*anagrapheus*) in writing up public documents. Here too no personal

prominent, there is rarely any sense that they had contributed financially.[68] It is clear enough from the literary record that office-holders might contribute financially and that this could, in some cases, be a contributory factor to the award of honours;[69] but the inscribed record reflects the strongly collectivist

expenses were entailed (it may be significant in this regard that he is not honoured for love of honour, *philotimia*, but for excellence, *arete*, and right conduct, *dikaiosyne*) albeit that, unsurprisingly given the nature of his duties (cf. the status of secretaries of the Council in table 1), he is otherwise known, including in contexts which probably imply, if not major prominence and wealth, reasonable levels of affluence (e.g. he is probably the Kallikratides of Steiria who was lender of 1,000 dr. with Philon of Rhamnous on the security of a house, SEG 21.657 = *Agora* 19 H98. For a discussion of him and his family, which is well documented in the hellenistic period, see Aleshire 1991, 133–37).

68 IG II^3 1, 348, honouring Phanodemos of Thymaitadai for substantial works at the Amphiaraion in 332/1 mentions that he had "supplied the means (or revenues) for these things" (πόρους πεπόριχεν εἰς ταῦτα). This phrase is, perhaps deliberately, slightly opaque as to the nature and extent of Phanodemos' personal contributions. One possibility is that he had donated land, the rental income from which was to fund the works at the Amphiaraion (cf. Papazarkadas 2011, 45–48). Cf., in the much more explicit catalogue of financial donations for the public good by the fabulously wealthy Eurykleides of Kephisia in the late 3rd century, IG II^3 1, 1160, 7–13, "… and when the country, because of its enemies, was fallow and unsown, he was responsible for it being worked and sown, having supplied money ([χρήματα πορί]σας) … and he supplied the money ([χρήμα]τα ἐπόρισεν) for the crown for [those forces] who with Diogenes returned [the garrisons]." Substantial expenditure is implied by IG II^3 1, 338, honouring the manager of the water supply, Pytheas of Alopeke, but the decree is not explicit on the extent of Pytheas' financial contributions. These two decrees (on which see now also Domingo Gygax 2016, 211) seem very gently to anticipate hellenistic practice, in which honorific decrees were much more explicit about financial contributions (cf. Lambert 2014). It may not be coincidental that neither Phanodemos nor Pytheas were contentious political figures, and that both these decrees were erected outside Attic territory at the Amphiaraion. A similar construction, however, can be put on IG II^3 1, 416, where in addition to four priests in Piraeus cults, ten *hieropoioi* chosen by the Council are honoured, because they finely and with *philotimia* took care of the provision (*parastasis*) of the sacrificial victims and took care of various other matters connected with sacrifices and heroes (text fragmentary) justly and with *philotimia* (23–27), though the extent of personal contributions by the *hieropoioi* is again opaque. On the other hand the managers of the Great Amphiaraia honoured by IG II^3 1, 355, were wealthy and prominent individuals, but there is no suggestion that they had contributed financially, though the decree does refer to financial transactions involving public funds. The reality of the situation is complex, however, and opaque, since it is implied by IG II^3 1, 348 that the costs of this festival is one of things for which Phanodemos had "supplied the means" and Phanodemos is himself one of the festival managers.

69 Most famously Demosthenes' personal contributions to costs of wall-building as commissioner of fortifications after the battle of Chaironeia, in the case of the crown for him proposed by Ktesiphon, Dem. 18.112–13, 117–19, 299, 311, cf. Aeschin. 3.17. This and a

ethos of the classical democracy, in which the wealthy were obliged to contribute of their wealth, could claim credit for it in forensic contexts, but could not expect public recognition for it in official citations for honours voted by the Assembly.[70] Such recognition was invidious and potentially elitist in a polity in which the contributions of all were valued, regardless of financial status. Though for the most part the connections between honorands and proposers are obscure,[71] it makes sense in general terms that those proposing honours for them should be commensurately of relatively modest status (it does not seem that there was any particular tendency for prominent and wealthy individuals to propose honours for the less prominent and wealthy, or vice versa); and that their proposals did not necessarily excite much debate in the Assembly.[72] Indeed there is an important key to understanding the dynamic here, namely that these decrees predominantly honoured councillors, Council officials or other city officials and priests who were ultimately responsible to the Council. As such, and given especially the limitation on tenure of office on the Council to twice in a lifetime, it is natural that the decrees should be initiated in the Council (some, as we have seen, are actually decrees of the Council alone), by proposers who were themselves by and large ordinary Athenian citizens. It is scarcely surprising, therefore, that relatively high numbers of decrees honouring Athenians at this period were proposed in the Council, and relatively low numbers of the proposers were wealthy and prominent.

---

number of other examples documented in the orators are discussed by Domingo Gygax 2016, 208–11.

70 On this cf. now Domingo Gygax 2016, 215, 254. Wealth was to be used for the public good, not boasted about (Pericles at Thuc. 2.40.1).

71 On the detectable points of contact (deme and healing cults) between Androkles, priest of Asklepios and the proposers of honours for him see above sect. 2; similar common interest in the Amphiaraion links Demetrios son of Euktemon of Aphidna with the honorand of his decree for Phanodemos (348). We are best informed about the background to what is perhaps the most high profile, albeit highly fragmentary, decree in this set, *IG* II^3 1, 336. In 335/4 Lykourgos proposed a decree with Aristonikos of Marathon providing for naval operations against pirates led by the general Diotimos (*IG* II^2 1623, 276–85); on his successful return he also proposed a decree honouring him in 334/3 ([Plut.] *Lives of the Ten Orators* 844a), which may be *IG* II^3 1, 336. The connection between honorand and proposer in this case is unusually clear.

72 It is no surprise that the two in this set that honoured especially prominent individuals, *IG* II^3 1, 355, for the board of managers of the Amphiaraia festival which included leading Athenians such as Lykourgos, Demades and Phanodemos, and the decree for the general Diotimos, *IG* II^3 1, 336, were non-probouleumatic. The decree for Phanodemos, *IG* II^3 1, 348, an uncontroversial figure who attracted uniform respect, is hybrid in form, i.e. perhaps probouleumatic, but also discussed in the Assembly (see further chapter 9).

Foreign honorands in inscribed decrees, on the other hand, mostly recipients of honours such as the citizenship and the proxeny, are on average of higher status at this period than Athenian honorands. Proposing such men for honours (and a fortiori proposing interstate treaties) generally presupposes that the proposer has a locus in high-status inter-polis networks in general, and close personal connections with the honorand in particular, even if, generally speaking, the state of our knowledge is such that we cannot pin these connections down with much confidence in specific cases.[73] Commensurately, the relevant decrees are commonly formulated in the Assembly rather than the Council.

Moreno has posited that Androtion (class A) and Polyeuktos of Krioa (class A), proposers of *IG* II^3 1, 298 for the Bosporan rulers, were part of an international elite network involving themselves, the rulers of the Bosporan kingdom, and others, including Isocrates and his school, though in this case, as in most others in the inscribed record, we have to be content with circumstantial evidence, indirect links and consonances, rather than specifically attested connections.[74] One case where we can fill in the background a little more is that of Archedikos of Lamptrai (class B1) comic poet (*PCG* II, 533–36) and proposer of a decree of the late 320s honouring friends of the (Macedonian) king and Antipater (*IG* II^3 1, 484). Not only is Archedikos later found in 320/19 as *anagrapheus*, a leading official (it seems) of the oligarchic regime imposed on Athens by Antipater, he is also on record as having satirised Demochares, Demosthenes' nephew, prominent democrat in the restored democracy after 307, and virulent opponent of elite intellectuals and oligarchs, such as Demetrios of Phaleron, and, as Polybios implies, Antipater and his friends.[75] Like some other theatrical personalities of this period,[76] the wealth, public profile, and not infrequently the political engagement of successful poets, not to mention their capacity to influence the historical record, meant that they commonly had a place among the elite on the international stage.

Demades is, of course, well attested in the literary record as a diplomat sans pareil, highly effective in constructive diplomacy with the Macedonians,

---

73 For proxenies as an aspect of high status inter-state networks across the Greek world as a whole, see now Mack 2015; Domingo Gygax 2016, 92, 108–14, 239–40, 251.

74 Moreno 2007, 175–77, and 269–75.

75 Polybios 12.13 = *FGH* 566 Timaios F35 = Archedikos F4K-A. See Habicht 1993. Polybios describes Archedikos as a nobody, but this merely suits his rhetoric.

76 Habicht 1993 draws parallels with Philippides, honorand of *IG* II^3 1, 877 (283/2 BC), and influential at the court of Lysimachos. On a comparable dynamic in relation to actors cf. Lambert 2008 (= *IALD* 337–62); 2012a (= this volume, chapter 4).

key negotiator of advantageous settlements for Athens with Philip II after Chaironeia[77] and Alexander after the sack of Thebes.[78] It is beyond my scope here to review his career in general, or all his many recorded decrees.[79] Suffice it to say that the inscribed record of his self-standing decrees at this period, all of which, where their content is discernible, honour foreigners, displays this high level diplomacy in action. We may lack what would have been the prize exhibit, the decree honouring Philip II himself with a bronze statue in the Agora, which may (or may not) have been proposed by Demades,[80] but *IG* II³ 1, 322 was certainly proposed by Demades and certainly honoured a courtier of Philip II; 335, also proposed by Demades, honoured an Amyntor who might (or might not) be the father of Alexander's friend, Hephaistion; and 319, the name of whose proposer does not survive, honoured an Alkimachos, which resonates with Hypereides' complaint (*Against Demades* F77 Jensen) that "we made Alkimachos [a Macedonian general and envoy] and Antipatros Athenians and proxenoi".[81] Not all his diplomatic capital was expended on this central issue of Athenian politics. As I noted in chapter 4 (= 2012a), two other policy themes loom large among the inscribed honorific decrees of the post-Chaironeia period: the promotion of Athens' theatrical heritage and of the security of her grain supply. Demades engaged with both, proposing, in rivalry (it can be assumed) with Lykourgos, a series of decrees bestowing honours connected with the theatre (346 for an unidentifiable son of Aristeides, 384 for an unknown honorand, and *IG* II³ 1, 929, for the Theban [pipe-player?] Ariston, reinscribed in the late 280s); and, though not in our corpus, there is epigraphical evidence also for his participation in the policy of seeking to secure the grain supply by honouring those traders and others on whose decisions it rested (see e.g. *IG* II²

77 Dem. 18.285; Brun 2000, 55–69.

78 E.g. Diod. 17.15.5; Brun 2000, 71–83. This was probably the occasion for the award of a statue and *sitesis* in the prytaneion vigorously opposed by Lykourgos (F9 Jensen) and Hypereides (see below) and later referred to by Dinarchos 1 *Against Demosthenes* 101.

79 22 dating up to 322/1 are conveniently listed by Hansen 1989a, 40; 18 epigraphically attested across his whole career by Brun 2000, 177–78; to which add *IG* II³ 1, 929.

80 Diod. 16.92.1–2, cf. Brun 2000, 64, who rates the chances as strong that Demades was behind the motion. As with most decrees providing for statues at this period we do not know whether the decree was inscribed. Demades was also attacked by *graphe paranomon* for proposing at this period a proxeny for (allegedly) an Olynthian partisan of Philip II, Euthykrates. Cf. Hyp. F14.76–86, chapter 7 n. 22; and for currying favour with Alexander by Hypereides, *Against Diondas* 7 (Carey et al. 2008, 10).

81 Cf. however my hesitations about the identification of this Alkimachos at 2006, 136 (= *IALD*, 126) n. 103. A similar thought is expressed, but without mentioning specific honorands, by Hypereides, *Against Diondas* 2.26–31 (Carey et al. 2008, 5).

400 = Engen 2010, 272 no. 33). *IG* II³ 1, 358, Demades' decree for Eurylochos of Kydonia, was not, so far as we can tell, connected with Macedon-directed diplomacy, the grain supply or the theatre, but recognised Eurylochos' work in ransoming Athenians from Crete, an alignment with the interests of fellow citizens in distress that, as we shall see in the next chapter, has an interesting echo in another decree for a Kydonian a century later.[82]

Consonant with his primary policy focus on domestic regeneration, honours for foreigners are less predominant among Lykourgos' inscribed laws and decrees, and tend to connect to aspects of his policies in that sphere: Eudemos of Plataia is honoured for help with one of Lykourgos' important projects, the construction of the Panathenaic stadium (*IG* II³ 1, 352),[83] and his intense interest in promoting the "classical" Athenian theatre is reflected in 345, for a relation of the honorand of 352, passed on the same day Demades' 346, and perhaps also in 470, mentioning the *skene* of the theatre, though the latter was is not certainly proposed by Lykourgos.[84] Like Demades he also engaged with the policy of deploying honorific decrees to support the grain supply. We have already noted this aspect of the background to his decree for the general Diotimos; it is also evidenced in 432, for Sopatros of Akragas (and cf. the fragmentary 495 for a possibly related man from Akragas[85]). *IG* II³ 1, 337 II, giving the Kitian merchants the right to found a temple of Aphrodite in the Piraeus, though not honorific in form, patently belongs in a comparable context of encouragement of the foreign trading community.

Another prominent anti-Macedonian politician who clearly belonged to the international elite and features as a proposer is Polyeuktos of Sphettos. He was active abroad as an envoy in 343 and 323[86] and the extent of his influence is indicated by his being among the politicians whose extradition was demanded by Alexander in 335.[87] We can not pin down the circumstances of his decree of 332/1 for one Theophantos, though we can draw inferences in general terms from the fact that a later decree for the same man (343 II) was passed during the Lamian War in the winter of 323/2 and, like the decree for Euphron of

---

82 The context of 356, for an unidentifiable Larisan, is obscure. 3rd-century decree: *IG* II³ 1, 1137, for Eumaridas of Kydonia, discussed chapter 9.11.

83 Cf. [Plut.] *Lives of the Ten Orators* 841d, 852, *IG* II² 457 + 3207, 5–7.

84 For (inconclusive and circumstantial) linguistic support for attributing this decree to Lykourgos see Lambert 2004b, 185 (= *IALD*, 318).

85 *IALD*, 402.

86 Dem. 9.72; [Plut.] *Lives of Ten Orators* 846c.

87 Arrian *Anab.* 1.10; Plut. *Dem.* 23.3. He lodged the *graphe paranomon* against Kephisodotos for proposing a statue and other high honours for Demades (Hansen 1974, 39 no. 31).

Sikyon, passed around the same time, seems to have been torn down at the behest of the victorious Macedonians and re-inscribed by the restored democracy in 318/7. 439 shows him engaging in the policy, pursued by leading politicians at this period regardless of their position on the Macedonian question, of deploying honorific decrees with the objective of securing the grain supply. This was also one of the spheres of activity of Telemachos of Acharnai, who was satirised by the comic poet Timokles as one of the busiest decree proposers of the period (see above). He took a leading hand in cultivating relations with the grain trader Herakleides of Salamis by securing a crown and practical assistance for him in recovering his sails after his first benefaction, actions which, as they were doubtless intended to, encouraged further benefactions from this trader. It is notable that, though the social status of these grain-trader honorands was not especially high – none of them are known to history outside these decrees honouring them – the social status of the Athenians who proposed the honours remained typically in the A/B1 range. It perhaps heightened the gratification of a Sopatros of Akragas (entirely unknown) to have been honoured by the likes of (the distinguished) Lykourgos of Boutadai.[88]

There are other cases where some kind of circumstantial link between proposer and foreign honorand can be detected.[89] Quite often, however, none is apparent, albeit that some kind of association, direct or indirect, must be assumed.[90] It was a rhetorical commonplace to accuse political opponents of

88 Cf. the remarks on this point of Engen 2010, 12.

89 It is probably not coincidental that it is a politician with a strong anti-Macedonian record, Demophilos of Acharnai, who proposes a decree for a citizen of that flashpoint in the history of relations between Athens and Macedon, Amphipolis; and there is a degree of extra-Attic, religiously flavoured, consistency between the activities of Epiteles of Pergase as *naopoios* and proxenos at Delphi, manager of the Amphiaraia festival at the Amphiaraion in Oropos, and proposer of a decree connected, shortly after the death of Alexander the Great, with the Athenian *theoria* to the Nemean Games at Kleonai and honouring Athens' *proxenos* there, Lapyris. Nor is it surprising to find Philodemos of Eroiadai, whose career displays strong patriotic military-financial engagement as guarantor of ships for Chalkis in 340, trierarch, and commissioner for the repair of walls after Chaironeia, active as proposer in one of the pair of inscriptions honouring Tenedos and its representative on the Council of the Second Athenian League, Aratos (401 II); cf. 313, which recognised Tenedos' help in 340/39 in supporting Byzantium and Perinthos against Philip II, arranging financial concessions for it, the last document of the Second Athenian League.

90 This applies to the decrees proposed by Demeas (class A); Demosthenes of Lamptrai (367 V) (C); Demosthenes of Paiania (A); Diopeithes of Sphettos (A); Diophantos of Myrrhinous (324) (A); Euboulides of Halimous (B1); Hierokleides of Alopeke (294) (B2); Hippostratos of Pallene (C); Kallikrates of Lamptrai (313) (B2 or C); Kephisodotos of

corruption in procuring honorific decrees for foreign allies.[91] This is in a sense mere rhetoric, but as Moreno points out, it can be interpreted as tapping into generalised anxiety and suspicion among ordinary Athenians about corrupt activities of a wealthy and prominent international elite, whether realistic or not.[92] The socio-economic statistics for decree proposers tend to confirm that the conduct of international relations via (treaties and) honorific decrees was indeed largely the preserve of an elite of prominence and wealth in the latest phase of the classical democracy; and it was an elite that operated primarily in the Assembly, rather than in the Council.

5 Conclusion

In concluding this chapter I would draw out three points from the foregoing analysis which are relevant to our overall understanding of the quality and character of the classical Athenian democracy in its final phase.

First there is the multiplicity of proposers, the fact, in other words, that so many different proposers are attested across a relatively small number of inscribed laws and decrees, and that, aside from Demades and Lykourgos, for whose prolific profile we have offered an explanation, most are attested as proposers of only one decree and none as proposers of more than two or three. This multiplicity was already apparent from Hansen's analysis, though, as we have seen, his explanation was not entirely satisfactory: the idea that it was common to put one's name to proposals that were in fact driven by "bigger" men, whether as a councillor or in the Assembly, is largely a product of rhetorical distortion and exaggeration of practices that were either unusual or more or less innocent, e.g. whereby a younger citizen would learn political techniques from a more experienced, or a citizen keen to propose a decree in the Assembly might arrange for a fellow demesman to put an appropriate *probouleuma* through the Council. It fails to account satisfactorily for the fact that, contrary to what was believed when Hansen wrote, most decrees of this period were either non-probouleumatic or discussed in the Assembly, or for the way that, as a matter of fact, "big" men are frequently attested as proposers in

Acharnai (367 II, *probouleuma*) (B2, where it is plausible that the main dynamic was his relationship with the main mover of this decree, Telemachos, see above); Kephisophon of Paiania (418 II) (A); Nothippos of Diomeia (B2); Phyleus of Oinoe (B2).

91 Alleged e.g. against Demosthenes: Din. 1.43; by Demosthenes against others: Dem. 23.185, 201–3.

92 Moreno 2007, 269–79.

their own name. What, then, is the correct explanation for this phenomenon? The explanation needs to account for the fact, apparent from the statistics in table 2, that this multiplicity applies both at higher and lower levels of wealth and prominence: to decrees honouring Athenians, proposed by relatively less wealthy and prominent men, and almost equally to decrees honouring foreigners (and treaties and laws) proposed by much more wealthy and prominent men. Analysis in terms of a dynamic as between "big men" and "small men" will not, therefore, meet the case. Given the predominance of honorific decrees in the statistics, one might perhaps suggest that it has something specifically to do with the personal nature of the dynamic linking proposer and honorand: what the epigraphical record shows us is, in a sense, the product of an aggregate of many such personal connections; though this does not fully explain why the same multiplicity should apply, as it seems to, to non-honorific decrees also. One might also think that it has to do with the strong networks that, along lines suggested by Ober, characterised the Athenian polity, though this does not seem quite to explain the applicability of the principle to decrees with a focus outside the city. What we can perhaps say is that such plurilocality or spreading widely and thinly of power and influence does seem consistent with a political culture that favoured the exercise of office by boards rather than individual officials; that induced the creation, in the early fourth century Council, of the *proedroi* in an attempt to offset any possibility that too much power might be exercised by a prytany, albeit that the latter was in office for only a tenth of a year, or its chairman, only in office for a single day;[93] that induced the prejudice in favour of political participation and against a "quiet life" famously articulated in Pericles' funerary oration;[94] and that induced Aeschines to assert the ideal of the "amateur" speaker in the Assembly. The statistics for proposers of laws and decrees do not perhaps indicate that the ordinary Athenian had as much political influence as someone of wealth and prominence; but it does suggest that, whether wealthy or not, it was an

93 In the 5th century the prytany and its chairman, who was in office for just a night and a day (*Ath. Pol.* 44.2), presided over Assembly meetings. Some time between 403/2 and 379/8 that function was transferred to a board of 9 *proedroi* selected from councillors not in prytany, one of whom was selected as its chairman to preside over Assembly meetings and "put to the vote" proposals. Hansen 1991, 140–41, regards it as significant that the chairman of the *proedroi* was appointed only on the morning of the meeting, not the previous evening (less time to be corrupted!). In any case the underlying passion for spreading power thinly is obvious.

94 "We alone regard the man who does not participate in these things [politics] not as retiring (ἀπράγμονα) but as useless (ἀχρεῖον)" Thuc. 2.40.2.

essential aspect of Athenian democratic culture that political power and influence should be spread between multiple individuals.[95]

Second, I would emphasise again in this context the significance of the inscribed decrees honouring Athenians. As we have seen, honouring of Athenian officials by the Council and Assembly had taken place before texts of the decrees began regularly to be inscribed in the 340s,[96] but it is only with the inscribing of the texts that they emerge fully-fledged into the historical record and we begin to obtain information on details such as proposers. As I argued in 2011 (= chapter 3), it is unlikely to be coincidental that they begin to be inscribed at around the same time as honorific decrees begin explicitly to praise and promote *philotimia* and to express a hortatory intention. The relative ordinariness of most of the recipients of such honours at this period reminds us of an important point about the culture of the classical Athenian democracy in its later phase: it was a culture in which *philotimia* was democratised both in the sense that ordinary Athenians had a share in it as honorands and in that it was not necessarily linked, in fact or in presentation, to expenditure of personal wealth. The data about the proposers of such decrees, also typically not especially wealthy or prominent, but rather ordinary Athenians serving their term on the Council, emphasises still further the decrees' "democratising" character.[97]

---

95 As Hansen 1991, 250, comments on the restriction of service as chairman of the prytany to once in a lifetime (*Ath. Pol.* 44.1), it "is a marvellous illustration of Aristotle's democratic principle that everyone must take part in the government by turns". Being a decree proposer was not precisely a "governmental" role, but it is unsurprising that the Athenians applied to it broadly the same culture of broad participation.

96 As implied e.g. by a number of the dedications collected at IG II^3 4, 20–220.

97 This trend may also help explain the *topos* in speeches of the orators objecting to proposed honours on the basis of the proliferation and devaluation of honorific decrees at this period, compared with the "good old days." E.g. at length, Aeschines 3.177–88 (objecting to Demosthenes' award), briefly Lykourgos F 9.2 (objecting to Demades'). To an extent this may also underlie the satire on the "seeker after petty honours" (*mikrophilotimos*), Theophrastos, *Char.* 21, among whose various small-scale attempts to draw attention to himself is obtaining from his fellow *prytaneis* the role of reporting to the Assembly on the *hiera*, coming forward, splendidly attired and crowned, to announce: "men of Athens, we *prytaneis* have sacrificed the *Galaxia* to the Mother of the gods, and the rites have turned out well (ἱερὰ καλά) and we bid you accept the favourable outcome (καὶ ὑμεῖς δέχεσθε τὰ ἀγαθά)". This type of wording occurs in our period e.g. in IG II^3 1, 416, 11–12, honouring priests and *hieropoioi*, and was to become common when decrees honouring prytanies came to be regularly inscribed in the hellenistic period (e.g. in 283/2 BC, IG II^3 1, 880, 8–20; Mother of the gods at 952, 6, ca. 280–265 BC; on the obscure *Galaxia* cf. Parker 2005, 470).

It is important, finally, to bear in mind the selectivity of the inscribed record. As we saw in chapter 2, even honorific decrees were not all inscribed, and broadly it was the more significant that were inscribed. Beneath the surface of the inscribed record there was most likely a mass of more routine honours for citizens involving, we may assume, a wide socio-economic range as well as the multiplicity of proposers and honorands that we have observed in the inscribed record.[98] As for non-honorific uninscribed decrees, as we saw in chapter 2 they were not necessarily unimportant, and the literary evidence makes clear that, as we might expect, the wealthy and prominent were active as proposers, but here too there will have been many opportunities for the engagement of a wide spectrum of Athenian society, and a multiplicity of proposers, in the decision-making process.

98 This applies particularly to honorific decrees of the Council, which, our evidence suggests, were not usually inscribed (cf. chapter 2 and chapter 9.3), but were most likely quite common and numerous.

APPENDIX 1 *Proposers of inscribed laws and decrees 354/3–322/1 BC*

Proposer	Law or decree proposed[a]	Date	Decree content[b]	Decree type[c]	Status and other features
1. Alkimachos son of – of Myrrhinoutta	331	335/4	H	PB	B2. *PAA* 121995. Age: ca. 55.
2. Androtion son of Andron of Gargettos	298 I	347/6	HF (Bosporan rulers)	A	A. *APF* 913. Politician and Atthidographer (*FGH* 324). Age: ca. 60–65.
3. Antidotos son of Apollodoros of Sypalettos	337 I	333/2	R (Kitian temple)	BP (open)	B1. *PAA* 132730 (cf. 143220). Among councillors who contributed to dedication to Amphiaraos, 328/7 (IG II^3 1, 360, 20).
4. Archedemos son of Archias of Paionidai	296	349/8	T? (or HF) (Echinaioi)	PB	B2 or C. *PAA* 209125 (cf. 120).

a Reference numbers are to *IG* II^3 1 unless stated otherwise. Included in this list are inscribed laws and decrees of which texts are preserved on stone and which are therefore included in *IG* II^3 1 fasc. 2. Those merely referred to in other inscriptions are not included.

b H = Honours; HA = Honours Athenian; HF = Honours Foreigner; R = Religious Regulation; T = Treaty or other foreign policy.

c B = Council decree; BP = Probouleuma; PB = Assembly decree based on probouleuma; A = Non-probouleumatic Assembly decree; R = Rider to a decree, passed in Assembly. For discussion of these decree types see chapter 9.

APPENDIX 1 *Proposers of inscribed laws and decrees 354/3–322/1 BC* (cont.)

Proposer	Law or decree proposed	Date	Decree content	Decree type	Status and other features
5. Archedikos son of Naukritos of Lamptrai	484	324–322/1	HF (Friends of king & Antipater)	A	B1. *PAA* 209325 ? = 209300 (comic poet *PCG* II 533–36) and 305. *Anagrapheus* in 320/19 under oligarchy. Satirised Demochares, nephew of Demosthenes.
6. Aristonikos son of Aristoteles of Marathon	447	ca. 335–30	R (Panathenaia)	Law	A. *PAA* 174070. Proposed decree on pirates with Lykourgos, 335/4 (*IG* II² 1623, 282).
7. Aristophon son of Aristophanes of Azenia	307	343/2	HF	A?	A. *APF* 2108. Prominent politician. Age: ca. 90.
8. [Aristox]enos son of Kephisodotos of Piraeus or Kephisia	347	332/1, same day as 344–6	HF (Poet)	A	Not identifiable. *PAA* 174440.
9. Blepyros son of Pei[thandros of Paionidai]	*IG* II² 189	ca. 353/2?[d]	?	R	B2. *PAA* 267030.
10. Brachyllos son of Bathyllos of Erchia	306 V	343/2	HA	B	B2. *PAA* 268840. See also *IG* II³ 1, 339, 5.

d Dated "before 353/2" in *IG* II², inclusion of father's name and demotic implies a date no earlier than 354/3.

Proposer	Law or decree proposed	Date	Decree content	Decree type	Status and other features
11. Chairionides son of Lysanias of Phlya	338 II	333/2	HA	A	C. *PAA* 978120.
12. Deinostratos son of Deiniades of Ankyle	306 III	343/2	HA	B	C. *PAA* 302610.
13. Demades son of Demeas of Paiania	1. 321	337/6, same day as next	?	A	A. *APF* 3263. Prominent politician. Age: ca. 50 in 337–ca. 65 in 322.
	2. 322	337/6, same day as previous	HF (courtier of Philip II)	A	
	3. 326	337/6	? (Lemnos?)	?	
?	4. 330	335/4	H?	?	
	5. 334	334/3, same day as next and ? 336 proposed by Lykourgos	?	A	
	6. 335	334/3, see previous	HF (Amyntor son of Demetrios)	A	
	7. 346	332/1, at same Assembly after City Dionysia as 344, 345 proposed by Lykourgos, 347	HF (son of Aristeides)	A	

APPENDIX 1 *Proposers of inscribed laws and decrees 354/3–322/1 BC* (cont.)

Proposer	Law or decree proposed	Date	Decree content	Decree type	Status and other features
	8. 356	329/8	HF (Larisan)	A	
	9. 358	328/7, probably same day as 357, proposed by Lykourgos	HF (Eurylochos of Kydonia)	?	
	10. 384	322/1, at Assembly after City Dionysia	HF?	A	
14. Demeas son of Demades of Paiania	480	ca. 325–322/1	HF (Plataian)	A	A (son of previous). *APF* 3263, *PAA* 306870. Age: a little over 30.
15. Demetrios son of Euktemon of Aphidna	348	332/1	HA (legislator for Amphiaraia, Phanodemos)	PB (hybrid)	B1 or B2. *PAA* 310410 = 400. Contributed to dedication to Amphiaraos, 328/7 (*IG* II³ 1 360, 18).
16. Demophilos son of Demophilos of Acharnai	419	ca. 340–320	HF (Amphipolitan)	A	A. *APF* 3675 ("a consistently anti-Macedonian politician")
17. Demosthenes son of Demokles of Lamptrai	355	329/8	HA (prominent managers of Amphiaraia)	A	C. Known only as proposer of these two decrees

Proposer	Law or decree proposed	Date	Decree content	Decree type	Status and other features
	367 V	325/4	HF (Herakleides of Salamis)	A	See previous.
18. Demosthenes son of Demosthenes of Paiania	312	340/39	HF	A	A. *APF* 3597. Prominent politician. Age: 44.
19. Diopeithes son of Diopeithes of Sphettos	302 II	346/5	HF (Abderites)	R	A. *APF* 4328, *PAA* 363695. Politician ("appeared one of most formidable in the city", Hyp. *Eux.* 29). No known link with Abdera.
20. Diophantos son of Phrasikleides of Myrrhinous	324 I	337/6	HF (Euenor of Akarnania, doctor)	PB	A. *APF* 4435, *PAA* 367500 (naval specialist). Probably also proposed decree in 337/6 on a naval matter (*IG* II^2 1623, 210–212).
	324 II	322/1	HF (as previous)	A	
	325	337/6	HA	PB	
21. Epikrates (son of -otetos of Pallene?)	Unpublished (Ag. I 7495)	354/3	R (Financing of a festival)	Law	A. Cf. *LGPN* II Ἐπικράτης 5 = ? 106; *APF* 4909; Hansen 1989a, 45, who identifies him with Epikrates the wealthy proposer of the law about ephebes, Lyk. F5.3.

APPENDIX 1 *Proposers of inscribed laws and decrees 354/3–322/1 BC* (cont.)

Proposer	Law or decree proposed	Date	Decree content	Decree type	Status and other features
22. Epiteles son of Soinomos of Pergase	375	323/2	HF (Lapyris of Kleonai)	A	B1. *PAA* 398510. Manager of Amphiaraia, with Lykourgos, Demades, Phanodemos, 329/8, *IG* II^3 1, 355, 26–27; *naopoios* at Delphi, 328/7–323/2, and proxenos, 327/6.
23. Euboulides son of Antiphilos of Halimous	302	346/5	HF (Abderites)	PB	B1. *PAA* 427825. Demarch and opponent of Euxitheos' claim to citizenship, Dem. 57 passim.
24. Euetion son of Autokleides of Sphettos	359 II	328/7	HA (Priest of Asklepios)	BP?	A. *APF* 5463 (mine lessee, trierarch). Age: 60. Contributed as councillor to dedication to Amphiaraos, 328/7 (*IG* II^3 1, 360, 12).
25. Eukrates son of Aristotimos of Piraeus	320	337/6	Other (Against tyranny)	Law	B1. *PAA* 437770 = 75. Executed by Antipater after Lamian war.
26. Euphiletos son of Euphiletos of Kephisia or Kikynna	378	323/2	HF (Euphron of Sikyon)	A	Not identifiable in light of uncertainty about deme (Kephisia, *APF* 6067; Kikynna, *Agora* 15.42, 326).

Proposer	Law or decree proposed	Date	Decree content	Decree type	Status and other features
27. Hegemachos son of Chairemon of Perithoidai	*IG* II^2 1156, 36.	334/3	HA (ephebes)	B (inscribed on ephebic dedication)	C. *PAA* 480507.
28. Hegemon son of – of – (?)	385	322/1	H?	A	A. *PAA* 480755 ? = 795 (politician with reputation for supporting Macedon).
29. Hegesippos son of Hegesias of Sounion	399	348 or 343?	T (Eretria and other allied cities)	A	A. *APF* 6351 (revised Davies 2011). Politician.
	316	338/7	HF (Akarnanians)	A	
30. Hierokleides son of Timostratos of Alopeke	294 I and II	349/8	HF (Theogenes of Naukratis)	PB + R	B2. *PAA* 531940.
	297	349/8	R? (Eleusis)	A?	
31. Hieronymos son of Oikopheles of Rhamnous	469 II	ca. 330	HA	PB	C. *PAA* 534235.
32. Hippochares son of – of Alopeke	327 II	336/5	HA	PB (hybrid?)	C. *PAA* 539220.
33. Hippostratos son of Etearchides of Pallene	309	341/0	HF (Elaious)	A	C. *PAA* 539190.
34. Kallikrates son of Charopides of Lamptrai	301	346/5	HA	PB	B2 or C. *PAA* 556845 (cf. 840).

APPENDIX 1 *Proposers of inscribed laws and decrees 354/3–322/1 BC* (cont.)

Proposer	Law or decree proposed	Date	Decree content	Decree type	Status and other features
	313	340/39	HF (Tenedos)	A	
35. [Kallipho?]n son of Antikrates of Pambotadai	306 IV	343/2	HA	B	B2 or C. Cf. *PAA* 563130–150.
36. Kallisthenes son of Charmylos (?) of Trinemeia	360	328/7	HA	B	B2. *PAA* 560035, cf. 988610.
37. Kephisodotos son of Euarchides of Acharnai	367 II	330/29–328/7	HF (Herakleides of Salamis)	BP	B2. *PAA* 567730 (= or father of inspector of soldiers [*exetastes*] at Sounion), cf. 567705, 713–715, 725, 745. Same deme as Telemachos, who commissioned the Council's proposal and proposed the eventual Assembly decree.
38. Kephisophon son of Kallibios of Paiania	306 I	343/2	HA	?	A. *APF* 8417 (p. 149) (+ honoured by *IG* II^3 1, 402).[e]

e Kephisophon of Paiania was a friend and associate of Chares (Aeschin. II 73), but this is Chares of Angele the general (*APF* 15292), not Chares of Aixone the trierarch (15294), so, *pace APF* p. 149, there do not seem strong grounds to link Kephisophon's proposal of a rider to the decree for Asklepiodoros, who fought (at a time and in circumstances that are unclear) on the trireme of Chares of Aixone (418, 7–9), with his friendship with Chares of Angele.

Proposer	Law or decree proposed	Date	Decree content	Decree type	Status and other features
	418 II	ca. 340–320 (337/6?)	HF (Asklepiodoros)	R	
39. Kephisophon son of Lysiphon of Cholargos	370	325/4	T	A	B1. *PAA* 569375. Among prominent Athenians who were honoured as managers of the Amphiaraia, *IG* II^3 1, 355, 30–31.
40. Lykourgos son of Lykophron of Boutadai	1. 329	336/5 or 335/4	HF	PB	A. *APF* 9251. Prominent politician. Age: ca. 55 in 335.
	2. 445	ca. 335	R (Cult objects)	Law	
	3. 336 (cf. [Plut.] *Lives of Ten Orators* 844a)	334/3?, same day as 334 and 335, proposed by Demades	HA (Diotimos the general?)	A	
	4. 337 II	333/2	R (Kitian temple)	A	
	5. 345	332/1, same day as 344, 346 (proposed by Demades), 347	HF (Plataian)	A	

APPENDIX 1 *Proposers of inscribed laws and decrees 354/3–322/1 BC* (cont.)

Proposer	Law or decree proposed	Date	Decree content	Decree type	Status and other features
	6. 352	330/29	HF (Eudemos of Plataia)	A	
	7. 357	328/7, probably same day as 358, proposed by Demades	H?	?	
	8. 432	337–325	HF (Sopatros of Akragas)	A	
41. Nothippos son of Lysias of Diomeia	351	331/0	HF (Rheboulas)	PB	B2. *PAA* 720955. Son = sec. of Council, 307/6.
42. Phanodemos son of Diyllos of Thymaitadai	306 II	343/2	HA	B	A. *PAA* 915640 + *Horos* 22–25 (2010–2013), 79–84. Historian of Attica (*FGH* 325). Special interest in religion richly documented in epigraphical record. Age: ca. 52
	349	332/1	H (Amphiaraos)	A	Age: ca. 63

Proposer	Law or decree proposed	Date	Decree content	Decree type	Status and other features
43. Philodemos son of Autokles of Eroiadai	401 II	345–338	HF (Tenedos)	R	A. *APF* 14488 + *PAA* 933905. Strong military engagement as guarantor of ships for Chalkis in 340, trierarch, and commissioner for repair of walls after Chaironeia, *IG* II^3 1, 429.45.
44. Philotades son of Philostratos of Pallene	*IG* II^2 136	354/3	HF (Halikarnassian)	PB	B1. *PAA* 958025.
45. Phyleus son of Pausanias of Oinoe	367 IV	325/4	HF (Herakleides of Salamis)	BP	B2. *PAA* 966535 + II^3 1, 327 (honoured 336–4 as secretary of Council and People)
46. Polyeuktos son of Sostratos of Sphettos	342 and 343	332/1	HF (Theophantos)	A	A. *PAA* 778285: prominent anti-Macedonian politician, envoy to Peloponnese and Akarnania 343/2, demanded by Alexander with other prominent politicians in 335, opposed hons. for Demades 335, associated with Demosthenes in Harpalos affair 324, envoy to Arcadia 323, proposer of honours 318/7, *IG* II^2 350 = Osborne 1981–83 D39, mine lessee, *Agora* 19 P16, 16, cursed, *SEG* 58.265, 63.

APPENDIX 1 *Proposers of inscribed laws and decrees 354/3–322/1 BC* (cont.)

Proposer	Law or decree proposed	Date	Decree content	Decree type	Status and other features
	439	337–322	HF (Dionysios)	A	
47. Polyeuktos son of Timokrates of Krioa	298 II	347/6	HF (Bosporan rulers)	R	A. *APF* 11946. Father was an associate of Androtion, who proposed 298 I. Age: ca. 30.
48. Polykrates son of Polykrates of -?	295	349/8 (?)	HF (Orontes)	A	Not identifiable.
49. Prokleides son of Panta- of Kerameis	359 I	328/7	HA (Priest of Asklepios)	A	B2. *PAA* 788752 = 45 = 50. Same deme as priest. Son dedicator to Asklepios. Age: 62
50. Stephanos son of Antidorides of Eroiadai	299	347/6	T (Mytilene)	PB	B1. *PAA* 834250. Husband of Neaira in [Dem.] 59. Age: ca. 50–55. Before ca. 370–66 had allegedly put his name to others' proposals (59.43).
51. Telemachos son of Theangelos of Acharnai	315	339/8	H?	PB (hybrid)	B1. *PAA* 881430. Satirised as overactive public speaker by Timokles F7 K-A (cf. F 21, F 23). Proposed tribal honours for Lykourgos. Cf. Lambert 2015, 10–11 (= this vol., 301–302).

Proposer	Law or decree proposed	Date	Decree content	Decree type	Status and other features
	367 I and III	330/29–328/7	HF (Herakleides of Salamis)	A and A	Cf. on no. 37.
52. –s son of Aristyllos of Steiria (or Keiriadai?)	293	351/0 or 348/7	HF (Lampsakene)	PB	Not identifiable. *PAA* 176685.
53. -les son of Hierokles of Philaidai	Unpublished (but see *SEG* 52.104)	354/3–344/3?	R (Brauron)	Law	B1. *PAA* 532494. Brother of Patrokles, hipparch in mid-iv BC on *IG* II^3 4, 249 l. 4.
54. – son of Oinobios of Rhamnous	304	344/3	HF (Pellana)	A	C. *PAA* 741140.
				TOTAL PER CLASS:	A: 19 (39%) B1: 9.5 (19%) B2: 11 (22%) C: 9.5 (19%) TOTAL: 49

APPENDIX 2 *Liturgists attested in IG II³ 1, 550 (333/2 OR 332/1) and SEG 25.177 (331/0)*

Name and reference[a]	Status as indicated by other evidence
1. Kephisodoros son of Meidias of Anagyrous, *IG* II³ 1, 550, 8.	A. *APF* 8362, cf. 9719.
2. Archebios son of Archebiades of Lamptrai, 9.	A. *APF* 2308.
3. Theopompos son of Pyrrhinos of Gargettos, 11.	B1. *APF* 7030.
4. Nikokles [son of Lysikles] of Kydantidai, 12.	B1. *APF* 10903 + *PAA* 715065. Probably = or related to Nikokles son of Lysikles who was proxenos of Kaunos ca. 330–300, *SEG* 47.1568.
5. Diophantos son of Diopeithes of Myrrhinous, 14.	A. *APF* 4435.
6. Pamphilos son of Chairephilos of Paiania, 15.	A. *APF* 15187.
7. Leukios son of Theokles of Sounion, 17.	A. *APF* 9057.
8. Python son of Pythokles of Sounion, 18.	A. *APF* 12478.
9. Androkles son of Xeinis of Sphettos, 20.	A. Brother of *APF* 11234 Xenokles of Sphettos. Cf. note ad *IG* II³ 1, 550, 20; *IG* II³ 4, 518; *IALD* p. 404.
10. Epiteles of Thorikos, 21.	A. *APF* 4959.
11. Smikros of Acharnai, 23.	C. *APF* 12758
12. Menippos son of Demokrates of Acharnai, 24.	Identity uncertain given size of deme, see *APF* 10037.
13. Charidemos son of Aischylos of Athmonon, 26.	B1. *APF* 15374 = 6, cf. *APF* 436.
14. Chares [son of Adeistos?] of Aixone, 27.	A. *APF* 15294.
15. Chairedemos of Oion, 29.	C. *APF* 15122.
16. Theomnestos of Rhamnous, 31.	B2. *APF* 6976 + seangb.org for up-to-date references.

Name and reference[a]	Status as indicated by other evidence
17. Sosistratos of Euonymon, *SEG* 25.177, 4–5	C. *APF* 13292.
18. Thymokles of Prasiai, 6–7.	A. *APF* 7401.
19. Aishchylos [son of Hippiskos] of Paionidai, 8–9.	A. *APF* 450.
20. Polyaratos [son of Periandros] of Cholargos, 10–11.	A. *APF* 11907.
21. Theophilos son of Tr- of Athmonon, 12–13.	B2. *APF* 7119, cf. *PAA* 511530, seangb.org.
22. Philokrates son of Phi- of Oinoe, 14–15.	B1. *APF* 14621 + seangb.org.
23. Kallikrates son of Aristokrates of Aphidna, 16–17.	A. *APF* 8157.
24. Leptines son of Olymp[iodoros] of Alopeke, 18–19.	B2. *APF* 9045 + seangb.org.
25. Lysikles son of Lysiades of Leukonoion, 23–24.	A. *APF* 9437.
26. Theophrastos son of Bathyllos of Cholargos, 27–28.	A. *APF* 11907.
27. Theophilos of Phrearrhioi, 36–37.	B2. *APF* p. 227 + seangb.org.
28. Philokles of Hagnous, 39–40.	C. *APF* p. 539.
29. Polyaratos [son of Periandros] of Cholargos, 41–42.	A. *APF* 11907 (see also above, 550, 10–11).
30. Nikoboulos of Prospalta, 43–44.	A. *APF* 10845.
Total per Class:	A: 17 (59%) B1: 4 (14 %) B2: 4 (14%) C: 4 (14%)

a Includes only those with at least two preserved name elements.

APPENDIX 3 *Secretaries of the Council, 354/3–322/1 BC*[a]

Year	Name	Status and other features
1. 354/3	Prokleides son of Anacharsis of Aphidna	A or B1. *PAA* 788725, cf. *APF* 1916.
2. 353/2	Philokedes son of Dorotheos of Pallene	B2 or C. *PAA* 934995, cf. 378140.
3. 352/1 (or 348/7?)	Chremes son of Ph[iloitios of Ioni]dai (or son of Ph[- of Eiresi]dai)	B2 or C. Cf. *PAA* 991340.
4. 349/8	Dieuches son of Demarchos of Phrearrhioi	B1 or B2. *PAA* 323920, cf. 915, 925, 306565. Age: 40.
5. 347/6	Lysimachos son of Sosidemos of Acharnai	A or B1. *PAA* 616370, cf. *APF* 9480.
6. 346/5	Kephisodoros son of Athenophanes of Phlya	B2. *PAA* 568755. Age: 44?.
7. 343/2	Kleostratos son of Timosthenes of Aigilia	B1. *PAA* 577930, *IG* II^3 4, 502.
8. 341/0	Onesippos son of Smikythos of Araphen	C. *PAA* 747560.
9. 340/39	Aspetos son of Demostratos of Kytherros	A. *PAA* 222515. *APF* 2638.
10. 338/7	Philippos son of Antiphemos of Eiresidai	B1. *PAA* 929925 ? = 920.
11. 337/6	Chairestratos son of Ameinias of Acharnai	C. *PAA* 974805, cf. *IG* II^3 1, 323.
12. 335/4	Proxenos son of Pylagoras of Acherdous	B2. *PAA* 789855.
13. 334/3	Mnesiphilos son of Mneson [of Phaleron]	C. *PAA* 657850.
14. 333/2	Archelas son of Chairias of Pallene	C. *PAA* 209900.
15. 332/1	Aristonous son of Aristonous of Anagyrous	C. *PAA* 174340.
16. 330/29	Antidoros son of Antinous of Paiania	C. *PAA* 132885.
17. 329/8	Sostratides son of Ekphantos of Eupyridai	B2 or C. *PAA* 865110.

Year	Name	Status and other features
18. 328/7	Pythodelos son of Pythodelos of Hagnous	C. *PAA* 794110.
19. 327/6	Autokles son of Autias of Acharnai	B1. *PAA* 239105 (cf. 238365, 370).
20. 325/4	Antiphon son of Koroibos of Eleusis	B1. *PAA* 138510 (cf. 498, 500, 505).
21. 324/3	Euphanes son of Phrynon of Rhamnous	A or B1. *PAA* 449245 (cf. 966010).
22. 323/2	Archias son of Pythodoros of Alopeke	B2. *PAA* 212380 (cf. 794472, 470).
23. 322/1	Euthygenes son of Hephaistodemos of Kephisia	C. *PAA* 432005.
	TOTAL PER CLASS:	A: 2.5 (11%)
		B1: 6 (26%)
		B2: 5 (22%)
		C: 9.5 (41%)

a Only secretaries with at least two out of three name elements attested are included.

APPENDIX 4 *Members of the Presiding Committee (Proedroi), 354/3–322/1.*[a]

Inscription[b]	Year	Name (C = Chairman)	Status
1. *IG* II^2 137	354/3	Tharrex of Lamptrai (C)	B2 or C. *PAA* 501040 (cf. 038).
2. 293	351/0 or 348/7	Aristaios of Phaleron (C)	C. *PAA* 163610.
3. 294	349/8	Sokerdes of Halai (C)	C. *PAA* 855130.
4. 296	349/8	Enmenides of Koile (C)	B2. *PAA* 387565 (cf. 560, 570 and *IG* II^3 1, 292.79)
5. 298	347/6	Theophilos of Halimous (C)	B2 or C. *PAA* 511640 (cf. 645).
6. 302	346/5	Protias of Acharnai (C)	C. *PAA* 791230.
7. 307	343/2	Archikleides of Paiania (C)	B2. *PAA* 213135 (= 213000).
8. 309	341/0	Aristomachos of Oion (C)	C. *PAA* 172820.
9. 312	340/39	Androkles of Hagnous (C)	C. *PAA* 127990.
10. 315	339/8	Kallias of Phrearrhioi (C)	B2 or C. *PAA* 555200 (cf. 205).
11. 321, 322, 323?	337/6	Antiphanes of Euonymon (C)	B2. *PAA* 137435 (cf. 430, 440, *SEG* 47.187, 48 and below no. 22).
12. 324 decree 1, 325	337/6	Euthykrates of Aphidna (C)	B1. *PAA* 433145 (cf. 150, 155, *IG* II^3 1, 360.5).
13. 330	335/4	Nikokles of Rhamnous (C)	B2 or C. *PAA* 715120 (cf. 125, 127, 130).
14. 334, 335, 336?	334/3	Demokr[ates or -itos] of Paiania 3 (C)	B2 or C. *PAA* 316190 (cf. 765, *SEG* 50.829 VIII 3).
15. 337 decree 1	333/2	Theophilos of Phegous (C)	C. *PAA* 512280.
16. 337 decree 2	333/2	Phanostratos of Philaidai (C)	B2. *PAA* 917270.
17. 333 decree 2	333/2	Thymochares of Teithras	C. *PAA* 519020.
18. 338	333/2	Nikias of Themakos (C)	C. *PAA* 712385.
19. 344, 345, 346, 347	332/1	Nikostratos of Kopros (C)	C. *PAA* 718510.
20. 348, 349	332/1	Epichares of Hagnous (C)	B2. *PAA* 399320 (cf. 330).

Inscription[b]	Year	Name (C = Chairman)	Status
21. 351	331/0	Dorotheos of Halai (C)	A or C. PAA 377650 (cf. 660).
22. 352	330/29	Antiphanes of Euonymon (C)	B2. = no. 11 above.
23. 355	329/8	Demochares of Phlya (C)	C. PAA 322075.
24. 357	328/7	Pamphilos of Phyle (C)	B2. PAA 763035 (cf. 065, SEG 58.265).
25. 359	328/7	Epigenes of Eroiadai (C)	C. PAA 391625.
26. 367	325/4	Philyllos of Eleusis (C)	B1. PAA 953220 (cf. 215).
27. 368	325/4	Archestratos of Athmonon (C)	B2. PAA 211360 (cf. 350, 355).
28. 324 decree 2	322/1	Eualkos of Phaleron (C)	B2 or C. PAA 426160 (cf. 020).
29. 466	332/1?	Chairedemos of Sounion	C. PAA 973555.
30. 467	333/2–320	Stratios of Acharnai	B2. PAA *Add.* 836570 (cf. 575).
31. 467		Lysikleides of Halai	C. PAA 614700.
32. 467		Diodoros of Piraeus	B2 or C. PAA 330945 (with 950–90).
33. 469 decree 2	ca. 330	Demetrios of Erchia	C. PAA 310628.
		TOTAL PER CLASS:	A: 0.5 (1%)
			B1: 2 (6%)
			B2: 12.5 (38%)
			C: 18 (55%)

a At this period for every meeting of the Council and Assembly a councillor from each tribe not in prytany was chosen by lot to be a member of the presiding committee (*proedroi*). One could be *proedros* once a prytany, chairman of the *proedroi* once a year (*Ath. Pol.* 44.2, cf. Develin 1989, 22, Rhodes 1972, 25 ff.). The table includes only *proedroi* attested in self-standing laws and decrees. I have omitted laws from this list as the *proedroi* of the *nomothetai* may have been a different body from the *proedroi* of the Council and Assembly (cf. RO p. 390).

b IG II^3 1 unless stated otherwise.

Bibliography and Abbreviations

Aleshire, S. B. 1991: *Asklepios at Athens: epigraphic and prosopographic essays on the Athenian healing cults*, Amsterdam.

APF: J. K. Davies, *Athenian propertied families*, Oxford, 1971.

Brun, P. 2000: *L'orateur Démade*, Bordeaux.

Canevaro, M. 2015: "Making and changing laws in ancient Athens", in E. M. Harris and M. Canevaro eds., *Oxford Handbook of Ancient Greek Law*, Oxford (forthcoming; this chapter published online, August 2015).

Canevaro, M. 2016: *Demostene, contro Leptine. Introduzione e commento storico*, Berlin.

Carey, C. et al. 2008: "Fragments of Hyperides' *Against Diondas* from the Archimedes palimpsest", ZPE 165, 1–19.

Cooper, C. 2000: "Philosophers, politics, academics. Demosthenes' rhetorical reputation in antiquity", in I. Worthington ed., *Demosthenes. Statesman and orator*, London.

Davies, J. K. 2011: "Hegesippos of Sounion: an underrated politician", in S. D. Lambert ed., *Sociable man. Essays on ancient Greek social behaviour in honour of Nick Fisher*, Swansea, 11–23.

Develin, R. 1989: *Athenian officials 684–321 BC*, Cambridge.

Domingo Gygax, M. 2016: *Benefaction and rewards in the ancient Greek city. The origins of euergetism*, Cambridge.

Engen, D. T. 2010: *Honor and profit. Athenian trade policy and the economy and society of Greece, 415–307 BCE*, Ann Arbor.

Flower, M. A. 1994: *Theopompos of Chios*, Oxford.

Habicht, C. 1993: "The comic poet Archedikos", *Hesp.* 62, 254–56.

Hansen, M. H. 1974: *The sovereignty of the people's court in the fourth century BC and the public action against unconstitutional proposals*, Odense.

Hansen, M. H. 1984: "The number of *rhetores* in the Athenian *ecclesia*, 355–322 BC", GRBS 25 (1984), 123–55, reprinted with addenda in Hansen 1989b, 93–127.

Hansen, M. H. 1987: *The Athenian Assembly in the age of Demosthenes*, Oxford.

Hansen, M. H. 1989a: "Updated inventory of *rhetores* and *strategoi* (1988)", in Hansen 1989b, 34–72.

Hansen, M. H. 1989b: *The Athenian ecclesia* II, Copenhagen.

Hansen, M. H. 1991: *The Athenian democracy in the age of Demosthenes*, Oxford.

Harris, E. M. 1994: "Demosthenes Loses a Friend and Nausicles Gains a Position: A Prosopographical Note on Athenian Politics after Chaeronea", *Historia* 43, 378–84.

Henry, A. S. 1977: *The prescripts of Athenian decrees. Mnemosyne Supplement 49*, Leiden.

IALD: S. D. Lambert, *Inscribed Athenian laws and decrees 352/1–322/1 BC. Epigraphical essays*, Leiden, 2012.

Kapparis, K. A. (ed.) 1999: *Apollodoros "Against Neaira" [D. 59]*, Berlin.

Kremmydas, C. 2012: *Commentary on Demosthenes, Against Leptines*, Oxford.

Lambert, S. D. 2001: "The only extant decree of Demosthenes", ZPE 137, 55–68 [= IALD 249–72].

Lambert, S. D. 2004: "Athenian State Laws and Decrees, 352/1–322/1: I Decrees Honouring Athenians", ZPE 150, 85–120 [= IALD 3–47].

Lambert, S. D. 2004b: "Greek Inscriptions in the University Museum, Oxford, Mississippi", ZPE 148, 181–86 [= IALD 311–20].

Lambert, S. D. 2006: "Athenian State Laws and Decrees, 352/1–322/1: III Decrees Honouring Foreigners. A. Citizenship, Proxeny and Euergesy", ZPE 158, 115–58 [= IALD 93–137].

Lambert, S. D. 2008: "Polis and theatre in Lykourgan Athens: the honorific decrees", in A. P. Matthaiou and I. Poinskaya eds., *Mikros Hieromnemon. Meletes eis mnemen Michael H. Jameson* (Athens) [= IALD 337–62].

Lambert, S. D. 2010a: "Inscribed treaties ca. 350–321: an epigraphical perspective on Athenian foreign policy", in G. Reger, F. X. Ryan and T. F. Winters eds., *Studies in Greek epigraphy and history in Honor of Stephen V. Tracy*, Bordeaux, 153–60 [= IALD 377–86].

Lambert, S. D. 2010b: "A polis and its priests: Athenian priesthoods before and after Pericles' citizenship law", *Historia* 59, 143–75.

Lambert, S. D. 2011: "What was the point of inscribed honorific decrees in classical Athens?", in S. D. Lambert ed., *Sociable man. Essays on ancient Greek social behaviour in honour of Nick Fisher*, Swansea, 193–214 [= this volume, chapter 3].

Lambert, S. D. 2012a: "Some political shifts in Lykourgan Athens", in V. Azoulay, P. Ismard eds., *Clisthène et Lycurgue d'Athènes. Autour du politique dans la cité classique*, Paris, 175–90 [= this volume, chapter 4].

Lambert, S. D. 2012b: "The social construction of priests and priestesses in Athenian honorific decrees from the fourth century BC to the Augustan period", in M. Horster, A. Klöckner eds., *Civic Priests. Cult personnel in Athens from the hellenistic period to late antiquity*, Berlin, 67–133.

Lambert, S. D. 2014: "Inscribed Athenian decrees of 229/8–198/7 BC (*IG* II^{3} 1, 1135–1255)", AIO *Papers* no. 4 (https://www.atticinscriptions.com/papers/aio-papers-4/).

Lambert, S. D. 2015: "The inscribed version of the decree honouring Lykourgos of Boutadai (*IG* II^{2} 457 + 3207)", AIO *Papers* no. 6 (https://www.atticinscriptions.com/papers/aio-papers-6/) [= this volume, chapter 11].

Liddel, P. 2016: "Honorific decrees of fourth-century Athens: trends, perceptions, controversies", in: C. Tiersch ed., *Die Athenische Demokratie im 4. Jahrhundert. Zwischen Modernisierung und Tradition*, Berlin, 335–57.

MacDowell, D. 2009: *Demosthenes the orator*, Oxford.

Mack, W. 2015: *Proxeny and polis. Institutional networks in the ancient Greek world*, Oxford.

Meyer, E. 2013: "Inscriptions as honors and the Athenian epigraphic habit", *Historia* 62, 453–505.

Moreno, A. 2007: *Feeding the democracy. The Athenian grain supply in the fifth and fourth centuries BC*, Oxford.

Ober, J. 2008: *Democracy and knowledge. Innovation and learning in classical Athens*, Princeton.

Osborne, M.J. 1981–83: *Naturalization in Athens*. Vols. 1–3.

PAA: J. S. Traill, *Persons of ancient Athens*, 21 vols., Toronto, 1994–2012.

Papazarkadas, N. 2011: *Sacred and public land in ancient Athens*, Oxford.

Parker, R. 2005: *Polytheism and society at Athens*, Oxford.

Rhodes, P.J. 1972: *The Athenian Boule*, Oxford.

Rhodes, P.J. 2016: "Demagogues and *Demos* in Athens", *Polis* 33, 243–64.

Taylor, C. 2008: "A new political world", in R. Osborne ed., *Debating the Athenian cultural revolution: art, literature, philosophy and politics 430–380 BC*, Cambridge.

Thomas, R. 1989: *Oral tradition and written record in classical Athens*, Cambridge.

Thomas, R. 2016: "Performance, audience participation and the dynamics of the fourth-century Assembly and jury-courts of Athens", in C. Tiersch ed., *Die Athenische Demokratie im 4. Jahrhundert. Zwischen Modernisierung und Tradition*, Stuttgart, 89–108.

Tracy, S.V. 2000: "Athenian politicians and inscriptions of the years 307 to 302", *Hesperia* 69, 227–33.

Tracy, S.V. 2011: "Athenian decrees of 404/3 to 86 BC passed at the same meeting", in O. Palagia and H.R. Goette eds., *Sailing to classical Greece. Papers … Petros Themelis*, Oxford.

CHAPTER 9

Council and Assembly in Late Classical and Hellenistic Athens: An Epigraphical Perspective on Democracy*

1 Introduction

It was a common feature of ancient Greek cities that there was both a citizen Assembly and a Council responsible for preparing the Assembly's business, but the size and composition of the Council, the respective powers of the two bodies, the frequency of their meetings and the balance between them in formulating decisions were key features differentiating democratic from oligarchic constitutions.[1]

In Aristotle's analysis, the size of the probouleutic body was a significant determinant of whether the constitution had a democratic or oligarchic character.[2] This was no doubt true in general terms, but, aside from the establishment of a board of 10 *probouloi* in the aftermath of the failure of the Sicilian expedition in 413[3] and a brief return to the Solonian number of 400 in 411, the size of the Council was not for the most part at issue in Athens, which retained the principle of 50 councillors per tribe established by Cleisthenes, thus producing a Council of 500 for most of the fifth and fourth centuries, 600 after the introduction of the two Macedonian tribes Antigonis and Demetrias in 307/6, 650 after the addition of the thirteenth tribe Ptolemais in 223/2, and 600 again after the reversion to 12 tribes with the abolition of the Macedonian tribes and

---

* This paper was first drafted at the Institute for Advanced Study, Princeton, where I enjoyed the privileges of Membership in 2012/3, supported by the Patrons' Endowment Fund and the Loeb Foundation. Versions of it were given at a conference in memory of David Lewis in Athens in 2014, at the University of Konstanz in 2014, and at the University of Paris in 2015. I am grateful to all who helped me to improve it by their comments on those occasions and to Peter Rhodes for reading an early draft.

1 Along with appointment by lot and accountability of officials, the relationship between Council and Assembly is implicitly among the three cornerstones of democracy (called "rule of the mass" or *isonomia*) according to Otanes in the debate on the constitutions in Persia in 522 BC dramatised by Herodotos 3.80: βουλεύματα δὲ πάντα ἐς τὸ κοινὸν ἀναφέρει ("all proposals are referred to the collective").

2 ἐὰν ὀλίγοι τὸν ἀριθμὸν ὦσιν, ὀλιγαρχικόν. *Pol.* 1299b 34.

3 Thuc. 8.1.3; *Ath. Pol.* 29.2; Lys. 12.65.

© KONINKLIJKE BRILL NV, LEIDEN, 2018 | DOI 10.1163/9789004352490_011

the addition of Attalis in 201/0. In 404/3 the Thirty retained a Council of 500, and changes to the number of councillors were not on the agenda of the oligarchic regimes of 321–318 and 317–308, or so far as we know during the tyranny of Lachares, ca. 300–296/5, or in the "oligarchy" of 294/3–288/7.[4]

Aristotle also identifies the frequency of meetings of the Assembly and payment for attendance at Assembly meetings as important democratic features, "for they are at leisure to gather frequently and determine everything themselves".[5] This certainly does reflect the situation in late classical Athens, when the Assembly usually met four times a prytany,[6] and Assembly pay had risen from one obol after the restoration of democracy in 403/2 to a full drachma for an ordinary meeting and one-and-a-half drachmas for the principal meeting of each prytany (the *kyria ekklesia*).[7] It is also plausible enough that the 5th-century oligarchic regimes at Athens reduced, or intended to reduce, the frequency of Assembly meetings and would have abolished Assembly pay, had it existed at the time, as comparable restrictions on pay for officials were introduced.[8] We shall consider below the issues of frequency of meetings of the Assembly and Assembly pay in the third century, on which the evidence is opaque.

If the number of councillors was not in practice generally an issue at Athens, the appointment and composition of the Council and the Assembly, and the relative powers of these bodies, were live issues affecting whether a regime was more or less democratic. A central plank of the oligarchic programme of 411, for example, was to replace Cleisthenes' Council of 500, appointed by lot,[9] with a Council of 400, initially co-opted,[10] subsequently to be appointed from a pre-elected group by tribes from those over 30.[11] The Assembly was to be replaced for practical purposes with a body of Five Thousand propertied citizens, and according to the *Ath. Pol.* the regime was overthrown by Aristokrates and Theramenes precisely because the Four Hundred decided everything themselves and referred nothing to the Five Thousand.[12] When in the aftermath of the restoration of democracy in 410 the Athenians decided to conduct

---

4 On the Athenian Council in the classical democracy see Rhodes 1972 and Hansen 1991, 246–65. On Lachares see most recently Osborne 2012a, 25–36; third century before 229 BC, 62–74.

5 σχολάζοντες γὰρ συλλέγονταί τε πολλάκις καὶ ἅπαντα αὐτοὶ κρίνουσιν. *Pol.* 1300a 3–4.

6 *Ath. Pol.* 43.3.

7 *Ath. Pol.* 62.2, cf. Hansen 1991, 150.

8 *Ath. Pol.* 29.5 (Four Hundred).

9 Thuc. 8.69.4; *Ath. Pol.* 32.1.

10 Thuc. 8.67.3.

11 *Ath. Pol.* 31.1.

12 *Ath. Pol.* 33.2.

a revision of Athenian law, it is unsurprising, against this background, that the laws about the Council were among those selected for inscription on stone, and that those laws resonate strongly with the events of 411.[13] They emphasise repeatedly, for example, the limitation of the Council's powers with respect to the "mass" of citizens: "without the Athenian People assembled en masse it shall not be permitted to raise war or to end war" (l. 35) was an especially pointed provision in the aftermath of the failed attempt by the Four Hundred to make peace with Sparta.[14] The more extreme oligarchy of the Thirty, which took power in 404/3 after Athens' defeat in the Peloponnesian War, also maintained a Council of 500, but appointed it, and the other officials, themselves (according to *Ath. Pol.* from a short-list of a thousand)[15] and presided over it in person, at least its judicial sessions.[16]

It is not controversial that, in the latest phase of the classical democracy, the Athens of Demosthenes and Lykourgos, the composition and powers of the Council were democratically normative.[17] Selected by a process involving allotment from those over 30, a quota from each deme in proportion to the deme's size, the Council held office for a year, members were paid a subsistence allowance, and tenure was limited for any individual to twice in a lifetime.[18] There are some indications that members might in practice have been a shade more affluent than the average citizen;[19] but together with the deme quota system, the limitation on serving more than twice in a lifetime acted as a brake on any tendency for the wealthy and prominent to predominate, and the statistics relating to liturgists, decree proposers, secretaries and members of the Council's presiding committee (*proedroi*) that we considered in chapter 8 (see table 1), confirm that the Council member was usually a more or less ordinary Athenian, of no particular wealth or prominence. Except for the fact that its members were over 30, broadly the Council can be conceived of, and was doubtless intended to be, the polis in microcosm.[20] The functions and powers of the Council are also clear enough: it oversaw the city's government,

13 *IG* I³ 105 = *OR* 183. See also Lambert and Rhodes, https://www.atticinscriptions.com/inscription/IGI3/105. It is unclear how far the text of this law reproduced the 6th century original.

14 Thuc. 8.70–71, 86; 9.90–91; *Ath. Pol.* 32.3.

15 Cf. Xen. *Hell.* 2.3.11.

16 Xen. *Hell.* 2.3.23–56, especially 50 (trial of Theramenes); Lysias 13.37 (trials of victims of Agoratos). Cf. Rhodes 1972, 30. There were also changes to the powers of the Council under the regime of Demetrios of Phaleron, see Habicht 1997, 55.

17 Cf. Rhodes 1972 (especially 1–16); Hansen 1991, chapter 10 (246–65).

18 5 obols per meeting/day at this period, *Ath. Pol.* 62.2. Twice in a lifetime: *Ath. Pol.* 62.3.

19 Rhodes 1972, 506; Hansen 1985, 58–60.

20 μικρὰ πόλις, in the words of schol. Aeschin. 3.4, cf. Rhodes 1972, 4.

including the work of other city officials; had significant roles in religious administration, jurisdiction, in public finance, and in the day-to-day conduct of foreign policy,[21] and it prepared the business of the Assembly, referring to it all major policy decisions (*probouleusis*).

My focus in this paper will not be on the Council's formal powers and functions, but on the balance between Council and Assembly in formulating decisions in practice. The Assembly could only pass decrees on the basis of a proposal from the Council, a *probouleuma*;[22] and from the fourth century onwards the wording of inscribed decrees usually enables us to distinguish between those which follow precisely the terms of the Council's proposal, probouleumatic decrees, and those where there are indications that the Council's proposal was reworked in the Assembly, non-probouleumatic decrees. The current orthodoxy, established by Rhodes 1972, is that, across the fourth-century democracy as whole, about 50% of the inscribed decrees were probouleumatic and 50% non-probouleumatic, and that there was accordingly a fair degree of balance between the Council and the Assembly in the formulation of policy decisions.[23] The recent publication of the third edition of the inscribed laws and decrees of 352/1 to 322/1 presents an opportunity to review the inscribed decrees of this period in this perspective. My principal argument will be that, in this last phase of the classical democracy, the balance in decree-making was much more heavily in favour of the Assembly than the current orthodoxy would suggest.[24] I shall conclude with some reflections on what this

21 Rhodes 1972, passim; Hansen 1991, 255–59; 259–65.

22 *Ath. Pol.* 45.4; Rhodes 1972, 52.

23 Fundamental on this topic is Rhodes 1972, 52–81 (his table, p. 79, shows 107 probouleumatic and 101 non-probouleumatic inscribed decrees in the period 403/2–322/1). His conclusions are repeated for example by Hansen 1991, 145; Oliver 2003, 45.

24 The Council also had a role in fourth-century lawmaking, but, on the reconstruction of that process by Canevaro 2015, sect. 7 (cf. 2016, 41–42), this consisted in *probouleusis* for the preliminary vote by the Assembly which set the lawmaking process in motion by permitting the proposal of new laws (cf. Dem. 24.25). Be that as it may, the laws were made by the *nomothetai*, on the basis of a proposal from an individual citizen, and there is no sign, in inscriptions or elsewhere, that a law might be "probouleumatic", in the sense of being the enactment of a *probouleuma* put forward by the Council. Exactly who the *nomothetai* were is obscure, but it is clear enough that they were appointed separately for each law. In Canevaro's analysis there are two passages in the literary record that may cast light on their identity, but neither of them is straightforward: (a) Dem. 20.93, where there is mention of "those who have sworn the oath", which might be a reference to the *nomothetai* enacting new laws, or to a body of jurors responsible for repeal of old laws inconsistent with the proposed new law (cf. Canevaro 2016). Only if it refers to the *nomothetai* will there be an implication that the *nomothetai* functioned like a jury (and were therefore

implies for the character of the Athenian democracy in its final phase and, by way of comparison, with a look at the extent to which this and some other key features of the 4th-century democracy had changed by the late-3rd century.

2 Overall Picture

To start with the overall statistics, the following table summarises the number of extant inscribed decrees from this period identifiable as belonging to the various different categories of decree:

TABLE 1 *Overall statistics*

Council decree or *probouleuma*	Probouleumatic Assembly decree	Non-probouleumatic Assembly decree	Non-probouleumatic (rider)
15	27	64–73 [+ 10[a]]	11

a See below sect. 6.

As these raw statistics clearly show, the balance in this period is much more skewed in favour of non-probouleumatic decrees than was apparent from Rhodes' 1972 work (which covered the fourth century as a whole). As we shall see when we explore the evidence in greater depth, there are indications that the Assembly was even more fully engaged than these raw data suggest. Let us begin, however, with a review of the Council decrees.

3 Council Decree or *Probouleuma*[25]

The 15 Council decrees/*probouleumata* in the first column of table 1 are as follows:

over 30 years old); (b) Aeschin. 3.39, where "the *prytaneis* shall hold an Assembly labelling it (*epigraphein*) *nomothetai*", which may imply that the Assembly should sit under a different name as "*nomothetai*" or (less likely?) that the appointment of *nomothetai* should be an item on the Assembly's agenda.

25 On decrees of the Council see also Rhodes 1972, 82–87 and table G.

TABLE 2 *Council decrees or probouleumata*

IG II^3 1	Year	Subject of decree	Decree type
1. 306 II	343/2	Dedication to Hephaistos and Athena Hephaistia	Council decree
2. 306 III	343/2	Honouring Phanodemos	Council decree and *probouleuma*
3. 306 IV	343/2	Honouring Eudoxos	Council decree
4. 306 V	343/2	Honouring Eudoxos	Council decree
5. 360	328/7	Honouring organisers of Council dedication	Council decree
6. *IG* II^2 1155b (see chapter 10)	339/8	Honouring taxiarch and soldiers of Kekropis	Council decree
7. *IG* II^2 1156 = *RO* 89 II	334/3	Honouring ephebes of Kekropis and their *sophronistes*	Council decree
8. 368	325/4	–	Council decree or *probouleuma* ?
9. 311 II	341/0	Honouring officials	*Probouleuma* ?
10. 327 I	336/5	Honouring Phyleus	*Probouleuma*
11. 337 I	333/2	Granting *enktesis* to Kitian merchants	Open *probouleuma*
12. 338 I	333/2	Honouring Pytheas of Alopeke	*Probouleuma*
13. 359 II	328/7	Honouring Androkles of Kerameis	*Probouleuma?*
14. 367 II	330/29–328/7	Honouring Herakleides of Salamis	*Probouleuma*
15. 367 IV	325/4	Honouring Herakleides of Salamis	*Probouleuma*

Like any other body of citizens, the Council was competent to make dedications and honour its own members and officials on its own authority, without reference to the Assembly, and though this rarely impacts on the inscribed record, there is an example in its dedication to Amphiaraos at the Amphiaraion in Oropos in 328/7 BC, *IG* II^3 1, 360, which is also inscribed with a decree of the Council honouring the councillors who had organised the dedication. In a rather different category are dedications by the Council commemorating honours awarded it by the People. There are two from this period which are not inscribed with the text of the decree: *IG* II^3 4, 3 (dedication of a statue of Democracy by the Council, having been crowned by the People, 333/2 BC); and *IG* II^3 4, 4 (dedication by the Council, having been crowned by the People, 332/1 BC). In principle similar to these is *IG* II^3 1, 306, dedicated by the Council to Hephaistos to commemorate the award of honours by the People for its management of the City Dionysia in 343/2; but this is in truth a hybrid, since it is inscribed not only with the People's decree (*IG* II^3 1, 306 I), but with four supplementary decrees of the Council, recording the decision, proposed by Phanodemos, to make the dedication (306 II), and honouring both Phanodemos (306 III) and the official in charge of its own administration (306 IV, crown funded from the Council's expense account, and V, funded by the councillors privately).

The Council was also competent to honour on its own authority officials and citizens over whose activities it exercised executive oversight, though such decrees seem not to have been usually inscribed, or at least not at the Council's own initiative and expense.[26] The examples from this period, which both relate to its oversight of military administration, are *IG* II^2 1155b I,[27] a very fragmentary decree of the Council from 339/8 honouring the taxiarch and soldiers of the tribe Kekropis, and which seems to have been inscribed, together with a decree of Kekropis, at the tribe's initiative (decree II, 14–15); and *IG* II^2 1156 = *RO* 89, a dedication by the ephebes of Kekropis of 334/3, inscribed with a list of their names and with honorific decrees of the Council, the tribe and two demes. The Council, like the two demes, stipulates that its decree was to be inscribed "on the dedication which the ephebes of Kekropis are dedicating",[28]

26 Again, however, there is evidence for such decrees in inscribed dedications, e.g. by a priest from Rhamnous (c. 350–300 BC): [– – – – –] ἀνέθηκεν Διονύσωι ἱερεὺς Ἥρω [Ἀρχηγέτου | ἐπαινεθεὶς] καὶ στεφανωθεὶς ὑπὸ τῆς βουλῆς καὶ τῶν δημοτῶν [καὶ τῶν στρατιωτῶν] ("the priest of the Hero Archegetes, …, dedicated to Dionysos, having been praised and crowned by the Council and the demesmen [and the soldiers]) *I Rham.* 82 = *IG* II^2 2849. Cf. Lambert 2010a, 166–67. Another example may be Kourouniotes 1927/28, 39 no. 3, a dedication from the temple of Apollo Zoster in Halai Aixonides of ca. 350 (?) commemorating the honouring of a priest, Eukles of Halai, by the Council and the *demos*, if *demos* here = deme. Some of the decrees honouring Lykourgos commemorated in *IG* II^2 3207, most likely including for the performance of his office in charge of the financial administration (*epi tei diokesei*), were also decrees of the Council alone (cf. Lambert 2015a = this volume, chapter 11, section 2).

27 Discussed, together with 1156, in Lambert 2015b = this volume, chapter 10.

28 ἐπιγράψαι δὲ τόδε τὸ ψήφισμα ἐπὶ τὸ ἀ[νάθημα]| ὃ ἀνατιθέασιν οἱ ἔφηβοι οἱ τῆς Κεκροπίδος (43–44).

but it makes no provision for payment for inscribing, and it seems that the initiative lay with the ephebes themselves, and with their tribe.

The Council might also forward decrees honouring its own members to the Assembly for further consideration, as in *IG* II^3 1, 306 III, honouring Phanodemos in 343/2 BC as the best speaker in the Council, though what is inscribed in this case is not the Assembly's eventual decree, but the Council's decree and *probouleuma*. Otherwise it is usually the Assembly's decree that is inscribed, though occasionally the Assembly decided to inscribe the *probouleuma* as well. This happened, for example, with *IG* II^3 1, 367 V (of 325/4 BC), where the Assembly instructed the secretary of the Council to inscribe not only the present decree honouring Herakleides of Salamis, but also previous decrees in his favour, and the secretary interpreted this conscientiously and inscribed not only a previous Assembly decree (367 III, of 330/29–328/7 BC), but also the *probouleumata* for that decree (367 II) and for 367 V (367 IV). In both cases the *probouleumata* provide for the award of a crown and for the decree to go forward to the Assembly as a basis for the honorand to seek further benefits from the People. There was also a retrospective aspect to *IG* II^3 1, 327, honouring Phyleus of Oinoe and his colleagues, where the eventual Assembly decree of 335/4 (327 III) specified explicitly not only that the earlier decree of the Assembly, "which Hippochares proposed" (327, 26), and dating to the end of the tenth prytany of Phyleus' year in office, 334/3 (327 II), but also the Council decree, "which Agasias proposed" (327, 25), should be inscribed. The Council decree, dating early in the ninth prytany of 334/3, is duly included on the stone (327 I) and (like the *probouleumata* for Herakleides) provides both that Phyleus be awarded a crown and that the decree go forward as a basis for Phyleus to seek further benefits from the Assembly.[29] Similarly *IG* II^3 1, 359 II, honouring Androkles priest of Asklepios in 328/7, may be the *probouleuma* on which the non-probouleumatic *IG* II^3 1, 359 I was based (unless it is a separate probouleumatic decree honouring the priest). These cases where the Council's original *probouleuma* is inscribed as well as the Assembly's resultant decree cast an interesting light on the extent to which, even in the case of apparently somewhat routine honours for relatively obscure honorands, the Assembly might play an active role.[30]

---

29 In this case Hippochares' decree (327 II) was not, apparently, based on this *probouleuma*. See further below.

30 There are indications that, at this period, the Council might award foliage crowns, which were not usually inscribed (*IG* II^2 1156 decree 2 being the exception which proves the rule), or gold crowns up to 500 dr., but that only the Assembly could award 1,000 dr. gold

IG II^3 1, 337 I is a unique case in this corpus of an "open" *probouleuma*, which simply put the matter at issue to the Assembly for consideration, and made neither a substantive provision, nor a specific recommendation. Normally such *probouleumata* were not inscribed. This, however, is a special case, in that the inscription, which conferred on the Kitian merchants the right of *enktesis* to found a sanctuary of Aphrodite, was erected not on the acropolis by the city but, it seems, on the site of the sanctuary at the initiative and expense of the Kitians themselves,[31] who were perhaps anxious to demonstrate that they had obtained ownership of the site by "due process". It is interesting that the Council decided not to formulate a substantive *probouleuma* on this issue, suggesting it was perhaps potentially a controversial matter best left to substantive debate in the Assembly.

The inscribed record of the Council's decrees and *probouleumata* is rather slight and presents an extremely limited picture of its decision-making. In particular it gives us almost no insight into the Council's wide range of executive and oversight functions, in the financial, military and religious spheres of the city's life, in relation to public works, or into its judicial activities.[32] Inscribed decrees of the Assembly do document functions in these areas, as for example *IG* II^3 1, 292, which places on the Council, amongst other bodies, responsibility for care of the sacred orgas and other sacred precincts,[33] and the many decrees in which the Council is charged with "taking care" of an honorand;[34] not to mention cases where the Council was explicitly commissioned or permitted by the Assembly to take measures to supplement the Assembly's decree;[35] but the decisions the Council took in pursuance of such functions did not generally result in inscribed decrees.[36] Overall, however, the impression conveyed by this material is that, while the Council clearly had a measure of executive discretion, the Assembly was firmly in control of the major decisions.

---

crowns (cf. Lambert 2004, 88 = *IALD*, 8; 2006, 133 = *IALD*, 122, n. 75; 2007, 123 = *IALD*, 171, n. 107; 2007, 127 = *IALD*, 178 n. 148).

31 This can be inferred from the absence of the secretary in the prescript and of the usual clause providing for inscription.

32 On all these matters see Rhodes 1972, 88–143 and 144–207; Hansen 1991, 257–65.

33 ἐπι]μελεῖσθαι [δ]ὲ τῆς ἱερᾶς ὀργάδος καὶ τῶν ἄλλω|[ν ἱερῶν τεμεν]ῶν τῶν Ἀθήνησιν … καὶ τὴν βουλὴν τὴν αεὶ βουλεύου|[σαν] …(16–22).

34 As e.g. *IG* II^3 1, 302, 17–18, for exiles from Abdera.

35 On these cases see chapter 7.2.

36 We do occasionally obtain a glimpse of the Council's executive functions in inscribed Council decrees from outside this period, e.g. *IG* II^2 120 + 1465, a Council decree of 353/2 (?) making provisions for an inventory of the Chalkotheke. Cf. Rhodes 1972, 92; *SEG* 37.74; and on the date Schweigert 1938, 286.

4 Criteria of Probouleumatic Decrees

Our next category is the Assembly decree which was formulated as an enactment of the Council's *probouleuma*, the "probouleumatic" decree.[37] *IG* II^3 1, 294 Decree I, a proxeny decree for Theogenes of Naukratis from 349/8 BC, supplies a well-preserved and characteristic example:

> Gods.
>
> *Decree 1*
>
> In the ninth prytany, of Pandionis, for which Dieuches son of Demarchos of Phrearrhioi was secretary. Sokerdes of Halai was chairman. Kallimachos was archon (349/8). The Council and the People decided. Hierokleides son of Timostratos of Alopeke proposed: since Theogenes of Naukratis is a good man with respect to the Athenian People and does what good is in his power, for those who come, both individually and collectively, both now and in time past, both himself and his ancestors, the Council shall decide: that the presiding committee allotted to preside at the next Assembly shall introduce Theogenes, and put his case on the agenda, and submit the opinion of the Council to the People, that it seems good to the Council, that Theogenes son of Xenokles of Naukratis be proxenos and benefactor of the Athenian People, both himself and his descendants; and he shall have right of ownership of a house; and the generals and the Council in office at any time shall take care of him.
>
> *Decree 2*
>
> Hierokleides son of Timostratos of Alopeke proposed: in other respects as proposed

37 In the main the distinction I draw between probouleumatic and non-probouleumatic decrees follows Rhodes 1972, 52–81.

> by the Council, but the secretary of the
> (30) Council shall inscribe this decree on the acropolis
> and stand it there within ten days; and
> the treasurer of the People shall give
> 20 drachmas for inscribing the stele
> from the People's fund for expenditure on decrees;
> (35) and to praise Theogenes
> and invite him to hospitality in the
> city hall tomorrow.[38]

The key indication that decree 1 is probouleumatic is the formulaic wording at ll. 14–20, implying that the Assembly's decree gives effect to the Council's proposal, the so-called "probouleumatic formula" ("PF"). This is echoed in the enactment formula, not simply "The People decided", but "The Council and the People decided" (5–6, "ετβκτδ"), and is confirmed by decree 2, a rider to decree 1 passed in the Assembly, introduced by "in other respects as proposed by the Council" ("RP"). In addition, in some probouleumatic decrees there is wording indicating that the *probouleuma* has been commissioned by the Assembly ("CPF").[39] A corollary of the probouleumatic character of a decree is that the man named as proposer of the decree in the Assembly was the councillor who had also proposed the decree in the Council. Unusually in 294 the same man also proposed the rider. It is impossible to tell whether this was because he had, deliberately, or conceivably by oversight, withheld the provisions in

---

38 θεο[ί]· | ἐπὶ τῆς Πανδιονίδος ἐνάτης π[ρυτα]|νείας, ἧι Διεύχης Δημάρχου Φρε[άρρ]| ιος^{IV} ἐγραμμάτευεν· Σωκέρδης Ἀλ[αιε]|(5)ὺς ἐπεστάτει· Καλλίμαχος ἦρχεν· [ἔδ]|οξεν τῆι βουλῆι καὶ τῶι δήμωι· Ἱε[ρο]|κλείδης Τιμοστράτου Ἀλωπεκῆθε[ν] | εἶπεν· ἐπειδὴ Θεογένης ὁ Ναυκρατί|της ἀνὴρ ἀγαθός ἐστιν περὶ τὸν δῆμ|(10)ον τὸν Ἀθηναίων καὶ ποεῖ ὅ τι δύνατ|αι ἀγαθὸν καὶ ἰδίαι τοὺς ἀφικνουμ|ένους καὶ δημοσίαι καὶ νῦν καὶ ἐν τ|ῶι πρόσθεν χρόνωι καὶ αὐτὸς καὶ οἱ | πρόγονοι αὐτοῦ, δεδόχθαι τῆι βουλ|(15)ῆι· τοὺς προέδρους, οἳ ἂν λάχωσιν πρ|οεδρεύειν εἰς τὴν πρώτην ἐκκλησί|αν, προσαγαγεῖν Θεογένην καὶ χρημ|[ατίσ]αι αὐτῶι, γνώμην δὲ ξυμβάλλεσ|θαι τῆς [β]ουλῆς εἰς τὸν δῆμον, ὅτ[ι] δο|(20)κεῖ τῆι βου[λῆι] εἶναι Θεογένην Ξε[ν]|οκλέος Ναυκ[ρατίτη]ν πρόξενον [κα]|ὶ εὐ[ερ]γέτην [τ]ο[ῦ δήμου τοῦ Ἀθηναίω]|ν καὶ αὐτὸν καὶ [ἐκγόνους καὶ εἶναι] | αὐτῶι οἰκίας ἔ[γκτησιν· ἐπιμελεῖσ](25)θαι δὲ αὐτοῦ το[ὺς στρατηγοὺς καὶ τ]|ὴν βουλὴν τὴν ἀ[εὶ βουλεύουσαν. *vvv*] Ἱεροκλείδης Τ[ιμοστράτου Ἀλωπεκ|ῆ]θεν εἶπεν· τὰ μὲ[ν ἄλλα καθάπερ τῆι] | βουλῆι, ἀναγράψ[αι δὲ τόδε τὸ ψήφισ](30)μα τὸν γραμματ[έα τῆς βουλῆς ἐν ἀκρ]|οπόλει καὶ στῆσ[αι δέκα ἡμερῶν, εἰς] | δὲ τὴν ἀναγραφὴ[ν τῆς στήλης δοῦνα]|ι τὸν [τ]αμίαν τοῦ [δήμου ΔΔ δραχμὰς ἐ]|κ τῶν κατὰ ψηφίσ[ματα ἀναλισκομέν](35)ων τῶι δήμωι· ἐπα[ινέσαι δὲ Θεογένη]|[ν κ]αὶ [κα]λέ[σ]α[ι] ἐ[πὶ ξένια εἰς τὸ πρυτ]|[ανεῖον εἰς αὔριον].

39 E.g. *IG* II^{3} 1, 301, 7–9: ἐπειδὴ ὁ δῆ[μ]ος ἐψήφιṣ[ται τὴν β]|ουλὴν προβ[ουλεύσασαν ἐξενεγ]κεῖν εἰς τὸ[ν δῆμον περὶ...("since the People resolved that the Council should formulate and bring forward to the People a proposal about..."). On such acts of commissioning see further below sect. 8.

the rider from his *probouleuma* or had originally included them, failed to get the Council to agree to them, but succeeded in getting them passed by the Assembly.[40] Though its content does not seem hugely contentious, it is not implausible in the culture of the classical democracy at this period that the Council might have regarded the rider's provisions as a "step too far" and best left to the discretion of the Assembly.[41]

5 Probouleumatic Decrees

Let us consider now the list of 27 identifiably probouleumatic decrees from this period:[42]

TABLE 3 *Probouleumatic decrees*[a]

IG II³ 1	Year	Description	E = "Assembly" heading[b] IC = bottom of inscription not preserved
1. 293	351/0 or 348/7	Proxeny for Demokrates of Lampsakos	IC.
2. 294 I	349/8	Proxeny for Theogenes of Naukratis	Followed by rider.
3. 296	349/8	Concerning the Echinaioi	IC.
4. 301	346/5	Honours an official	IC.
5. 302 I	346/5	Honours Abderans	Followed by rider.
6. 303	345/4	Honours Elaiousians?	IC.
7. 310	341/0	Honours Theoklos of Corinth	IC.
8. 324 I	**337/6**	**Proxeny for Euenor of Akarnania**	
9. 325	337/6	Honours Kalliteles of Kydantidai	IC.

40 It is notable that this man also proposed what appears to be a non-probouleumatic decree (ετδ) on Eleusinian affairs during his year on the Council (297), unless this is a probouleumatic decree with "hybrid" formulation, like 348 (see below sect. 6).

41 Compare the implication of the "open" *probouleuma* at *IG* II³ 1, 337 I. See further below sect. 10.

42 This list updates Rhodes 1972, Table C.

IG II³ 1	Year	Description	E = "Assembly" heading[b] IC = bottom of inscription not preserved
10. 327 II	336/5	Honours Phyleus of Oinoe and fellow officials	E.
11. 329[c]	336/5 or 335/4	Honorific	IC.
12. 331	335/4	Honours Nikostratos	IC.
13. 351	331/0	Honours Rheboulas, brother of Kotys, king of the Odrysai	IC.
14. 390 I	c. 350–340	Proxeny for Kleomis of Methymna	Followed by rider.
15. 398	348?	Proxeny for Euboeans	IC?[d]
16. 401 I	c. 345–338	Honours Tenedos, Aratos of Tenedos and others	Followed by rider
17. 411 I[e]	342?	Honours Arybbas	Followed by rider
18. 416	**c. 340–330**	**Honours Priests and *Hieropoioi***	
19. 417	c. 340–325	Honours prytany treasurer of Leontis?	IC.
20. 426	c. 340–320?	Proxeny	IC?
21. 428	c. 340–300	Honours Philomelos	IC.
22. 444	c. 336–330	About repair of statue of Athena Nike and honouring the statue-maker	IC.
23. 454	c. 334/3–322	Honours a Coan	IC.
24. 459	c. 334/3–314/3	Honorific	IC.
25. 469 II[f]	c. 330	Honours Kallikratides of Steiria, the *anagrapheus*	IC.
26. 472	c. 330–300	Honorific	IC.
27. 514	mid-iv?	?	IC.

a In addition to those listed below there are three fragmentary cases which may be Council decrees (or *probouleumata*) or probouleumatic decrees: 402 (c. 345–335) honouring Kephisophon of Paiania (IC), 403 I (c. 345–320) for Apelles of Byzantium, followed by a non-probouleumatic decree, 482 I (c. 325–300) relating to Tenos, followed by rider.

b On the significance of this see section 6.

c This probouleumatic decree implies that its proposer, Lykourgos of Boutadai, was on the Council in this year.

d ἐὰν καὶ τῶι δήμ|[ωι δοκῆι ("if it also seems good to the People") (18–19) implies a probouleumatic decree.

e The clause at 33–35 providing that Arybbas' statement be placed on the agenda of the Assembly, and decree II, which begins τὰ μὲν ἄλλ|α καθάπερ τῆι βουλῆι ("in other respects as proposed by the Council") (35–36) imply that the decree was probouleumatic. Cf. RO 70.

f The status of the fragmentary decree I is uncertain. In *IG* II³ I suggested it might be the *probouleuma* for II (cf. the *probouleuma* 327 I, followed on the stone by the probouleumatic 327 II), but it might alternatively be an independent Assembly decree.

We come now to another significant new observation in relation to the balance between Council and Assembly. It is quite common for probouleumatic decrees to be followed on the stone by riders, and these riders are good evidence that the Council's proposal was discussed in the Assembly. Such cases are indicated in the right column of the table by the rubric "followed by rider". There are five. A notable feature of the probouleumatic decrees, however, not recognised in the literature on this topic hitherto, is that nearly all of the rest of them do not preserve the bottom of the stone, and the lost portion may therefore have included a rider (these cases are marked IC in the table).[43]

In fact the two decrees printed in heavy type in the table, no. 8 and no. 18, are the only two in this corpus which are unequivocally probouleumatic in formulation, which are not followed on the stone by a rider, and where the stone is completely preserved at the bottom. *IG* II³ 1, 324 I, of 337/6, awarded the proxeny to the famous Akarnanian doctor, Euenor. Euenor was honoured again in 322/1 (by a second decree preserved on the same stone, inscribed in a different hand) and was awarded the Athenian citizenship a little later (*IG* II² 374 = Osborne 1981–1983, D50). Interestingly the decree that interests us, the one of 337/6, was passed on the last day of the year, a not uncommon feature of honorific decrees, and might perhaps have been got through without specific debate in a mass of decrees passed at this Assembly. It was proposed by an active member of the liturgical class, Diophantos of Myrrhinous (*APF* 4435), at the end of his year on the Council, who also proposed another probouleumatic decree, honouring an Athenian official, on the same day (*IG* II³ 1, 325).

We do not know on what day of the year, *IG* II³ 1, 416, honouring a group of priests in the Piraeus and *hieropoioi*, was passed, or by whom it was proposed, but it is perhaps relevant here that this decree belongs to a genre, honouring priests and religious officials, for which we have evidence only in the epigraphical record. The literary evidence at this period, mainly the orators, contains of

43 Another likely case is the hybrid *IG* II³ 1, 315, of 339/8 (ε[τδ]. PF. IC). On this type of hybrid see below, section 6, on *IG* II³ 1, 348; cf. Rhodes 1972, 77 and Guagliumi 2004, 46 no. 1 (where this inscription is listed as *SEG* 16.52).

course many references to honorific decrees, but none of these honours a religious official;[44] and the reason for this is surely precisely that such decrees were relatively uncontentious, and as such make no impact on the literary record.

A famous doctor such as Euenor was also perhaps a politically uncontroversial figure, honours for whom might have been expected to attract little opposition. Doctors and priests: both general benefactors of mankind, neither, in different ways, discriminating as between individuals. Precisely the sort of people whose honours might be expected to be uncontentious and to have been rubber-stamped by the Assembly.

By definition a non-probouleumatic decree was handled in the Assembly. It is less certain that a probouleumatic decree was debated in the Assembly. Though our evidence on the point is somewhat obscure, there seems to have been a procedure for nodding through the Assembly some proposals coming up from the Council, the *procheirotonia*.[45] The decrees for Euenor and the Piraeus priests are the only two plausible candidates in this corpus for having been passed at the *procheirotonia*.

The number of inscribed probouleumatic decrees, therefore, is relatively small. Moreover, most were modified in the Assembly by riders and most, perhaps all, of them, were discussed in the Assembly.

6 "Assembly" Headings as Indicators that Decrees were Non-probouleumatic or Discussed in the Assembly

We come now to another fresh observation impacting on the balance between Council and Assembly. From c. 340 BC inscribed Athenian decrees began sporadically to include headings indicating the type of meeting at which they were passed: those attested up to 322/1 BC are, for Council meetings, "Council in the Council chamber" (βουλὴ ἐν βουλευτηρίωι, e.g. *IG* II³ 1, 368, 5); for Assemblies,

44 Cf. Liddel 2016, 319.

45 The clearest testimony is Harp. (cf. Phot., Suid. Π 2933) s.v. προχειροτονία = Lysias F181 Sauppe = F 227 Carey: "it appears that something of this sort happens at Athens, whenever the opinion of the Council, having formulated its proposal, is brought before the People: first of all a vote takes place in the Assembly to decide whether the People will scrutinise the *probouleumata*, or if the *probouleuma* is sufficient. These things are indicated in the speech of Lysias against the writ of Meixidemos". Consistent with that are Aeschin. 1.23 and Dem. 24.11, which both seem to imply that the *procheirotonia* entailed selection of matters for debate; *Ath. Pol.* 43.6 (obscurely) that some matters were dealt with without *procheirotonia* (cf. Rhodes 1981, 529–31). Hansen 1983, 123–30, suggests that a *probouleuma* incorporating a specific recommendation would be debated only if in the *procheirotonia* somebody voted against automatic acceptance.

"Assembly" (ἐκκλησία), "Principal Assembly" (ἐκκλησία κυρία) or "Assembly in the (theatre) of Dionysos" (ἐκκλησία ἐν Διονύσου).[46] The earliest certain examples occur in *IG* II[3] 1, 327 I ([βουλὴ ἐν βουλευτ]ηρίωι) and II (ἐκκλησία) of 336/5 BC,[47] and in 1994 R. M. Errington suggested that the rubrics should be taken to indicate that the arrangement whereby there was one "Principal Assembly" and three other "Assemblies" in each prytany, attested by *Ath. Pol.* 43.4–6, was introduced in that year. In 1995, however, P. J. Rhodes argued persuasively that "It may be ... that the decision to include these rubrics ... is simply an instance of the tendency, with the passage of time, to give more information in the prescripts of decrees, and that the relevant parallels are such matters as the change from personal name alone to personal name, patronymic and demotic for the proposers of decrees, and the dating of decrees by the number of the prytany, and the day within the prytany, and the month and day in the archontic calendar, as well as by the name of the tribe in prytany."[48] There is support for Rhodes' argument in the fact that the meeting headings only occur sporadically;[49] and the introduction of headings for Council meetings at the same time as headings for Assemblies makes it implausible that the rationale lay specifically in a change in the system of Assembly meetings.[50] As with other aspects of the tendency for information in prescripts to become progressively more detailed, the introduction of meeting headings is perhaps an instance of the penetration into the epigraphic record of information that had previously been contained in the papyrus copies of decrees stored in the state archive in the Metroon.

It would seem a natural implication that a decree headed "Assembly" was discussed in the Assembly, and under the classical democracy there is indeed a rather close correlation between the appearance of such headings and other

---

46 See *IG* II[3] 1, 2, Index, pp. 213 and 219.

47 There is, however, a plausible, albeit wholly restored, example at *IG* II[3] 1, 314, 3, now dated to 340/39 BC.

48 Rhodes 1995 (quotation, p. 189). Fathers' names and demotics of proposers begin to be supplied from 354/3 (cf. Henry 1977, 32); the number of the prytany begins to appear in the early fourth century (first case: *IG* II[2] 18, of 394/3. See *RO* 10 with Henry 1977, 24–25); supply of other dating information tends also to increase over the course of the fourth century (*IG* II[3] 1, 316 = *RO* 77, of 338/7, is perhaps the earliest decree that gives the date in full in both lunar and prytany calendars).

49 Cf. Tracy 1998, 221, who, in publishing *IG* II[3] 1, 331, of 335/4 BC, noted the absence of meeting specification from the prescript of this decree, and that "the change [i.e. to occasional inclusion of meeting specifications] was as likely to be in the style of preambles as one that had legal or constitutional substance".

50 Cf. Henry 1977, 39.

indicators that a decree was non-probouleumatic.[51] The following twenty decrees from this period identifiable conventionally as non-probouleumatic carry one of the "Assembly" headings:[52]

TABLE 4 *Non-probouleumatic decrees with "Assembly" headings*

IG II^3 1	Year	Honorand	Rubric
1. 327 III	335/4	Phyleus of Oinoe	*ekklesia*
2. 334	334/3	–	*ekklesia*
3. 335	334/3	Amyntor	*ekklesia*
4. 339	333/2	Mnemon and Kallias of Herakleia	[*ekklesia*]
5. 355	329/8	*Epimeletai* of Amphiaraia	*ekklesia*
6. 359	328/7	Androkles of Kerameis	*ekklesia*
7. 366	326/5	–	*ekklesia*
8. 324 II	322/1	Euenor of Akarnania	*ekklesia*
9. 385	322/1	–	*ekklesia*
10. 419	c. 340–320	Amphipolitan	*ekklesia*
11. 467	c. 333/2–320	–	*ekklesia*
12. 344	332/1	– son of Onoma–	*ekklesia en Dionysou*
13. 345	332/1	– son of -emos of Plataia	*ekklesia en Dionysou*
14. 384	322/1	–	*ekklesia en Dionysou*
15. 333 I	334/3	Archippos of Thasos	*ekklesia kyria*
16. 349	332/1	Amphiaraos	*ekklesia kyria*
17. 361	327/6	–	*ekklesia kyria*
18. 376	323/2	–	*ekklesia* [*kyria*]
19. 378 I	323/2	Euphron of Sikyon	[*ekklesia kyria*]
20. 439	337–322	Dionysios	[*ekklesia kyria*]

Three cases are less straightforward. *IG* II^3 1, 348, honouring Phanodemos in 332/1 for his legislation for the Amphiaraia festival, is hybrid in formulation, displaying the probouleumatic formula (17–23), but introduced not, as one

51 The correlation seems less well observed after 322/1. See Rhodes 1972, Table C, 250–58 (where probouleumatic decrees with an "Assembly" heading are marked "E").

52 *IG* II^3 1, 379 might be a further case, but the heading, *ekklesia kyria*, depends on an uncertain restoration.

would normally expect of probouleumatic decrees, by "The Council and People decided", ἔδοξεν τῆι βουλῆι καὶ τῶι δήμωι, but, as one would normally expect of non-probouleumatic decrees, by "The People decided", ἔδοξεν τῶι δήμωι. There are 16 hybrids of this type, two from our period,[53] and the rest hellenistic, and the current consensus is that ἔδοξεν τῶι δήμωι in these cases should be attributed to "secretarial carelessness."[54] It is notable, however, that this decree also carries the heading, "Principal Assembly" (ἐκκλησ|ία κυρία) (6–7). As we have seen, probouleumatic decrees might be, but were not necessarily, discussed in the Assembly, and a possible explanation of this combination of formulae – probouleumatic, but with two headings emphasising the Assembly – is that it implies precisely that, though probouleumatic, this decree was discussed in the Assembly.

The same explanation might apply to the two other exceptions. *IG* II³ 1, 327 II (336/5 BC), honouring Phyleus of Oinoe, is probouleumatic in formulation, but includes the heading, ἐκκλησία, and is divergent in content from the *probouleuma* inscribed before it, suggesting perhaps that the Council's proposal had, in fact, been substantively reworked in the Assembly. *IG* II³ 1, 341 (333/2 BC), which has the probouleumatic, [ἔδοξεν τῆι βουλῆ]ι καὶ τ[ῶι | δήμωι] (9–10), combined with [ἐ|κκλησία κυρία] (6–7) is too fragmentary to press.

In the light of this it seems we may infer that, in the ten other cases in this period in which one of the "Assembly" headings occurs and there is no other formulaic indication as to whether or not the decree was probouleumatic, the measure was probably non-probouleumatic, or, if probouleumatic, was discussed in the Assembly:

TABLE 5 *Assembly headings on decrees whose bouleumatic status is uncertain*

IG II³ 1	Year	Honorand	Rubric
21. 333 II	333/2	Archippos of Thasos	[*ekklesia*][a]
22. 342 = 343 I	332/1	Theophantos	[*ekklesia kyria*]
23. 353	330/29	–	*ekklesia* [*kyria*]
24. 357	328/7	–	*ekklesia* [*kyria*][b]
25. 364	326/5	–	*ekklesia kyria*
26. 372	324/3	–	*ekklesia* [*kyria*]
27. 373	324/3	–	[*ekklesia*]

53 The other case is *IG* II³ 1, 315, on which see above n. 43. *IG* II³ 1, 297, is also a candidate (see n. 40).

54 Rhodes 1972, 77–78; Guagliumi 2004, 46–48, supplies an updated list, and is inclined to a similar explanation ("trascuratezza formale", 46).

IG II³ 1	Year	Honorand	Rubric
28. 415	After c. 340	–	*ekklesia*
29. 436	337–323	–	*ekklesia* [*en Dionysou*]
30. 476	326/5–324/3	*Proedroi*?	[*ekklesia*]

a ἐν τῶι δήμωι ἔν|νομα] ἱκετεύειν ("made lawful supplication in the Assembly") does not of itself necessarily imply a non-probouleumatic decree. Cf. Rhodes 1972, 73 with n. 1.

b The latest inscribed decree proposed by Lykourgos. There is a further indication that the decree was non-probouleumatic in that he had probably already had his two terms on the Council before this, i.e. in 336/5 or more likely 335/4 BC (*IG* II³ 1, 329), and 329/8 or shortly before (*IG* II² 1672, 302).

7 Non-probouleumatic Decrees

The large majority of the decrees in our corpus are non-probouleumatic. They show no trace of any underlying *probouleuma*, and instead contain formulae implying that the decree represents a decision specifically of the Assembly, rather than of the Council and Assembly, so ἔδοξεν τῶι δήμωι (ετδ) ("The People decided") and δεδόχθαι or ἐψηφίσθαι τῶι δήμωι (δ/ψτδ) ("that the People shall decide *or* resolve"); and any riders are introduced by τὰ μὲν ἄλλα καθάπερ ὁ δεῖνα (RI) ("in other respects as proposed by *name*") rather than τὰ μὲν ἄλλα καθάπερ τῆι βουλῆι (RP) ("in other respects as proposed by the Council").[55] Occasionally the decree may also mention the *probouleuma* (περὶ ὧν ἡ βουλὴ προεβούλευσεν…); or commission a *probouleuma* (CP). The following 64 decrees can be identified on these criteria, or others mentioned in the notes, as non-probouleumatic:[56]

TABLE 6 *Non-probouleumatic decrees*

IG II³ 1	Year	Description (E = Assembly heading)
1. 295	349/8?	Honours Orontes (citizenship)
2. 297	349/8	On an Eleusinian matter (but see above n. 40)
3. 298 I	347/6	Honours Bosporan rulers (citizenship)[a]
4. 304 II	344/3?	Honours Pellanians

55 Rhodes 1972, 64–65. There is only one case of RI in this corpus: *IG* II³ 1, 298.

56 The table in effect updates for this period Rhodes 1972, Table D.

TABLE 6 *Non-probouleumatic decrees* (cont.)

IG II³ 1	Year	Description (E = Assembly heading)
5. 308	343/2	Treaty with Messene
6. 309	341/0	Honours Elaiousians
7. 311 I	341/0	Honours officials
8. 312	340/39	Proxeny for Phokinos and others
9. 313	340/39	Honours Tenedos and Aratos of Tenedos
10. 316	338/7	Honours Akarnanians (citizenship)
11. 321	337/6	?
12. 322	337/6	Honours courtier of Philip II
13. 323	337/6?	Honours official
14. 327 III	335/4	Honours Phyleus of Oinoe (E)
15. 333 I	334/3	Honours Archippos of Thasos (E) (citizenship)
16. 334	334/3	? (E)
17. 335	334/3	Honours Amyntor (E) (citizenship)
18. 336	334/3?	Honours Diotimos?
19. 337 II	333/2	*Enktesis* for Kitian merchants' sanctuary
20. 338 II	333/2	Honours Pytheas of Alopeke
21. 339	333/2?	Honours Mnemon and Kallias of Herakleia (E)
22. 344	332/1	Proxeny for an actor? (E)
23. 345	332/1	Honours a Plataian (E)
24. 346 II	332/1	Honours the son of Aristeides
25. 347	332/1	Proxeny for Amphis of Andros
26. 349	332/1	Honours Amphiaraos (E)
27. 352	330/29	Honours Eudemos of Plataia
28. 355	329/8	Honours *epimeletai* of Amphiaraia (E)
29. 356	329/8	Honours Larisan
30. 359 I	328/7	Honours Androkles of Kerameis, priest (E)
31. 361	327/6	Honours Thymondas? (E)
32. 362	327/6	?
33. 363	327/6	Honours Phanostratos
34. 366	326/5	? (E)
35. 367 III	330/29–328/7	Honours Herakleides of Salamis
36. 367 V	325/4	Proxeny for Herakleides of Salamis
37. 370	325/4	On dispatch of colony to Adriatic
38. 375	323/2	Honours Lapyris of Kleonai

IG II³ 1	Year	Description (E = Assembly heading)
39. 376	323/2	On Phokians (E)
40. 377=378 I	323/2	Honours Euphron of Sikyon (citizenship) and People of Sikyon (E)
41. 379	323/2?	Proxeny Apollonides of Sidon (E?)
42. 380	323/2	Honours a son of Demetrios
43. 384	322/1	? (E)
44. 385	322/1	? (E)
45. 399	348 or 343?	Decree against those attacking Eretria or other allies (CP)
46. 405	c. 345–320	Proxeny a Phaselite
47. 414	c. 340	Honours a city
48. 419	c. 340–320	Honours an Amphipolitan (E)
49. 421	c. 340–320	Honorific decree
50. 430	c. 337 ?	Honours a Salaminian
51. 432	337–325	Proxeny for Sopatros of Akragas
52. 439	c. 337–322	Honours Dionysios (E)
53. 440	c. 337–320	Honours Potamon
54. 441	c. 337–320?	Honours Pandios of Herakleia
55. 466	after 333/2	Honorific
56. 467	c. 333/2–320	? (E)
57. 473	329–322?	Honours Nikostratos
58. 479	after 325?	Proxeny for Hestiaian
59. 480	c. 325–322	Honours a Plataian (citizenship)
60. 484	324–322/1	Honours friends of king and Antipater
61. 485	c. 323/2?	Honours Kythnos
62. 493	mid-iv	Proxeny
63. 498	mid-iv	Honorific
64. 519	350–300	Honorific

a It is clear from the fact that the proposer, Androtion, cannot have been on the Council this year (he had already been a councillor twice before 347/6), and from the formulation of the rider as amending Androtion's (rather than the Council's) proposal (RI), that the decree is non-probouleumatic. See Rhodes 1972, 73–74; *RO* 64.

To these can be added a further 9 possible cases, making a total of between 64 and 73 non-probouleumatic decrees altogether:

TABLE 7 *Possible non-probouleumatic decrees*

IG II³ 1	Year	Description	Formulae
1. 292	352/1	On sacred orgas	–[a]
2. 299	347/6	Treaty with Mytilene	ετβκτδ. δτδ.[b]
3. 307	343/2	Honours Kephallenians or Lampsakenes	–[c]
4. 367 I	330/29–328/7	Commissions a *probouleuma* to honour Herakleides of Salamis	–[d]
5. 404	c. 345–320	Honours exiles	–[e]
6. 410	c. 345–320	Honorific	[δ]τδ ?
7. 418 I	c. 340–320	Honours Asklepiodoros	RP.[f]
8. 433	c. 337–325 ?	Agreement with Sokles about exploitation of a resource	[δ]τδ ?[g]
9. 507	mid-iv	Honorific	[ψ]τδ ?

a The correction at the end (84–86) empowering the Council to make any necessary supplementary provisions might imply that the decree itself was non-probouleumatic. Cf. the comparable provision in the non-probouleumatic 370, 95–100, and below on 404. In the case of a long and complex decree of this kind, however, it is not inconceivable that the Council might have inserted such a clause into a *probouleuma* on its own initiative.

b Perhaps a late case of an earlier tendency (normal practice c. 462/1–405/4 BC) to use ἔδοξεν τῆι βουλῆι καὶ τῶι δήμωι for any enactment of the Assembly. Cf. Rhodes 1972, 64 (3 ii), 71, 76–77; Guagliumi 2004, 43–44.

c The latest dated decree proposed by the major politician, Aristophon of Azenia (*APF* 2108), in 343/2 at the age of ca. 90. There is nothing in the text to indicate that it is non-probouleumatic, but one would have expected such a figure to have served his two terms on the Council before reaching this age, and perhaps, like most decrees proposed by major politicians, this one was non-probouleumatic. Cf. Rhodes 1972, 70–71 with Table F.

d This decree, which simply commissions a *probouleuma*, was perhaps itself non-probouleumatic. Though the evidence is inconclusive (cf. Rhodes 1972, 52–57), the Assembly could perhaps commission a *probouleuma* without a *probouleuma* for the commission. This is suggested by the parallel of procedures for initiating judicial proceedings in the Assembly, εἰσαγγελίαι and προβολαί, and by the procedures for supplication (ἱκετηρίαι), which could, it seems, sometimes be made directly to the Assembly (Rhodes 1972, 55–56), though we do not know whether a supplication from Herakleides underlay the Assembly's commission in this case. The power to commission a *probouleuma* independently of the Council would not contradict the principle, οὐδὲν ἀπροβούλευτον, since any substantive Assembly decision would still be based on a *probouleuma*; and it is notable in this case that, though the secretary seems to have been rather conscientious in inscribing other *probouleumata* relating to Herakleides, there is no *probouleuma* for the Assembly's commissioning decree on the stone.

e As with IG II³ 1, 292 (above no. 1), the clause at 7–9 empowering the Council to make supplementary provisions might imply that the decree was non-probouleumatic.

f The fact that it is followed by a rider introduced by τὰ μὲν ἄλλα καθάπερ τεῖ βου|λεῖ (24–25) suggests that decree I was probouleumatic, and this is also consistent with ἐν τεῖ βο]υλεῖ ἔννομα ἱ[κετεύειν (5). However, [ἐψ|ηφίσθαι] τῶι δήμωι (5–6) would normally indicate a non-probouleumatic decree. Perhaps we may infer that decree I was probouleumatic, but adapted somewhat in the Assembly. Cf. Rhodes 1972, 72–73.

g If δεδόχθαι Δ[- (5) conceals a corruption of δεδόχθαι [τῶι δήμωι.

To these 64–73 decrees can tentatively be added the ten which I identified in section 1 as being non-probouleumatic, or at least debated in the Assembly, on the basis that they carry one of the "Assembly" headings.

8 Riders and Proposals Commissioned by the Assembly

A "rider" is a sub-class of non-probouleumatic decree which explicitly amends another Assembly decree, and is normally inscribed beneath the decree it amends. Usually, riders amend probouleumatic decrees (RP). Decree 2 of the inscription honouring Theogenes of Naukratis, discussed above, is a good example; and as we have seen, riders can add quite substantially to the provisions in a probouleumatic decree. The examples in this corpus (several of which are very fragmentary) are:

TABLE 8 *Riders*

IG II³ 1	Year	Description
1. 294 II	349/8	Proxeny for Theogenes of Naukratis
2. 298 II (= *RO* 64)	347/6	Honours Bosporan rulers

TABLE 8 *Riders* (cont.)

IG II^3 1	Year	Description
3. 302 II	346/5	Honours Abderans
4. 403 II	c. 345–320	Proxeny for Apelles of Byzantium
5. 411 II	342?	Honours Arybbas
6. 390 II	c. 350–340	Proxeny for Kleomis of Methymna
7. 401 II	c. 345–338	Honours Tenedos and Tenedians
8. 418 II	c. 340–320	Honours Asklepiodoros
9. 482 II	c. 325–300	On Tenians
10. 324 II	322/1	Honours Euenor
11. 447 II	c. 335–330	Provides for sacrifices at Little Panathenaia

In the decrees for Theogenes and for Tenedos the inscribing provision is included in the rider; in those for Arybbas and Asklepiodoros it is in the main decree (I). *IG* II^3 1, 302 I and 390 I contain no inscribing provision, and we may probably assume that in both cases it was contained in the incompletely preserved rider.

IG II^3 1, 298 II is the only case in this corpus of a rider to a non-probouleumatic decree, introduced not by "in other respects as proposed by the Council…", but "in other respects as proposed by Androtion." It honours Apollonios, a brother of the honorands of Androtion's decree, Spartokos and Pairisades, rulers of the Bosporan kingdom, and depicted on the relief at the top of the decree as standing next to them, while his two brothers are enthroned. It seems that Apollonios did not share in his brothers' rule; and it is likely also that this arrangement of the decrees was the product of some advance planning. The proposer of the rider was a young man, Polyeuktos of Krioa, son of a known associate of Androtion, and he can plausibly be seen as proposing his rider under the aegis of the older man.[57]

There are two cases in which the "rider", though introduced by the "in other respects as proposed by the Council, but…" formulation, does not conventionally amend a decree inscribed above it. *IG* II^3 1, 324 II awards *enktesis* and protection to the doctor, Euenor. It does in effect supplement the proxeny granted by the (probouleumatic) decree I on the stone, but it is not formally a rider to that decree, which was passed 15 years previously and is inscribed in a different

57 See *RO* pp. 323 and 325. For this type of dynamic see chapter 8.2.

hand. *IG* II³ 1, 447 II provides for the application to fund sacrifices at the Little Panathenaia of the income raised by the provisions of the law inscribed before it (447 I), but 447 II is not formally a "rider" to that law. Both these "pseudo-riders" have the character of straightforward, substantive, non-probouleumatic decrees. Perhaps the "rider" formula was used in these cases simply to signal that the *probouleuma* had been completely recast in the Assembly.[58]

The Assembly had the power to take the initiative in commissioning *probouleumata*. As we saw above (Table 7, note d), though our evidence is inconclusive in the one instance we have of a simple commissioning decree, *IG* II³ 1, 367 I, a case can be made that such a decree did not itself need to be probouleumatic. In any case these commissions imply once again an active Assembly. They are attested in three cases of honours for Athenian officials: the fragmentary *IG* II³ 1, 301, 7–9, for an unknown office-holder of the year 347/6, honoured in 346/5, and where the decree on the stone is not only probouleumatic, it is stated to result from the Assembly's commission. This is an interesting case as it is the earliest in the regular series of decrees honouring Athenian officials. We should like to know more, for example whether the initiative for the honours in fact lay with the honorand, but we have no means of telling this.[59] The same process is implied for another official honorand ten years later, in *IG* II³ 1, 325, of 337/6, for Kalliteles of Kydantidai. Again the decree is fragmentary; again probouleumatic. 338 honouring Pytheas of Alopeke, the manager of the water supply, in 333/2, is better preserved and differs from the other two cases only in being non-probouleumatic, though the *probouleuma* the Assembly had commissioned is also inscribed under it. That the same procedure was also available for foreign honorands is implied by 367 I (commission) and II (resulting *probouleuma*, referred to also in IV, 69–71), though in this case there is no back-reference to the commission in the Assembly's resulting (non-probouleumatic) decree, 367 III. This is valuable evidence as it implies that, where, as was more normal, only the Assembly's final decree is inscribed, it may have

58 I owe this suggestion to Peter Rhodes.

59 *IG* II³ 1, 469 (unfortunately not precisely datable), shows that Athenian officials who had passed their *euthynai* were encouraged by the law to "seek benefits from the People", i.e. implicitly over and above the 500 dr. crown proposed by the Council (l. 27), and this implies that in some cases, at least, officials applied to be honoured by the Assembly. Whether the commissioning of honours by the Assembly, in cases where it is attested, was the result of such an application, or was initiated by a alternative route, however, is obscure. Assumptions of uniform procedures may be misplaced. In 306 III an individual councillor is crowned, and a *probouleuma* goes forward recommending that the Assembly should also crown him, not as a result of any application for honours, but of a competition and vote by his fellow councillors (cf. also 402).

resulted from a *probouleuma* commissioned by the Assembly without that being made clear in the text. 331, 11–14 for Nikostratos, who may or may not be an Athenian official, adds nothing, and 351, 10 for Rheboulas, member of the royal house of the Odrysai, is too fragmentary and uncertain an attestation of this process to be significant. We see the commissioning process at work in a non-honorific context in 399, where Hegesippos of Sounion commissions a *probouleuma* for the punishment of those who had attacked Eretria. This is not only non-probouleumatic, it is a highly personal, rhetorical decree which is sui generis in the corpus. The initiative for the commission patently lay with Hegesippos speaking in the Assembly.[60]

9 Contrasting Features of the Content of Probouleumatic and Non-probouleumatic Decrees

The most striking feature as far as the content of the decrees is concerned is that while all the probouleumatic decrees are or may have been honorific,[61] the non-probouleumatic category includes other types of decree: treaties (Mytilene, Messene), (probably) religious decrees (292?, 297?, 337 II also has a strong religious aspect), and several items that are sui generis: the decree on the foundation of the colony in the Adriatic (370); Hegesippos' decree directed against those attacking Eretria or other allied cities (399); and perhaps the decree providing for Sokles to exploit a resource (433). We may infer that at this period there was a routine aspect to the award of honours that meant that some of the decrees could be passed by the Assembly on the basis of the Council's proposal, but that once an inscribed decree left this honorific "beaten track" it was likely, or even certain, that the Council's *probouleuma* would be reworked in the Assembly.

---

60 *IG* II³ 1, 298, 57 (non-probouleumatic), proposed by Androtion in Elaphebolion 347/6, uses probouleumatic language rather than commissioning language, but the net effect is the same, i.e. the Council is commissioned by the Assembly to come forward with a proposal at the Assembly on the 18th (scil. Elaphebolion) for how to settle the Bosporan rulers' complaints about money apparently owed them by the Athenians.

61 *IG* II³ 1, 296 related to the Akarnanian Echinaioi and mentioned *symbola* (14), but whether it was itself a *symbola* agreement is unclear. Athens must have had a very large number of *symbola* agreements (mutual agreements with other cities on the judicial treatment of citizens of the other city, cf. Gauthier 1972) and they were perhaps somewhat routine. The decree may in any case have included an honorific element. *IG* II³ 1, 444 contained provisions relating to a statue of Athena Nike, but also honoured the statue-maker.

As regards the honorific decrees, the pattern is as one would expect, in other words decrees awarding weightier and/or potentially more contentious honours tend to be non-probouleumatic. As we saw in chapter 8 (table 2), most decrees awarding honours to Athenians are Council decrees, *probouleumata* or probouleumatic decrees; the six exceptions are mostly decrees for officials which have come forward from the Council and where the Council's honours are (or may have been) also recorded on the stone (311 I, 323 for a secretary, 327 III for a secretary, 338 II for a curator of the water supply, 359 I for a priest of Asklepios). In the case of *IG* II^3 1, 355, the decree honours the board of prominent Athenians who managed the first celebration of Phanodemos' new Great Amphiaraia, including Phanodemos himself, Lykourgos and Demades, the most prominent Athenian honorands of any inscribed decree of this period. With decrees honouring foreigners there is some overlap between the probouleumatic and non-probouleumatic categories. With a proxeny decree, for example, one could not predict whether it was going to be probouleumatic or not. Again, however, there is a definite bias in the non-probouleumatic decrees to weightier honours and higher status honorands, while there is only one probouleumatic decree, *IG* II^3 1, 411, that awards, or rather confirms, the highest honour normally awarded to foreigners, the Athenian citizenship.[62] The non-probouleumatic decrees also include the one decree honouring a god (349) and most or all of the decrees honouring whole cities.

As Rhodes observed,[63] there was an inevitable tendency, given that it was only possible to serve on the Council twice in a lifetime, for decrees proposed by major political figures to be non-probouleumatic. It is unsurprising that such decrees also tended to deal with weightier matters. Thus the non-probouleumatic decrees include the one proposed by Demosthenes (*IG* II^3 1, 312); six proposed by Demades (321, 322, 334, 335, 346, 356; 326, 330 and 358 are too fragmentary to determine); and all but one of those proposed by Lykourgos (336, 337 II, 345, 352, 357, 432; only 329 is probouleumatic). They also include decrees proposed by other major figures such as Androtion (298 I), Phanodemos (349, 306 II arises from his term on the Council), Hegesippos of Sounion (316 and 399) and Polyeuktos of Sphettos (342, 343, 439).

62 *IG* II^3 1, 351, honouring Rheboulas, is also probouleumatic and related to a prominent foreigner (brother of Kotys, king of the Odrysai) who was already an Athenian citizen, but only the prescript is preserved and we do not know what the decree was about.

63 Rhodes 1972, table F.

10 Interpretation

My main conclusion is that the current orthodoxy, based on the inscribed record, that Council and Assembly were broadly in balance in formulating decisions in the fourth-century democracy requires radical modification in relation to the period 352/1–322/1.[64]

First, the large majority of Assembly decrees in this period were non-probouleumatic (between 64 and 73, plus 11 riders), in other words formulated in the Assembly rather than the Council, and of those which are probouleumatic (27) all but two are or may have been followed on the stone by riders, implying that they were actively debated and amended in the Assembly. Ten further decrees of indeterminable bouleumatic character carry "Assembly" headings, which, I have suggested, indicate that they were either non-probouleumatic or were debated in the Assembly. As regards content, there is a clear division between the probouleumatic decrees, all of which are or may have been honorific, either for Athenian officials or, insofar as for foreigners, mostly awarding less weighty honours and/or for less prominent honorands, and the non-probouleumatic, which include also non-honorific decrees, and insofar as they are honorific tend to award weightier honours and/or be for more prominent honorands and/or proposed by more prominent Athenians. This not only confirms the liveliness of the Assembly in late classical Athens as a forum for decision-taking, it indicates a clear tendency for the Assembly to reserve to itself more significant decisions. There are also numerous other indications of the subordination of the Council to the Assembly: in the limitation in scope of the Council's independent decree-making capacity (section 3); in the practice whereby the Assembly might initiate discussion of a topic by commissioning a *probouleuma* from the Council (which, as we saw in section 8, might have been more common than is apparent on the surface of the decree); and in the delegation to the Council of responsibility for "tidying up" the detail of an Assembly's decree (discussed chapter 7, section 2). We do not know how common it was for non-probouleumatic

64 I am not concerned here with the literary evidence, discussed by Rhodes 1972, 52–64. As he notes (pp. 63–64), "[literary] texts, where they give us enough detail, show a heavy bias towards genuine debates in the Assembly and towards decrees proposed by non-councillors, but this is inevitable: the evidence is mostly for controversial issues in the fourth century, where the Council's suggestions are least likely to have been adopted without change by the Assembly, and since our most voluble informant is Demosthenes we ought not to be surprised at the prominent appearance of his own decrees in many years when he was not councillor. For a fairer estimate of the part played by the Council and Assembly we must turn to the preserved texts of inscribed decrees, selected not for their importance to the orators but by the chance of discovery".

decrees to be based on "open" *probouleumata* that, in effect, put a topic on the agenda of the Assembly without making a substantive recommendation, but it is unlikely to be coincidental that, in the one case we have, *IG* II³ 337 I, the issue, an application for the foundation of a temple in Attica by a non-Greek community (the Kitians), was patently potentially rather contentious. It may be that the pressures, democratic-cultural and perhaps practical also (the quantity of business that the Council had to handle was patently formidable) were such that this "easy option" was taken by the Council more frequently than is apparent on the surface of the epigraphical record.[65]

That said, we must continue to bear in mind that, as we established in chapter 2, the inscribed record gives us only a partial impression of the Assembly's decision-taking, one that is dominated by honorific decrees. As we have seen in earlier chapters there are other indications that such decrees formed a significant element of the policy agenda,[66] which is some reassurance as to their representative quality. As we have just seen, some of the inscribed ones are probouleumatic, some non-probouleumatic, with the former tending to be the less weighty cases. As we saw in chapter 2, however, whole categories of honorific decree were not usually inscribed, e.g. those awarding merely crowns to foreigners, and no substantive honours, and those awarding foliage crowns to Athenians. One would expect such decrees to be probouleumatic (or indeed decrees of the Council alone) to a greater extent than the inscribed decrees; and it would not be surprising if some were nodded through the Assembly at the *procheirotonia*. As for non-honorific decrees, we have seen that all those that were inscribed at this period were non-probouleumatic, but in absolute terms the number of such inscribed decrees is not large and it is possible that they are not representative in this respect of the generality of non-honorific decrees. It would be unjustified to infer from the inscribed examples that uninscribed non-honorific decrees were all or mostly non-probouleumatic. Probably there was a good number of more routine decisions on non-honorific matters taken by the Assembly that were probouleumatic in form, and some that were nodded through at the *procheirotonia*, but in the absence of evidence this is impossible to quantify.

What are we to conclude in this perspective about the character of the classical Athenian democracy in its final phase? Especially since the Assembly was on any account composed predominantly of men whose time was largely taken up with other occupations rather than by "professional" politicians, to have some body which prepared the Assembly's business was a practical necessity

65 On this cf. also section 4, on *IG* II³ 1, 294.

66 Chapter 7; chapter 8 sect. 3.

even in the most democratic regime.[67] It was patently important from a democratic perspective that its composition and appointment should be optimally representative of the citizen body as a whole, and this was achieved in this period via a combination of the deme quotas, the use of allotment for appointment to office, the availability of subsistence payments for attendance and, above all perhaps, by the limitation on tenure to a maximum of twice in a lifetime. As the statistics we looked at in chapter 8 confirm, aside from its members being over 30, the Council was broadly a microcosm of the adult male citizen population. What is remarkable to our minds, however, used to ideas of representative democracy, is that it was not enough that decisions should be taken by a body that accurately represented the collective; the very fact (it seems) that only 500 citizens at any one time were entitled to participate in the Council (its debates and votes) meant that it was an unsuitable body for taking important policy decisions. The extent to which the Assembly (= *demos*) was predominant over the Council in decision-taking in the final phase of the classical democracy would have been regarded by most contemporary Athenians as a healthy sign of a vigorous "democracy";[68] but from our perspective, it is a notably radical feature.

This, I suggest, is consonant with the observations about the multiplicity of decree proposers that we made in the last chapter. It was intrinsic to the democratic idea that the many should predominate, whether this was a matter of the relative roles in decision-taking of the Council and Assembly, or the number of individuals who came forward with successful proposals to be inscribed on stone. That those proposers were predominantly wealthy and prominent individuals when it came to making laws or to making decrees in the sphere of foreign relations was less important than that the decisions to pass their proposals had been made by the citizens as a whole, in a forum in which everyone was equally entitled to contribute to the debate. Similarly, though the reservation of important decisions to the Assembly, and the subordination of the Council to it, in effect made the Assembly the principal forum in which the prominent

---

67 I take it that this, or something like it, is what Aristotle means at *Pol.* 1299b 32–33: δεῖ μὲν γὰρ εἶναί τι τοιοῦτον ᾧ ἐπιμελὲς ἔσται τοῦ δήμου προβουλεύειν, ὅπως ἀσχολῶν [ἄσχολον some MSS] ἔσται.

68 συλλέγονταί τε πολλάκις καὶ ἅπαντα αὐτοὶ κρίνουσιν, as Aristotle remarks (above n. 5). The subordination of Council to the Assembly = *Demos* in "democracy" at this period is concisely but eloquently acknowledged in the inscription on the base of the statue of Demokratia dedicated by the Council of 333/2: "Demokratia. The Council in the archonship of Nikokrates dedicated, having been crowned by the *Demos* for its excellence and justice" (*IG* II^3 4, 3).

and wealthy could exercise influence, it was more important that the Council should be representative of the citizen body, thereby excluding the prominent and wealthy from dominance, and that the prominent and wealthy should exercise their influence in a forum in which every citizen could participate.

11 Postscript: Comparison with Late-3rd century[69]

The dynamics of relations between Council and Assembly in the last phase of the classical democracy can be further illuminated by taking a look at the situation over a comparable span of time just over a century later, between 229/8 and 198/7 BC.[70] The character of Athenian democracy, and Greek democracy more broadly, in the hellenistic period is a live topic, and to do it full justice would require a broader and more focussed discussion than would be appropriate here, taking in the (albeit limited) literary evidence, and analysing in greater depth Athens' relations with the successor kingdoms.[71] The impression one would gather from recent scholarship on this subject is that little changed,

69 Looking in the other direction chronologically I note that a comparison of the figures presented here with those in Rhodes 1972, 79, with tables C and D, suggests that there was probably an increase in the proportion of inscribed decrees that were non-probouleumatic as the fourth-century democracy progressed, but full analysis of this must await the publication of *IG* II³ 1 fasc. 1. Appreciation of the situation in the fifth century is rendered difficult by the fact that a single enactment formula, first "The People decided", later "The Council and People decided" was apparently used for all decrees regardless of their bouleumatic quality (Rhodes 1972, 64, 66) and that motion formulae ("… that it be decided by the Council/People") are not used at all (66), so it is unclear in most cases whether or not a decree is probouleumatic. Rhodes 1972, 79, counted 29 probouleumatic and 6 non-probouleumatic decrees to 404/3 BC, but mostly the criterion is the form of the rider (i.e. whether "in other respects as proposed by X" or "in other respects as proposed by the Council" see Rhodes 1972, table C, pp. 246–247, table D, p. 259) and since, by definition, any rider indicates debate and discussion of an issue in the Assembly, this is not very significant as regards the balance between the Council and Assembly in formulating decisions.

70 I reviewed the inscribed decrees of this period in Lambert 2014. This section represents a consolidation and expansion of some of the points made there.

71 For an overview of scholarship on hellenistic democracy see Mann 2012. Particularly influential has been the analysis of Gauthier 1984, 1985 and 1993, who emphasised the mid-2nd century as the point at which Greek cities became oligarchic, following the displacement of the hellenistic kings by the Romans and the substitution of the kings by super-wealthy citizens as sources of major benefaction. In Gauthier's view, before that, and in contrast to earlier assumptions about the "decline" of the polis in the hellenistic period, the polis

at Athens, between the fourth-century democracy and the hellenistic period. Grieb 2008, 42–47, emphasises the continuities in the organisation and powers of the Athenian Council and Assembly from the fourth century through to the second. Bayliss 2011 passionately defends the continuity of democratic ideology and institutions in hellenistic Athens, while Osborne 2012a, chapter 2,[72] also emphasises the extent to which the "Government and Institutions" of 3rd-century Athens continued to follow the model described in the *Ath. Pol.*. Chaniotis 2010, while showing how, in the hellenistic period, the term "democracy" can be used of constitutions in which power was in the hands of a tight elite and that were in no way democratic according to the usual understanding of the term, nevertheless writes (p. 6):

> .... the democratic institutions in the hellenistic period are ... comparable to those of the moderate Athenian democracy of Demosthenes' times ... in this period the foundation of the People's sovereignty, the popular Assembly, regularly met in hundreds of city-states to elect annual magistrates, to approve of all proposals of the Council ... proposals of the Council could be amended after considering the discussions in the Assembly. In this respect, moderate democracy is the most widespread constitutional form in the hellenistic period.

Hellenistic democracy and fourth-century Athenian democracy are presented here as much of a piece, and indeed Chaniotis gives a number of examples illustrating the points he is making, from the fourth century Athenian democracy and from hellenistic Athens, as if nothing had changed. Habicht 1997 similarly emphasises the continuity of Athenian institutions from the classical period. There continued to be an Assembly, which was sovereign, and so it would be proper in that sense to describe the constitution as formally a democracy, and there continued to be a Council, appointed from the tribes.[73] This, of course, is true; but Assemblies and Councils were common institutions across the Greek world at all periods, and, as we saw in section 1, continued to operate under avowedly non-democratic regimes. We need to dig deeper if we are to determine the extent to which Assembly and Council were constituted on a democratic basis.

---

had remained a vital institution in which democracy had been sustained. It is not clear to me that this model suits the Athenian case.

72 Pp. 55–102; Assembly and Council, 56–74. Bayliss 2011, 96–97.

73 Habicht 1997, 4–5.

The inscribed decrees of 229/8–198/7 clearly imply that Assembly and Council continued to operate within the same formal constitutional structure as existed in 352/1–322/1. The Council performed the probouleutic function as it did in 352/1–322/1; the Assembly made decisions on the basis of the Council's *probouleuma*, either accepting it, or amending it, again as in 352/1–322/1. As we saw above, the Council was also large, larger in fact in the periods of 12 and 13 tribes, than it had been in the classical democracy; deme quotas continued to operate and, as far as we know, there was no change in the method of appointment by lot, or to age limits. These features are "democratic" and to this extent the current scholarship on this topic is correct. The interesting question, however, is whether this continuity of form covered discontinuities of substance. As we explored in the two chapters of Part III,[74] the Lykourgan period marked the point at which Athens began deliberately cultivating and projecting an image of itself that reflected its 5th-century heritage, including its democracy. By the late-third century one is bound to ask whether the reality had crumbled behind the classical façade.

If we consider the two key factors tending to make for a more democratic regime mentioned by Aristotle in the *Politics* (1299b–1300a) the situation is much less clear. There seems to be no clear evidence as to the frequency of Assembly meetings in the late third century. It is commonly assumed[75] that, in line with the shortening of the prytany consequential upon the increase in the number of tribes in 307/6 BC, the normal frequency of Assembly meetings was reduced pro rata to three times per prytany, and that that continued to be the case through the third century; but the explicit basis for this is weak, i.e. a set of confused and inaccurate comments in scholia and other late sources that there were three principal Assemblies (sic) per *month* (not per prytany).[76] It is suggested that this reflects Assembly frequency in the hellenistic period, but this is not especially plausible given that the commentaries all, explicitly or

74 See also my remarks on this point in the Introduction to this volume.

75 E.g. recently by Grieb 2008, 42–45, Osborne 2012a, 56–61, and in more detail, Osborne 2012b.

76 Schol. to Aristophanes *Acharnians* 19 (3 Assemblies a month, called *kyriai*, on the first, tenth and thirtieth), to Aeschin. 1.60 (3 Assemblies a month, called *kyriai*), 3.24 (3 Assemblies a month), to Dem. 18.73, 19.123 (3 Assemblies a month), 24.20 (3 Assemblies a month, on the eleventh, about the twentieth, about the thirtieth), Phot. s.v. κυρία ἐκκλησία (reports a view that there were three Assemblies a month), Sud. s.v. κυρία ἐκκλησία (3 Assemblies a month, called *kyriai*, on the first, tenth and thirtieth). These sources commonly distinguish the *kyria ekklesia* from the *synkletos ekklesia*, the extraordinary Assembly, specially summoned e.g. in emergencies. Note that, where specific days are named, these are inconsistent and do not correspond to the actual situation in the classical democracy or at any other time.

implicitly, relate to 5th or 4th century sources. These commentators are misleading as regards the classical democracy; there is no reason to suppose they are any less misleading as regards the hellenistic period. The continued use of the term κυρία ἐκκλησία in 3rd-century inscriptions rather implies that there was usually at least one Assembly per prytany, and the use of other headings, including ἐκκλησία without qualification, that there might be more than one; but there are only two prytanies in the 3rd century in which two Assembly meetings are explicitly attested, prytany 12 in 271/0, when there were meetings on 23rd and 31st of the prytany,[77] and prytany 3 in 225/4, when there was a meeting in the theatre specially summoned by decree on 20th and another one in the theatre on 27th;[78] and it is quite possible that there were, in fact, usually less than three meetings per prytany, and/or that the number of meetings was variable.[79]

Whether there continued in the 3rd century to be payment for attendance at the Assembly, or the Council for that matter (see further below), is also uncertain. Aristotle was clearly right to highlight this as an important issue, with a potential impact on the numbers and socio-economic backgrounds of those attending Council and Assembly meetings. Whether or not Assembly pay was re-introduced in 307/6 (it was patently abolished by Demetrios of Phaleron) is not stated in our sources. In any case it might seem unlikely, given the economic stringencies of the 3rd century, and the shift away from a collective ethos in public financing that can be observed in early hellenistic Athens, that Council and Assembly pay was sustained through this period, certainly at the generous level that obtained at the end of the classical democracy. On the other hand

---

77 *IG* II^3 1, 909, 21 Skirophorion = pryt. XII 23 (fragmentary, type of meeting not specified), 910, ἕνει καὶ νέαι προτέραι Skirophorion = pryt. XII 31 ("Assembly"). Cf. Osborne 2012b, 154.

78 *IG* II^3 1, 1146, 2nd intercalated 22 Metageitnion = pryt. III 20; 1147, 29 Metageitnion = pryt. III 27.

79 *Prima facie* this might be an implication of the fact that, in 300/299–230/229, as many inscribed decrees were passed at the κυρία ἐκκλησία (43) as at an ἐκκλησία of unspecified type (43); in addition 6 were passed in the theatre (or ἐν Διονύσου). See *IG* II^3 1, 4 index p. 262. This might, however, also be to an extent because the principal Assembly of a prytany was more likely to produce an inscribed decree. On the other hand κυρία may sometimes simply have been omitted from the headings of Assemblies that were in fact κύριαι. In the period 229/8–168/7 more meetings are designated as taking place in the Piraeus or the theatre or as being specially summoned. Overall 36 inscribed decrees of this period are designated as passed at principal Assemblies (including principal Assemblies in the theatre or the Piraeus), 49 are designated simply "Assembly" (including in the theatre or Piraeus) and 6 as specially summoned in some way (e.g. in accordance with a decree or oracle). See *IG* II^3 1, 5, index pp. 261–262.

it is clear enough that public funding of public institutions continued at some level;[80] and there are indications that Assembly pay and Council pay continued to be available in hellenistic Rhodes, which might be thought suggestive for Athens also.[81]

Until recently it was thought that the rule prohibiting tenure of office as councillor more than twice in a lifetime, which was a crucial factor in the fourth century in ensuring a Council that was broadly representative of the citizen population, continued to apply through the third century, but it has now become clear that this was not the case.[82] Four men are now attested as three-time councillors in the mid-3rd century.[83] Our data about councillors, largely consisting of prytany inscriptions for particular tribes separated by a number of years, is too patchy for large number of explicit attestations to be expected; but, as Byrne 2009 clearly demonstrates, there are also many more men attested as two-time councillors than in the fourth-century democracy, and than would be expected, given our patchy evidence, if they had in fact only served twice.[84] Byrne suggests this change took place in 286 BC. A contributing factor here may be the increase in the size of the Council commensurate

80 Implicit for example in the wording of decrees praising the curators of the Mysteries and the ephebes, *IG* II^3 1, 1176, 19–20 (203/2 BC); *IG* II^3 1, 1164 (214/3 BC), 17–19 (see further below).

81 The question of Assembly pay, though patently important, seems to have been ignored in recent standard literature on hellenistic Athens (e.g. Grieb 2008, 42–45, Osborne 2012a, 56–61). We can not, it seems, infer anything for hellenistic Athens from the fact that payment for Assembly attendance (on the classical Athenian model?) is attested epigraphically in Iasos in the late-fourth century (*I Iasos* 20 = RO 99, see Gauthier 1990, Fabiani 2012, 115). On the Rhodian case see de Ste Croix 1975, 50–52. Rhodes 2013, 207, finds it hard to believe that, given the large numbers involved, "the jury courts and the Council could have been manned unless payment at least for these was retained". The reality of attendance levels on these bodies in the hellenistic period, however, is obscure.

82 See Tracy 2003b, 60; Rhodes 2006, 33; Byrne 2004, 313–25; Byrne 2009; Osborne 2012a, 63.

83 Byrne 2009, 221 names: Kallistratos son of Telesinos of Erchia, *IG* II^3 1, 921.27 (265/4); 1011.7 (248/7); 1018.8 (245/4); Lykomedes son of Diochares of Konthyle, *IG* II^3 1, 983.23 (259/8); 987.9 (256/5); 996.6 (252/1, largely restored). Osborne 2012a, 63, adds Epicharmos son of Kallistratides of Kolonai (286/5, 276/5, a little after 263/2) and Philippos son of Astygenes of Thymaitadai (280/79, 275/4, 271/0).

84 The pattern is being confirmed by newly published inscriptions. In *IG* II^3 1, 1162, first fully published in *IG* II^3 (2012) and honouring the prytany of Aiantis in 214/3, on which all but two of the councillors' names are preserved (ll. 80–81), Demophon of Marathon (l. 66) also appears in the very fragmentary prytany list of Aiantis as far back as ca. 240–230 (1070 = *Agora* XV 113, 6), five men (lines 69, 71, 77, 93 and 97) also appear in the Aiantis list of perhaps eight years previously (cf. 1152, 54, 51, 46, 60, 58) and three names (ll. 88–89 and

with the increase in the numbers of tribes, to 600 from 307/6 (and to 650 in 223). Whether, however, there were concommitant adjustments for example in the socio-economic circumstances of councillors (which might not be the direct consequence of the introduction of a property qualification, which seems unlikely, but an indirect consequence of removal of subsistence allowances, which is much more plausible) requires further analysis.

There are a total of 121 inscribed decrees of 229/8–198/7 (*IG* II³ 1, 1135–1255). Excluding the large number of prytany decrees (depending on whether uncertain cases are included, there are ca. 45) and those whose bouleumatic status is not discernible, 40 (87%) of these are probouleumatic and 6 (13%) are non-probouleumatic.[85] All those erected at public initiative and expense were honorific. The only exceptions are the (probouleumatic) decrees providing for *kathairesis* in sanctuaries, i.e. the melting down of dedications to produce one or more larger ones, which were erected not at public expense, but from the proceeds of the melting down operation.[86] Since the bulk of the inscribed decrees of 352/1–322/1 were also honorific, and, as we have seen, there is reason to think that honorific decrees formed a significant component of the bread-and-butter decisions of the Assembly, this patently represents a very significant shift in the balance towards the Council and away from the Assembly in formulating the content of the city's decisions. In a further important, and consonant, shift from the classical democracy, no decree, whether probouleumatic or non-probouleumatic, is accompanied on the stone by a rider proposed in the Assembly; and none results from a *probouleuma* commissioned by the Assembly. It is at least possible that the narrowing of the subject matter of inscribed decrees erected at public expense to honorific decrees reflects a narrowing of the policy agenda of the Assembly. In any case, the data would seem to indicate clearly the decline of the Assembly as a forum for substantive debate, when compared with the period 352/1–322/1.

---

112) recur in the list of 180/79 (1307, 84, 86, 70). Some of this may be due to homonyms in different generations, but the general thrust is clear.

85 Not four, as I wrote in 2014. Osborne 2012a, 69 gives the following figures, excluding prytany decrees, for 286–63: probouleumatic 81%, non-probouleumatic 19%; for 262–28: probouleumatic 85%, non-probouleumatic 15%. This suggests that there was no significant shift in this regard across the period 286–198/7. Oliver 2003, analysing the decrees of 321–318 from this perspective, will need revising in the light of this chapter when *IG* II³ 1 fasc. 3 has been published. His finding that non-probouleumatic decrees predominated in these years, however, if confirmed, would be an interesting indication that the character of this oligarchy did not significantly affect the balance between Council and Assembly.

86 *IG* II³ 1, 1154; 1151; 1220. Cf. Lambert 2014, 31.

In chapter 8 we explored in some depth the situation as regards the numbers, wealth and prominence of decree proposers in the period 352/1–322/1. Direct comparison with 229/8–198/7 is rendered difficult by the decrease in overall numbers of surviving decrees, differences in their types (e.g. the prevalence in the later period of the prytany decree), the higher proportion of probouleumatic decrees in the later period, and shifts in the quantity (much reduced; there are three times more known Athenians in the 4th century than in the 3rd century, see Lambert 2010b, 149) and quality (almost entirely derived from inscriptions in the later period) of the background prosopographical data. For what it is worth, however, the only men attested as proposers of more than one decree in these years are proposers of prytany decrees: Aristion son of Aristokles of Xypete, *IG* II³ 1, 1162, 10 and 50 (214/3); Ekphantos son of Euphanes of Thria, 1168, 7 and 42 (211/0); Xenophon son of Euphantos of Berenikidai, 1246, 6 (ca. 200), 1263, 9–10 and 37–38 (192/1); Chares son of Eucharistos of Aphidna, 1139, 8 (227/6), 1155, 5 and 42 (219/8). These men are scarcely otherwise known, but the most notable feature of the list of decree proposers at this period is that it does not include the brothers, Eurykleides and Mikion, the dominant political figures of the period. This highlights another crucial shift in comparison with 352/1–322/1, in the locus of real power away from the formal public nexus of Council and Assembly, towards Athenians who dominated more-or-less extra-constitutionally and essentially through wealth rather than, as in the classical democracy, rhetorical skill, and towards external powers, whether foreground figures such as the Antigonids at earlier periods of the successor kingdoms, or, as in this period, background figures such as the Ptolemies.

Of the non-probouleumatic decrees, *IG* II³ 1, 1136 (228/7), an honorific decree mentioning king A[ntigonos?] and the Aitolians, and passed in the aftermath of the liberation of Athens from the Macedonians, is too fragmentary for us to be able to discern precisely why it might have been non-probouleumatic, but it may not be coincidental that it was passed in the same prytany, and possibly at the same Assembly, as 1137 decree I, also non-probouleumatic, on which see further below. 1146, of 225/4, is also rather fragmentary, but awarded honours to someone who seems to have been a major figure, Kastor friend of king Ptolemy, and moreover at a specially convened Assembly in the theatre on the second of a series of intercalary days in Metageitnion. This was patently an unusual occasion. 1159, of 217/6, is so fragmentary that the honorand is not discernible. It is likely to be relevant that 1190, of 229/8–203 BC, again passed at a special Assembly in the theatre, honours Kydonia, the home city of the honorand of 1137 I, also non-probouleumatic. The honours for Byzantines, including Eris, bestowed by 1238, of ca. 200 BC or later, if they belong in this period at all,[87] may belong in a context of unusual tension at the time of the Second Macedonian War.

The most fully preserved non-probouleumatic decrees, 1137 I and II, honouring Eumaridas of Kydonia, are the most illuminating as to the underlying dynamic (III, honouring his son, Charmion, in 193/2 is probouleumatic, and was the occasion for also inscribing I and II). Decree 1, of 228/7, honours Eumaridas with a statue on the acropolis, to be paid for from public funds, a very rare honour; but from decree 2, also non-probouleumatic, and dating to 211/0, it becomes apparent that the statue had never been put up, and provides for it to be erected now in the sanctuary of Demos and Graces. Ll. 4–10 of decree 1 make clear that what gave rise to the decree was Eumaridas' intervention on behalf of Athenians and others captured in raids on Attica and shipped to Crete and sold as slaves.[88] This was clearly an issue of mass popular interest. In the second decree, however, passed seventeen years later, we read that: "the People previously voted to erect (*anatheinai*) a statue of him (sc. Eumaridas), and now Eurykleides and Mikion, drawing attention to the services he has rendered, think it right (*axiousi*) that he be granted the erection (*anathesin*) in the precinct of the People and the Graces, for good fortune, the People shall decide, (40) that Eumaridas be granted erection of the statue, which the People voted for him previously, in the precinct of the People and the Graces, as Eurykleides and Mikion request for him." (ll. 35–42). Eurykleides and Mikion were the vastly wealthy brothers who had been instrumental in the liberation of Athens by buying off the Macedonian garrison in 229, and were dominant in Athenian policy-making thereafter, pursuing a consistent policy of neutrality.[89] It had been on their initiative that the cult of the People and the Graces had been founded, commemorating the liberation of 229.[90] What is remarkable, however, from our perspective, is that the People's original decision to erect a statue to Eumaridas has not been put into effect.[91] What the People decide at this period is not necessarily done, it seems. Remarkably, too, when

87 Note Tracy's tentative suggestion (*IG*), based on letter forms, of a mid-2nd cent. date.

88 "Eumaridas ... at a time when Boukris, having raided (*katadramonta*) the country, brought to land (*katagagein*) in Crete many of the citizens and others from the city, did the People many great services and advanced (*proeisēnenke*) money from his own resources towards the twenty talents which had been negotiated (*synphōnēthenta*) for (10) the prisoners (*aichmalōtōn*), and loaned the captives travelling expenses...". For the dynamic cf. in our period, *IG* II³ 1, 358, of 328/7, proposed by Demades for Eurylochos, another Kydonian who had saved Athenians from capture.

89 Cf. *IG* II³ 1, 1160 with Lambert 2014, 28–29.

90 Parker 1996, 269, 272–73.

91 Why this was we do not know. Cost would seem to be a possible factor.

the Assembly returns to this topic seventeen years later, the stated reason why the erection of the statue is now after all to go ahead is not because this is the will of the People, but because Eurykleides and Mikion "think it right". Such a craven and explicit subordination of itself to the will of two individual citizens would have been unthinkable in an Assembly decree of the classical democracy.[92] The new cult of the People and the Graces was implicitly a celebration of democracy, and indeed in the theatre of Dionysos, the priest of the new cult was seated next to the priest of Democracy.[93] This episode, however, highlights that we are here rather close to the territory of Chaniotis' democratic illusion.[94]

We might add a word about the prytany decrees, by far the most numerous category of inscribed decree in the period 229/8–198/7, since these touch on the same territory. Conventionally these inscriptions consisted of a Council decree honouring the officials of the prytany and a decree of the Assembly honouring the prytany as a whole, non-probouleumatic as a matter of form. Prytany lists had been inscribed on dedications in the classical democracy,[95] but with the exception of one early outlier,[96] these were not usually inscribed with the relevant decrees until after the restoration of democracy in 307/6. What was the purpose of such inscriptions? Partly it is straightforwardly about the commemoration of the good service of those named, and the encouragement of others to do likewise;[97] but partly also, and this became more obvious with the inscribing of the decrees, it was precisely about celebrating the Athenian political system as a

---

92 A consonant impression is created by literary sources for the period, which report that in foreign policy the Athenians maintained a neutral stance and "followed the wishes and initiatives of their leaders" (Polyb. 5.106) and that, though most citizens favoured supporting the Achaean League in response to its request for help in 225, Eurykleides and Mikion successfully maintained the city's neutrality (Plut. *Aratus* 41.3).

93 *IG* II^2 4676 and 5029a, cf. Parker 1996, 273. As he points out it was significant that, on the other side of the priest of Demos and the Graces, sat the priest of Ptolemy III and Berenice, Athens' major patrons among the hellenistic monarchs.

94 Cf. the remarks of Green 1990, 40 and 50, and O'Neill 1995, 105, on the plutocratic character of hellenistic Athens. The common response (thus e.g. Bayliss 2011, 52–53) that leading Athenians had always tended to be wealthy individuals, that in reality Athens was ruled or led by a perpetual oligarchy of wealth, is superficial and unsatisfactory, as Mann 2012, 22–23, has noted.

95 Those dating to the 4th cent. democracy are now accessible conveniently among the *dedicationes magistratuum*, *IG* II^3 4, 20–105.

96 *IG* II^3 1, 417 (Ca. 340–325 BC).

97 Though explicit hortatory intention clauses were not part of the formulaic wording of these decrees in the 3rd century, that intention is clear enough from the very first example, *IG* II^3 1, 417, which was to be stood "in front of the Council chamber", and paid for from public funds, "so that others may also [show love of honour (*philotimōntai*)],

showcase of democracy, in which the Council delicately acknowledged its formal subordination to the Assembly in the context of a continuously and unwaveringly harmonious relationship and common appreciation of the supporting work of the Council's executive committee and its officers. There was, I suggest, a considerable element of illusion here. The evidence we have reviewed above suggests that, in comparison with the latest phase of the classical democracy, the Council had become more influential in formulating the Assembly's decisions and the Assembly had become a less vigorous and independent forum for debate; but it is not perhaps very surprising that continuity of form should be emphasised, just as the substance was shifting.[98]

Finally, we might briefly review some other continuities and discontinuities in the inscribed record relevant to the general theme of "democracy".[99] Accountability of officials was a cornerstone of a democratic constitution.[100] Though less emphasised in the inscriptions than had been the case in 352/1–322/1, this apparently continued to apply in the last decades of the third century, as we learn from *IG* II^3 1, 1164, 27–30, honouring the managers of the Mysteries in 214/3, who had both submitted financial accounts (*logoi*) to the *logistai* and "rendered their accounts (*euthynai*) in the jury court (*dikasterion*) according to the laws"; and from the more fragmentary, 1213, 9–10, for a public doctor?, ca. 210.[101] As 1164 and other references show, jury courts were also maintained in the later period, though the extent of continuity in detail of organisation, actual numbers of jurors, frequency of meetings, pay etc., is

in speaking and acting excellently, knowing that they will obtain due thanks from the Council and the People". Cf. chapter 1, p. 34.

98 I might also note the possibility (there seems no evidence) that the regular and systematic public honouring of councillors partly reflected the fact that, with the (putative) withdrawal of pay for attendance, service on the Council had become to a greater extent than in 352/1–322/1 both voluntary and costly.

99 See also Lambert 2012, 86–88; 2014.

100 As Otanes had emphasised in (dramatically) the earliest discussion of rule of the mass = "democracy" in Greek literature, the debate on the constitutions in Hdt. 3.80 (ὑπεύθυνον δὲ ἀρχὴν ἔχει). By the hellenistic period, at least, accountability had become a widespread phenomenon in the Greek world. Cf. Fröhlich 2004.

101 For the earlier 3rd century see Osborne 2012a, 89–90. The fact that references to *euthynai* are less common in this period than in the decrees of 352/1–322/1 may not be especially significant, since the practice of conditional award of crowns to officials "when they have rendered their accounts", common in the earlier period (cf. chapter 7), does not seem to have been maintained in the later one.

obscure.[102] A key shift, however, is that decrees of the later period honouring Athenians, whether (unusually) individuals, or more commonly boards, tend to be for wealthier citizens than in 352/1–322/1, and explicitly refer to (voluntary) financial expenditure on the part of the honorands as praiseworthy.[103] Characteristic is the switch from a compulsory, publicly funded, ephebate (*Ath. Pol.* 42) to a voluntary one, accompanied by a radical reduction in the numbers of ephebes, and a raising of the highest level at which they were honoured from the Council, in fairly terse wording (see above section 3), to the Assembly in much more extravagant wording, including explicit reference to their having funded themselves.[104] There is similar reference to self-funding in the best-preserved of the decrees honouring the managers of the Eleusinian Mysteries;[105] and *IG* II^3 1, 1160, honouring Eurykleides of Kephisia, lists explicitly his extensive financial benefactions.[106]

To summarise our main conclusions: formally the Council and Assembly continued to have the same constitutional functions and relationship in the late third century as in the classical period. The size of the Council was also democratically large, though on two important criteria of "democracy", frequency of Assembly meetings and pay for attendance at Assembly or Council, the evidence is at best opaque. On the other hand, it now seems clear that one of the crucial features that made for a Council that was broadly representative of the citizen body as a whole, the ban on serving more than two terms, had been lifted, potentially (and especially if there was no continuing pay for Council attendance) opening the door to a Council in which the wealthy and prominent tended to dominate the body. The evidence is quite clear that, in stark contrast to the last period of the classical democracy, the Council also predominated in decision-taking and the Assembly was much less lively as a forum for debate. Alongside these changes there was a shift in the political culture in which Athenian honorands tended to a greater extent to be wealthy and prominent individuals and to be praised for expenditure of that wealth in the course of their official duties. At the same time, there was some shift of

102 *IG* II^3 1, fasc. 5, index p. 260 s.v. δικαστήριον, δικαστής. The *thesmothetai* continue to be responsible for conducting a scrutiny (*dokimasia*) of citizens newly created by decree, "whenever they fill the jury courts with the 501 jurors", *IG* II^3 1, 1218 etc. On jury pay in the hellenistic period cf. above n. 81.

103 For the situation in this regard in the earlier period see chapter 8 sect. 4D.

104 *IG* II^3 1, 1176, 19–20 (203/2 BC).

105 At *IG* II^3 1, 1164 (214/3 BC), 17–19, they had "prepared the cart at their own expense for the conveyance of the holy things, and donated to the Council what (money) had been allocated to them for the cost of the cart."

106 Cf. Lambert 2014, 28–29.

effective power away from the constitutional nexus of Council and Assembly. On the one hand what the Assembly decided was not any longer invariably put into effect, and its decisions were heavily influenced by the super-rich Eurykleides and Mikion even to the extent, if our literary sources are to be believed, that the brothers could in effect overrule the majority, or at least decisively sway its opinion. On the other hand, though the Assembly is careful to take account of what the brothers "thought right", Eurykleides and Mikion are not attested as proposers of a single decree of the Council and Assembly.

Politically, years of ultimate dependency, voluntary or involuntary, on the good-will of more powerful polities and rulers, the Antigonids since 307/6 and particularly at this period the Ptolemies,[107] made foreign policy choices less vital and contentious than they had been when Athens had been a powerful and fully independent agent on the Greek political stage, or in the case of the post-Chaironeia years, when there was a scope for significant differences of view about the best route to recovering that position. Whatever the rhetoric about freedom, democracy and independence after 229 BC, real power ultimately lay now with the hellenistic kings, and the small number of men, whether Athenians or not, who had their ear. Within Athens there was also a shift away from the collective as source of power, and towards the wealthy in general and the super-rich Eurykleides and Mikion in particular. Significant here is the shift, marked crucially by the abolition of liturgies in 317–307 by Demetrios of Phaleron, from a collectivist system of public financing entailing imposition on the wealthy of compulsory obligations, the performance of which was not regarded (in honorific decrees at least) as praiseworthy, to a system reliant on voluntary euergestism in which expenditure of personal wealth for the public good was explicitly honoured.[108] Whatever the formal constitutional situation, the ordinary citizens of the Assembly had ceased to be, in reality or in aspiration, the master, and become, instead, dependents, both internally on the benefactions of their wealthier fellow-citizens, and externally on the good-will of foreign patrons.

---

107 The extent to which Athens was dependent on the Ptolemies, and to which relations with them was guided crucially by small numbers of wealthy and prominent go-betweens, including, but only, Athenian citizens, is clear from Habicht 1992 (e.g. earlier in the third century Kallias of Sphettos, Habicht 1992, 70).

108 If my interpretation of the *Rationes Centesimarum* is correct, this shift was preceded by a massive shift of Attic landed resources from collective ownership into the hands of, mainly, wealthy individuals. See Lambert 1997 chapter 8; most recently, https://www.atticinscriptions.com/inscription/Rationes/stele-1; Fawcett 2016, 171–73.

Bibliography and Abbreviations

APF: J. K. Davies, *Athenian propertied families*, Oxford, 1971.

Bayliss, A. J. 2011: *After Demosthenes. The politics of early hellenistic Athens*, London.

Byrne, S. G. 2004: "Proposers of Athenian state decrees, 286–261 BC", in A. P. Matthaiou, G. E. Malouchou eds., *Attikai Epigraphai. Praktika ... Wilhelm*, Athens, 313–25.

Byrne, S. G. 2009: "*Agora* XV and iteration of Council service in hellenistic Athens", in A. Themos, N. Papazarkadas eds., *Attika Epigraphika. Meletes ... Habicht*, Athens, 215–23.

Canevaro, M. 2015: "Making and changing laws in ancient Athens", in E. M. Harris and M. Canevaro eds., *Oxford handbook of ancient Greek law*, Oxford forthcoming (this chapter published online, 2015).

Canevaro, M. 2016: "The procedure of Demosthenes' *Against Leptines:* how to repeal (and replace) an existing law", *JHS* 136, 39–58.

Chaniotis, A. 2010: "Illusions of democracy in the hellenistic World", Athens Dialogues. Democracy and Politeia. Period Two. http://athensdialogues.chs.harvard.edu/cgi-bin/WebObjects/athensdialogues.woa/wa/dist?dis=43.

Culasso Gastaldi, E. 2004: *La prassi della democrazia ad Atene. Voci di un seminario*, Alessandria.

Errington, R. M. 1994: "Ἐκκλησία κυρία in Athens", *Chiron* 24, 135–60.

Fabiani, R. 2012: "Protagonisti e prassi della procedura deliberativa a Iasos", in C. Mann, P. Scholz (eds.), *"Demokratie" im Hellenismus. Von der Herrschaft des Volkes zur Herrschaft der Honoratioren?*, Mainz.

Fawcett, P. 2016: "Taxes and tax policy in classical Athens", *Hesperia* 85, 153–99.

Fröhlich, P. 2004: *Les cités grecques et le contrôle des magistrats (IVe–Ier siècle avant J.-C.)*, Geneva.

Gauthier, P. 1972: *Symbola. Les étrangers et la justice dans les cités grecques*, Nancy.

Gauthier, P. 1984: "Les cités hellénistiques: épigraphie et histoire des institutions et des régimes politiques, in *Praktika of the 8th international congress of Greek and Latin epigraphy* 1, Athens.

Gauthier, P. 1985: *Les cités grecques et leurs bienfaiteurs (IVe-Ier siècle avant J.-C.). BCH Supplément 12*, Paris.

Gauthier, P. 1990: "L'inscription d'Iasos relative à l'*ekklesiastikon* (*I Iasos* 20)", *BCH* 114, 417–43.

Gauthier, P. 1993: "Les cités hellénistiques", in M. H. Hansen ed., *The ancient Greek city-state*, Copenhagen.

Green, P. 1990: *Alexander to Actium: the historical evolution of the hellenistic age*, London.

Grieb, V. 2008: *Hellenistische Demokratie. Politische Organisation und Struktur in freien griechischen Poleis nach Alexander dem Großen. Historia Einzelschrift 199*, Stuttgart.

Guagliumi, B. 2004: "Tra approvazione e mozione: corrispondenza e irregolarità delle formule epigrafiche", in Culasso Gastaldi 2004, 27–52.
Habicht, C. 1992: "Athens and the Ptolemies", *Classical Antiquity* 11, 68–90.
Habicht, C. 1997: *Athens from Alexander to Antony*, Cambridge Mass.
Hansen, M. H. 1983: *The Athenian ecclesia*, Copenhagen.
Hansen M. H. 1985: *Demography and democracy*, Herning.
Hansen, M. H. 1989, Updated inventory of *rhetores* and *strategoi* (1988), in *The Athenian ecclesia* II, Copenhagen, 34–72.
Hansen, M. H. 1991: *The Athenian democracy in the age of Demosthenes*, Oxford.
Henry, A. S. 1977: *The prescripts of Athenian decrees. Mnemosyne Supplement* 49, Leiden.
IALD: S. D. Lambert, *Inscribed Athenian laws and decrees 352/1–322/1 BC. Epigraphical essays*, Leiden, 2012.
Kourouniotes, K. 1927/28: "Τὸ ἱερὸν τοῦ Ἀπόλλωνος τοῦ Ζωστῆρος", *Arch. Delt.* 11, 9–53.
Lambert, S. D. 1997: *Rationes Centesimarum. Sales of public land in Lykourgan Athens*, Amsterdam.
Lambert, S. D. 2004: "Athenian state laws and decrees, 352/1–322/1: I Decrees honouring Athenians", *ZPE* 150, 85–120 (= *IALD*, chapter 1).
Lambert, S. D. 2006: "Athenian state laws and decrees, 352/1–322/1: III Decrees honouring foreigners. A. Citizenship, proxeny and euergesy", *ZPE* 158, 115–58 (= *IALD*, chapter 3).
Lambert, S. D. 2007: "Athenian state laws and decrees, 352/1–322/1: IV Decrees honouring foreigners. B. Other awards", *ZPE* 159, 101–54 (= *IALD*, chapter 4).
Lambert, S. D. 2010a: "A polis and its priests: Athenian priesthoods before and after Pericles' citizenship law", *Historia* 59, 143–75.
Lambert, S. D. 2010b: "LGPN and the epigraphy and history of Attica", in R. W. V. Catling and F. Marchand eds., *Onomatologos. Studies in Greek personal names presented to Elaine Matthews*, Oxford, 143–52.
Lambert, S. D. 2012: "The social construction of priests and priestesses in Athenian honorific decrees from the fourth century BC to the Augustan period", in M. Horster, A. Klöckner eds., *Civic Priests. Cult personnel in Athens from the hellenistic period to late antiquity*, Berlin, 67–133.
Lambert, S. D. 2014: "Inscribed Athenian decrees of 229/8–198/7 BC (*IG* II³ 1, 1135–1255)", *AIO Papers* no. 4 (https://www.atticinscriptions.com/papers/aio-papers-4/).
Lambert, S. D. 2015a: "The inscribed version of the decree honouring Lykourgos of Boutadai (*IG* II² 457 + 3207)", *AIO Papers* no. 6 (https://www.atticinscriptions.com/papers/aio-papers-6/) (= this volume, chapter 11).
Lambert, S. D. 2015b: "Dedication and Decrees commemorating military action in 339/8 BC (*IG* II² 1155)", in A. P. Matthaiou and N. Papazarkadas eds., *Axon. Studies in Honor of Ronald S. Stroud*, Athens, 233–46 (= this volume, chapter 10).

Liddel, P. 2016: "Honorific decrees of fourth-century Athens: trends, perceptions, controversies", in C. Tiersch ed., *Die Athenische Demokratie im 4. Jahrhundert. Zwischen Modernisierung und Tradition*, Berlin, 335–57.

Mann, C. 2012: "Gleichheiten und Ungleichheiten in der hellenistischen Polis: Überlegungen zum Stand der Forschung", in C. Mann, P. Scholz (eds.), *"Demokratie" im Hellenismus. Von der Herrschaft des Volkes zur Herrschaft der Honoratioren?*, Mainz.

Oliver, G. J. 2003: "Oligarchy at Athens after the Lamian war: epigraphic evidence for the *Boule* and the *Ekklesia*", in: O. Palagia and S. V. Tracy eds., *The Macedonians in Athens, 322–229 BC*, Oxford, 38–51.

O'Neill, J. L. 1995: *The origins and development of ancient Greek democracy*, Lantham.

Osborne, M. J. 1981–83: *Naturalization in Athens*, Brussels.

Osborne, M. J. 2012a: *Athens in the third century BC*, Athens.

Osborne, M. J. 2012b: "Months, prytanies and the meeting times of the Athenian Assembly (300/299–228/7)", ZPE 183, 141–70.

Parker, R. C. T. 1996: *Athenian religion. A history*, Oxford.

Rhodes, P. J. 1972: *The Athenian Boule*, Oxford.

Rhodes, P. J. 1981: *Commentary on the Aristotelian Athenaion Politeia*, Oxford.

Rhodes, P. J. 1995: "*Ekklesia kyria* and the schedule of Assemblies in Athens", *Chiron* 25, 187–98.

Rhodes, P. J. 2006: "Classical and hellenistic in Athenian history", in E. Dąbrowa ed., *Electrum* 11, 27–43.

Rhodes, P. J. 2013: "The organization of Athenian public finance", *Greece and Rome* 60, 203–31.

RO: P. J. Rhodes and R. Osborne, *Greek historical inscriptions 404–323 BC*, Oxford, 2003.

Schweigert, E. 1938: "Inscriptions from the north slope of the acropolis", *Hesperia* 7, 265–310.

de Ste Croix, G. E. M. 1975: "Political pay outside Athens", CQ 69, 50–52.

Tracy, S. V. 1998: "An Athenian decree of the year 335/4 BC", *Hesperia* 67, 219–21.

Tracy, S. V. 2003a: *Athens and Macedon. Attic letter cutters of 290 to 230 BC*, Berkeley.

Tracy, S. V. 2003b: "Antigonos Gonatas, King of Athens", in O. Palagia and S. V. Tracy eds., *The Macedonians in Athens, 322–229 BC*, Oxford, 56–60.

PART 5

Postscripts

CHAPTER 10

Dedication and Decrees Commemorating Military Action in 339/8 BC (*IG* II^2 1155)[1]

Introduction

As currently presented in the Corpus, *IG* II^2 1155 is a dedication to Athena by the citizen soldiers of the tribal regiment of Kekropis in 339/8 BC, and their commander, the taxiarch, Boularchos son of Aristoboulos of Phlya, followed by decrees of the Council and of the tribe honouring the taxiarch. In *IG* it is grouped, reasonably enough, with the tribal decrees rather than the decrees of the Council and People, and was not, therefore, included in fascicule 2 of *IG* II^3 1. Since, however, it includes a decree of the Council, I listed it in the catalogue of "state" decrees honouring Athenians of the years 352/1–322/1 BC

1 [This chapter was first published in A. P. Matthaiou and N. Papazarkadas eds., *Axon. Studies in Honor of Ronald S. Stroud* (Athens, 2015), 233–46.] I am delighted to offer this article on an honorific inscription in honour of a profound scholar, and a wonderfully wise, kind and generous colleague. I completed the article in 2012/3 while a Member of the Institute for Advanced Study, Princeton, where I enjoyed the privilege of support from the Patrons' Endowment Fund and the Loeb foundation, and of being able to consult relevant squeezes in the Institute's collection. I thank Angelos P. Matthaiou for kindly reporting to me the results of his examination of *IG* II^2 1155b = EM 7742, and Stephen Tracy for very helpful comments on a draft of the paper. Any remaining errors are my responsibility. I use the following abbreviations:
IALD: S. D. Lambert, *Inscribed Athenian Laws and Decrees, 352/1–322/1 BC. Epigraphical Essays*, Leiden and Boston, 2012.
Jones 1995: N. F. Jones, "The Athenian Phylai as Associations", *Hesperia* 64, 503–542.
Lawton 1995: C. L. Lawton, *Attic Document Reliefs*, Oxford.
Oliver 2007a: G. J. Oliver, *War, Food and Politics in Early Hellenistic Athens*, Oxford.
Oliver 2007b: G. J. Oliver, "Space and the Visualization of Power in the Greek Polis. The Award of Portrait Statues in Decrees from Athens", in P. Schultz and R. von den Hoff eds., *Early Hellenistic Portraiture. Image, Style, Context*, Cambridge, 181–204.
Rangabé: A. R. Rangabé, *Antiquités Helléniques* vol. II, Athènes, 1855.
Rhodes-Osborne: P. J. Rhodes and Robin Osborne, *Greek Historical Inscriptions 404–323 BC*, Oxford 2003, revised paperback edition 2007.
Tracy, *ADT*: S. V. Tracy, *Athenian Democracy in Transition. Attic Letter Cutters of 340 to 290 BC*, Berkeley 1995.
For the dates of archons between 300/299 and 228/7 I have used M. J. Osborne, "The archons of Athens 300/299–228/7", *ZPE* 171 (2009), 83–99.

© KONINKLIJKE BRILL NV, LEIDEN, 2018 | DOI 10.1163/9789004352490_012

which I published in 2004,[2] in the category (E), "Inscriptions on which a decree of the Council is inscribed together with decree(s) of subgroup(s) of the polis" (no. 27). The other inscription in that category, *IG* II² 1156 (no. 28), is one of several relating to the ephebes of 334/3, the earliest epigraphically attested year-group after the ephebate was reformed by Epikrates' law. It honours the ephebes of Kekropis and their *sophronistes*, and also includes a decree of the Council, together with decrees of the tribe and of the demes Eleusis (where the ephebes were stationed) and Athmonon (the deme of the *sophronistes*). *IG* II² 1156 is well preserved, there are no significant textual problems, and it has recently been re-published by Rhodes and Osborne, together with a helpful historical commentary.[3] Both 1155 and 1156 were found on the acropolis, and it is not coincidental that both relate to the tribe Kekropis. 1156 was set up in the sanctuary of Kekrops there (l. 35), the location used by this tribe for posting its decrees, and it seems likely that 1155 derives from the same context.[4] In contrast to 1156, however, 1155 has languished in relative obscurity. In fact a search of the indices of that indispensable publication to which our honorand has contributed so much, the *Supplementum Epigraphicum Graecum*, reveals no entry for it. It is worth a fresh look.

1155 has two fragments, fr. a (itself composed of two joining pieces) and fr. b. The current Corpus text presents them as follows, in a way that makes them appear to be part of the same inscription:

---

2 "Athenian State Laws and Decrees 352/1–322/1: I. Decrees Honouring Athenians", *ZPE* 150 (2004), 85–120, at p. 110 = *IALD* 46.

3 Rhodes-Osborne no. 89. See also J. L. Friend, *The Athenian Ephebeia in the Lycurgan Period, 334/3–322/1 BC* (PhD diss. University of Texas).

4 Jones 1995, 508–509, lists three other tribal decrees of Kekropis (all honorific): *IG* II² 1141, of 376/5 BC, recorded by Fourmont "in basilica S. Nicolai Borealis" and recording in its prescript that the decree was passed by secret ballot of the tribesmen voting at their principal meeting on the acropolis (τῆι κυρίαι ἀγορᾶι κρύβδην ψηφισαμένων τῶ[ν φυλετῶν] | ἐν ἀκροπόλει); *SEG* 2.8, an extremely fragmentary inscription of "iv BC", also apparently found on the acropolis and restored somewhat speculatively by A. Salaç in 1923 as containing two decrees, one of the Council and People providing for an honorific statue and the second of the tribesmen allocating a location for the statue in the sanctuary of Kekrops (but it is possible that the first decree, which apparently placed an obligation on the tribal secretary, was also tribal. On this statue see also Oliver 2007b, 184 S2, 190–191); *IG* II² 1158, post-med. s. iv, found on the acropolis and, as restored, to be erected in the sanctuary of Kekrops. On the sanctuary of Kekrops and its location see also *IG* II³ 1, 392, a proxeny decree of c. 350–335?, to be erected ἀκροπόλει ἐ]|πὶ τῆς Κεκρο[π...... 9......] (8–9), with G. E. Malouchou, Δύο τιμητικά ψηφίσματα ἀπὸ τὴν Ἀκρόπολη, *ΗΟΡΟΣ* 14–16 (2000–2003), 55–59, no. 1, and Lambert, *ZPE* 158 (2006), 128 = *IALD* 115 no. 20.

339/8 ***a*** Κεκροπίδος οἱ στρατευ[σ]άμενοι ἐπὶ Λυσιμαχίδου ἄρχοντος
[κ]αὶ ὁ ταξίαρχος Βούλαρ[χος] Ἀριστοβούλου Φλυεύς Ἀθηνᾶι.
margo

non-stoich. 46–52

b [- - - - - - - - - - - - - - εἶπε]ν· δεδόχθα[ι τῆι βουλῆι· ἐπειδὴ ὁ]
[ταξίαρχος τῆς Κεκροπίδος φ]υλῆς Βο[ύλ]α[ρχος Ἀριστοβούλου]
[ἀνὴρ ἀγαθὸς γεγένηται περ]ὶ τοὺς σ[τρατευσαμένους, ἐπαι]-
[νέσαι Βούλαρχον Φλυέα κα]ὶ στεφ[α]νῶ[σαι αὐτὸν θαλλοῦ στ]-
[εφάνωι ἀνδραγαθίας ἕνεκα καὶ] φιλοτιμίας [τῆς εἰς τὸν δῆμον· εἶν]-
[αι δὲ αὐτῶι καὶ ἄλλο ἀγαθὸν εὑρέσ]θαι παρά τῶ[ν φυλετῶν?].
vacat 0.032
- - - - - - - - - - - - εὺς εἶπεν· ἐπει[δὴ Βούλαρχος Φλ]-
[υεὺς ἀνὴρ ἀγαθὸς γεγένηται πε]ρὶ τὴν φυλὴν τὴ[ν Κεκροπίδα καὶ]
[τοὺς στρατευσαμένους, δεδό]χθαι τοῖς φυλέτ[αις ἐπαινέ]σα[ι]
[Βούλαρχον Ἀριστοβούλου Φλυ]έα καὶ στεφανῶ[σαι χρυσῶι] στε[φ]-
[άνωι ἀπὸ – – δραχμῶν ἀνδρ]αγαθία[ς ἕ]νεκα κα[ὶ φιλοτ]ιμία[ς]
[τῆς περὶ ἑαυτούς· παραλαβεῖν] δὲ τόδε τὸ ψήφισμ[α τὸν γρ]αμμα[τ]-
[έα τὸν κατὰ πρυτανείαν καὶ] ἐπὶ τὸ ἀνάθημα ἐπιγρ[άψ]αι καθάπ[ερ]
[τὸ ψήφισμα τῆς βουλῆς?].
in corona
ἡ βουλή
in corona
οἱ φυλ[έται].

One of the principles of epigraphical work of which our honorand is a champion is autopsy of the stones. It is a principle that we have applied in *IG* II³ and the case in hand illustrates its importance well. Unfortunately, when I visited the Epigraphical Museum to examine this inscription in July 2011, I was able to see only the upper fragment (fr. a). The lower one could not be extracted from behind boards set up in connection with a temporary exhibition. I am accordingly extremely grateful to Angelos Matthaiou for examining fr. b and for generously sharing with me his advice.

Relationship of fr. a and fr. b

Fr. a is inscribed with a two-line dedication in large lettering, fr. b in a different hand with two inscribed decrees in smaller lettering followed by two crowns. Rangabé published them in 1855 as separate inscriptions. Köhler, when he published fr. b in 1877, as *IG* II 562, noted with approval that Kirchhoff had in the meantime (in 1863) drawn attention to a connection between them ("Kirchhoffius ... adposite contulit titulum votivum in arce et ipsum repertum", *scil.* fr. a). Köhler had examined both fragments himself, and wrote in 1880: "Die ... Weihinschrift ist von dem Stein mit den Dekreten schwerlich zu trennen, beide Steine werden von demselben Denkmal herrühren", and he carried this view over into his publication of fr. a in 1888 as *IG* II 1214, noting in that publication: "562, quem lapidem eiusdem monumenti cum his [1214] partem formasse manifestum est". Köhler, therefore, took the two stones to belong to the "same monument (Denkmal)", but stopped short of specifying exactly how they related to eachother. He was no doubt encouraged to think in these terms by the wording in line 13 of decree II, ἐπὶ τὸ ἀνάθημα ἐπιγρ[άψ]αι. If this is taken to refer to the inscription on which the words are inscribed, it might naturally follow that that inscription was part of the dedication to which fr. a manifestly belonged. It was Kirchner, however, in *IG* II^2 1155 who first published the two fragments together, specifying that fr. a was part of a "base" ("pars baseos ex duobus fragmentis composita") and repeating Köhler's view that it belonged to the same monument as fr. b ("... quae ad idem monumentum pertinere significavit Koehler"). He printed the two fragments as a single continuous text, with the indication "*margo*" between the two.

Fr. a is a rectangular dedication base. Fr. b on the other hand is a stele. As is apparent from the photograph, and as Angelos Matthaiou confirms from autopsy, the top of the stele is original and there is trace of a crowning moulding which has been chiseled away. These facts about the stones undermine the hypothesis that fr. a was positioned above fr. b as part of the same inscription. An obvious alternative is that fr. a functioned as a base for the stele (fr. b); in other words that Kirchner's order of the fragments should simply be reversed. So far as I can judge, this would seem possible, as far as the dimensions and physical features of the stones are concerned.[5] It is also possible, however, that the base supported something else (e.g. a statue) and that the stele was a separate, self-standing inscription, though collocated with the base and forming part of the same monumental complex (Köhler's "Denkmal"); and it can not be altogether ruled out (though it seems unlikely) that the two stones were

5 The width of the base is 0.725, and of the present cutting in the top of the base (which may or may not be original) ca. 0.6. This seems consistent with Kirchner's measurement of the surviving maximum width of the stele (perhaps a little over half the original width) as 0.315. The compatibility of the stones in such an arrangement should ideally be verified at autopsy of the two together.

originally located at different places, the stele e.g. in the sanctuary of Kekrops, the dedication with other dedications to Athena on the acropolis.[6]

New Edition

I present below a fresh edition of the two inscriptions. I present them separately, though, as we have seen, it is possible that no. 2 was the base for no. 1:

1 ***Honorific Decrees of the Council and the Tribe Kekropis***

EM 7742. Acropolis. Stele of grey marble, damaged right side and top, with trace of original moulding, preserved, h. 0.73, w. 0.315, th. 0.34 (Kirchner). L. h. 0.005–0.007 (χ 0.004, β 0.008), "Cutter of *IG* II² 244", 340/39–ca. 320 (Tracy, *ADT* 99).[7]

Edd. Rangabé 2283; A. Kirchhoff, *Monatsberichte der Berliner Akademie*, 1863, pp. 9 ff. (ex schedis Velsen) (non vidi); *IG* II 562 (1877, exscripsit Köhler in area aedis Minervae Erganae); E. L. Hicks and G. F. Hill, *A Manual of Greek Historical Inscriptions* (Oxford, 1901), no. 148; *IG* II² 1155 fr. b (1916, Kirchner).

Cf. U. Köhler, "Inschriften von der Akropolis", *Ath. Mitt.* 5 (1880) 319 note 1. Princeton squeeze. Fig. 10.1.

---

6 Commemoration of honours at more than one location was not uncommon. In 333/2, for example, copies of the stele honouring Pytheas of Alopeke as superintendent of the water supply (ἐπὶ τὰς κρήνας), were erected at two locations where he had carried out works, the Amphiaraion in Oropos and the sanctuary of Ammon in Piraeus (*IG* II³ 1, 338, the Amphiaraion copy, is the only one to survive). A more complex case involving multiple monuments is *IG* II³ 1, 306, a dedication to Hephaistos (base) relating to the work of the Council in 343/2 and inscribed with five decrees. The original location of the dedication is uncertain, but the dedication to Hephaistos does not suggest an acropolis location, and indeed it was found not on the acropolis, but built into the foundations of a church to the east of the tower of the winds. Decree III, a Council decree honouring Phanodemos of Thymaitadai, was to be inscribed on the dedication (ἀναγ[ρ]άψαι δὲ καὶ ἐπὶ τὸ ἀνάθημα τῆς βουλῆς τόδε τὸ ψήφισμα τοὺς αἱρεθέντας ποήσασθαι τὸ ἀνάθημα, l. 8), but was also to go forward as a *probouleuma* to the Assembly, whose resulting decree was to be inscribed on a stele on the acropolis (ll. 14–15) ([ἀναγράψαι τόδε τὸ ψήφισ]μα τόν γραμμ[α|τέα] τὸν κατὰ πρυτανείαν ἐν στήληι λιθ[ίνη]ι καὶ στῆσαι ἐν ἀκροπόλει). The stele does not, in this case, survive. From the surviving text of decree II, proposed by Phanodemos, and providing for the dedication, it would seem that this series of decrees generated a third commemorative monument, containing a list of councillors (l. 20) (ἐπιγρ[άψαι δὲ – –c. 16 – – τοὺς βουλ]ẹụṭὰς πατρόθεν καὶ τοῦ δήμ|[ου – –). *Agora* XV 37, a small fragment from what seems to have been a list of councillors of this year, might or might not be from this list. It was found in the Agora, but its original location is unknown.

7 Tracy noted that *IG* II² 1155 fr. a was "done in larger letters by a different cutter", but also remarked that "Köhler seems to have been correct to associate these fragments".

FIGURE 10.1 *IG II*[2] 1155 *fr.* b = EM 7742
PHOTOGRAPH COURTESY OF EPIGRAPHICAL MUSEUM

339/8 *vac. c.* 0.015

I [- - - - - - - ca. 19 - - - - - - - εἶπε]ν· δεδόχθα[ι τῆι βουλῆι - - ca. 8 - -]non-stoich.
[- - ca. 9 - - τῆς Κεκροπίδος φ]υλῆς Βο[ύλ]α[ρχο - - - -ca. 13 - - - - - -]
[- - - - - ca. 24 - - - -]ι τοὺς σ[τρατευσαμένους? - ca. 6 -]
[- - - - - - -ca. 23 - - - - - -]ι στεφ[α]νω[- - - - -ca. 19 - - - - - -]
[- - ca. 6 - - ἀνδραγαθίας ἕνεκα καὶ] φιλοτιμίας [- - - -ca. 15 - - - - -]
[- - - - - - - - ca. 19- - - - - - - - εὑρέσ]θαι παρὰ τῶ[ν φυλετῶν?].

vac. 0.032

II [- - - - - - - - ca. 24- - - - - - - -]εὺς εἶπεν· ἐπει[δὴ Βούλαρχος -ca. 2-]-
[- - - - - - - ca. 22- - - - - -πε]ρὶ τὴν φυλὴν τη[- - -ca. 13- - -]
[- - - - - - ca. 20- - - - - δεδό]χθαι τοῖς φυλέτ[αις ἐπαινέ]σα[ι]
[Βούλαρχον Ἀριστοβούλου Φλυ]έα καὶ στεφανῶ[σαι χρυσῶι] στε[φ]-
[άνωι ἀπὸ - - δραχμῶν ἀνδρ]αγαθία[ς ἕ]νεκα κα[ὶ φιλοτ]ιμία[ς]
[- - - - - - - ca. 24- - - - - - -] δὲ τόδε τὸ ψήφισμ[α τὸν γρ]αμμα[τ]-
[έα τῆς φυλῆς ? - - ca. 14- -] ἐπὶ τὸ ἀνάθημα ἐπιγρ[άψ]αι καθάπ[ερ]
[τὸ ψήφισμα τῆς βουλῆς?].

[*One or two crowns* ?] *Crown*
ἡ βουλή
Crown
οἱ φυλ[έται].

Translation

Decree 1

.... proposed: that it be decided [by the Council. ... the taxiarch of the Kekropid] tribe Bo[ul]a[rchos...] those who [have served on campaign? ...] crown [...(5) ... for their courage and] love of honour [... and that he *or* they be permitted] to find from the [tribesmen? ...].

Decree 2

.... of – proposed: since [Boularchos] ... concerning the tribe ... that it be decided by the tribesmen to praise (10) [Boularchos son of Aristoboulos of Phl]ya and crown him with a [gold] crown [of – drachmas] for his courage and love of honour ... and the secretary [of the tribe? shall...] this decree ... inscribe it on the dedication as well as [the decree of the Council?].

[*In crown*: ?. *In crown*: ?]. *In crown*: the Council. *In crown*: the tribesmen.

2 *Dedication by Soldiers of Kekropis and their Taxiarch, Boularchos of Phlya*

EM 10663 (fr. a) + EM 10664 (fr. b). Acropolis, fr. b north of the Propylaia, 1834. Rectangular base of whitish grey marble, h. 0.24, w. 0.725, th. 0.62, consisting of two fragments which have been cemented together, preserving inscribed front face, uninscribed left face and parts of uninscribed right face (extending 0.18 from front face) and uninscribed back face (extending 0.325 from left face). Top surface hollowed out. L. h. 0.015.

Edd. *a* K. Pittakis, *Eph. Arch.* 1856, 2876; *b* K. Pittakis, *Eph. Arch.* 1853, 1819; Rangabé 2368. *ab* Rangabé 1160; A. Kirchhoff, *Monatsberichte der Berliner Akademie* 1863, p. 5 (non vidi); IG II 1214 (1888, exscripsit Köhler); IG II^2 1155 fr. a (Kirchner). Cf. Tracy, *ADT* 99. Autopsy (July 2011). Fig. 10.2.

a *b*

339/8 Κεκροπίδος οἱ στρατευ[σ]άμενοι ἐπὶ Λυσιμαχίδου ἄρχοντος
[κ]αὶ ὁ ταξίαρχος Βούλαρ[χος] Ἀριστοβούλου Φλυεὺς Ἀθηνᾶι.

Translation

Of Kekropis those who served on campaign in the archonship of Lysimachides, and their taxiarch Boularchos son of Aristoboulos of Phlya, to Athena.

Number of Decrees on No. 1

The original top of the stone has been reworked for a subsequent use in a process which also removed the surface in the upper right area of the first preserved decree. However, above the preserved remains of line 1 there is a *vacat* of c. 1.5 cm, and above that remains of part of an original moulding. The first preserved decree was thus the first decree on the stone. Köhler, who had seen the stone, seems at one point to have thought otherwise. In IG II 562 he restored the first preserved decree as of the Council, corresponding with the body mentioned in the first crown, but in 1880 he wrote, "Ich vermuthe, dass das Decret des Rathes, auf welches sich die Kranzinschrift bezieht, an einer anderen Stelle des jetzt verstümmelten Steines stand und dass das erste der erhaltenen Decrete, wie Kirchhoff annahm, von dem Regiment herrürte". The evidence of the stones seems to indicate that we should set Köhler's 1880 view to one side. There were, it seems, only two decrees inscribed on this stele.

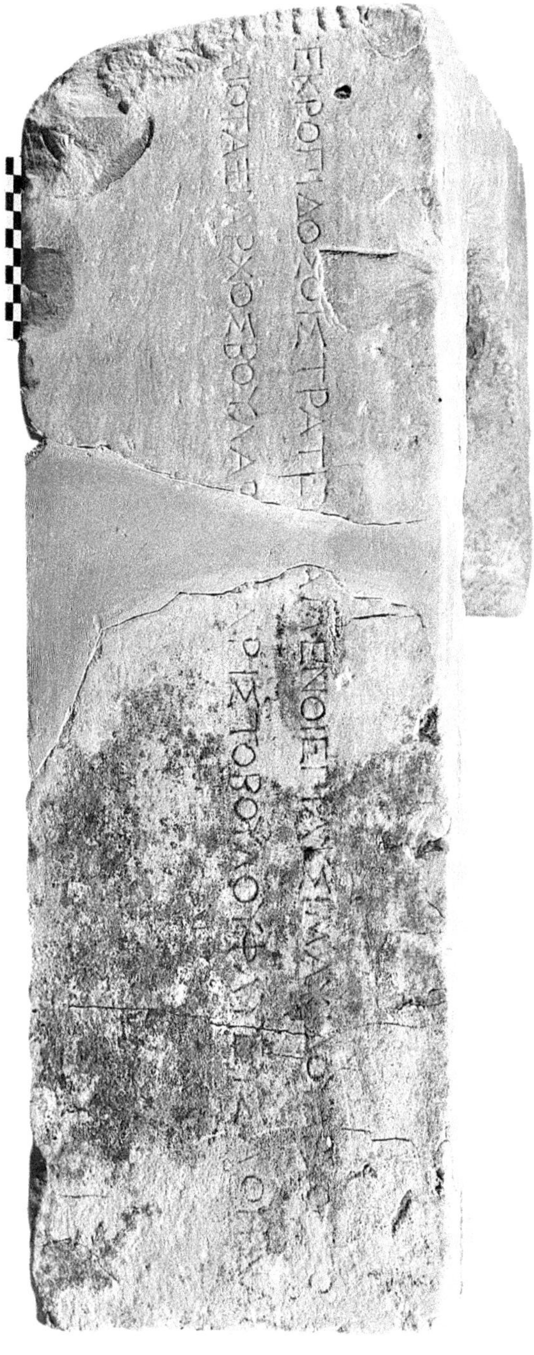

FIGURE 10.2 *IG II² 1155 fr. a = EM 10663 + 10664*
PHOTOGRAPH COURTESY OF EPIGRAPHICAL MUSEUM

Textual Notes

Given that the left side of no. 1 is not preserved and the spacing of the non-stoichedon script is quite variable, line lengths can only be approximately determined. The identification of these decrees as belonging to the same honorific process as no. 2 depends crucially on the reading of the name of the taxiarch in lines 2 and 10. On the Princeton squeeze the initial two letters of Βο[ύλ]α[ρχος are clearly legible in l. 2 (after that the surface of the stone seems not now to be preserved); and there are faint traces of the epsilon and alpha of Φλυ]έα at the preserved start of l. 10. The tau in φυλέτ[αις] (l. 9) is also legible on the Princeton squeeze and on the photograph.

Decree 1

That this is a Council decree is indicated by Crown 3 and it would seem from the surviving text and comparison with the dedication that the decree mentioned both Boularchos, taxiarch of Kekropis (l. 2), and, probably, his co-dedicator, i.e. those who served under him on campaign (οἱ στρατευσάμενοι, l. 3). [ἀνδραγαθίας] in l. 5 is supported by [ἀνδρ]αγαθία[ς] in the tribal decree (l. 11).[8] In l. 6 we have an example of the formulaic invitation to "seek what good he (or they) can", most likely, as Köhler saw, from the tribesmen (cf. decree II). In detail, however, restoration is uncertain. In particular it is not clear whether Köhler's scheme was correct or whether, as the wording of the dedication might rather suggest, we have δεδόχθαι τῆι βουλῆι ἐπαινέσαι with the objects being both the taxiarch and the soldiers under his command, in which case perhaps κα]ὶ τοὺς σ[τρατευσαμένους in l. 3.[9]

Decree 2

The scheme and thrust of Köhler's restoration of this decree up to l. 12 seems sound, though again we can not press the detail. The inscribing clause, however, presents a puzzle. Köhler's restoration is ingenious, but looks questionable on two grounds. There seems to be no parallel for παραλαβεῖν] δὲ τόδε τὸ ψήφισμ[α (one expects ἀναγράψαι, though that is uncertain here), and, more seriously, a tribe was surely not competent to give inscribing instructions to

---

8 Cf. C. Veligianni-Terzi, *Wertbegriffe in den attischen Ehrendekreten der klassischen Zeit*, Stuttgart 1997, 110 B 6. The context here implies the connotation of physical courage. Cf. D. Whitehead, "*Andragathia* and *Arete*", in L. Mitchell and L. Rubinstein (eds.), *Greek History and Epigraphy. Essays in Honour of P.J. Rhodes*, Swansea 2009, 47–58.

9 For this type of structure in tribal decrees cf. for example *IG* II² 1140, of Pandionis (... εἶπε· ἐπαινέσαι ... καὶ στεφανῶσαι...) and 1143, of Kekropis (... εἶπεν· ἐπαινέσαι...).

the secretary of the Council. When a tribe wants to inscribe something it commissions its own secretary to do it (as e.g. 1158, also Kekropis, "post med. s. IV": στῆσαι δὲ στή]λην εἰς τ||[ὸ ἱερὸν τοῦ Κέκροπος ἀναγρ]άψαντα τ||[όδε τὸ ψήφισμα τὸν γραμματ]έα τῆς φυ||[λῆς]. For this tribal official see also *Agora* XV 86). In this case it seems that the secretary of the tribe is to do something with the decree, and also to inscribe it, together with the Council decree, on the present dedication (in fact a stele). It is interesting to consider the sense of this inscribing provision alongside *IG* II^2 1156. The tribal decree, which is inscribed first on that stone, under the list of the ephebes, is to be "inscribed (not specified by whom, but the initiative surely lies with the ephebes, who are responsible for the dedication as a whole) on a stone stele and stood in the sanctuary of Kekrops" (ll. 34–35).[10] The other three decrees (of the Council and the two demes) are to be inscribed (again unspecified by whom) "on the dedication which the ephebes of Kekrops are dedicating" (ἐπὶ τὸ ἀνάθημα ὃ ἀνατιθέασιν οἱ ἔφηβοι οἱ τῆς Κεκροπίδος). It seems that in 1156, as in 1155, the stele and the *anathema* are both, in practice, the same thing, i.e. the inscription that survives; but as far as the Council's decree in 1156 is concerned, and the decrees of the demes, it also seems from this wording that the Council and the demes are not so much taking the initiative in inscribing the decrees –there is no provision for meeting the expense of inscription – but permitting the ephebes to inscribe them on their dedication, together with their own tribal decree. In 1155 too, though it may be the secretary of the tribe who takes responsibility for the inscribing, it is perhaps the honorands that are taking the initiative and carrying the expense of inscribing the Council's decree, as well as the tribal one, on their "dedication". In this case, however, the Council does not specify its permission in so many words, but, in effect, refers the matter to the tribe in a manner which permits it to provide for the Council's decree to be inscribed.

It would seem from the positioning of the two surviving crowns in the right half of the stone that there may have been one or two more in the lost part of the stone to the left, though no trace of them is apparent and it is unclear what wording they would have contained (perhaps designations of the two honorands, Boularchos and οἱ στρατευσάμενοι).

10 ἀναγράψαι δὲ τόδε τὸ ψή[φι]|σμα ἐν στήληι λιθίνηι καὶ στῆσαι ἐν τῶι τοῦ Κέκροπος ἱερ[ῶι].

Honorand

The family of the taxiarch, Boularchos son of Aristoboulos of Phlya (J. S. Traill, *Persons of Ancient Athens* no. 268235 = *LGPN* II Βούλαρχος no. 5),[11] is not attested in the liturgical class, but neither was it obscure. His father was perhaps the Aristoboulos son of Boularchos of Phlya who appears as representative of his tribe on the dedication (with tripod), *IG* II^2 2814 [= *IG* II^3 4, 66] l. 8, while another relation (his son on Kirchner's scheme, *PA* 1770) was the Boularchos son of Boularchos of Phlya who was selected by the hierophant to strew a couch for Plouton ca. 330–320, *IG* II^2 1933 l. 9, and another (grandson?) was Kallitheos son of Boularchos of Phyla who was *epimeletes* of the procession at the City Dionysia in 266/5 (*IG* II^2 668 [= *IG* II^3 1, 920] ll. 25–26).

Context

Insofar as *IG* II^2 1155 has attracted the interest of historians, this has arisen from the suggestion, first made by Kirchhoff in 1863, that it commemorates military action connected with the successful engagements of the allies in Phocis against Philip II in the winter of 339–8, in the lead-up to the battle of Chaironeia. These are alluded to in retrospect by Demosthenes in 330 (18.216–217):

> Twice marshalled with them (scil. the Thebans) in the two first battles, the one by the river and the winter battle (τὴν τ' ἐπὶ τοῦ ποταμοῦ καὶ τὴν χειμερινήν),[12] you not only showed yourselves irreproachable, but even admirable in your discipline, equipment and determination; which gave rise to praises from others (ἐφ' οἷς παρὰ μὲν τῶν ἄλλων ὑμῖν ἐγίγνοντ' ἔπαινοι),[13] and on your side sacrifices and processions to the gods. (217) And I should like to ask Aeschines, when these things were being done and the city was full of enthusiasm and rejoicing and praises (ζήλου καὶ χαρᾶς καὶ ἐπαίνων),[14] whether he joined the many in the sacrifices and celebrations, or sat at home grieving and groaning and bemoaning the public successes.

11 In the revision of *LGPN* II dated 14.3.2013, at www.seangb.org, this is Βούλαρχος no. 6.

12 On the winter campaign of 339–8 and these battles see N. G. L. Hammond and G. T. Griffith, *A History of Macedonia*, Oxford 1979, 591.

13 This perhaps implies an honorific decree (passed by the Thebans?). For ἔπαινοι = honorific decrees, cf. e.g. *IG* II^3 1, 367, 24.

14 This might include the decrees in *IG* II^2 1155.

Because of this famous possible context, 1155 found its way into Hicks' and Hill's, *Manual of Greek Historical Inscriptions* (no. 148 in the 1901 edition), though in 1948 it was dropped from Tod's successor volume, *A Selection of Greek Historical Inscriptions* vol. II and has remained excluded from Rhodes-Osborne. This context has continued to be registered as a possibility from time to time. Thus Harvey Yunis, in his recent commentary on Demosthenes' *Crown* speech: "nothing further is recorded of these battles (*scil.* the "battle by the river and the winter battle"), though a pair of honorary decrees of 339/8 for an Athenian taxiarch may relate to them (*IG* II^2 1155)".[15] The association of 1155 with these campaigns remains attractive, but, in the absence of specific wording in the decrees referring to the campaigns, it can not be established with certainty.

Whether or not this association is correct, the wording of the dedication makes it clear enough that it is service of the taxiarch on a military campaign that is being commemorated. This is remarkably unique in the inscribed record, as becomes apparent when one considers 1155 in the context of other dedications by, and decrees honouring, taxiarchs.[16] The city did not normally honour its own citizens with decrees inscribed on stone before the mid-340s,[17] but the series of dated dedications by officials stating explicitly that they had been honoured by the Council and People begins a little earlier, and one of the first examples is *SEG* 21.668,[18] a dedication by the taxiarchs of 356/5, found in the Agora (its original location is unknown): ταξίαρχοι ἀνέθεσαν οἱ ἐπὶ Ἐλπίνο ἄρχοντο[ς] | στεφανωθέντες ὑπὸ τõ δήμο καὶ τῆς βολῆς, followed by a list of three of the taxiarchs of that year. The precise duties for which they were honoured are unfortunately unspecified. Only one other inscription honouring a taxiarch certainly predates the end of the classical democracy in 321, *IG* II^2 3201 (found on the acropolis, broken on all sides except the bottom), of which only three inscribed crowns survive, and which commemorated, in the left crown, the honouring by the People of an (unnamed) taxiarch of 346/5, and in the right crown, the honouring by his tribe of (presumably) the same man for his service as gymnasiarch at the Hephaisteia. The central crown associates the Council with the honours. Whether the stone was inscribed above with the

---

15 H. Yunis, Demosthenes. *On the Crown*, Cambridge 2001, 231.

16 I pass over here inscriptions relating to the ephebic taxiarchs, attested from 333/2 onwards. On these see now conveniently J. L. Friend, *The Athenian Ephebeia in the Lycurgan Period: 334/3–322/1 B.C.*, PhD. University of Texas, 2009, 115–116.

17 See Lambert, *op. cit.* in n. 2. There were a few decrees awarding statues to very prominent Athenians (and foreigners) from before the 340s, including generals, but it is not clear in how many of these cases the decrees were inscribed (cf. Oliver 2007b, 184, S1–S13).

18 B. D. Meritt, Greek Inscriptions, *Hesp.* 32 (1963) 36–37 no. 33 [= *IG* II^3 4, 246].

texts of the relevant decrees, as Kirchner suggests, or merely with a dedicatory formula, is unclear. In any case, what the taxiarch had done to merit the honours is again obscure.

The next securely dated inscriptions honouring taxiarchs are a series of, mostly quite well preserved, state decrees from after 307/6.[19] The duties for which they are honoured are broadly of two types: those connected with religious processions and festivals, mainly, it seems, the maintenance of good order, but also sometimes the conduct of sacrifices themselves;[20] and those connected with the defence of Attica, including guarding the walls.[21] *SEG* 3.116, a decree of the senior *epilektoi* of Antiochis, erected, it seems, in the tribal sanctuary of Antiochis, has commonly been dated c. 330, but it probably postdates the classical democracy. Lawton (1995, 150, no. 157) has now assigned the relief on stylistic grounds to "towards the end of the [fourth] century"; and the wording, with its emphasis on guard duties and obedience to the general (ἐπιμε[μέ]ληται [κ|αλῶς κα]ὶ φιλοτί[μως τῆ[ς] τε | [φυλα]κῆς καὶ τῶν [ἄ]λλω[ν], ὅ[σ]α | [προσέ]ταξεν ὁ στρατηγὸ[ς α|ὐτῶι, ll. 6–10) recalls that of the state decrees of the period after 307/6. Similarly *SEG* 17.85,[22] a dedication by taxiarchs to Demeter and Kore, though not firmly datable more closely than ca. 350–300, recalls the circumstances of *Agora* XVI 123, of 302/1.[23] *IG* II² 1155 is the only inscription (or pair of inscriptions) which relate directly and explicitly to services connected

19 In addition to Woodhead's useful notes on the relevant inscriptions in *Agora* XVI there is also helpful discussion in Oliver 2007a.

20 *Agora* XVI 123 (302/1, set up in the Eleusinion) for maintaining *eukosmia* in the rites for Demeter (perhaps the Mysteries); *Agora* XVI 182 [= *IG* II³ 1, 882] (281/0, set up near the *strategion*) for sacrifices conducted by taxiarchs sent as delegates to Lebadeia in Boeotia for the Basileia festival. The single taxiarch honoured by the fragmentary *Agora* XVI 295 (163/2, archon Erastos), had apparently performed services at the Panathenaia and the Eleusinia. Later second-century decrees honouring taxiarchs are noted by Oliver 2007a, 178 n. 30.

21 *IG* II² 500 (302/1, honouring taxiarchs of 305/4, set up in front of the *strategion*. Oliver 2007a, 116, notes that Athens was fighting Kassander around the city and in Attica in 305/4); *Agora* XVI 185 (275/4) [= *IG* II³ 1, 897] and the similarly worded *Agora* XVI 187 [= *IG* II³ 1, 907] (271/0, set up in front of the *strategion*) refer both to sacrifices funded from their own resources, and to duties connected with the defence of Attica (the fragmentary *IG* II² 685 [= *IG* II³ 1, 893], of 276/5, begins with the same wording as XVI 185). Cf. Oliver 2007a, 178; 188–189.

22 B. D. Meritt, Greek Inscriptions, *Hesp.* 26 (1957) 206 no. 52 = *Agora* XXXI 189 no. 9 [= *IG* II³ 4, 258].

23 One can do little with the extremely fragmentary *IG* II² 2972 (iv BC) [= *IG* II³ 4, 325], from the acropolis, [οἱ στρατιῶται – ἀνέ]θεσαν | [- - - - - - - - - - - - ἐκ Κοί]λης ἐταξιάρχε[ι]. Complete to the right and below, it was clearly not inscribed with a decree.

with a military campaign, as opposed to more general duties for the defence of Attica, and, if the specific connection with the campaign against Philip in the winter of 339/8 is correct, it is one of only two which relate to activities of the taxiarchs beyond the borders of Attica. As Graham Oliver remarks (2007a, 126), the releasing of the taxiarchs of 281/0 to sacrifice in Lebadeia (*Agora* XVI 182 [= *IG* II^3 1, 882] ll. 9–11), far beyond the northern borders of Attica, suggests a level of confidence in security at home; if Kirchhoff's identification of the context of our inscriptions is correct, the activities, also beyond the northern borders of Attica, for which our taxiarch of 339/8 was commemorated, were of a rather different kind.[24]

24 For English translations and concordances of inscriptions in *IG* II^3 mentioned in this paper, see *Attic Inscriptions Online* (www.atticinscriptions.com). [*IG* II^2 1155 fr. a, the base, separated from fr. b, the stele, is now published alone at *IG* II^3 4, 260.]

CHAPTER 11

The Inscribed Version of the Decree Honouring Lykourgos of Boutadai (*IG* II² 457 and 3207)[1]

1 The Association of *IG* II² 457 and *IG* II² 3207

The two non-joining fragments of *IG* II² 457 (EM 7249) preserve sections of the upper part of the inscribed version of the decree honouring posthumously the orator Lykourgos of Boutadai, proposed by Stratokles of Diomeia in 307/6 BC. A complete version of the same decree, deriving from the application of Lykourgos' eldest son, Lykophron, for dining rights (*sitesis*) in the city hall (*prytaneion*) under the terms of the decree, and perhaps ultimately from the papyrus version of the decree in the city archive in the Metroon, is preserved in an Appendix to the *Life of Lykourgos* attributed to Plutarch ([Plut.] *Lives of the Ten Orators* 851e–852).

IG II² 3207 (EM 10679) preserves the lower portion of a stele inscribed with crowns in three columns. Within each crown the awarding body is given, followed by the name of the proposer. Of the first column of crowns nothing substantive is legible beyond the demotic of the proposer of crown 1, who was from Myrrhinous. The second and third columns record the following decrees:

---

1 [This paper was first published as *AIO Papers* no. 6 (2015), https://www.atticinscriptions.com/papers/aio-papers-6/]. I am grateful to Athanasios Themos for permission to examine the stones in the Epigraphical Museum in December, 2014, to him, Eleni Zavvou and Stergios Tzanekas for discussion of the association of 457 and 3207; to Angelos P. Matthaiou for joining in the examination, for his wise observations and for comments on a draft of this paper; to Adele Scafuro for an account of her own consultations about this inscription earlier in 2014, for reading a draft of this paper and showing me a draft of a paper of her own which will discuss the commemoration of decrees on *IG* II² 3207 in the context of comparable monuments. I acknowledge with thanks a contribution of Utrecht University towards the cost of my visit to Athens and thank Josine Blok and P. J. Rhodes for reading a draft. This paper should be read in conjunction with the translation on AIO of *IG* II² 457 + 3207 and the accompanying notes, which have been revised to coincide with its issue. *IALD* = *Inscribed Athenian Laws and Decrees, 352/1–322/1 BC. Epigraphical Essays* (2012). *Polis and Theatre* = "Polis and Theatre in Lykourgan Athens. The Honorific Decrees", in A. P. Matthaiou and I. Polinskaya eds., *Mikros Hieromnemon. Meletes eis mnemen Michael H. Jameson* (2008), 53–85. *IG* II² references for inscriptions in *IG* II³ can be traced via the main AIO site.

© KONINKLIJKE BRILL NV, LEIDEN, 2018 | DOI 10.1163/9789004352490_013

col. 2
crown 5
The Council.
Demeas of Sphettos proposed.
crown 6
The Council.
Diophanes of Kephisia proposed.
crown 7
The Council.
Ktesikles of Bate proposed.
crown 8
The tribesmen.
Telemachos of Acharnai proposed.

col. 3
crown 9
The Council.
Theomenes of Oe proposed.
crown 10
The People.
Theomenes of Oe proposed.
crown 11
The People in Samos.
Epiktetos of Epikephisia proposed.
crown 12
The People in Lemnos.
Timodemos of Acharnai proposed.

This stele commemorated, in brief, multiple awards of crowns to someone who was, it seems, quite prominent. Crown 11 must have been awarded in the period of the Athenian cleruchy on Samos (i.e. before 322/1). In 1911 the great Austrian epigraphist, Adolf Wilhelm, suggested that the honorand was Lykourgos of Boutadai, whose career peaked 336–325,[2] and that 3207 might be from the same stele as 457.[3] In 1925 he justified that opinion more fully.[4]

We may eagerly anticipate Graham Oliver's fresh edition of this inscription for *IG* II^3, which will offer a fully considered revision of the text. My more limited purpose here is to report the results of a brief examination of the stones in December 2014, directed at reviewing whether 3207 belongs to the same stele as 457, and to make a few remarks about the decrees commemorated on 3207.

As Wilhelm noted, the rather abraded script on 3207, though it makes a somewhat more careless impression, is similar in style to that on the well preserved 457 fr. b. Assuming the stones thickened and widened towards the bottom, the fragments display compatible thickness (as recorded by Wilhelm: 457

2 The dating of the decrees to about this time is confirmed by the prosopography of the proposers (see further below). Moreover, Lykourgos's tribe (Oineis) corresponds with the tribe which awarded crown 8 (Oineis, implied by the demotic of the proposer, Telemachos of Acharnai).

3 *Zeitschrift für die österreichischen Gymnasien* 1911, 1030 (non vidi).

4 *Attische Urkunden* III = *Sitzungsberichte der Akademie der Wissenschaften in Wien* 202 (1925), 3–6 = *Akademieschriften zur griechischen Inschriftenkunde* I (1974), 463–66.

a, 0.115; 457 b, 0.12; 3207, 0.135) and width (as calculated by Wilhelm: 457 b, 0.45; 3207, over 0.48), and the marble is also of the same type (white, "Pentelic"). Angelos Matthaiou and I concur with Wilhelm that 3207 is compatible with 457 in these respects and that the stones may belong to the same inscription. In our opinion, however, this is not a necessary inference.[5] The fragments of 457 have a rough-picked back. The back of 3207, on the other hand, is different. At some point it acquired a highly smoothed finish. Later, apparently as part of a secondary use which created a socket in the back, behind the left edge of the front surface, roughly half way down, numerous cuts have been made in the reverse face of the stele to roughen the surface. These cuts extend about half way across the back of the stele from the edge with the socket. If the smooth back of 3207 is original (which is unclear), the stone does not belong to the same inscription as 457. If it is not original, and an original rough-picked back has been smoothed in a secondary use, the full thickness of the bottom of the stele must originally have been rather greater than 0.135, implying a very significant thickening of the stele towards the bottom. Moreover, there are extensive vertical fault-lines in 3207 which are not present in the fragments of 457; and Mr Tzanekas suggests that there are slight differences in the working of the right sides of 457 fr. b and 3207.[6] None of these points is decisive, but they do raise the possibility that 457 and 3207 belong to two separate, but associated, stelai. Such pairs of stelai are not unexampled. *IG* II^3 1, 448, for example, providing for a festival, and referring to the "stele about the Peace" (ten *stelen tes peri tes eirenes*), complements physically (script, thickness, same smoothly finished back) and in content the stele recording the Peace of Corinth, *IG* II^3 1, 318. Moreover, there is not always correspondence between the number of stelai provided for, or implicit, in the inscribing clause of a decree, and the number that were actually inscribed. *IG* II^2 140, the law of Meid- amending the law of Chairemonides, and specified to be added to the stele recording that law, was actually erected on a separate stele. *IG* II^3 1, 375, the decree honouring Lapyris of Kleonai, specified for erection *eis ten stelen* for Echenbrotos of Kleonai (= *IG* II^2 63) was also inscribed on a separate stele.

The inscribed version of Stratokles' decree does not preserve the inscribing clause. The version in [Plut.], however, concludes as follows:

---

5 I am especially grateful to Mr Tzanekas of the Epigraphical Museum for discussing his reservations about whether 457 and 3207 belong to the same stele.

6 In Mr Tzanekas' opinion a tooth chisel has been used on 457 fr b, and a tongue chisel on 3207.

> and the secretary of the People shall set up for him (or about him, MSS of him), and there shall be valid, all the decrees on stone stelai and erect them on the acropolis near the dedications; and the treasurer of the People shall give for inscribing the stelai fifty drachmas from the People's fund for expenditure on decrees.[7]

The decrees in question are the decree of Stratokles and the decrees inscribed in brief on 3207. There is a clear implication that there are to be multiple stelai. This may not have been followed through; in the event only one stele may have been erected, with Stratokles' decree at the top, and the other decrees honouring Lykourgos commemorated in abbreviated form in crowns inscribed underneath. 50 drachmas is possible provision for a single inscription at this period.[8] On other occasions, however, 20 or 30 dr. is provided for a single stele and 50 dr. is accordingly also possible provision for two stelai. In 323/2 (as reinscribed in 318) 50 dr. was provided for two copies of the decree honouring Euphron of

7 ἀναθεῖναι δ' αὐτῷ *or* περὶ αὐτοῦ (Lambert, *Polis and Theatre* 77 = *IALD* 355 n. 40, αὐτοῦ MSS) καὶ εἶναι κύρια πάντα τὰ ψηφίσματα τὸν γραμματέα τοῦ δήμου ἐν στήλαις λιθίναις καὶ στῆσαι ἐν ἀκροπόλει πλησίον τῶν ἀναθημάτων· εἰς δὲ τὴν ἀναγραφὴν τῶν στηλῶν δοῦναι τὸν ταμίαν τοῦ δήμου πεντήκοντα δραχμὰς ἐκ τῶν εἰς τὰ ψηφίσματα ἀναλισκομένων τῷ δήμῳ. The text is peculiar, and may have been corrupted in the course of transmission from the Athenian city archive to the medieval manuscripts of [Plut.], but the sense of the provision seems clear enough: all the decrees honouring Lykourgos are to be inscribed and erected on the acropolis "near the dedications". As noted *IALD* 355, n. 40, the language used here usually expresses the thought that decrees voted *for* or *about* someone should be valid (*IG* II^2 275 [= *IG* II^3 1, 501], 5–7, and other examples cited n. 40), not decrees *proposed by* them. That this is the correct interpretation is confirmed not only by *IG* II^2 3207 but by the fact that the clause needs also to have covered the inscribing of Stratokles' own decree. *Pace* what I wrote there, laws and decrees might be referred to by the names of their proposers, as e.g. "the law of Chairemonides", *IG* II^2 140, though use of a pronoun ("his decrees") in such a sense in this context seems to me difficult; and in the Lykourgan period note the characteristically both more correct and more collectivist formulation at *IG* II^3 1, 327, 25–26, "the [decree] of the Council, which Agasi- proposed, and the one of the People which Hippochares proposed".

8 W. T. Loomis, *Wages, Welfare Costs and Inflation in Classical Athens* (1998), 143–44, no. 137, notes that 50 dr. was provided in this same year for inscribing the law on the repair of the long walls (*IG* II^2 463, 33–34) and, no. 146, in ca. 307–302 50 dr. for a citizenship decree (*IG* II^2 518 + Osborne, *Naturalization* D54, 5–9; also for the decree honouring ambassadors from Carthage, *IG* II^2 418 = Loomis no. 127, work of Tracy's "Cutter of *IG* II^2 1262", ca. 320–296, *Athenian Democracy in Transition* [1995], 138).

Sikyon.[9] It is therefore also quite plausible that this inscribing provision was put into effect by erecting a pair of stelai, one carrying Stratokles' decree (457) and one carrying the other decrees honouring Lykourgos (3207).

The stipulation that the stelai be set up on the acropolis "near the dedications" is remarkable on two counts. First, because it would seem that no copy of Stratokles' decree was to be erected alongside the bronze statue of Lykourgos in the Agora, provided for in the decree.[10] Though we know of several earlier awards of statues to Athenians,[11] this is the earliest extant inscribed decree making such an award. In the case of the early fourth-century statue for Konon, it seems that there was an inscribed decree, as Demosthenes 20.69 quotes "from the stele"; but it may not have been usual, or at least not invariable, practice to inscribe decrees awarding statues alongside the statue.

Second, specific locations on the acropolis were rarely named in inscribing clauses of decree stelai,[12] and the stipulation, "near the dedications", is unique. It was normal in decree language to distinguish between a "stele" and a "dedication" (*anathema*), the former typically thinner and taller and bearing the text

9 IG II^3 1, 378, 31. M. J. Osborne, ZPE 42 (1981), 173–74, noted the possibility that 50 dr. in Stratokles' decree was intended to cover two stelai in connection with his theory (since refuted, see SEG 49.107 and S. V. Tracy, *Athens and Macedon* [2003], 70–73) that IG II^2 513 was a second copy of Stratokles' decree for Lykourgos.

10 The statue was to be erected in the Agora except where the laws forbid (852e), probably a reference to the prohibition on erection next to the statues of Harmodios and Aristogeiton stipulated in our earliest surviving text of a decree awarding a statue, IG II^2 450 of 314/3 for Asandros of Macedon, = Lambert, *ABSA* 95 (2000), 486–89 no. E1. According to [Plut.] 843c Lykourgos' statue was located in the Kerameikos. One wonders if this was deliberately in proximity to the public funerary monuments in the Kerameikos for Lykourgos' ancestors, Lykomedes and Lykourgos (852a) (on which see A. P. Matthaiou, *Horos* 5 [1987], 31–44, and most recently N. T. Arrington, *Hesperia* 79 (2010), 499–539 at 520). The statue was seen by Paus. 1.8.2 (mentioned after the statues of the eponymous heroes in the Agora, but not precisely located). A fragment of what is apparently its base, inscribed with Lykourgos's name, was discovered at the "Agora gate" (IG II^2 3776). The statue is S20 in the catalogue of Athenian portrait statues compiled by G. J. Oliver, "Space and the Visualization of Power in the Greek Polis. The award of portrait statues in decrees from Athens", in P. Schultz and R. von den Hoff, *Early Hellenistic Portraiture* (2007), 181–204, at 185.

11 Oliver, *op. cit.*

12 On the rare occasions they are specified it is usually because specific factors in the decree drew the inscription to particular location on the acropolis, as e.g. the decree concerning objects in the *chalkotheke*, IG II^2 120, to be set up "in front of the *chalkotheke*", see P. Liddel, ZPE 143 (2003), 79–93, at 81 with 86, table 2.

of a decree, the latter more squat and thick and carrying the object dedicated.[13] There is some conceptual overlap, however, and there are ambiguous cases and hybrids.[14] This is one such hybrid, as not only are the stelai to be located "near the dedications" (rather than, it seems implied, with other decree stelai on the acropolis), the inscribing clause uses both the verb *anatheinai*, "set up", cognate with and normally used for dedications (*anathemata*), and *stesai*, "stand", normally used of stelai. To understand the background here we need to bear in mind that decrees honouring Athenians (never those honouring foreigners) with the more routine award of a crown were sometimes inscribed not on regular "stelai", but, from the 340s onwards, on dedications, usually, but not always, bases for statues. Where such dedications were provided for in the decree, however, though they might be *funded by* the city, they were not usually *made by* the city, but by the honorands.[15] In this case the honorand is dead and not in a position to make a dedication; the responsibility is taken over by the city. Though the decrees for Lykourgos were to be inscribed on stelai, therefore, language and location assimilates them to dedications made by Athenian officials commemorating, and inscribed with, decrees awarding them crowns.

There is also, however, another possible factor in the background here, for the honorand had a special connection with the acropolis as member of the *genos* Eteoboutadai, which supplied the priests of Poseidon Erechtheus and the priestesses of Athena Polias. Broadly contemporary with this bronze statue (the precise timing can not be pinned down), there were wooden statues of Lykourgos and his sons in the Erechtheion, made by Timarchos and Kephisodotos, sons of Praxiteles, and Lykourgos' son Habron set up a tablet (*pinax*) there illustrating the succession of the priests of Poseidon Erechtheus

---

13 The distinction is observed, for example, in the five decrees inscribed on the dedication by the Council of 343/2, set up at the initiative of Phanodemos, *IG* II^3 1, 306, where the Council's decree honouring Phanodemos for his performance as councillor (decree 3), is both to be inscribed "on the dedication" (l. 8, i.e. the surviving monument), and also to go forward as a *probouleuma* to the Assembly, which, if passed by the Assembly, was to be inscribed on a stele on the acropolis (l. 15, no such monument survives).

14 E.g. *IG* II^3 1, 360, a base in the form of a thick stele, referred to as a dedication in l. 1, a stele in l. 54; 417, a block from a dedication of uncertain physical type, apparently referred to as a stele in l. 24 (unless this decree was also inscribed separately on a stele, cf. previous note); *IG* II^2 1156, same monument apparently referred to as a stele l. 35, a dedication ll. 43–44, 49–51, 62–63.

15 For a catalogue and discussion of decrees honouring Athenians of the period before 322/1, including physical format, see *ZPE* 150 (2004), 85–120, and 154 (2005), 125–29 = *IALD* 1–55. Examples of dedications at public expense, but made by the honorands: *IG* II^3 1, 311, 6; 355, 36–37; 369, 48; 416, 36.

([Plut.] 843e–f).[16] Perhaps the (or a) point of the inscribing clause of Stratokles' decree was to clarify that the inscription was not to be placed among the monuments of the Eteoboutadai, but in public space alongside the regular dedications.

The findspot of 3207, on the acropolis, is compatible with the inscribing clause of Stratokles' decree. So are the findspots of the two fragments of 457, which can be assumed, as not uncommonly with fragments of inscriptions originally set up on the acropolis, to have wandered down from it, fr. a to the church of Panagia Pyrgiotissa, south of the Stoa of Attalos, fr. b to the theatre of Dionysos.

To summarise the key points: *IG* II^2 3207, inscribed with summaries of decrees honouring Lykourgos of Boutadai passed in his lifetime, either (a) belongs to the same stele as *IG* II^2 457, containing Stratokles' decree honouring him posthumously, or (b) to a separate stele associated with it. The stele or stelai give effect to the inscribing clause of Stratokles' decree, which provides for erection of decrees for Lykourgos (i.e. both Stratokles' decree and the decrees passed in his lifetime) on "stelai" on the acropolis near the dedications. The use of the plural, "stelai", is prima facie more consistent with (b), but does not rule out (a), given that it was not uncommon for numbers of stelai implied by inscribing clauses of decrees to differ from numbers of stelai actually erected. The unique stipulation "near the dedications" resonates with other decrees honouring Athenians, some of which, since the 340s, had been inscribed on dedications rather than regular stelai, but may also signify that the decrees were to be erected in the area of the acropolis normally used for dedications rather than the area of the acropolis (the Erechtheion) in which monuments were located relating to Lykourgos' *genos*, the Eteoboutadai, which already included, or was shortly to include, a wooden statue of him.

2 The Decrees Commemorated in *IG* II^2 3207

The great political rivals of the post-Chaironeia period, Demades and Lykourgos, proposed, by a considerable margin, more extant inscribed laws and decrees than any other Athenian politician of the classical democracy;[17]

16 Monuments relating to the priestesses of Athena Polias, including the earlier fourth-century statue of the long-serving priestess, Lysimache, *IG* II^2 3453, may also have been erected in Eteoboutad space. See now C. M. Keesling, *Hesperia* 81 (2012), 476–505.

17 Demades proposed eight or nine extant self-standing decrees erected before 321/0: (1) *IG* II^3 1, 321, of 337/6; (2)* 322, of 337/6, honouring a courtier of Philip II; (3)* possibly 330,

and on two or three occasions extant decrees were proposed by both men at the same Assembly.[18] Both these phenomena can plausibly be interpreted to an extent as a product of their rivalry, for at this period the practice begins of highlighting proposers' names on inscribed decrees via devices such as allocating the name a line to itself and leaving space before or after it;[19] and successful proposing of decrees in the Assembly, prominently displayed on inscribed stelai, erected by the decision, and at the expense, of the Assembly, can increasingly be regarded as an intentional expression of political influence. Moreover, in a political culture driven by *philotimia* (a value more explicitly embraced in decrees since the 340s[20]), this "decree-proposer rivalry" can be identified as a

of 335/4; (4) 334, of 334/3; (5) 335, of 334/3, honouring Amyntor son of Demetrios; (6) 346 decree 2, of 332/1, for a son of Aristeides; (7) 356, of 329/8, for a man from Larisa; (8)* 358, of 328/7?, for Eurylochos of Kydonia; (9)* 384, of 322/1. Lykourgos proposed at least eight: (1) *IG* II³ 1, 329, of 336/5 or 335/4, honouring a son of Eupor-, probably a foreigner, and, since it is probouleumatic in formulation, implying that Lykourgos was on the Council this year; (2) 336, of 334/3?, perhaps honouring the general Diotimos for his expedition against pirates; (3) 337 decree 2, of 333/2, granting the merchants of Kition the right to own a plot of land on which to build a temple of Aphrodite; (4) 345, of 332/1, honouring a son of [Eud?]emos of Plataia; (5) 352, of 330/29, honouring Eudemos of Plataia for his contribution to the building of the Panathenaic stadium; (6)* 357, of 328/7, content unknown; (7) 432, of 337–325, honouring Sopatros of Akragas for his contribution to the Athenian grain supply (cf. 495, with *IALD* 402); (8) 445, of ca. 335, law(s) on sacred objects. Among possible cases note 470, mentioning the *skene* (of the theatre of Dionysos?), with E. Csapo and P. Wilson, "The Finance and Organisation of the Athenian Theatre in the Time of Eubulus and Lycurgus", in E. Csapo, H. Goette, J. R. Green and P. Wilson eds., *Greek Theatre in the Fourth Century BC* (2014), 415–17. No other Athenian proposed more than 3 or 4 extant inscribed decrees before 321/0.

18 These are: at an Assembly in 334/3, *IG* II³ 1, 334 and 335 (Demades) and probably 336 (Lykourgos); at the special Assembly in the theatre following the City Dionysia in Elaphebolion 332/1, 345 (Lykourgos), 346 (Demades); at an Assembly in Gamelion 328/7, 357 (Lykourgos), 358 (Demades).

19 See A. S. Henry, *The Prescripts of Athenian Decrees* [*Mnemosyne Supplement* 49] (1977), 63–66. Those decrees marked * in the lists in n. 17 display this feature, which was to become more marked in the years after 307/6 (S. V. Tracy, *Hesperia* 69 [2000], 227–33). Cf. Lambert, "Some Political Shifts in Lykourgan Athens", in V. Azoulay and P. Ismard eds., *Clisthène et Lycurgue d'Athènes. Autour du politique dans la cité classique* (Paris, 2011), 175–90, at 184–85 [= this volume, chapter 4.].

20 On this see Lambert, "What was the point of honorific decrees in Lykourgan Athens", in Lambert ed., *Sociable Man. Essays on Ancient Greek Social Behaviour in Honour of Nick Fisher* (2011), 193–214 [= this volume, chapter 3].

factor underlying the increase in the numbers of extant decrees in the years after 338.[21]

The large majority of inscribed decrees at this period were honorific, and political rivalry was also apparent in the pursuit by politicians of honours for themselves, and in challenging proposals of honours for opponents, most famously in Aeschines' challenge to Ktesiphon's proposal to bestow a crown on Demosthenes, a challenge which came to court in 330, at the height of the "Lykourgan" era, and elicited from Demosthenes what was to become the most famous speech in Greek oratory, Demosthenes 18 *On the Crown*. At the key moment in the rivalry between Lykourgos and Demades it was Lykourgos who was cast in the role of Aeschines, vehemently opposing the proposal of Kephisodotos to award a bronze statue and *sitesis* to his rival. The occasion is not explicitly attested, but was probably in 335 following the latter's remarkable diplomatic coup in securing a favourable deal for Athens following Alexander's destruction of Thebes.[22] Four fragments of Lykourgos' speech survive (Lykourgos F9 Conomis). In the first he undertook to demonstrate that "the decree was illegal and that the man was not worthy of the grant",[23] and in the second he compared the extravagant honours claimed for Demades' modest achievements unfavourably with the outstanding achievements of Pericles and the modest honours with which he had contented himself:

> Pericles, having captured Samos and Euboea and Aegina, and built the Propylaia and the Odeion and the Hekatompedon, and having brought

21 This can be illustrated by a simple statistic: 25 extant inscribed decrees with identifiable proposers are datable to the 16 years, 354/3–339/8; nearly twice as many, 48, to the 17 years, 338/7–322/1. Another factor underlying this statistic is the increasingly deliberate use of the inscribed honorific decree as a political lever to manipulate the performance of officials and the behaviour of foreigners in relation e.g. to the grain supply and the theatrical life of the city. Cf. Lambert, in G. Reger et al. eds., *Studies ... Stephen V. Tracy* (2010), 153–60 = *IALD* 377–86.

22 In the Harpalos affair of 324/3 Dinarchos 1 *Against Demosthenes* 101 was to criticise Demosthenes for having condoned erection of a bronze statue of Demades in the Agora and permitted Demades to share *sitesis* in the *prytaneion* with the descendants of Harmodios and Aristogeiton. Cf. P. Brun, *L'orateur Démade* (2000), 78–83.

23 καὶ παράνομον τὸ ψήφισμα ἐπιδείξω καὶ ἀνάξιον τὸν ἄνδρα δωρεᾶς. Lyk. F9.1. On these and other fragments of Lykourgos see the helpful translation and notes of E. M. Harris in I. Worthington et al. transl., *Dinarchus, Hyperides, and Lycurgus* (2001), 204–18.

10,000 talents of silver up to the acropolis, was crowned with a foliage crown.[24]

What of Lykourgos' own honours? The award of a statue and *sitesis* in Stratokles' decree was doubtless seen by Stratokles and Lykourgos' sons as an opportunity posthumously to even up the score against Demades; and it is notable in this context that Lykourgos' actions are presented in the decree as explicitly in opposition to Alexander, in contrast, implicitly, to Demades, whose success had been based on a policy of constructive diplomacy with the Macedonians. It is also notable that the only extant inscribed decree honouring Lykourgos in his lifetime is *IG* II³ 1, 355, of 329/8, proposed by Demosthenes of Lamptrai. Characteristically given the fierce commitment to the collective over the individual apparent in Lykourgos' *Against Leokrates*, he is honoured there, with a gold crown and money for sacrifice and a dedication, not as an individual, but as member of the board responsible for the management of the first celebration of the new Great Amphiaraia festival. Strikingly, his name appears in the list (l. 23) immediately before that of Demades (l. 24); joint service on such a board did not, of course, exclude political rivalry, as Demosthenes (of Paiania) and Aeschines had demonstrated on the embassies to Philip II in 346.[25]

How do the decrees commemorated on 3207 fit into the picture? The requirement at the end of Stratokles' decree to inscribe the decrees honouring Lykourgos follows through the claim earlier in the decree, that "having been deemed to have administered all these things justly, he was crowned many times by the city".[26] "All these things" refers to Lykourgos' financial responsibilities and achievements as "treasurer of the public revenue" (τῆς κοινῆς προσόδου ταμίας) as Stratokles's decree terms it, for three quadrennia.[27] So,

24 Περικλῆς δὲ ὁ Σάμον καὶ Εὔβοιαν καὶ Αἴγιναν ἑλών, καὶ τὰ Προπύλαια καὶ τὸ Ὠιδεῖον καὶ τὸ Ἑκατόμπεδον οἰκοδομήσας, καὶ μύρια τάλαντα ἀργυρίου εἰς τὴν ἀκρόπολιν ἀνενεγκών, θαλλοῦ στεφάνῳ ἐστεφανώθη. Lyk. F9.2.

25 Lykourgos and Demades also served together as *hieropoioi* on the Pythais of ca. 330–325, *Syll.*³ 296 (a new edition of which will shortly be published in *IG* II³ 4 fasc. 1 [= *IG* II³ 4, 18]), where again they are listed in consecutive lines (5 and 6), perhaps because they were about the same age.

26 δόξας δὲ ἅπαντα ταῦτα δικαίως διῳκηκέναι πολλάκις ἐστεφανώθη ὑπὸ τῆς πόλεως. 852b.

27 [Plut.] explains (841b–c) that Lykourgos held the office for the first quadrennium (probably 336/5–332/1) in his own person, and subsequently, because tenure was prohibited for more than four years, through friends. Lykourgos' office is elsewhere described as ἐπὶ τῇ διοικήσει, "in charge of the financial administration", most clearly at Hyp. F118, cf. D. Whitehead, *Hypereides* (2000), 448–50, but also implicitly e.g. in Lykourgos F5 and at

the implication seems to be that some or all of the decrees commemorated on 3207 had recognised Lykourgos' tenure of this office. Awards of crowns to office-holders were subject to the satisfactory rendering of accounts (*euthynai*), and Lykourgos had not enjoyed an easy ride at the hands of his opponents. At some point he had to defend himself against Demades at a *euthynai* (Lykourgos F4); and his speech *On the Administration*, Περὶ τῆς διοικήσεως (Lykourgos F5) was also apparently delivered at a *euthynai* (cf. Dinarchos F4), perhaps after his first quadrennium in office. Most famously, on his deathbed Lykourgos had been carried into the Council-chamber and the Metroon to defend himself, "wishing to give an account of his political actions" (βουλόμενος εὐθύνας δοῦναι τῶν πεπολιτευμένων, 842f). This seems to have been Lykourgos' "On *the Crown*" and the surviving fragments of his speech (Lykourgos F1) confirm that he ranged broadly across his career.[28] The precise legal context is unclear; [Plut.] gives the impression that it was a *euthynai*, and it is usually thought to have been connected with Lykourgos' third quadrennium as "treasurer of the public revenue". If (what is not quite clear) the office was actually filled by one of his friends in his third term, it may have been formally a *euthynai* for the office-holder. According to [Plut.] 842f, he was vindicated on this occasion, and indeed on every other occasion according to Stratokles,[29] but his opponent, Menesaichmos, pursued his sons after his death for non-payment of public debts owed by their father (842d–e), and they were saved by the intervention, among others, of Hypereides, and of Demosthenes from exile.[30] Significantly, Lykourgos had clashed with Menesaichmos before; as we learn from his F14, he seems, characteristically, to have sought to condemn Menesaichmos at an *eisangelia* (the same heavy-handed process of "impeachment", intended for

---

IG II³ 1, 445, 28. Perhaps ἐπὶ τῇ διοικήσει was the formal office, while τῆς κοινῆς προσόδου ταμίας was looser language comprehending the oversight Lykourgos exercised when his friends held office on his behalf. Cf. P. J. Rhodes, *Chiron* 37 (2007), 349–62.

28 This speech presumably relates in some way to the account of his financial administration which he inscribed on a stele in front of the *palaistra* he had built ([Plut.] 843f). One may guess that this inscription and/or Lykourgos' speech on this occasion was a source for Stratokles' decree, whether directly or mediated via the biography of Lykourgos by his contemporary Philiskos (Olympiodoros, *Comm. in Plat. Gorg.* 515c, cf. M. Cuvigny [et G. Lachenaud], *Plutarque. Oeuvres Morales* XII 1, Traités 54–57 (Budé edition), 2nd ed. Paris, 2003, 33). Philiskos was probably also a source for [Plut.] (who appears to have been a writer of the Augustan period, perhaps Caecilius of Cale-Acte, see Cuvigny, *loc. cit.*).

29 852d, cf. 842e.

30 Hyp. F 118; Dem. *Epist.* 3; [Plut.] 842e. Cf. J. K. Davies, *Athenian Propertied Families* (1971), p. 351.

treasonable offences, that he had used against Leokrates) for sacrificing improperly on Delos.

Some of the crowns on 3207, therefore, will have commemorated Lykourgos' tenure of financial office, and been awarded following or subject to successful completion of the *euthynai* to which these speeches relate. The number of crowns was at least 12, possibly more, even if Stratokles' decree was inscribed above the crowns; indeed, since 3207 can scarcely preserve as much as half the height of a stele, if the entire stele was occupied by crowns, the total number may have been up to 24 or more. In any case there are good grounds here for Stratokles' claim that he had been crowned "many times".

Crowns 9 and 10, proposed by Theomenes of Oe in the Council and the Assembly respectively seem likely to belong to a single honorific process, culminating in a probouleumatic Assembly decree, originally proposed by Theomenes in the Council. Theomenes had been amphiktyon in accounts from Delos in 345/4 (ID 104–24, 5), which is consistent with the possibility that the honours recognised Lykourgos' financial performance. One can only speculate that Theomenes might also have colluded with Lykourgos' prosecution of Menesaichmos on the matter of the Delian sacrifice.

The two cleruchic decrees, of Samos and Lemnos, are intriguing. Epiktetos of Epikephisia, proposer of 11 (Samos) is otherwise unknown; the proposer of 12 (Lemnos), was Timodemos of Acharnai, councillor in ca. 321 BC (*Agora* XV 54, 5) and apparently a descendant of the Timodemos of Acharnai whose victory in the *pankration* in the 480s was celebrated by Pindar, *Nemean* 2. Pindar's Timodemos was Salamis-bred, and might have been a member of the Athenian cleruchy on Salamis and/or of the *genos* Salaminioi, which probably implied landholding, but not necessarily residence, on the island.[31] It is interesting indeed that the family seems also to have been a member of the Athenian community on another offshore possession, Lemnos; but there is scarcely a hint here of a connection with Lykourgos, unless it be a case of solidarity between old *genos* families, or unless these two cleruchic decrees were generated by appreciation for Lykourgos' measures against pirates.[32]

The proposer of the tribal decree commemorated by crown 8, Telemachos of Acharnai, is a name to conjure with. A well-known enough figure to be satirized by the comic poet Timokles for his busy politicking ("is the Acharnian Telemachos still making speeches?"[33]), and also, rather obscurely, for his consumption of beans – according to Athenaios he was always eating

---

31 See Lambert, *ZPE* 125 (1999), 118, cf. 128–30.

32 See *IG* II³ 1, 336 with II² 1623, 276–85 and [Plut.] 844a.

33 ὁ δ' Ἀχαρνικὸς Τηλέμαχος ἔτι δημηγορεῖ; Timokles *PCG* 7 p. 760 F7 = Athen. 9.407e.

cooking pots of beans and celebrated the "Beanboiling" festival, Pyanopsia, as "festival of flatulence",[34] – he is indeed well-attested in the epigraphical record as proposer in the Assembly of three non-probouleumatic decrees: a very fragmentary decree of 339/8 for one Theophantos, *IG* II³ 1, 315; and two of the decrees (dating to between 330/29 and 328/7) honouring the grain trader, Herakleides of Salamis, that were inscribed under the terms of Demosthenes of Lamptrai's decree of 325/4 BC awarding Herakleides the proxeny (*IG* II³ 1, 367). The first of the two (decree 1, ll. 47–51) commissions the Council to come forward with a decree honouring Herakleides, and the second (decree 3, ll. 29–46) builds in the Assembly on the resultant *probouleuma*, adding to the Council's proposed award of a crown provision for an embassy to Dionysios, tyrant of Herakleia Pontica, seeking the return of Herakleides' sails, which had been confiscated there.[35] Lykourgos had also participated in the policy of honouring grain traders to encourage them to supply Athens in the difficult years after Chaironeia,[36] and one may perhaps detect here a common purpose with Telemachos. Demosthenes of Lamptrai may supply another point of connection, since, as we have seen, he was also the proposer of the decree honouring Lykourgos and other managers of the Great Amphiaraia in 329/8. It is possible that the Pyanopsia supplies another. Lykourgos had included a disquisition on this festival in his speech *Against Menesaichmos* (F14.2–3); and one wonders whether Telemachos' reputation in connection with bean-pots at this festival might have related to his appearance in the same case, or to proposals (satirized as flatulent?) made by him in the Assembly for reform or enhancement of the festival. Such proposals would not be unexpected in this period of intense preoccupation with

34 ἐκ τούτων δῆλόν ἐστιν ὅτι Τηλέμαχος κυάμων χύτρας ἀεὶ αιτούμενος ἦγε Πυανέψια πορδὴν ἑορτήν Athen. 9.407e–408a. Athenaios quotes not only F7 of Timokles, but also F18 (407f) and F23 (407d–e). All three fragments connect Telemachos with pots of beans.

35 It is notable that the proposer of the *probouleuma*, Kephisodotos son of Euarchides of Acharnai, was from Telemachos' deme, pursuing his fellow demesman's proposal in a nice illustration of the way deme representation on the Council worked in practice. Telemachos of Acharnai was also a buyer of confiscated property sold by the *poletai* in *Agora* 19 P26, 496. The case for a connection between this Telemachos and the Telemachos who founded the Athenian cult of Asklepios in 420 BC is tenuous. See Lambert, *Historia* 59 (2010), 156–57.

36 See *IG* II³ 1, 432, for Sopatros of Akragas, and the references to the grain supply in *Against Leokrates*.

the festival life of the city, including measures attested in the epigraphical record relating to the Panathenaia, Amphiaraia and Dipolieia.[37]

The decrees commemorated in the remaining three crowns, 5, 6 and 7, are of the Council only, so will have honoured Lykourgos for his conduct as councillor or in an office in which he was responsible to the Council.[38] Ktesikles of Bate (crown 7) is otherwise unknown, though the demotic suggests a connection with Lykourgos' wife, Kallisto daughter of Habron of Bate, and/or with the branch of the Eteoboutadai which supplied the priestess of Athena Polias, which was based in that deme.[39] Demeas of Sphettos (crown 5) is unknown, and Diophanes of Kephisia (crown 6) is known only as (or perhaps more likely as son of) the Diophanes son of Diophanes of Kephisia who was councillor in 367/6 (*Agora* XV 14.23 [= IG II^3 4, 54]). The relative obscurity of these three proposers of Council decrees is not very surprising. They may well have been more or less ordinary Athenians, taking the opportunity of their turn on the Council to associate themselves with a "big man."[40]

For a man whose public persona radiated austere moral integrity, and who sought indeed to emulate Pericles' example, his remarks on the latter's contentment with a foliage crown would not perhaps have been consistent with his having frequently sought or accepted the award of gold crowns. We may perhaps infer that most, if not all, the crowns commemorated in 3207 had been of foliage. Few, if any, of the decrees had probably been inscribed before. The process for Lykourgos parallels in some respects that which can be observed on another inscription we have already mentioned: Demosthenes of Lamptrai's decree of 325/4 for the grain trader, Herakleides of Salamis (IG II^3 1, 367, 1–28), according to which the prytany secretary was to inscribe not only his own decree, awarding Herakleides the proxeny, but also the "other praises that there have been for him" (τοὺς ἄλλους ἐπαίνους τοὺς γεγενημένους αὐτῶι). The proxeny decree is duly followed on the stone by the text of four earlier decrees (fully transcribed on this occasion), which had patently not been

37 See the translation on AIO of IG II^3 1, 447, with notes.

38 As for example the Council decrees, decrees II–V of IG II^3 1, 306. Note also the Council decrees included in IG II^2 1155 and 1156.

39 Cf. J. Blok and S. D. Lambert, ZPE 169 (2009), 95–121, at 105–14.

40 The sort of dynamic in play here is illustrated by Aeschin. 3.125, where Aeschines portrays Demosthenes as prevailing on a councillor to put a *probouleuma* of his through the Council, "taking advantage of the proposer's inexperience" (προσλαβὼν τὴν τοῦ γράψαντος ἀπειρίαν). On the relative obscurity of proposers in the Council see M. H. Hansen, *The Athenian Democracy in the Age of Demosthenes* (1991), 145–46 [See now this volume, chapter 8].

inscribed previously, and the texts of which had, it seems, been obtained from the papyrus archive of decrees in the Metroon. Insofar as the decrees honouring Lykourgos were of the Council or Assembly, the information about them on which 3207 was based perhaps also derived from the Metroon archive. The decrees honouring Herakleides had not previously been inscribed because, at this period, it was simply not normal to inscribe awards of crowns to individual foreigners without substantive accompanying honours such as the proxeny or citizenship [See this volume, chapter 2.]. In the case of Athenian citizens, decrees awarding crowns only were sometimes inscribed from the 340s onwards, but for the inscribing to be at public expense, the crowns had at this period normally to be of gold, rather than foliage.[41] Crowns awarded by the Council on its own authority (crowns 5, 6 and 7) were also usually of foliage and the decrees awarding them were not usually inscribed.[42]

41 Cf. *ZPE* 150 (2004), 88 = *IALD* 8.

42 *IG* II² 1155 decree 1 (?) and 1156 decree 2 are exceptions which prove the rule in that they both record awards of foliage crowns by the Council on its own authority, but were inscribed not at the Council's initiative, but that of the honorands or their tribe (Kekropis in both cases). See the translations on AIO.

Index of Ancient Sources

1 Literary texts

Index of Persons

Index of Gods, Heroes, Festivals and Sanctuaries

Index of Places

Index of Subjects

www.ingramcontent.com/pod-product-compliance
Ingram Content Group UK Ltd.
Pitfield, Milton Keynes, MK11 3LW, UK
UKHW022209051026
15624UKWH00001B/67

9 789004 352483